A New Star-Rating System & Other Exciting News from Frommer's!

In our continuing effort to publish the savviest, most up-to-date, and most appealing travel guides available, we've added some great new features.

Frommer's guides now include a new **star-rating system**. Every hotel, restaurant, and attraction is rated from 0 to 3 stars to help you set priorities and organize your time.

We've also added **seven brand-new features** that point you to the great deals, in-the-know advice, and unique experiences that separate travelers from tourists. Throughout the guide, look for:

Finds	Special finds—those places only insiders know about
Fun Fact	Fun facts—details that make travelers more informed and their trips more fun
Kids	Best bets for kids—advice for the whole family
Moments	Special moments—those experiences that memories are made of
Overrated	Places or experiences not worth your time or money
Tips	Insider tips—some great ways to save time and money
Value	Great values—where to get the best deals

We've also added a **"What's New"** section in every guide—a timely crash course in what's hot and what's not in every destination we cover.

D1257457

Here's what the critics say about Frommer's:

"Amazingly easy to use. Very portable, very complete."

—*Booklist*

"Detailed, accurate, and easy-to-read information for all price ranges."
—*Glamour Magazine*

"Hotel information is close to encyclopedic."
—*Des Moines Sunday Register*

"Frommer's Guides have a way of giving you a real feel for a place."
—*Knight Ridder Newspapers*

Other Great Guides for Your Trip:

Frommer's The Carolinas & Georgia

Frommer's Nashville & Memphis

Frommer's Portable Savannah

Frommer's Portable Charleston

*Unofficial Guide to Bed & Breakfasts and Country Inns
in the Southeast*

*Unofficial Guide to the Best RV and Tent Campgrounds
in Florida & the Southeast*

Unofficial Guide to the Great Smoky & Blue Ridge Region

Unofficial Guide to the Southeast with Kids

Atlanta

8th Edition

by K. K. Snyder

Wiley Publishing, Inc.

About the Author

K. K. Snyder, former Bureau Chief and features writer for *The Albany Herald*, spends every available hour in search of a new destination to enjoy and share with readers. She admits that while she wasn't born in the South, she got there as quickly as she could and has lived there for the past 20 years. She has written for *Albany* magazine and coauthored *The Flood of the Century*, depicting the devastation of the 1994 flood in Southwest Georgia. She now works as a writer for the marketing department of a major hospital and continues freelance travel writing for a number of publications.

Published by:

Wiley Publishing, Inc.

909 Third Ave.
New York, NY 10022

ISBN 0-7645-2537-9
ISSN 1540-6806

Editor: Liz Albertson
Production Editor: Donna Wright
Cartographer: Roberta Stockwell
Photo Editor: Richard Fox
Production by Wiley Indianapolis Composition Services

Front cover photo: A Buckhead mansion
Back cover photo: Midtown Atlanta at night

For information on our other products and services or to obtain technical support, please contact our Customer Care Department within the U.S. at 800-762-2974, outside the U.S. at 317-572-3993 or fax 317-572-4002.

Wiley also publishes its books in a variety of electronic formats. Some content that appears in print may not be available in electronic formats.

Manufactured in the United States of America

5 4 3 2 1

Contents

Index 237

List of Maps

*This book is dedicated to Tom—my best friend, my true love,
and my travel companion for life.*

Acknowledgments

This project would not have been possible without the input from dozens of people, few of which I remember names for. Lauren Kenworthy's knowledge of the tourist industry in Atlanta was a tremendous help. Liz Albertson is appreciated dearly for taking a chance. Thanks to my children, Garret and Caitlin, who don't gripe about having to share me with the computer.

An Invitation to the Reader

In researching this book, we discovered many wonderful places—hotels, restaurants, shops, and more. We're sure you'll find others. Please tell us about them, so we can share the information with your fellow travelers in upcoming editions. If you were disappointed with a recommendation, we'd love to know that, too. Please write to:

Frommer's Atlanta, 8th Edition
Wiley Publishing, Inc. • 909 Third Ave. • New York, NY 10022

An Additional Note

Please be advised that travel information is subject to change at any time—and this is especially true of prices. We therefore suggest that you write or call ahead for confirmation when making your travel plans. The authors, editors, and publisher cannot be held responsible for the experiences of readers while traveling. Your safety is important to us, however, so we encourage you to stay alert and be aware of your surroundings. Keep a close eye on cameras, purses, and wallets, all favorite targets of thieves and pickpockets.

New! Frommer's Star Ratings & Icons

Every hotel, restaurant, and attraction listing in this guide has been ranked for quality, value, service, amenities, and special features using a star-rating scale. In country, state, and regional guides, we also rate towns and regions to help you narrow down your choices and budget your time accordingly. Hotels and restaurants in the Very Expensive and Expensive categories are rated on a scale of one (highly recommended) to three stars (exceptional). Those in the Moderate and Inexpensive categories rate from zero (recommended) to two stars (very highly recommended). Attractions, towns, and regions are rated according to the following scale: zero stars (recommended), one star (highly recommended), two stars (very highly recommended), and three stars (must-see).

In addition to the rating system, we also use seven icons to highlight insider information, useful tips, special bargains, hidden gems, memorable experiences, kid-friendly venues, places to avoid, and other useful information:

Finds	*Fun Fact*	*Kids*	*Moments*	*Overrated*	*Tips*	*Value*

The following abbreviations are used for credit cards:

AE	American Express	DISC	Discover	V	Visa
DC	Diners Club	MC	MasterCard		

FROMMERS.COM

Now that you have the guidebook to a great trip, visit our website at **www.frommers.com** for travel information on nearly 2,500 destinations. With features updated regularly, we give you instant access to the most current trip-planning information available. At Frommers.com, you'll also find the best prices on airfares, accommodations, and car rentals—and you can even book travel online through our travel booking partners. At Frommers.com, you'll also find the following:

- Online updates to our most popular guidebooks
- Vacation sweepstakes and contest giveaways
- Newsletter highlighting the hottest travel trends
- Online travel message boards with featured travel discussions

What's New in Atlanta

The land of the rising phoenix is continually evolving and reinventing itself. Today's Atlanta is a mecca for entertainment, fine dining, professional and college sports, and shopping. It is also one of the largest convention cities in the country. There is always something new on the horizon here in terms of construction and development. From a new retro clothing store to a restaurant opened by an internationally recognized chef, Atlanta is home to an ever-changing, ever-improving list of places to explore and things to experience. Here's a smattering of some recent additions to Atlanta, as well as a rundown of upcoming changes.

ACCOMMODATIONS Despite the huge decline in convention business following the September 11, 2001 terrorist attacks, developers continue to construct and renovate hotels in Hotlanta as if we were preparing to host another Olympic Games. Atlanta is preparing for its first Inter-Continental hotel (which is also its first five-star hotel since 1992) as **Six Continents Hotels, Inc.** plans to build a new hotel tower in Buckhead. The tower will be built across Peachtree Road from the Grand Hyatt Atlanta. Scheduled to open in 2004, the new facility and its 421 rooms will focus on service for business travelers.

With renovations of the Presidential Suite, Governor's Suite, and Swiss Executive Club Lounge complete, guests at **Swissôtel Atlanta,** 3391 Peachtree Rd. NE (© **800/63-SWISS**), can enjoy their stay in enhanced luxury (the hotel was pretty luxurious even *before* the renovations). The Swiss Executive Club Lounge now includes updated dining options such European continental breakfast, hors d'oeuvres, cocktails, aperitifs, cordials and afternoon tea. In addition, Swissotel announced a new $2.7 million renovation of its Grand Ballroom, the largest ballroom in Buckhead.

The **Westin Peachtree Plaza** hotel, located in the heart of downtown at 210 Peachtree St. NW (© **800/228-3000**), recently unveiled its entirely new look upon completion of a $30 million renovation. The comprehensive project included improvements to all the hotel's guestrooms, meeting facilities, restaurants and public spaces. A new dining facility, The Café, serves a buffet breakfast with stations for freshly prepared omelets and other breakfast items.

DINING Atlanta is quickly embracing its new role as a fine dining city. The Buckhead Life Restaurant Group, which is responsible for the celebrated culinary ventures of Pricci, Pano's and Paul's, and Bluepointe, has now brought fine Greek dining to Atlanta's table. **Kyma,** 3085 Piedmont Rd. (© **404/262-0702**), is a contemporary Greek seafood tavern unlike any other. The restaurant offers a unique presentation of authentic Greek food and wine that's flavorful and surprisingly healthy. Design elements are both dramatic and subtle, featuring solid marble columns, a ceiling lit by twinkling stars, a broken plate wall mosaic and a fountain cascading over a marble display of iced fresh fish.

Much to the delight of Atlantans and visitors, nightlife spot **Dante's Down the Hatch,** 3380 Peachtree Rd. NE (© **404/266-1600**), has reopened and is serving specialty fondue dinners, including that ultimate sweet tooth fantasy—chocolate fondue—for dessert. The Paul Mitchell Jazz Trio and the John Robertson Trio play live jazz aboard the restaurant's home—a fantasy 18th century ship.

For ice cream lovers and families traveling with children, **Jake's Ice Cream & Sorbets,** located in historic Inman Park at 970 Piedmont Rd. (© **404/685-3101**), offers their famous flavors in a cozy atmosphere with high ceilings, exposed brick and a view of the spectacular Atlanta skyline. Try "chocolate slap yo' mama", brown sugar vanilla, cinnamon apple pie or honey fig. In addition to the amazing ice cream, Jake's recently added fresh sandwiches, salads and soups to the menu and now offers a weekend brunch.

ATTRACTIONS The Coca-Cola Company has donated land across from Centennial Olympic Park in downtown Atlanta for the **Georgia Aquarium** and a new **World of Coca-Cola** (© **404/676-5151**)—creating a major entertainment destination in Atlanta's convention corridor. The new World of Coca-Cola, and the 5-million gallon Georgia Aquarium, slated to open its doors to the public in 2005, is expected to make the northwest section of downtown Atlanta—already occupied by a half dozen major attractions—the ultimate tourist area. Additionally, the plans should help foster 24-hour activity in the area around Centennial Olympic Park, much like the atmosphere during the 1996 Olympics.

Georgia's Stone Mountain Park (© **800/317-2006**) recently completed its largest expansion ever, with the opening of two fun-filled family attractions. The **Great Barn** is Atlanta's newest and largest children's attraction. Children can experience 1800s Southern farm life through interactive adventures. Inside the Barn, kids will find a gigantic climbing structure with rope nets, mazes, interactive games, and a 40-foot ultimate super slide. The second attraction, **Crossroads,** is a significant addition to family entertainment in Atlanta. The new attraction re-creates a small Georgia town from the 1870s, bringing the old South to life. Guests can immerse themselves in Southern culture and heritage. "Townspeople," dressed in period costumes, invite visitors to experience the past through craft demonstrations and other activities. The town features Thompson's Grist Mill and Bakery, a blacksmith shop, Tweedle's Candle Shop, glass blowing demonstrations, Miss Katie's Sideboard and the Tall Tales 4-D Theater, among other activities.

The **Atlantic Station** project is a 140-acre environmental redevelopment and reclamation of the former Atlantic Steel Mill in Midtown. Once complete, the development will include 12 million square feet of retail, office, residential and hotel space as well as 11 acres of public parks. The grand opening of this $2 billion venture is scheduled for fall of 2003.

The **Georgia World Congress Center's** (no phone) Phase IV expansion will add 75,000 square feet of meeting space and 420,000 square feet of exhibit space, and will maintain the center's rank as one of the top five largest convention centers in the nation. It is estimated that it will generate $1 billion in economic impact, $53 million in new tax revenue and 400,000 additional out-of-state visitors to the Atlanta area.

The **CNN Studio Tour** (© **404/827-2300**) now offers a better-than-ever overview of the art, science and technology of news reporting. Tourgoers can now look back at CNN's history-making coverage of news events and get a behind the scenes look at the state-of-the-art studios where world events are reported daily to more than one billion people.

Celebrating 35 seasons in Atlanta, **Six Flags Over Georgia** (© 770/ **948-9290**) opened an astonishing, next-generation roller coaster in 2002. Superman–Ultimate Flight is the South's only "flying" roller coaster. Passengers tilt face-first into flying position before climbing a 115-foot hill with a bird's-eye view below and entering a series of sharp dives, high-banked curves and spirals designed to enhance the flying experience. The signature feature is the first-ever 78-foot pretzel shaped inverted loop, that riders sail through.

The **Atlanta Symphony Orchestra** (© **404/733-5000**) announced that it was developing a new facility and would break ground in 2005. The $240 million new home of the symphony will sit on 6 acres at Peachtree and 14th streets. Plans include a living, working, and learning environment with two 30-plus story mixed-use residential/hotel and restaurant towers, green space and retail space.

Groundbreaking is scheduled for 2003 on a $130 million project to turn the **Woodruff Arts Center** and the **HIGH Museum of Art** (© **404/ 733-HIGH**) into world-class cultural destinations. The expansion will add 177,000 square feet to the HIGH museum—more than doubling the size of the facility. The expanded museum is scheduled to open in spring 2005.

AtlanTIX, the South's first day-of-show, half-price ticket booth, now offers full-price online ticket sales. Their site, www.atlantaperforms.com, provides consumers with a user-friendly, online box office selling tickets to shows and cultural arts events throughout greater Atlanta. The new online service compliments the existing day-of-show, half-price, walk-up ticket booth service located at Underground Atlanta.

1

The Best of Atlanta

"How do I get to Tara?"
"Where are Scarlett and Rhett buried?"
"Why on earth would you put sugar in iced tea but not on grits?"
"Just what is a grit anyway?"

Some visitors come to Atlanta looking for the Old South stereotypes—white-columned mansions surrounded by magnolias, owned by slow-moving folks with accents as thick as molasses. What they find is a lot more cosmopolitan and a heck of a lot more interesting.

When Gen. William Sherman burned Atlanta to the ground in 1864, the city rose from those bitter ashes and hasn't looked back since. Instead, it has spent the last 136 years or so building what's been described as the Capital of the New South and the Next Great International City. Atlanta's heritage may be Southern, but the current dynamic is brashly Sunbelt, and now it's economic vitality that drives the city's engines.

Atlanta is and always has been a city on the move. Longtime mayor William B. Hartsfield called it the city "too busy to hate," and the spirit of Atlanta is one of working together to get the job done. The dramatic downtown skyline, with its gleaming skyscrapers, is testimony to Atlanta's inability to sit still—even for a minute. And its role as host for the Centennial Olympic Games in 1996 finally convinced the rest of the world that Atlanta is a force to be reckoned with—and a great place to visit. Recent projects have only reinforced that notion. These new ventures include the $214 million, 70,500 seat Georgia Dome, which hosted the Super Bowl in 2000 and will host basketball's Final Four in 2002 and 2007; and the $213 million Philips Arena, which opened in 1999 and is home to the Atlanta Hawks basketball team and the Atlanta Thrashers hockey team.

Consistently ranked as one of the best cities in the world in which to do business, Atlanta is headquarters for hundreds of corporations, including Coca-Cola, Delta Air Lines, UPS, Holiday Inn, Georgia-Pacific, The Home Depot, BellSouth, and Cox Enterprises, and has recently become a magnet for many Internet-related companies. A major convention city and a crossroads where three interstate highways converge, it's home to the country's busiest airport and is the shopping capital of the Southeast. Although the city limits are only 131 square miles, the metro area is vast and sprawling. With 4.1 million in population and still counting, there seems to be no limit to its growth.

But commerce and development are not the only things that characterize this bustling metropolis. Its success is due in no small part to its quality of life, which is hard to beat. Atlanta is often called the City of Trees, and anyone who's ever strolled its streets when the dogwoods and azaleas are in bloom knows that the city has a small-town quality to it, with dozens of lush and beautiful neighborhoods and parks. A temperate climate makes it a magnet for anyone who enjoys the outdoors, and its Southern roots ensure a pleasant mix of graciousness and hospitality. As Atlanta has grown in stature, it has attracted residents from across the continent and around the world, further enriching the city's social fabric. You'll still hear gentle Southern accents here, but at least half of Atlanta's citizens were born outside the South. Those transplants, though, find themselves bending to the local customs, saying "please" and "ma'am" and holding doors open for each other.

When H. L. Mencken came south earlier in the century, he branded Atlanta a cultural wasteland. He should visit now.

In 1980, the revitalized black neighborhood called Sweet Auburn became a National Historic District, its 10 blocks of notable sites including Martin Luther King, Jr.'s boyhood home, his crypt, the church where he preached, a museum, and the Martin Luther King, Jr., Center for Nonviolent Social Change. It is probably *the* major black historical attraction in the country, and in the last several years it has undergone a major revitalization and restoration.

Media mogul Ted Turner inaugurated CNN here in 1980, and subsequently launched Superstation TBS, Headline News, and TNT. The High Museum of Art opened its doors in 1983. And in 1989, Underground Atlanta, a retail/restaurant/entertainment complex with a historical theme, garnered national attention.

The city is also home to major art, science, nature, and archaeology museums; a vibrant theater community; an outstanding symphony; a well-regarded ballet company; opera; blues; jazz; Broadway musicals; a presidential library; Confederate and African-American heritage sites; and dozens of art galleries. Add to that such entertaining attractions as Georgia's Stone Mountain Park, a regional theme park, a botanical garden, and major league sports teams, and you have the makings of a lively and sophisticated city. The culinary spectrum ranges from grits and biscuits to caviar and sushi. Sure, you can still feast on fried chicken and barbecue, but Atlanta also serves up Thai, Ethiopian, and Russian cuisine.

Of great significance is the recent development downtown. For years, city leaders have tried to encourage central city living, and it's finally beginning to take hold as developers are remaking old buildings into attractive apartments and lofts. The mark of a great city is an attractive and vital downtown area where people live as well as work, and Atlanta finally appears to be headed in that direction.

Atlanta now has Shirley Franklin, the first African-American female elected as mayor of this busy city. Her vision for this heart of the New South is expansive, and she's not too shy to tell you all about it.

So if it's hoop skirts and plantations you've got your heart set on, go on down to your local bookstore and pick up a copy of *Gone With the Wind.* But if you want to visit a vibrant, energetic city that's rich in heritage, culture, entertainment, and commerce, Atlanta runs right up there with the big dogs.

1 Frommer's Favorite Atlanta Experiences

• **Stepping Back in Time at the Atlanta History Center.** A re-created farm (with original buildings from the 1840s) shows how rural Southern folks really lived before the Civil War, and the 1928 Swan House, an estate on the property, gives a fascinating glimpse into the lifestyle enjoyed by upper-crust Atlantans in the early 20th century. Kids can explore the walking trails after they take in the exhibits, which include hands-on discovery areas at the history

The Atlanta Region

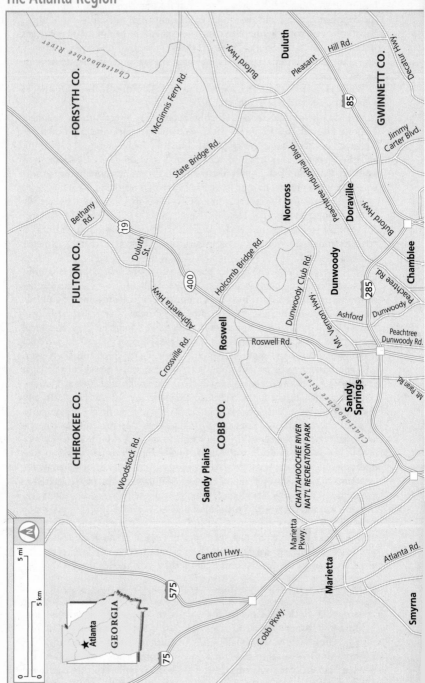

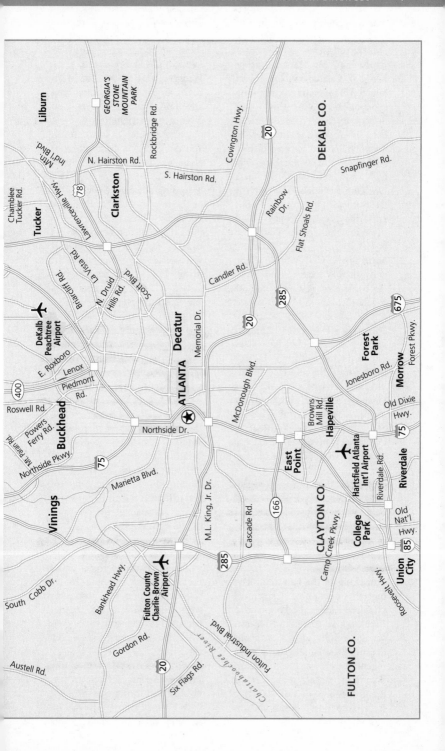

museum. A great look at the rich tapestry of Atlanta's past and present. See p. 147.

- **Exploring the Martin Luther King, Jr. Center for Nonviolent Social Change.** It's an inspiring experience to visit this living memorial to a true American hero, where you'll see lots of King memorabilia and a video display on his life and works. Especially moving is Freedom Plaza, where Dr. King is buried. The tomb is inscribed with his words: "Free at Last. Free at Last. Thank God Almighty I'm Free at Last." See p. 164.

- **Touring the CNN Studios.** The network that started around-the-clock television news lets you take a peek behind the scenes to see how it's all done. See p. 152.

- **Spending a Day at the Ballpark.** Pack up the kids and take them out to the old ball game. Even if there isn't a Braves game scheduled, you can take a tour of Turner Field, which was completed in 1996 and served as the Olympic Stadium for the Centennial Olympic Games before it was converted to a baseball park. See p. 194.

- **Trekking Through Virginia-Highland.** Atlanta's version of SoHo, this trendy neighborhood is full of coffee bars, galleries, cafes, and funky little shops. It all makes for a pleasant stroll on a sunny afternoon.

- **Frolicking in the Fountain.** The biggest attraction at Centennial Olympic Park is the Fountain of Rings, where young and old can get delightfully soaked on warm days. The fountain is a simple but ingenious design on the plaza floor that consists of 251 water jets in the shape of the 5 Olympic rings. Take a deep breath and zip in and around the 12-foot water bursts or just sit and watch the timed light- and sound-effects show, when the water bursts 35 feet into the air. See p. 150.

- **Hanging Out at the Zoo.** Ever since the giant pandas, Yang Yang and Lun Lun, arrived at Zoo Atlanta in late 1999, this has been one of the hottest tickets in town. You don't have to be a kid to be fascinated by the adorable duo. See p. 185.

- **Shopping at Lenox Square.** One of the most popular malls in the Southeast, Lenox Square is a mecca for upscale shoppers. It's hard to visit every store, even if you spend the whole day, but many visitors think it's a worthy goal. You'll find good restaurants and great people-watching, too. See p. 210.

- **Getting a Breath of Fresh Air in Piedmont Park.** Atlanta's favorite public park is fun and funky and a terrific place to watch the world go by. Take your in-line skates or pack a lunch and find a shady spot for a picnic. See p. 179.

- **Bargain-Hunting at the Lakewood Antiques Market.** Crammed with everything from precious antiques to objets-de-junque, this huge once-a-month flea market is not to be missed if you're lucky enough to be in town on the right weekend. See p. 212.

- **Taking in a Chastain Park Amphitheatre Concert.** Big-name entertainers perform under the stars, and everyone brings elaborate picnic fare, complete with tablecloth and a candelabrum, for the picnic table. Even the entertainers seem dazzled by the setting. See p. 221.

- **Spending the Morning at the Market.** Atlanta is home to two gigantic indoor farmers markets, both jammed with locals who are shopping in earnest and visitors

Aquarium for the Future

With downtown revitalization at the top of the list for Atlanta leaders and developers, the proposal for a Georgia Aquarium was a big hit with Atlantans when announced in 2001. Governor Roy Barnes projects that the new aquarium will be "the single biggest attraction in the state of Georgia."

Planned for construction on 9 acres donated by the Coca Cola Co., next to Centennial Olympic Park, the proposed $200 million facility will be connected by a plaza to the soon-to-be-relocated World of Coca-Cola, and the two attractions will open simultaneously in 2005.

These two projects, along with a planned children's museum and the existing CNN Center, Philips Arena, and the Tabernacle—the latter two being popular entertainment venues—should be a much-needed shot in the arm for the downtown residential and commercial markets. These developments will no doubt make the downtown area *the* place to be in this city, for tourists, residents, and convention-goers.

who are having a hard time keeping their eyes from bugging out. Choose from the DeKalb Farmers Market, which has an international flavor, and Harry's, which is a little more upscale. Each has loads of gourmet goodies you can take home or consume on the spot. See p. 214 for the Dekalb Farmers Market and p. 214 for Harry's.

- **Strolling Around Oakland Cemetery.** This 88-acre cemetery is a peaceful place, and its Victorian graves are of aesthetic, historic, and symbolic interest. The guided tour is recommended. Bring a picnic lunch. See p. 168.

- **Discovering the Fox Theatre.** This Moorish-Egyptian palace exemplifies the glamorous movie-theater architecture of the 1920s, complete with onion domes, minarets, and a twinkling starlit sky over the auditorium. See p. 156.

- **Touring the World of Coca-Cola.** Atlanta is Coke's hometown, so it's only fitting that there's a monument here to the world's most renowned beverage. There's a replica of a 1930s soda fountain, a gigantic collection of memorabilia, interactive exhibits, and Club Coca-Cola, where you can sample all the beverages Coke has to offer, including many not marketed in the United States. It might seem pretty commercial, but it's also fascinating. See p. 169.

- **Relaxing in Georgia's Stone Mountain Park.** Take a hike to the top of the big granite rock or spend a leisurely day seeing the sights. You can also choose from an array of activities—golf, tennis, swimming, hiking, boating, and more. See p. 156.

- **Time-Traveling at Fernbank Museum of Natural History.** Check out the 45-foot-long model of a Giganotosaurus, then travel back 15 billion years and experience the "Big Bang" that jump-started the formation of the universe. The museum's stunning architecture is notable. IMAX films are shown here, too. See p. 154.

2 Best Hotel Bets

- **Best for Business Travelers:** All the major downtown megahotels—which cater largely to a business and convention clientele—are fully equipped to meet your business needs. The finest is the **Ritz-Carlton Atlanta,** 181 Peachtree St. NE (ℂ **800/241-3333**), which combines a full business center and a can-do concierge with superb service. See p. 75.

- **Best for Families:** The **Marriott Residence Inn Buckhead,** 2960 Piedmont Rd. NE (ℂ **800/331-3131**), offers accommodations large enough to ensure privacy for all, plus fully equipped kitchens, washers and dryers, indoor and outdoor swimming pools, barbecue grills, and basketball, volleyball, and paddle tennis courts. Many rooms have fireplaces. See p. 94.

- **Best for a Romantic Getaway:** You'll be pampered beyond belief at the luxurious **Ritz-Carlton Buckhead,** 3434 Peachtree Rd. (ℂ **800/241-3333**).

- **Best Moderately Priced Hotel:** It's hard to beat the **Marriott Residence Inn Atlanta-Downtown,** 134 Peachtree St. NW (ℂ **800/331-3131**). It offers large rooms and a bundle of amenities for a very reasonable price. See p. 78.

- **Best Inexpensive Accommodations:** It's nothing fancy, but the convenient Buckhead location of the **Sleep Inn,** 800 Sidney Marcus Blvd. (ℂ **800/753-3746**), makes this a good deal. See p. 97.

- **Best Location:** Buckhead is one of the loveliest parts of town and has exceptional nightlife, dining, and shopping. There are two MARTA stations (Buckhead and Lenox) where you can connect to other parts of the city, and any hotel within walking distance of either of those stations is a sure bet. A good example is the **J.W. Marriott Hotel Lenox,** 3300 Lenox Rd. NE (ℂ **800/228-9290**), adjacent to the upscale Lenox Square mall. See p. 87.

- **Best Service:** The **Ritz-Carlton Atlanta** and the **Ritz-Carlton Buckhead** (see addresses and telephone numbers above) are in a class by themselves. A close second is the **Four Seasons,** 75 Fourteenth St. (ℂ **800/332-3442**). See p. 75, p. 90, and p. 80 for each hotel, respectively.

- **Best Architectural Digest Interior:** The most exquisite interior in town can be found at the **Gaslight Inn,** 1001 St. Charles Ave. (ℂ **404/876-1001**), a bed-and-breakfast where the rooms might inspire you to redecorate your own home. See p. 98.

- **Best Trendy Hotel:** The **Swissôtel,** 3391 Peachtree Rd. NE (ℂ **800/63-SWISS**), with its clean Euromodern style, is a favorite among visiting celebrities. See p. 90. The chic **W Atlanta,** 111 Perimeter Center West (ℂ **770/396-6800**), is another trendy fave. See p. 95.

- **Best for Travelers with Disabilities:** The **Embassy Suites Atlanta Buckhead,** 3285 Peachtree Rd. NW (ℂ **800/362-2779**), is fully accessible, with 10 suites completely equipped for disabled visitors and some with roll-in showers. The hotel is just a block away from the Buckhead MARTA station. See p. 93.

- **Best for Pets:** Some hotels can get downright snooty if you try to check in with your pooch, but not the lavish **Four Seasons Hotel** (see address and phone number above). Small pets are welcome (just call ahead) and even get special treats to make them feel at home. The more modest **Cheshire Motor Inn,** 1865 Cheshire Bridge Rd. (© **800/827-9628**), also wel-

comes pets. See p. 80 for the Four Seasons and p. 86 for Cheshire Motor Inn.

3 Best Dining Bets

- **Best Spot for a Romantic Dinner:** There's no better spot than the tree-shaded terrace at **Horseradish Grill,** 4320 Powers Ferry Rd. (© **404/255-7277**). See p. 130.
- **Best Spot for a Business Lunch:** The power brokers head for **Bone's,** 3130 Piedmont Rd. NE (© **404/237-2663**), in Buckhead, where the food is serious and the service is impeccable and unobtrusive. See p. 120.
- **Best Spot for a Celebration:** Why not pick one of the most sought-after tables in town? That would be at **Bacchanalia,** 1198 Howell Mill Rd. (© **404/365-0410**). See p. 110.
- **Best Newcomer: Joel,** 3290 Northside Parkway (© **404/233-3500**), as in Chef Joel Antunes, formerly of the famed Ritz-Carlton Buckhead, is a chic and simple French brasserie featuring Mediterranean and Asian influences in a Johnson Studio–designed minimal, contemporary space. See p. 125.
- **Best View: Canoe,** 4199 Paces Ferry Rd., in Vinings (© **770/432-2663**), is perched on the side of the Chattahoochee River. Ask for a table on the large, canopied patio, surrounded by landscaped gardens, and watch the river go by. See p. 140.
- **Best Wine List: The Dining Room** at the Ritz-Carlton Buckhead, 3434 Peachtree Rd. NE (© **404/237-2700**), is Atlanta's premier dining venue, and its cuisine is complemented by a vast wine cellar. See p. 121.

- **Best Italian Cuisine:** It's noisy as the devil, but **Sotto Sotto,** 313 N. Highland Ave. (© **404/523-6678**), gets my vote for its inspired Northern Italian cuisine. See p. 137.
- **Best Italian on a Budget: Pasta da Pulcinella,** 1123 Peachtree Walk (© **404/876-1114**), serves gourmet pasta for next to nothing. See p. 117.
- **Best Seafood:** The **Atlanta Fish Market,** 265 Pharr Rd. (© **404/262-3165**), is the ticket, with an enormous selection of fresh seafood dishes that are done to perfection. See p. 127.
- **Best New Southern Cuisine:** The competition is stiff, but the **Horseradish Grill** (see "Best Spot for a Romantic Dinner," above) wins by a hair. See p. 130.
- **Best Traditional Southern Cuisine:** It's a tie between **Colonnade,** 1879 Cheshire Bridge Rd. NE (© **404/874-5642**), keeper of the best heirloom recipes; and **Thelma's Kitchen,** 768 Marietta St. NW (© **404/688-5855**), the city's premier soul food spot. See p. 109 and 110.
- **Best Southwestern Cuisine: Nava,** 3060 Peachtree Rd. (© **404/240-1984**), is a stunning restaurant with food to match. See p. 130.
- **Best Steakhouse:** There's quite a turf war going on, but **Bone's,** that powerhouse for powerbrokers, gets my vote (see "Best Place for a Business Lunch," above). See p. 120.
- **Best Desserts: Bacchanalia** (see "Best Spot for a Celebration,"

The Importance of P.C.

P.C. is a big priority in Atlanta. No, no. Not P.C. as in political correctness. P.C. as in pimento cheese. And let's get the pronunciation down right off the bat. It's puh-MEN-uh cheese, an utterly simple but delightful mixture, usually consisting of just three main ingredients—canned pimentos, cheese, and some sort of binder, probably mayonnaise—slapped between two pieces of white bread. Southern cooks have hot debates over the fine points. Cheddar or Monterey Jack? Sharp or extra sharp? Duke's mayonnaise or Hellmann's? Is onion OK? How about red pepper flakes?

Regardless of the mixture, a pimento cheese sandwich is right up there with grits as one of the ultimate Southern comfort foods. It's usually a homemade concoction, not on many restaurant menus. But the renowned Scott Peacock, executive chef of Watershed in Decatur, has seen fit to include it among his lunch *and* dinner offerings. Here's his take on the venerable Southern classic. We recommend adding a little more mayonnaise.

Watershed's Pimento Cheese

2½ cups (10 oz.) extra sharp cheddar cheese, grated
⅛ teaspoon cayenne pepper, or to taste
salt to taste, if needed
5 or 6 grinds of black pepper
¾ cup homemade mayonnaise
3 tablespoons finely chopped pimento

In a mixing bowl, stir together all of the ingredients until well mixed and creamy. Taste carefully for seasoning and adjust as needed. Cover and store refrigerated until ready to use. Makes about 2 cups.

above) wins this category with its warm Valrhona chocolate cake with vanilla bean ice cream, a flourless confection with a sinful, gooey center. They tried to take it off the menu once, but the public outcry was too great. See p. 110.

- **Best Fried Chicken:** There are lots of New Southern restaurants trying to invent newfangled ways to cook fried chicken. Well, they should just cut it out. And you should head to the **Colonnade** or **Thelma's Kitchen** (see "Best Traditional Southern Cuisine," above) for some of the best fried chicken you've ever tasted. These two establishments have been turning it out for years, and they

know what they're doing. See p. 110 and 109.

- **Best Brunch:** Can be no other than **Murphy's,** 997 Virginia Ave. (© **404/872-0904**), where the serving of American and Continental cuisine has transitioned right along with this funky neighborhood. See p. 136.

- **Best Breakfast:** The fun and funky **Flying Biscuit Cafe,** 1655 McLendon Ave. (© **404/687-8888**), fulfills all the usual breakfast expectations, but there's also a great selection of offbeat specialties. See p. 139.

- **Best Late-Night Dining:** Head downtown to **Mumbo Jumbo Bar & Grill,** 89 Park Place NE

(© **404/523-0330**); the folks there stay up very late. See p. 106.

- **Best Decor: Bluepointe,** 3455 Peachtree Rd. (© **404/237-9070**), is an energy-filled multi-level restaurant in a soaring contemporary space. Its dramatic decor feels very of the moment and full of class. See p. 128.

- **Best People-Watching:** Famous beefeaters flock to **Bone's** (see "Best Steakhouse," above), which has welcomed the likes of Bob Hope, George Bush, and the Atlanta Braves. See p. 120.

- **Best Afternoon Tea:** Fresh-baked scones with Devonshire cream, finger sandwiches, pastries, and tea are served every afternoon in the posh lobby lounge of the **Ritz-Carlton Buckhead** (see "Best Wine List," above). See p. 121.

- **Best Pre- and Post-theater Dining:** If you're attending a show at the Woodruff Arts Center—Atlanta's major performance facility—dine at **Veni Vidi Vici,** 41 Fourteenth St. (© **404/875-8424**), which opens early enough to have a relaxing meal. For post-theater noshing, try **South City Kitchen,** 1144 Crescent Ave. (© **404/873-7358**). See p. 115 and p. 111, respectively.

2

Planning Your Trip to Atlanta

In the pages that follow, you'll find practical information that will help you make travel arrangements, pick a time to visit, find local resources for specialized needs, and even access megabytes of useful information on the Internet.

1 Visitor Information

As soon as you know you're going to Atlanta, write or call the **Atlanta Convention & Visitors Bureau (ACVB),** 233 Peachtree St. NE, Suite 2000, Atlanta, GA 30303 (© **800/ ATLANTA** or 404/222-6688). They'll send you a copy of *Atlanta Now* (a visitors' guide), a book of discount coupons, a *Metro Atlanta Map and Attractions Guide,* and a 2-month calendar of events; they can also advise you on anything from Atlanta's hotel and restaurant scene to the best tour packages available. For information, visit the ACVB website at **www. atlanta.net**.

You can also learn a lot about the city and its latest happenings by visit-ing **www.AccessAtlanta.com**, a web-site whose partners include *The Atlanta Journal-Constitution* and WSB-TV and radio. There, you'll find current local news, a 5-day weather forecast, street maps, and up-to-date information about special events, the arts, entertainment, sports, recreation, restaurants, shopping, and more. There's even a link to the Atlanta Yellow Pages.

Another site worth checking out is **www.Atlanta.Citysearch.com**. Although it's not as complete as www. AccessAtlanta.com, it still has lots of useful information about arts, entertainment, attractions, restaurants, shopping, and hotels.

2 Money

ATMS

ATMs are linked to a network that most likely includes your bank at home. **Cirrus** (© **800/424-7787;** www.mastercard.com) and **PLUS** (© **800/843-7587;** www.visa.com) are the two most popular networks in the U.S.; call or check online for ATM locations at your destination. Be sure you know your four-digit PIN before you leave home and be sure to find out your daily withdrawal limit before you depart. You can also get cash advances on your credit card at an ATM. Keep in mind that credit card companies try to protect themselves from theft by limiting the funds someone can withdraw away from home. It's therefore best to call your credit card company before you leave and let them know where you're going and how much you plan to spend. You'll get the best exchange rate if you withdraw money from an ATM, but keep in mind that many banks impose a fee every time a card is used at an ATM in a different city or bank. On top of this, the bank from which you withdraw cash may charge its own fee.

Destination: Atlanta—Red Alert Checklist

- Do any theater, restaurant, or travel reservations need to be booked in advance?
- Did you pack your camera and an extra set of camera batteries, and purchase enough film? If you packed film in your checked baggage, did you invest in protective pouches to shield film from airport x-rays?
- Do you have a safe, accessible place to store money?
- Did you bring your ID cards that could entitle you to discounts such as AAA and AARP cards, student IDs, etc.?
- Did you bring emergency drug prescriptions and extra glasses and/or contact lenses?
- Do you have your credit card PINs?
- If you have an E-ticket, do you have documentation?
- Did you leave a copy of your itinerary with someone at home?

TRAVELER'S CHECKS

These days, traveler's checks seem less necessary because most cities have 24-hour ATMs that allow you to withdraw small amounts of cash as needed. However, keep in mind that you will likely be charged an ATM withdrawal fee if the bank is not your own, so if you're withdrawing money every day, you might be better off with traveler's checks—provided that you don't mind showing identification every time you want to cash one.

You can get traveler's checks at almost any bank. **American Express** offers denominations of $20, $50, $100, $500, and (for cardholders only) $1,000. You'll pay a service charge ranging from 1% to 4%. You can also get American Express traveler's checks over the phone by calling ✆ **800/221-7282**; Amex gold and platinum cardholders who use this number are exempt from the 1% fee. AAA members can obtain checks without a fee at most AAA offices.

Visa offers traveler's checks at Citibank locations nationwide, as well as at several other banks. The service charge ranges between 1.5% and 2%; checks come in denominations of $20, $50, $100, $500, and $1,000. Call ✆ **800/732-1322** for information. **MasterCard** also offers traveler's checks. Call ✆ **800/223-9920** for a location near you.

CREDIT CARDS

Credit cards are invaluable when traveling. They are a safe way to carry money and provide a convenient record of all your expenses. You can also withdraw cash advances from your credit cards at any bank (though you'll start paying hefty interest on the advance the moment you receive the cash.) At most banks, you don't even need to go to a teller; you can get a cash advance at the ATM if you know your PIN access number. If you've forgotten yours, or didn't even know you had one, call the number on the back of your credit card and ask the bank to send it to you. It usually takes 5 to 7 business days, though some banks will provide the number over the phone if you tell them your mother's maiden name or pass some other security clearance.

WHAT TO DO IF YOUR WALLET GETS STOLEN

Be sure to block charges against your account the minute you discover a credit card has been lost or stolen. Then be sure to file a police report.

Almost every credit card company has an emergency 800-number to call if your card is stolen. They may be able to wire you a cash advance off your credit card immediately, and in many places, they can deliver an emergency credit card in a day or two. The issuing bank's 800-number is usually on the back of your credit card—though, of course, if your card has been stolen, that won't help you unless you recorded the number elsewhere.

Citicorp Visa's U.S. emergency number is ⓒ **800/336-8472.** American Express cardholders and traveler's check holders should call ⓒ **800/ 221-7282.** MasterCard holders should call ⓒ **800/307-7309.** Otherwise, call the toll-free number directory at ⓒ **800/555-1212.**

Odds are that if your wallet is gone, the police won't be able to recover it for you. However, it's still worth informing the authorities. Your credit card company or insurer may require a police report number or record of the theft.

If you choose to carry traveler's checks, be sure to keep a record of their serial numbers separate from your checks. You'll get a refund faster if you know the numbers.

If you need emergency cash over the weekend when all banks and American Express offices are closed, you can have money wired to you from **Western Union** (ⓒ **800/325-6000;** www.westernunion.com). You will be asked to present a valid ID to pick up the cash at the Western Union office. However, you can usually pick up a money transfer even if you don't have valid identification, as long as you can answer a test question provided by the sender. Be sure to let the sender know in advance that you don't have ID. If you need to use a test question instead of ID, the sender must take cash to his or her local Western Union office, rather than transferring the money over the phone or online.

3 When to Go

Although there is no high season for tourism here, Atlanta is a major convention and trade show destination. Before choosing travel dates, it's wise to ask the Atlanta Convention & Visitors Bureau (ACVB) or your travel agent what major events will be taking place in Atlanta when you plan to visit. Large conventions can mean an increase in hotel prices and longer waits at popular restaurants.

Spring and autumn are long seasons, and in terms of natural beauty and moderate temperatures, they're ideal times to visit. April, when the dogwoods and azaleas put on a brilliant, colorful display, is especially lovely, but May and October are excellent months here, too.

If you come during July and August, when Atlanta gets a little steamy, you may find some hotels offering summer discounts. Almost all accommodations offer reduced rates during the Christmas holiday season.

THE WEATHER

Atlanta's climate is mostly temperate year-round. The city enjoys four distinct seasons, but the variations are less extreme than in other parts of the United States.

It does get cold here in winter. The mercury dips below freezing—usually at night—an average of 50 days a year, and at least once a year there's a snowfall or an ice storm. (Northern transplants think it's pretty hilarious the way an inch or two of snow can paralyze the city.) But for the most part, winter days are mild, and it's often possible to enjoy the parks and even the outdoor restaurants in the middle of January or February.

Don't let the low average daytime temperatures for July, August, and early September fool you. Summers can be hot and humid, with daytime highs reaching into the 90s, although the really stifling spells usually last just a few days at a time. Annual rainfall is about 48 inches, and the wettest months are December through April, and July.

Atlanta's Average Daytime Temperature & Rainfall

	Jan	Feb	Mar	Apr	May	June	July	Aug	Sept	Oct	Nov	Dec
Temp. °F/°C	41/5	45/7	54/12	62/17	69/21	76/24	79/26	78/26	73/23	62/17	53/12	45/7
Rainfall (in.)	4.8	4.8	5.8	4.3	4.3	3.6	5.0	3.7	3.4	3.1	3.9	4.3

ATLANTA CALENDAR OF EVENTS

Note: Some events, such as the Georgia Renaissance Festival and the Georgia Shakespeare Festival, begin in one month and continue for several months thereafter. These are listed in the month that they start, so do look back and ahead a few months for information on ongoing events. The ACVB's website also offers a terrific calendar of events.

January

Martin Luther King, Jr., Weekend. This is a major happening that begins with an interfaith service and includes musical tributes, seminars, awards dinners, and speeches by notables (including Coretta Scott King). There are also concerts by major performers (in past years Stevie Wonder and the Neville Brothers, among others, have performed). For details, contact the **King Center** (© **404/526-8900**) or visit www.the kingcenter.org. Second weekend of January.

Cathedral Antiques Show. For 4 days, 30 to 35 high-quality antiques dealers display their wares at the Cathedral of St. Philip, 2744 Peach-tree Rd. at W. Wesley Rd. The merchandise ranges from 18th- and 19th-century furnishings to vintage jewelry and Oriental rugs. Admission is $10 per day. On the first day of the show, a tour of homes and mansions in Buckhead is offered for an additional fee. For details, call © **404/365-1000.** Last week in January.

February

Southeastern Flower Show. One of the South's premier gardening events, the flower show takes place for 5 days toward the beginning of the month at the Atlanta Exposition Center, 3650 Jonesboro Rd. SE. It offers nearly 4 acres of stunning landscapes and gardens displaying both flowers and plants. Garden-related products are sold at the 90-vendor marketplace, and there are events for children and demonstrations of gardening techniques. Adult admission is $11 in advance, $15 at the door, with discounts for seniors and children. For information, directions, and tickets, call © **404/888-5638** or visit www. flowershow.org. Five days in early February.

March

Lasershow Spectacular. This sight-and-sound extravaganza of laser lights and fireworks, held at Georgia's Stone Mountain Park, is choreographed to popular, patriotic, country, and classical music. Admission is free, but you must pay $6 for a parking permit to the park. For details, call © **770/498-5690** or visit www.stonemountainpark. com. Beginning in March, the show can be seen Saturdays at 8:30pm. From Memorial Day Weekend through Labor Day, the show takes place nightly at 9:30pm, and then it resumes its Saturday 8:30pm schedule through October.

April

Easter Sunrise Services. The service is held at the top and the base of Georgia's Stone Mountain at 30 minutes before sunrise. Park gates open at 4am, and the skylift begins operating at 5am. For details, call ℂ 770/498-5690 or visit www.stonemountainpark.com On Easter Sunday (April 20th in 2003; April 11th in 2004).

Atlanta Dogwood Festival. Held in Piedmont Park, this huge festival includes concerts, food booths, kite-flying contests, children's activities, a juried arts-and-crafts show, and the National Disc-Dog Championship (a canine Frisbee tournament). Particularly exciting is the display of hot-air balloons. For details, call ℂ 404/329-0501. Three days in mid-April.

Inman Park Spring Festival. This Atlanta suburb (the city's oldest) is noted for its gorgeous turn-of-the-century Victorian mansions and Craftsman-style cottages. Activities include a tour of homes, live entertainment (theater, jazz bands, cloggers, Irish music, country music, and more), an arts-and-crafts festival/flea market, a parade, and food vendors. Tickets to the tour of homes are $10 in advance, $12 the day of the tour. All other events are free. For more information, call ℂ 770/242-4895. Last weekend in April.

Spring Campaign. Although there are several Civil War re-enactments at Stone Mountain Park during the year, this full-scale encampment of both Union and Confederate soldiers is the most ambitious. It's staged near the Antebellum Plantation, and lots of participants in uniforms and other period costumes demonstrate what life was like during the Civil War. Admission is free, but you must pay $6 for a parking permit to the park. For details, call ℂ 770/498-5690 or visit www.stonemountainpark.com. Late April (April 24–27 in 2003).

Georgia Renaissance Festival. This re-creation of a 16th-century English county fair (held in Fairburn—8 miles south of the airport on I-85, Exit 61) in a 30-acre "village," features a juried crafts show and marketplace with over 100 craftspeople (many of them demonstrating 16th-century skills); continuous entertainment on 12 stages (there are more than 100 shows each day); period foods; a birds of prey show; and a cast of costumed characters including jousting knights, jugglers, storytellers, giant stilt-walkers, minstrels, magicians, and choral groups. King Henry VIII and one of his wives oversee the festivities. Admission is $12.95 for adults, $11 for seniors, $5.75 for ages 6 to 12; free for ages 5 and under. For details, call ℂ 770/964-8575 or visit www.garenfest.com. On seven weekends, from the next to last Saturday in April through the first Sunday in June (plus Memorial Day).

May

Gardens for Connoisseurs Tour. If you're a gardening buff, this is an excellent tour, allowing you a peek into several outstanding private gardens. Tickets, which benefit the Atlanta Botanical Garden, are around $20 for the entire tour, $5 per garden. For details, call ℂ 404/876-5859 or visit www.atlantabotanicalgarden.org. Weekend of Mother's Day.

Music Midtown—An Atlanta Festival. This musical extravaganza takes place in Midtown at the beginning of May. Events—starting Friday night—include dozens of concerts on several stages (many of them big-name performers such as the Indigo Girls, Etta James, Al Green, Joan Baez, and blues artist Buddy Guy), an artists' market, and food booths from regional restaurants. There are kids' activities too, from live performances to hands-on activities. Admission is $25 for 1 day, $30 for all 3 days; free for children under age 10 accompanied by an adult. You may buy tickets at the gate, but they're also available through Ticketmaster at ℂ **404/249-6400.** Call ℂ **770-MIDTOWN** or contact www.musicmidtown.com for locations and more information. Early May.

Decatur Arts Festival and Garden Tour. This 3-day event features an art show on the south lawn of the Old Courthouse in Decatur, various juried shows nearby, garden tours, mimes, jugglers, puppet shows, clowns, children's art activities, great food, and performances by music, dance, and theater groups. The literary arts are celebrated with storytelling, readings, and book signings. Events are free, except for the garden tour, which is $10 for eight gardens. For details, call ℂ **404/371-8386.** Memorial Day weekend, but most events take place on Saturday and Sunday.

Atlanta Jazz Festival. This is a week of jazz in different venues around the city, beginning the week before Memorial Day and continuing through the holiday weekend. Concerts might include such major stars as Wynton Marsalis, Nancy Wilson, Shirley Horn, Cyrus Chestnut, Max Roach, or Sonny Rollins. Admission is charged to most events, but concerts in Piedmont Park on Memorial Day Weekend are free. The celebration in the park also includes artists'

booths and food vendors. For details call the **Festival Hotline** at ℂ **404/817-6851,** visit www.atlantafestivals.com, or call the city's **Bureau of Cultural Affairs** at ℂ **404/817-6815.** Begins the week before Memorial Day and continues through the holiday weekend.

Atlanta Film & Video Festival. The IMAGE Film/Video Center, 75 Bennett St. NW, features more than 150 films and videos by some of the country's most important independent media artists. Admission is $7.50 per film for most films, which are shown at several venues around the city. Discounts are available for students and seniors. Call ℂ **404/352-4225** for details or visit **www.imagefv.org**. Eight or 9 days in late May or early June.

June

Virginia-Highland Summerfest. Held one weekend in the middle of the month, this neighborhood arts and music festival takes place along Virginia Avenue near the intersection of North Highland Avenue. There's a juried arts-and-crafts show, an artists market, food booths, and plenty of free entertainment in John Howell Park. Afterward, take a stroll through Virginia-Highland, which has lots of galleries and shops. All events are free. For more information, call ℂ **404/222-8244, ext. 9** or visit www.vahi.org. One weekend in the middle of June.

Georgia Shakespeare Festival. Five productions are held mid-June through November on the campus of Oglethorpe University, 4484 Peachtree Rd., in the intimate 510-seat Conant Performing Arts Center. Before the summer performances, audiences enjoy farcical vignettes on the lawn. Everyone brings a pre-performance picnic or arranges in advance to purchase it on the premises. The company, made up of Actors Equity pros for the most part, offers both traditional and innovative Shakespearean productions as well as other classics. Picnic grounds open an hour-and-a-half before summer performances, and the pre-show begins 1 hour before curtain time. There are both matinees and evening performances. Admission is $20 to $26.50 for adults, $3 less for seniors and students. Call for tickets as far in advance as possible, especially for weekend performances. For information about tickets or picnic lunches, call © **404/264-0020** or visit www.gashakespeare.org. Mid-June through November.

Stone Mountain Village Annual Arts & Crafts Festival. This family-oriented festival has something for everyone. More than 125 Southeastern craftspeople display their wares in a juried show, and entertainment (cloggers, clowns, country music, and more) is offered continually in the Village. There are food booths and lots of activities for kids. Admission is $1 for adults; free for children under age 12. For details, call © **770/879-4971.** Father's Day weekend.

July

Asian Cultural Experience. The Atlanta Botanical Garden celebrates Asian culture with demonstrations of crafts, musical performances, children's activities, an art show, and dancing, among other things. Admission is included with Garden admission price. For details, call © **404/876-5859** or visit www. atlantabotanicalgarden.org. One weekend in early July.

Independence Day. If you're willing to get up early on July 4th, you can start the day's celebrations by watching 55,000 runners pound the pavement in the **Peachtree Road Race,** a 10K run down Peachtree Road from Lenox Square to Piedmont Park. For details, call © **404/231-9064.** Later in the afternoon, take in Atlanta's star-spangled Salute 2 America Parade. The floats, marching bands, and giant, helium-filled balloons start at Centennial Olympic Park at 1pm, then travel down Marietta St. to Five Points. For information, call © **404/897-7855.** Afterward, there's more free entertainment and music in the park, but the best part is the stunning fireworks display at night. For more information call © **404/222-7275.** The big attraction at Stone Mountain Park's **Fantastic Fourth Celebration** is the extravagant fireworks displays after the star-spangled laser show. Picnickers come early in the day and stay for the grand finale. For details, call © **770/498-5690** or visit www.stonemountainpark.com. July 4th. An old-fashioned **Fourth of July Parade,** complete with floats, bands, baton twirlers, cloggers, and more, also takes place in Stone Mountain Village, from Mountain Street at the foot of the west gate of Stone Mountain Park along Main Street through the Village shop area. The stores are open, and when the parade's over, there's free watermelon for everyone at the Visitor Center. The parade begins at 10am, preceded by a 5K run at 7am.

For details, call © **770/879-4971.** About 100,000 people gather every July 4th at Underground Atlanta for a multicultural celebration featuring live entertainment from a variety of cultural backgrounds. Call © **404/523-2311** for details.

National Black Arts Festival. More than 150 events (most of them free) take place throughout

Impressions

We're going to ride these buses desegregated in Atlanta, Georgia, or we're going to ride a chariot in heaven or push a wheelbarrow in hell.
—Rev. William Holmes Borders, civil rights leader (1957)
Atlanta is like Los Angeles was before it went bad.
—Jane Fonda, activist (1996)

the city. Billed as "a celebration of the sights, sounds, and expressions of the African Diaspora," it features concerts (including such big names as Abbey Lincoln and Wynton Marsalis), theater, film, dance, storytelling, poetry readings, performance art, art and folk-art exhibitions, children's activities, workshops, African puppet shows, and more. For details call ℂ **404/730-0177** or visit www.nbaf.org. A 10-day affair (even-numbered years only) in late July and early August.

August

Montreux Atlanta Music Festival. Jazz, blues, gospel, reggae, and zydeco music is performed in different venues around the city, including Centennial Olympic Park and Piedmont Park. Both regional and internationally known artists perform. Admission is charged to most events, but concerts in Piedmont Park on Labor Day Weekend are free. The celebration in the park also includes artists' booths and food vendors. For details call the **Festival Hotline** at ℂ **404/817-6851,** visit www.atlantafestivals.com, or call the city's **Bureau of Cultural Affairs** at ℂ **404/817-6815.** A weeklong affair ending on the Monday of Labor Day weekend).

September

Art in the Park. This Labor Day weekend art show, on the historic square in Marietta (just northwest of Atlanta), offers fine art by more than 120 artists, plus food and antiques. Free. Call ℂ **770/429-1115** for details. Labor Day weekend.

Yellow Daisy Festival. Georgia's Stone Mountain Park hosts a vast outdoor arts-and-crafts show (more than 400 exhibitors) with musical entertainment, a flower show, great food, clogging, and storytellers. About 175,000 people attend each year. For details, call ℂ **770/498-5690** or visit www.stonemountainpark.com. Held the weekend after Labor Day.

October

American Association of University Women's Annual Book Fair. At this 4-day event in Lenox Square mall, the AAUW collects, categorizes, and sells over 75,000 used books each year. All are in good condition, some are valuable, and prices are low. Proceeds go to scholarships for women. Admission is free. Hours are 10am to 9:30pm. Call ℂ **404/355-1861** for details. Held in early October.

Annual Scottish Festival and Highland Games. This gathering of the clans at Stone Mountain comprises 2 days of Highland dancing, pipe and drum concerts, Scottish harping and fiddling, sword dancing, reel dancing, lilting, and athletic events such as the hammer throw and caber toss. For details and admission charges, call ℂ **770/498-5690** or visit www.stonemountainpark.com. Mid-October.

ArtScape. Woodruff Park, in the heart of downtown, is the scene for this mid-month gathering of more than 125 artists and craftspeople. Though the emphasis is on local and regional art, there are also artists from around the country, as well as musical entertainment, festival food, and children's activities. There's a small admission charge. For more information, call ℂ **404/577-7477** or visit www.artscape atlanta.com. Mid-October.

Sunday in the Park at Oakland Cemetery. On an annually selected October Sunday, this graveyard party features storytellers, historians, guided tours, a hat and costume contest, turn-of-the-century music, and Victorian boutiques. Admission is free. For a small charge, you can reserve a picnic lunch. Call ℂ **404/688-2107** for details. Sunday in October (changes yearly).

November

Veterans Day Parade. Atlanta mounts an impressive version of this parade each year, with floats, drill teams, marching bands, clowns, color guards, and more. The parade begins at 11am at Sixteenth Street and Peachtree Street in Midtown and proceeds south to Tenth Street. Veterans Day.

An Olde Fashioned Christmas. Things kick off with an array of events at Stone Mountain Park from mid-November through December 30. Tour the authentically decorated Antebellum Plantation, where you'll find a 5-story poinsettia Christmas tree, crafters, carolers, storytellers, and a live nativity. The open-air Scenic Railroad is decorated to the hilt, too, and travels through a spectacular array of Christmas light displays as it makes its way around the base of Stone Mountain. Santa Claus is here, and there's also an animated children's program with a talking Christmas tree. Events are open daily 6 to 10pm, except for December 24 and 25. There is a $10 charge for adults and $5 for children, in addition to the park's $6 parking charge. For details, call ℂ **770/498-5690** or visit www.stonemountainpark.org. Begins in mid-November.

Stone Mountain Village Candlelight Shopping. Every Thursday and Friday night until 9pm, beginning the Thursday before Thanksgiving and continuing until Christmas, this charming shopping village is candlelit, and visitors are lured into decorated shops by the aroma of mulled cider. A jolly St. Nick, strolling carolers, gaily lighted trees, and carriage rides are part of the fun. No admission fee. The Village also hosts the **Sugar Plum Festival,** a breakfast with Santa Claus from 7 to 11am on the first Saturday of December. The $5 admission includes breakfast and a photograph with Santa. Call ℂ **770/879-4971** for details. Every Thursday and Friday night, beginning the Thursday before Thanksgiving and continuing until Christmas.

Holiday High Lights. When Rich's department store decided to move its giant Christmas tree to Lenox Square from Underground Atlanta, it looked as if a long-time Atlanta holiday fixture would be history. But World of Coca-Cola and Underground Atlanta quickly stepped in to continue the tradition of an enormous, exquisitely decorated tree and an accompanying holiday celebration in the heart of downtown. Festivities kick off with the tree lighting in the plaza between Underground and World of Coca-Cola on the Saturday after Thanksgiving. Other family-friendly activities featuring the Underground Express Train and the Coca-Cola Polar Bear continue through Christmas Eve. For details, call © **404/676-5151.** Take MARTA to the Five Points station for the lighting, which is usually attended by thousands. Tree lighting takes place on the Saturday after Thanksgiving.

Christmas at Callanwolde. Noted interior and floral designers decorate the Callanwolde Fine Arts Center, 980 Briarcliff Rd. NE, and shops (sweets, toys, pottery, garden) are set up in different rooms. Activities include concerts on a 3,742-pipe Aeolian organ, children's breakfasts with Santa, caroling and hymn singing, and other entertainment. Admission at the door is $10 adults, $8 seniors, $6 children ages 4 to 12; free for children age 3 and under. For details, call © **404/872-5338** or visit www.callanwolde. org. Usually held for 2 weeks in late November or early December.

December

Country Christmas. The Atlanta Botanical Garden is beautifully decorated, and highlights of the afternoon include carolers, bell ringers, children's theater, entertainers, chestnuts roasting on an open fire, pony rides, cranberry and popcorn stringing, and strolling mimes, musicians, and magicians. Christmas crafts such as wreath-making are demonstrated, and you can shop for handcrafted gifts and homemade baked goods. Admission is free. For details and to inquire about off-site parking and shuttle buses, call © **404/876-5859** or visit www.atlantabotanical garden.org. The first Sunday in December.

Children's Healthcare of Atlanta Christmas Parade and Festival of Trees. The parade is a major to-do with award-winning bands, lavish holiday-themed floats, helium-balloon comic characters, and, of course, Santa Claus. The parade kicks off the 9-day Festival of Trees at the Georgia World Congress Center, for which Atlanta artists and designers lavishly decorate trees, wreaths, and Christmas vignettes that are exhibited and auctioned off to benefit Children's Healthcare of Atlanta. The festival also features live entertainment, cooking demonstrations, an antique carousel, a roller coaster, a giant slide, a balloon ride, international holiday displays, and more. Admission to the festival is $8 for adults, $5 for seniors and children ages 2 to 12; free for children under age 2. For tickets, call © **404/264-9348, ext. 108.** The parade begins at 10:30am, and the festival follows. For information, call © **404/325-NOEL** or visit www.choa.org/ festival. First Saturday in December.

Peach Bowl Game. Held annually at the Georgia Dome. Tickets are hard to come by; reserve well in advance. Call © **404/586-8499** for information. Sometime between Christmas and New Year's (occasionally in early Jan).

New Year's Eve. The Big Peach that rings in Atlanta's New Year is dropped at the stroke of midnight from the 138-foot light tower at Underground Atlanta. But festivities begin earlier (about 8pm) with live music for dancing in the streets, a pyrotechnic display and laser show, balloons, and usually a marching band. Call © **404/523-2311** for details.

4 Insurance, Health & Safety

TRAVEL INSURANCE AT A GLANCE

Check your existing insurance policies before you buy travel insurance to cover trip cancellation, lost luggage, medical expenses, or car rental insurance. You're likely to have partial or complete coverage. But if you need more insurance, ask your travel agent about a comprehensive package. The cost of travel insurance varies widely, depending on the cost and length of your trip, your age and overall health, and the type of trip you're taking.

And keep in mind that in the aftermath of the World Trade Center attacks, a number of airlines, cruise lines, and tour operators are no longer covered by insurers. *The bottom line:* Always, always check the fine print before you sign on; more and more policies have built-in exclusions and restrictions that may leave you out in the cold if something does go awry.

For information, contact one of the following popular insurers:

- **Access America** (© **800/284-8300;** www.accessamerica.com/)
- **Travel Guard International** (© **800/826-1300;** www.travel guard.com)
- **Travel Insured International** (© **800/243-3174;** www.travel insured.com)
- **Travelex Insurance Services** (© **800/228-9792;** www.travelex-insurance.com)

TRIP-CANCELLATION INSURANCE (TCI)

There are three major types of trip-cancellation insurance—one, in the event that you pre-pay a cruise or tour that gets cancelled, and you can't get your money back; a second if you or someone in your family gets sick or dies, and you can't travel (but beware that you may not be covered for a pre-existing condition); and a third,

when bad weather makes travel impossible. Some insurers provide coverage for events like jury duty; natural disasters close to home, like floods or fire; even the loss of a job. A few have added provisions for cancellations due to terrorist activities. Always check the fine print before signing on, and don't buy trip-cancellation insurance from the tour operator that may be responsible for the cancellation; buy it only from a reputable travel insurance agency. Don't overbuy. You won't be reimbursed for more than the cost of your trip.

MEDICAL INSURANCE

Most health insurance policies cover you if you get sick away from home—but check, particularly if you're insured by an HMO. Members of **Blue Cross/Blue Shield** can now use their cards at select hospitals in most major cities worldwide (© **800/810-BLUE** or www.bluecares.com for a list of hospitals).

Some credit cards (American Express and certain gold and platinum Visa and MasterCards, for example) offer automatic flight insurance against death or dismemberment in case of an airplane crash if you charged the cost of your ticket.

If you require additional insurance, try one of the following companies:

- **MEDEX International,** 9515 Deereco Rd., Timonium, MD 21093-5375 (© **888/MEDEX-00** or 410/453-6300; fax 410/453-6301; www.medexassist.com)
- **Travel Assistance International** (© **800/821-2828;** www.travel assistance.com), 9200 Keystone Crossing, Suite 300, Indianapolis, IN 46240 (for general information on services, call the company's Worldwide Assistance Services, Inc., at © **800777-8710**).

The cost of travel medical insurance varies widely. Check your existing policies before you buy additional coverage. Also, check to see if your medical insurance covers you for emergency medical evacuation: If you have to buy a one-way same-day ticket home and forfeit your nonrefundable roundtrip ticket, you may be out big bucks.

LOST-LUGGAGE INSURANCE

On domestic flights, checked baggage is covered up to $2,500 per ticketed passenger. On international flights (including U.S. portions of international trips), baggage is covered to approximately $9.07 per pound, up to approximately $635 per checked bag. If you plan to check items more valuable than the standard liability, you may purchase "excess valuation" coverage from the airline, up to $5,000. Be sure to take any valuables or irreplaceable items with you in your carry-on luggage. If you file a lost luggage claim, be prepared to answer detailed questions about the contents of your baggage, and be sure to file a claim immediately, as most airlines enforce a 21-day deadline. Before you leave home, compile an inventory of all packed items and a rough estimate of the total value to ensure that you're properly compensated if your luggage is lost. You will only be reimbursed for what you lost, no more. Once you've filed a complaint, persist in securing your reimbursement; there are no laws governing the length of time it takes for a carrier to reimburse you. If you arrive at a destination without your bags, ask the airline to forward them to your hotel or to your next destination; they will usually comply. If your bag is delayed or lost, the airline may reimburse you for reasonable expenses, such as a toothbrush or a set of clothes, but the airline is under no legal obligation to do so.

Lost luggage may also be covered by your homeowner's or renter's policy. Many platinum and gold credit cards cover you as well. If you choose to purchase additional lost-luggage insurance, be sure not to buy more than you need. Buy in advance from the insurer or a trusted agent (prices will be much higher at the airport).

CAR-RENTAL INSURANCE (LOSS/DAMAGE WAIVER OR COLLISION DAMAGE WAIVER)

If you hold a private auto insurance policy, you probably are covered in the U.S., but not abroad, for loss or damage to the car and liability in case a passenger is injured. The credit card you use to rent the car also may provide some coverage.

Car-rental insurance probably does not cover liability if you caused the accident. Check your own auto insurance policy, the rental company policy, and your credit card coverage for the extent of coverage: Is your destination covered? Are other drivers covered? How much liability is covered if a passenger is injured? (If you rely on your credit card for coverage, you may want to bring a second credit card with you, as damages may be charged to your card and you may find yourself stranded with no money.)

Car-rental insurance costs about $20 a day.

THE HEALTHY TRAVELER

What To Do If You Get Sick Away From Home If you worry about getting sick away from home, consider purchasing **medical travel insurance** (see suggested insurers above) and carry your ID card in your purse or wallet. In most cases, your existing health plan will provide the coverage you need. See the section on insurance above for more information.

If you suffer from a chronic illness, consult your doctor before your departure. For conditions like epilepsy, diabetes, or heart problems, wear a **Medic Alert Identification Tag** (✆ 800/825-3785; www.medicalert.org), which will immediately alert doctors to your

---

> **Tips**   Quick ID
>
> Tie a colorful ribbon or piece of yarn around your luggage handle, or slap a distinctive sticker on the side of your bag. This makes it less likely that someone will mistakenly appropriate it. And if your luggage gets lost, it will be easier to find.

---

condition and give them access to your records through Medic Alert's 24-hour hot line.

Pack **prescription medications** in your carry-on luggage, and carry prescription medications in their original containers. Also bring along copies of your prescriptions in case you lose your pills or run out. And don't forget sunglasses and an extra pair of contact lenses or prescription glasses.

The United States **Centers for Disease Control and Prevention** (© 800/ 311-3435; www.cdc.gov) provides up-to-date information on necessary vaccines and health hazards by region or country. If you get sick, consider asking your hotel concierge to recommend a local doctor—even his or her own. You can also try the emergency room at a local hospital; many have walk-in clinics for emergency cases that are not life-threatening. You may not get immediate attention, but you won't pay the high price of an emergency room visit (usually a minimum of $300 just for signing your name).

THE SAFE TRAVELER

General Safety Suggestions While tourist areas are generally safe, crime is on the increase everywhere, and U.S. urban areas tend to be less safe than those in Europe or Japan. You should always stay alert. This is particularly true of large U.S. cities. It is wise to ask your hotel front desk staff or the city's or area's tourist office if you're in doubt about which neighborhoods are safe.

Avoid deserted areas, especially at night, and don't go into public parks at night unless there's a concert or similar occasion that will attract a crowd.

Atlanta's neighborhoods are relatively safe, but it's wise to exercise caution at night near Underground Atlanta, and around the major venues for sporting events. Most of the central city is primarily a business district that closes up after dark, so it's a good idea to stay within the downtown hotel and entertainment district, which is likely to be much busier.

Buckhead, a major restaurant and bar scene, is safe as long as the crowds are out. Recently, however, a few square blocks of Buckhead's entertainment district—where most of the bars are located—have been plagued by overly rowdy behavior and incidents of violent crime. Much of the undesirable activity takes place after midnight or in the wee hours as the bars are winding down, so be alert.

Avoid carrying valuables with you on the street, and don't display expensive cameras or electronic equipment. If you are using a map, consult it inconspicuously—or better yet, try to study it before you leave your room. Hold onto your pocketbook, and place your billfold in an inside pocket. In theaters, restaurants, and other public places, keep your possessions in sight.

Remember also that hotels are open to the public, and in a large hotel, security may not be able to screen everyone entering. Always lock your room door—don't assume that once inside your hotel you are automatically safe and no longer need to be aware of your surroundings.

Driving Safety Driving safety is important, too. Question your rental agency about personal safety and ask for a traveler-safety brochure when you pick up your car. Obtain written directions—or a map with the route clearly marked—from the agency showing how to get to your destination. (Many agencies now offer the option of renting a cellular phone for the duration of your car rental; check with the rental agent when you pick up the car.) And, if possible, arrive and depart during daylight hours.

Recently, more and more crime has involved cars and drivers. If you drive off a highway into a doubtful neighborhood, leave the area as quickly as possible. If you have an accident, even on the highway, stay in your car with the doors locked until you assess the situation or until the police arrive. If you're bumped from behind on the street or are involved in a minor accident with no injuries and the situation appears to be suspicious, motion to the other driver to follow you. Never get out of your car in such situations. Go directly to the nearest police precinct, well-lit service station, or 24-hour store.

Always try to park in well-lit and well-traveled areas if possible. Never leave any packages or valuables in sight. If someone attempts to rob you or steal your car, don't try to resist the thief/carjacker—report the incident to the police department immediately by calling © **911**.

5 Tips for Travelers with Special Needs

TRAVELERS WITH DISABILITIES

Most disabilities shouldn't stop anyone from traveling. There are more options and resources out there than ever before. Before planning a trip to Atlanta, travelers with disabilities should send for a copy of *The Atlanta Accessibility Guide,* available from the Shepherd Center, a nationally renowned Atlanta hospital specializing in the treatment of spinal cord injuries and diseases. The guide rates the accessibility of local museums, parks, restaurants, hotels, theaters, sports venues, and other popular tourist stops. Accessibility is assessed in several categories, including restrooms, parking, main entrance, and telephone. The booklet also lists services and information of interest to travelers with disabilities. For a free copy, contact the **Noble Learning Resource Center, Shepherd Center,** 2020 Peachtree Rd. NW, Atlanta, GA 30309 (© **404/350-7330**). The guide is also available at **www.shepherd.org**.

AGENCIES/OPERATORS

- **Flying Wheels Travel** (© **800/535-6790;** www.flyingwheels travel.com) offers escorted tours and cruises that emphasize sports and private tours in minivans with lifts.
- **Access Adventures** (© **716/889-9096**), a Rochester, New York–based agency, offers customized itineraries for a variety of travelers with disabilities.
- **Accessible Journeys** (© **800/TINGLES** or 610/521-0339; www.disabilitytravel.com) caters specifically to slow walkers and wheelchair travelers and their families and friends.

ORGANIZATIONS

- **The Moss Rehab Hospital** (© **215/456-9603**; www.moss resourcenet.org) provides friendly, helpful phone assistance through its **Travel Information Service.**
- **The Society for Accessible Travel and Hospitality** (© **212/447-7284;** fax 212/725-8253; www. sath.org) offers a wealth of travel resources for all types of disabilities and informed recommendations on destinations, access guides, travel agents, tour operators, vehicle rentals, and companion services. Annual membership costs $45 for adults; $30 for seniors and students.

- **The American Foundation for the Blind** (© 800/232-5463; www.afb.org) provides information on traveling with Seeing Eye dogs.

PUBLICATIONS

- **Mobility International USA** (© 541/343-1284; www.miusa. org) publishes *A World of Options,* a 658-page book of resources, covering everything from biking trips to scuba outfitters, and a biannual newsletter, *Over the Rainbow.* Annual membership is $35.
- **Twin Peaks Press** (© 360/694-2462) publishes travel-related books for travelers with special needs.
- *Open World for Disability and Mature Travel* magazine, published by the Society for Accessible Travel and Hospitality (see above), is full of good resources and information. A year's subscription is $13 ($21 outside the U.S.).

GAY & LESBIAN TRAVELERS

Atlanta has a large gay community and one publication that caters to it is *Southern Voice,* a newspaper that covers gay issues across the Southeast. Call © 404/876-1819 for a free issue, a distribution point near your hotel, or additional information.

Once you arrive, you might want to visit **Outwrite Bookstore and Coffeehouse,** 991 Piedmont Ave. (© 404/607-0082). It's a popular Midtown gathering spot for gay men and lesbians and a sort of unofficial clearinghouse for information on local gay and lesbian resources.

The **International Gay & Lesbian Travel Association (IGLTA)** (© 800/448-8550 or 954/776-2626; fax 954/776-3303; www.iglta.org) links travelers up with gay-friendly hoteliers, tour operators, and airline and cruise-line representatives. It offers monthly newsletters, marketing mailings, and a membership directory

that's updated once a year. Membership is $200 yearly, plus a $100 administration fee for new members.

AGENCIES/OPERATORS

- **Above and Beyond Tours** (© 800/397-2681; www.above beyondtours.com) offers gay and lesbian tours worldwide and is the exclusive gay and lesbian tour operator for United Airlines.
- **Now, Voyager** (© 800/255-6951; www.nowvoyager.com) is a San Francisco–based gay-owned and operated travel service.

PUBLICATIONS

- *Out and About* (© 800/929-2268 or 415/644-8044; www.out andabout.com) offers guidebooks and a newsletter 10 times a year packed with solid information on the global gay and lesbian scene.
- *Spartacus International Gay Guide* and *Odysseus* are good, annual English-language guidebooks focused on gay men, with some information for lesbians. You can get them from most gay and lesbian bookstores, or order them from **Giovanni's Room** bookstore, 1145 Pine St., Philadelphia, PA 19107 (© 215/923-2960; www.giovannisroom. com).
- *Gay Travel A to Z: The World of Gay & Lesbian Travel Options at Your Fingertips,* by Marianne Ferrari (Ferrari Publications; Box 35575, Phoenix, AZ 85069) is a very good gay and lesbian guidebook series.

SENIOR TRAVEL

Mention the fact that you're a senior citizen when you first make your travel reservations. All major airlines and many hotels offer discounts for seniors. Major airlines also offer coupons for domestic travel for seniors over sixty. Typically, a book of four coupons costs less than $700, which means you can fly anywhere in the continental U.S. for under $350 round-trip. In most cities, people over the age of 60 qualify for reduced admission to theaters, museums, and other attractions, as well as discounted fares on public transportation.

Members of **AARP** (formerly known as the American Association of Retired Persons), 601 E St. NW, Washington, DC 20049 (𝄢 **800/424-3410** or 202/434-2277; www.aarp.org), get discounts on hotels, airfares, and car rentals. AARP offers members a wide range of benefits, including *Modern Maturity* magazine and a monthly newsletter. Anyone over 50 can join.

The Alliance for Retired Americans, 8403 Colesville Rd., Suite 1200, Silver Spring, MD 20910 (𝄢 **301/578-8422;** www.retiredamericans.org), offers a newsletter six times a year and discounts on hotel and auto rentals; annual dues are $13 per person or couple. *Note:* Members of the former National Council of Senior Citizens receive automatic membership in the Alliance.

The **U.S. National Park Service** offers a **Golden Age Passport** that gives seniors 62 years or older lifetime entrance to U.S. national parks for a one-time processing fee of $10. It must be purchased in person at any NPS facility that charges an entrance fee. Besides free entry, a Golden Age Passport also offers a 50% discount on federal-use fees charged for such facilities as camping, swimming, parking, boat launching, and tours. For more information, click onto www.nps.gov/fees_passes.htm or call 𝄢 **888-GO-PARKS.**

AGENCIES/OPERATORS

• **Grand Circle Travel** (𝄢 **800/221-2610** or 617/350-7500; www.gct.com) offers package deals for the 50-plus market, mostly of the tour-bus variety, with free trips

thrown in for those who organize groups of 10 or more.

• **Elderhostel** (𝄢 **877/426-8056;** www.elderhostel.org) arranges study programs for those aged 55 and over (and a spouse or companion of any age) in the U.S. and in more than 80 countries around the world. Most courses last 5 to 7 days in the U.S. (2–4 weeks abroad), and many include airfare, accommodations in university dormitories or modest inns, meals, and tuition.

• **Interhostel** (𝄢 **800/733-9753;** www.learn.unh.edu/interhostel), organized by the University of New Hampshire, also offers educational travel for seniors. On these escorted tours, the days are packed with seminars, lectures, and field trips, with sightseeing led by academic experts. **Interhostel** takes travelers 50 and over (with companions over 40), and offers 1- and 2-week trips, mostly international.

PUBLICATIONS

• *The Book of Deals* is a collection of more than 1,000 senior discounts on airlines, lodging, tours, and attractions around the country; it's available for $9.90 by calling 𝄢 **800/460-6676.**

• *101 Tips for the Mature Traveler* is available from Grand Circle Travel (𝄢 **800/221-2610** or 617/350-7500; fax 617/346-6700).

• *The 50+ Traveler's Guidebook* (St. Martin's Press).

• *Unbelievably Good Deals and Great Adventures That You Absolutely Can't Get Unless You're Over 50* (Contemporary Publishing Co.).

FAMILY TRAVEL

The family vacation is a rite of passage for many households, one that in a split second can devolve into a

National Lampoon farce. But as any veteran family vacationer will assure you, a family trip can be among the most pleasurable and rewarding times of your life. Page 180 highlights some of Atlanta's best bets on attractions for kids. A list of kid-friendly hotels can be found on p. 79 and restaurants that cater to tots are on p. 108.

AGENCIES/OPERATORS

- **Familyhostel** (*©* **800/733-9753;** www.learn.unh.edu/familyhostel) takes the whole family on moderately priced domestic and international learning vacations. All trip details are handled by the program staff, and lectures, fields trips, and sightseeing are guided by a team of academics. For kids ages 8 to 15 accompanied by their parents and/or grandparents.

PUBLICATIONS

- *How to Take Great Trips with Your Kids* (The Harvard Common Press) is full of good general advice that can apply to travel anywhere.
- *Frommer's Unofficial Guide to the Southeast with Kids* (John Wiley Inc.) includes information on kid-friendly attractions in and around Atlanta.

WEBSITES

- **Family Travel Network** (www. familytravelnetwork.com) offers travel tips and reviews of family-friendly destinations, vacation deals, and thoughtful features such as "What to Do When Your Kids Are Afraid to Travel" and "Kid-Style Camping."
- **Travel with Your Children** (www.travelwithyourkids.com) is a comprehensive site offering sound advice for traveling with children.
- **The Busy Person's Guide to Travel with Children** (http://wz. com/travel/TravelingWithChildren.html) offers a "45-second newsletter" where experts weigh in on the best websites and resources for tips for traveling with children.

STUDENT TRAVEL

Council Travel Service (*©* **800/ 226-8624;** www.counciltravel.com) is the biggest student travel agency in the world. **STA Travel** (*©* **800/ 781-4040;** www.statravel.com) is another travel agency catering especially to young travelers, although their bargain-basement prices are available to people of all ages.

In Canada, **Travel CUTS** (*©* **800/ 667-2887** or 416/614-2887; www. travelcuts.com) offers similar services. In London, **Campus Travel** (*©* **020/ 7730-2101**), opposite Victoria Station, is Britain's leading specialist in student and youth travel.

PUBLICATIONS

The Hanging Out Guides (www. frommers.com/hangingout), published by Frommer's, is the top student travel series for today's students, covering everything from adrenaline sports to the hottest club and music scenes.

6 Getting There

BY PLANE

Hartsfield Atlanta International Airport (*©* **404/768-4100**), 10 miles south of downtown, is the world's largest and busiest passenger airport and transfer hub, accommodating 78 million passengers a year. It serves 186 U.S. cities with nonstop service.

Delta Air Lines (*©* **800/221-1212** or **www.delta.com** for reservations and flight information), which is based at Hartsfield, is the major carrier to Atlanta, connecting the city to pretty much the entire country as well as 62 countries internationally. It carries 80% of the air passengers who come into Atlanta and serves over 350 international cities.

Other major carriers include **Airtran** (© 800/247-8726; www.air tran.com), **America West** (© 800/235-9292; www.americawest.com), **American Airlines** (© 800/433-7300; www.aa.com), **British Airways** (© 800/247-9297; www.british-air ways.com), **Continental** (© 800/732-6887; www.flycontinental.com), **Japan Airlines** (© 800/525-3663; www.jal.com), **KLM** (© 800/374-7747; www.nwa.com), **Lufthansa** (© 800/645-3880; www.lufthansa-usa.com), **Northwest** (© 800/225-2525; www.nwa.com), **United Airlines** (© 800/241-6522; www.ual.com), and **USAirways** (© 800/428-4322; www.usairways.com).

Generally, the least expensive fares (except for specially promoted discount fares announced in newspaper travel sections) are advance-purchase fares that involve certain restrictions. For example, in addition to paying for your ticket 3 to 21 days in advance of your trip, you may have to leave or return on certain days, stay a maximum or minimum number of days, and so on. Advance-purchase fares are often nonrefundable. Nonetheless, the restrictions are usually within the framework of normal vacation plans. The further in advance you reserve, the better your options, since sometimes there are a limited number of seats sold at discounted rates.

When you reserve, be sure to inquire about money-saving packages that include hotel accommodations, car rentals, tours, and other similar expenses, with your airfare.

GETTING INTO TOWN FROM THE AIRPORT

Those flying into Atlanta have several options for getting from the airport to the downtown area. Most large hotels offer shuttle service to their guests, accessible through a courtesy phone located near the baggage claim area at Hartsfield International Airport. Other options include taxi, MARTA rapid-rail or bus service, and rental cars. See "Orientation," in chapter 4, for details on getting from the airport to your destination.

AIR TRAVEL SECURITY MEASURES

In the wake of the September 11, 2001, terrorist attacks, the airline industry implemented sweeping security measures in airports. Expect a lengthier check-in process and possible delays. Although regulations vary from airline to airline, you can expedite the process by taking the following steps:

- **Arrive early.** Arrive at the airport at least 2 hours before your scheduled flight.
- **Try not to drive your car to the airport.** Parking and curbside access to the terminal may be limited. Call ahead and check.
- **Don't count on curbside check-in.** Some airlines and airports have stopped curbside check-in altogether, whereas others offer it on a limited basis. For up-to-date information on specific regulations, check with the individual airline.
- **Be sure to carry plenty of documentation.** A government-issued photo ID (federal, state, or local) is now required. You may need to show this at various checkpoints. With an E-ticket, you may be required to have with you printed confirmation of purchase, and perhaps even the credit card with which you bought your ticket (see "All About E-Ticketing," below). This varies from airline to airline, so call ahead to make sure you have the proper documentation. And be sure that your ID is **up-to-date:** an expired driver's license, for example, may keep you from boarding the plane altogether.

Tips <u>What You Can Carry On—And What You Can't</u>

The Transportation Security Administration (TSA), the government agency that now handles all aspects of airport security, has devised new restrictions for carry-on baggage, not only to expedite the screening process but to prevent potential weapons from passing through airport security. Passengers are now limited to bringing just one carry-on bag and one personal item onto the aircraft (previous regulations allowed two carry-on bags and one personal item, like a briefcase or a purse). For more information, go to the TSA's website, **www.tsa.gov**. The agency has released an updated list of items passengers are not allowed to carry onto an aircraft:

Not permitted: knives and box cutters, corkscrews, straight razors, metal scissors, golf clubs, baseball bats, pool cues, hockey sticks, ski poles, ice picks.

Permitted: nail clippers, nail files, tweezers, eyelash curlers, safety razors (including disposable razors), syringes (with documented proof of medical need), walking canes and umbrellas (must be inspected first).

The airline you fly may have **additional restrictions** on items you can and cannot carry on board. Call ahead to avoid problems.

- **Know what you can carry on— and what you can't.** Travelers in the United States are now limited to one carry-on bag, plus one personal bag (such as a purse or a briefcase). The Transportation Security Administration (TSA) has also issued a list of newly restricted carry-on items; see the box "What You Can Carry On— and What You Can't."
- **Prepare to be searched.** Expect spot-checks. Electronic items, such as a laptop or cellphone, should be readied for additional screening. Limit the metal items you wear on your person.
- **It's no joke.** When a check-in agent asks if someone other than you packed your bag, don't decide that this is the time to be funny. The agents will not hesitate to call security.
- **No ticket, no gate access.** Only ticketed passengers will be allowed beyond the screener checkpoints,

except for those people with specific medical or parental needs.

HOW TO HAVE AN (ALMOST) FIRST-CLASS EXPERIENCE IN COACH

Anyone who has traveled in coach or economy class in recent years can attest to the frustrating reality of cramped seating. But with a little savvy and advance planning, you can make an otherwise unpleasant coach experience downright comfy.

Here are some tips for finding the right seat:

- For more legroom, check in early and ask for an aisle seat in an emergency-exit row or bulkhead.
- To have two seats for yourself, try for an aisle seat in a center section toward the back of coach.
- To sleep, avoid the last row or the row in front of the emergency exit, as these seats are the least likely to recline. You also may want to reserve a window seat so

Tips All About E-Ticketing

Only yesterday **electronic tickets (E-tickets)** were the fast and easy ticket-free alternative to paper tickets. E-tickets allowed passengers to avoid long lines at airport check-in, all the while saving the airlines money on postage and labor. With the increased security measures in airports, however, an E-ticket no longer guarantees an accelerated check-in. You often can't go straight to the boarding gate, even if you have no bags to check. You'll probably need to show your printed E-ticket receipt or confirmation of purchase, as well as a photo ID, and sometimes even the credit card with which you purchased your E-ticket. That said, buying an E-ticket is still a fast, convenient way to book a flight; instead of having to wait for a paper ticket to come through the mail, you can book your fare by phone or on the computer, and the airline will immediately confirm by fax or e-mail. In addition, airlines often offer frequent flier miles as incentive for electronic bookings.

that you can rest your head and avoid being bumped in the aisle.

- If you're traveling with a companion, book an aisle and a window seat. Middle seats are usually booked last, so chances are good you'll end up with three seats to yourselves. And in the case that a third passenger is assigned the middle seat, they'll probably be more than happy to trade for a window or an aisle.
- Unless you love noise, avoid seats in the very back, or near toilets and pantries.

Here are some tips for making yourself comfortable during your flight:

- Wear comfortable, low-heeled shoes and dress in loose-fitting layers that you can remove as cabin temperature fluctuates. Don't underdress: Airline cabins can be notoriously chilly and blankets may be unavailable. Wear breathable natural fabrics instead of synthetics.
- Hydrate before, during, and after your flight to combat the lack of humidity in airplane cabins—

which can be as dry as the Sahara Desert. Bring a bottle of water on board.

- Pre-order a special meal. The airlines' vegetarian and kosher meals are usually fresher than standard plane fare. Or brown-bag your own meal.
- Get up and walk around whenever you can or perform stretching exercises in your seat to keep your blood flowing.
- Bring a toothbrush and moisturizer to stay fresh.
- If you're flying with kids, don't forget a deck of cards, toys, extra bottles, pacifiers, diapers, and chewing gum to help them relieve ear pressure buildup during ascent and descent. Let each child pack his or her own backpack with favorite toys.
- If you're flying with a cold or chronic sinus problems, use a decongestant 10 minutes before ascent and descent, to minimize pressure buildup in the inner ear.
- Try to acclimate yourself to the local time as quickly as possible. Stay up as long as you can the first

day, then try to wake up at a normal hour the next morning.

FLYING FOR LESS: TIPS FOR GETTING THE BEST AIRFARE

Passengers within the same airplane cabin are rarely paying the same fare. Business travelers who need to purchase tickets at the last minute, change their itinerary at a moment's notice, or get home for the weekend pay the premium rate. Passengers who can book their ticket long in advance, who can stay over Saturday night, or who are willing to travel on a Tuesday, Wednesday, or Thursday after 7pm, will pay a fraction of the full fare. On many flights, even the shortest hops, the full fare is close to $1,000 or more, while a 7- or 14-day advance purchase ticket may cost less than half that amount. Here are a few other easy ways to save.

- Airlines periodically lower prices on their most popular routes. Check the travel section of your Sunday newspaper for advertised discounts or call the airlines directly and ask if any **promotional rates** or special fares are available. You'll almost never see a sale during the peak summer vacation months of July and August, or during the Thanksgiving or Christmas seasons; but in periods of low-volume travel, you should pay no more than $400 for a domestic cross-country flight. If your schedule is flexible, say so, and ask if you can secure a cheaper fare by staying an extra day, by flying midweek, or by flying at less-trafficked hours. If you already hold a ticket when a sale breaks, it may even pay to exchange your ticket, which usually incurs a $100 to $150 charge.

   Note: The lowest-priced fares are often nonrefundable, require advance purchase of 1 to 3 weeks and a certain length of stay, and

carry penalties for changing dates of travel.

- **Consolidators,** also known as bucket shops, are a good place to find low fares. Consolidators buy seats in bulk from the airlines and then sell them back to the public at prices usually below even the airlines' discounted rates. Their small ads usually run in Sunday newspaper travel sections. And before you pay, request a confirmation number from the consolidator and then call the airline to confirm your seat. Be aware that bucket shop tickets are usually nonrefundable or rigged with stiff cancellation penalties, often as high as 50% to 75% of the ticket price. Protect yourself by paying with a credit card rather than cash. Keep in mind that if there's an airline sale going on, or if it's high season, you can often get the same or better rates by contacting the airlines directly, so do some comparison shopping before you buy. Also check out the name of the airline; you may not want to fly on some obscure Third World airline, even if you're saving $10. And check whether you're flying on a charter or a scheduled airline; the latter is more expensive but more reliable.

   Council Travel (© 800/226-8624; www.counciltravel.com) and **STA Travel** (© 800/781-4040; www.statravel.com) cater especially to young travelers, but their bargain-basement prices are available to people of all ages. **The TravelHub** (© 888/AIR-FARE; www.travelhub.com) represents nearly 1,000 travel agencies, many of whom offer consolidator and discount fares. Other reliable consolidators include **1-800-FLY-CHEAP** (www.1800flycheap.com); **TFI Tours International** (© 800/745-8000 or 212/736-

---

Tips Cancelled Plans

If your flight is cancelled, don't book a new fare at the ticket counter. Find the nearest phone and call the airline directly to reschedule. You'll be relaxing while other passengers are still standing in line.

1140; www.lowestairprice.com), which serves as a clearinghouse for unused seats; or "rebators" such as **Travel Avenue** (© **800/333-3335;** www.travelavenue.com) and the **Smart Traveller** (© **800/448-3338** in the U.S., or 305/448-3338), which rebate part of their commissions to you.

• Search **the Internet** for cheap fares. Great last-minute deals are available through free weekly e-mail services provided directly by the airlines. See "Planning Your Trip Online," below, for more information.

• Look into **courier flights**—though they are usually not available on domestic flights. These companies hire couriers to hand-deliver packages or mail, and use your luggage allowance for themselves; in return, you get a deeply discounted ticket—for example, $300 round-trip to Europe in winter. Flights often become available at the last minute, so check in often. **Halbart Express** has offices in New York (© **718/656-8189**), Los Angeles (© **310/417-9790**), and Miami (© **305/593-0260**). **Jupiter Air** (www.jupiterair.com) has offices in New York (© **718/656-6050**), Los Angeles (© **310/670-5123**), and San Francisco (© **650/697-1773**).

• Join a travel club such as **Moment's Notice** (© **718/234-6295;** www.moments-notice.com) or **Sears Discount Travel Club** (© **800/433-9383,** or 800/255-1487 to join; www.travelersadvantage.com), which supply unsold tickets at discounted prices. You pay an annual membership fee to get the club's hot line number. Of course, you're limited to what's available, so you have to be flexible.

• Join **frequent-flier clubs.** It's best to accrue miles on one program, so you can rack up free flights and achieve elite status faster. But it makes sense to open as many accounts as possible, no matter how seldom you fly a particular airline. It's free, and you'll get the best choice of seats, faster response to phone inquiries, and prompter service if your luggage is stolen, your flight is canceled or delayed, or if you want to change your seat.

BY CAR

Three major interstate highways (I-20, I-75, and I-85) converge near the center of downtown Atlanta.

Below is a list of approximate mileages from other major cities in the region:

Birmingham, AL: 148
Charleston, SC: 320
Charlotte, NC: 240
Jacksonville, FL: 346
Louisville, KY: 417
Nashville, TN: 244
New Orleans, LA: 473
Norfolk, VA: 555
Orlando, FL: 441
Savannah, GA: 252
Tampa, FL: 458

BY TRAIN

Amtrak operates the *Crescent* daily between Atlanta and New York, with stops in Washington, D.C., Philadelphia, and other intermediate points. Travel time between New York and

Package Tours

Package tours are simply a way to buy airfare and accommodations at the same time. For popular destinations such as Atlanta, they are a smart way to go, because they save you a lot of money. In many cases, a package that includes airfare, hotel, and transportation to and from the airport will cost you less than just the hotel alone would have, had you booked it yourself. That's because packages are sold in bulk to tour operators—who resell them to the public at a cost that drastically undercuts standard rates.

Packages, however, vary widely. Some offer a better class of hotels than others. Some offer the same hotels for lower prices. Some offer flights on scheduled airlines, while others book charters. In some packages, your choice of accommodations and travel days may be limited. Some packages let you choose between escorted vacations and independent vacations; others will allow you to add on just a few excursions or escorted day trips (also at lower prices than you could locate on your own) without booking an entirely escorted tour. If you take the time to shop around, you will save money in the long run.

Here are a few suggestions to help you find a good package deal for Atlanta:

- The best place to start your search is the travel section of your local Sunday newspaper. Also check the ads in the back of national travel magazines like *Travel & Leisure, National Geographic Traveler,* and *Condé Nast Traveler.* **Liberty Travel** (© **888/271-1584** to be connected

Atlanta is approximately 18½ hours. The *Crescent* also goes beyond Atlanta to many points south each day, terminating in New Orleans. And other Amtrak trains connect with most of the country. To find out if your city connects via rail with Atlanta, call © **800/USA-RAIL** or check the company's website at www.amtrak.com.

Like the airlines, **Amtrak** offers several discount fares, and though not all are based on advance purchase, you may increase your options by reserving early. At this writing, **full round-trip coach fares and discount fares** are as follows between Atlanta and these cities:

City	Full Fare	Discount Fare
Boston–Atlanta	$416	$236
Chicago–Atlanta	$534	$274
Los Angeles–Atlanta	$1224	$684
Miami–Atlanta	$792	$424
New Orleans–Atlanta	$184	$104
New York–Atlanta	$394	$222

Call **Amtrak's Great American Vacations** (© **800/321-8684; www. amtrak.com**) to inquire about money-saving packages that include hotel accommodations and attraction tickets with your train fare. **Amtrak** trains arrive in Atlanta at 1688 Peachtree St., just off I-85. From this central with the agent closest to you; www.libertytravel.com), one of the biggest packagers in the Northeast, often runs a full-page ad in the Sunday papers. You won't get much in the way of service, but you will get a good deal.

- **Online Vacation Mall** (© 800/839-9851; www.onlinevacation mall.com) allows you to search for and book packages offered by a number of tour operators and airlines. The **United States Tour Operators Association's** website (www.ustoa.com) has a search engine that allows you to look for operators that offer packages to a specific destination.
- **American Express Vacations** (© 800/241-1700; www.leisureweb.com) is another good option. Check out its Last Minute Travel Bargains site, offered in conjunction with Continental Airlines (http://travel.americanexpress.com/travel/lmt/), with deeply discounted vacation packages and reduced airline fares that differ from the E-savers bargains that Continental e-mails weekly to subscribers.
- An excellent resource is the airlines themselves, which often package their flights together with accommodations. Since Delta makes its home in Atlanta, **Delta Dream Vacations** (© 800/872-7786) usually offers the best airline packages to Atlanta. Among the other airline packagers, your options include **American Airlines FlyAway Vacations** (© 800/321-2121), and **US Airways Vacations** (© 800/455-0123).

location, you can take a taxi to your hotel or to the nearest MARTA station (Arts Center). For information, call © **800/USA-RAIL** or 404/881-3060.

BY BUS
Greyhound buses (© **800/231-2222** or 404/584-1731 for reservations and information; **www.greyhound.com**) connect the entire country with Atlanta. The bus terminal is located at 232 Forsyth St., at the Garnett Street MARTA station, one stop south of

Five Points, the main MARTA station downtown. Taxis are available, but it's convenient and inexpensive to take MARTA into the central city.

The fare structure on buses is complex and not always based on distance traveled. The good news is that when you call Greyhound, they'll always give you the lowest-fare options. Once again, advance-purchase fares booked 3 to 21 days prior to travel represent big savings.

7 Planning Your Trip Online

Researching and booking your trip online can save time and money. Then again, it may not. It is simply not true that you always get the best deal online. Most booking engines do not include schedules and prices for budget airlines, and from time to time

you'll get a better last-minute price by calling the airline directly, so it's best to call the airline to see if you can do better before booking online.

On the plus side, Internet users today can tap into the same travel-planning databases that were once accessible only to travel agents—and do it at the same speed. Sites such as **Frommers.com**, **Travelocity.com**, **Expedia.com**, and **Orbitz.com** allow consumers to comparison shop for airfares, access special bargains, book flights, and reserve hotel rooms and rental cars.

But don't fire your travel agent just yet. Although online booking sites offer tips and hard data to help you bargain shop, they cannot endow you with the hard-earned experience that makes a seasoned, reliable travel agent an invaluable resource, even in the Internet age. And for consumers with a complex itinerary, a trusty travel agent is still the best way to arrange the most direct flights to and from the best airports.

Still, there's no denying the Internet's emergence as a powerful tool in researching and plotting travel time. The benefits of researching your trip online can be well worth the effort.

Last-minute specials, such as weekend deals or Internet-only fares, are offered by airlines to fill empty seats. Most of these are announced on Tuesday or Wednesday and must be purchased online. They are only valid for travel that weekend, but some can be booked weeks or months in advance. Sign up for weekly e-mail alerts at airline websites or check mega-sites that compile comprehensive lists of last-minute specials, such as **Smarter Living** (smarterliving.com) or **WebFlyer** (www.webflyer.com).

Some sites, such as Expedia.com, will send you **e-mail notification** when a cheap fare becomes available to your favorite destination. Some will also tell you when fares to a particular destination are at their lowest.

TRAVEL PLANNING & BOOKING SITES

Keep in mind that because several airlines are no longer willing to pay commissions on tickets sold by online travel agencies, these agencies may either add a $10 surcharge to your bill if you book on that carrier—or neglect to offer those carriers' schedules.

The list of sites below is selective, not comprehensive. Some sites will have evolved or disappeared by the time you read this.

- **Travelocity** (www.travelocity.com or www.frommers.travelocity.com) and **Expedia** (www.expedia.com) are among the most popular sites, each offering an excellent range of options. Travelers search by destination, dates, and cost.
- **Orbitz** (www.orbitz.com) is a popular site launched by United, Delta, Northwest, American, and Continental Airlines. With this site, you're granted access to the largest data bank of low rates, airline tickets, rental cars, hotels, vacation packages, and other travel products. You get, among other offerings, available fares from more than 450 airlines.
- **Qixo** (www.qixo.com) is another powerful search engine that allows you to search for flights and accommodations from some 20 airline and travel-planning sites (such as Travelocity) at once. Qixo sorts results by price.
- **Priceline** (www.priceline.com) lets you "name your price" for airline tickets, hotel rooms, and rental cars. For airline tickets, you can't say what time you want to fly—you have to accept any flight between 6am and 10pm on the dates you've selected, and you may have to make one or more stopovers. Tickets are nonrefundable, and no frequent-flier miles are awarded.

SMART E-SHOPPING

The savvy traveler is armed with insider information. Here are a few tips to help you navigate the Internet successfully and safely.

Frommers.com: The Complete Travel Resource

For an excellent travel-planning resource, we highly recommend **Frommers.com** (www.frommers.com). We're a little biased, of course, but we guarantee that you'll find the travel tips, reviews, monthly vacation giveaways, and online-booking capabilities thoroughly indispensable. Among the special features are our popular **Message Boards,** where Frommer's readers post queries and share advice (sometimes even our authors show up to answer questions); **Frommers.com Newsletter,** for the latest travel bargains and inside travel secrets; and Frommer's **Destinations Section,** where you'll get expert travel tips, hotel and dining recommendations, and advice on the sights to see for more than 2,500 destinations around the globe. When your research is done, the **Online Reservation System** (www.frommers.com/booktravelnow) takes you to Frommer's favorite sites for booking your vacation at affordable prices.

- **Know when sales start.** Last-minute deals may vanish in minutes. If you have a favorite booking site or airline, find out when last-minute deals are released to the public. (For example, Southwest's specials are posted every Tuesday at 12:01am central time.)
- **Shop around.** If you're looking for bargains, compare prices on different sites and airlines—and against a travel agent's best fare. Try a range of times and alternative airports before you make a purchase.
- **Stay secure.** Book only through secure sites (some airline sites are not secure). Look for a key icon (Netscape) or a padlock (Internet Explorer) at the bottom of your web browser before you enter credit card information or other personal data.
- **Avoid online auctions.** Sites that auction airline tickets and frequent-flier miles are the number-one perpetrators of Internet fraud, according to the National Consumers League.
- **Maintain a paper trail.** If you book an E-ticket, print out a confirmation, or write down your confirmation number, and keep it safe and accessible—or your trip could be a virtual one!

ONLINE TRAVELER'S TOOLBOX

Following is a selection of online tools to bookmark and use.

- **Visa ATM Locator** (www.visa.com), for locations of PLUS ATMs worldwide, or **MasterCard ATM Locator** (www.mastercard.com), for locations of Cirrus ATMs worldwide.
- **Intellicast** (www.intellicast.com) and **Weather.com** (www.weather.com). Give weather forecasts for all 50 states and for cities around the world.
- **Mapquest** (www.mapquest.com). This best of the mapping sites lets you choose a specific address or destination, and in seconds, it will return a map and detailed directions.
- **Cybercafes.com** (www.cybercafes.com) or **Net Café Guide** (www.netcafeguide.com/mapindex.htm). Locate Internet cafes at hundreds of locations around the globe. Catch up on your e-mail and log onto the Web for a few dollars per hour.
- **Universal Currency Converter** (www.xe.net/currency). See what your dollar or pound is worth in more than 100 other countries.

Tips Easy Internet Access Away from Home

There are a number of ways to get your e-mail on the Web, using any computer.

- Your **Internet Service Provider (ISP)** may have a web-based interface that lets you access your e-mail on computers other than your own. Just find out how it works before you leave home. The major ISPs maintain local access numbers around the world so that you can go online by placing a local call. Check your ISP's website or call its toll-free number and ask how you can use your current account away from home, and how much it will cost. Also ask about the cost of the service before you leave home. If you're traveling outside the reach of your ISP, you may have to check the Yellow Pages in your destination to find a local ISP.

- You can open an account on a free, web-based **e-mail provider** before you leave home, such as Microsoft's **Hotmail** (hotmail.com) or **Yahoo! Mail** (mail.yahoo.com). Your home ISP may be able to forward your home e-mail to the web-based account automatically.

- Check out **www.mail2web.com**. This amazing free service allows you to type in your regular e-mail address and password and retrieve your e-mail from any web browser, anywhere, so long as your home ISP hasn't blocked it with a firewall.

- Call your hotel in advance to see whether Internet connection is possible from your room.

8 Tips on Accommodations

TIPS FOR SAVING ON YOUR HOTEL ROOM

The **rack rate** is the maximum rate that a hotel charges for a room. It's the rate you'd get if you walked in off the street and asked for a room for the night. Hardly anybody pays these prices, however, and there are many ways around them.

- **Don't be afraid to bargain.** Most rack rates include commissions of 10% to 25% for travel agents, which some hotels may be willing to reduce if you make your own reservations and haggle a bit. Always ask whether a room less expensive than the first one quoted is available, or whether any special rates apply to you. You may qualify for corporate, student, military, senior, or other discounts. Be sure to mention membership in AAA, AARP, frequent-flier programs, or trade unions, which may entitle you to special deals as well. Find out the hotel policy on children— do kids stay free in the room or is there a special rate?

- **Rely on a qualified professional.** Certain hotels give travel agents discounts in exchange for steering business their way, so if you're shy about bargaining, an agent may be better equipped to negotiate discounts for you.

- **Dial direct.** When booking a room in a chain hotel, compare the rates offered by the hotel's local line with that of the toll-free number. Also check with an agent and online. A hotel makes nothing on a room that stays empty, so

Tips **Renting a Cellphone**

In Atlanta, **RentCell Inc.,** located at 28107 Plantation Dr. NE (☏ **404/ 467-4508**), and **Discount Cellular Inc.,** located at 2221 Peachtree Rd. NE (☏ **404/367-0303**), both offer cellphone rental services. Another highly recommended wireless rental company is **InTouch USA** (☏ **800/872- 7626;** www.intouchusa.com). Give them your itinerary and they will tell you which wireless products and services you need. InTouch will also evaluate your own phone's calling capabilities before you leave home. For this free evaluation, call ☏ **703/222-7161** between 9am and 4pm.

Renting a cellphone is much like renting a car: It comes fully equipped and ready to use; you just pick it up and go.

Most companies charge a basic rental fee (which may include activa- tion and shipping fees) of $40 to $75, plus a per-minute rate for both outgoing and incoming calls. Know that if you plan to travel in differ- ent countries with different networks, you may need a separate phone for each. In addition, air-time rates vary from network to network and country to country. Bottom line: Shop around for the best deal.

the local hotel reservation desk may be willing to offer a special rate unavailable elsewhere.

- **Remember the law of supply and demand.** Resort hotels are most crowded and therefore most expensive on weekends, so dis- counts are usually available for midweek stays. Business hotels in downtown locations are busiest during the week, so you can expect big discounts over the weekend. Avoid high-season stays whenever you can: planning your vacation just a week before or after official peak season can mean big savings.
- **Look into group or long-stay discounts.** If you come as part of a large group, you should be able to negotiate a bargain rate, since the hotel can then guarantee occu- pancy in a number of rooms. Likewise, if you're planning a long stay (at least 5 days), you might qualify for a discount. As a general rule, expect 1 night free after a 7- night stay.
- **Avoid excess charges.** When you book a room, ask whether the

hotel charges for parking. Many hotels charge a fee just for dialing out on the phone in your room. Find out whether your hotel imposes a surcharge on local and long-distance calls. A pay phone, however inconvenient, may save you money, although many call- ing cards charge a fee when you use them on pay phones. Finally, ask about local taxes and service charges, which could increase the cost of a room by 25% or more.
- **Watch for coupons and adver- tised discounts.** Scan ads in your local Sunday newspaper travel sec- tion, an excellent source for up-to- the-minute hotel deals.
- **Consider a suite.** If you are trav- eling with your family or another couple, you can pack more people into a suite (which usually comes with a sofa bed), and thereby reduce your per-person rate. Remember that some places charge for extra guests.
- **Book an efficiency.** A room with a kitchenette allows you to shop for groceries and cook your own

meals. This is a big money-saver, especially for families on long stays.

- Join hotel **frequent-visitor clubs,** even if you don't use them much. You'll be more likely to get upgrades and other perks.
- Many hotels offer **frequent-flier points.** Don't forget to ask for yours when you check in.
- **Investigate reservations services.** These outfits usually work as consolidators, buying up or reserving rooms in bulk, and then dealing them out to customers at a profit. You can get 10% to 50% off; but remember, these discounts apply to the inflated rack rates that savvy travelers rarely end up paying. You may get a decent rate, but always call the hotel as well to see if you can do better.

Among the more reputable reservations services, offering both telephone and online bookings, are: **Accommodations Express** (© **800/950-4685;** www.accommodationsexpress.com); **Hotel Reservations Network** (© **800/715-7666;** www.hoteldiscounts.com or www.180096HOTEL.com); and **Quikbook** (© **800/789-9887,** includes fax on demand service; www.quikbook.com). Online, try booking your hotel through **Frommers.com** (www.frommers.com). **Microsoft Expedia** (www.expedia.com) features a "Travel Agent" that will also direct you to affordable lodgings.

LANDING THE BEST ROOM
Somebody has to get the best room in the house. It might as well be you.

Always ask about a corner room. They're often larger and quieter, with more windows and light, and they often cost the same as standard rooms.

When you make your reservation, ask if the hotel is renovating; if it is, request a room away from the construction. Ask about nonsmoking rooms, rooms with views, rooms with twin, queen-, or king-size beds. If you're a light sleeper, request a quiet room away from vending machines, elevators, restaurants, bars, and discos. Ask for one of the rooms that have been most recently renovated or redecorated. If you aren't happy with your room when you arrive, talk to the front desk. If they have another room, they may be willing to accommodate you. Join the hotel's frequent visitor club; you may qualify for upgrades.

9 Recommended Reading

Many books have been written—fiction and non-fiction—about this beloved city. And while most fiction can be taken for fact, many natives will also tell you that a lot of the non-fiction holds nearly as many truths (and some not-so-secret skeletons) about Atlanta and the folks who've lived here through the decades.

Archival Atlanta: Forgotten Facts and Well-Kept Secrets from Our City's Past, by Perry Buffington and Kim Underwood, is a light read, packed with fascinating historical tidbits, some of which are sure to surprise even the most knowledgeable Atlanta history buff. The book also includes its share of humorous anecdotes, shining a new light on this beloved capital city.

For those more interested in looking at pictures than reading, Andy Ambrose, deputy director of the Atlanta History Center, compiled *Atlanta: An Illustrated History,* filled with images from Atlanta's archives. From the days of saloons and brothels in the early 1800s to the city's renaissance beginning in the 1960s, this account explores everything from the city's troubling racial past to the celebrated, historically rich neighborhoods of Ansley Park and Buckhead.

Michael Rose's **Atlanta Then and Now** delivers an illustrated juxtaposition of Atlanta's past and present. The photos allow first time visitors as well as old friends to see just how far this southern city has come in the past century.

For an account of some of the down-and-dirty backroom dealings, which brought Hotlanta quickly to the forefront as an international city, many readers swear by Frederick Allen's **Atlanta Rising: The Invention of an International City of 1946–1996.** This mainly objective account of Atlanta's dealings over the past 50 years describes the relationships among Atlanta's decision-makers as various events unfold.

Atlanta is also home for many of the writers who've etched out those beloved tales of the "city too busy to hate." Of course, Margaret Mitchell's **Gone with the Wind** is a given for those who wish to take in a Civil War era depiction of this area.

Author Fred Willard has a big following, which began with his Atlanta-based satirical mystery, **Down on Ponce,** and continued with **Princess Naughty and the Voodoo Cadillac.** Those folks who are intimately associated with Atlanta will swear to the authenticity of Willard's Deep South social outcast characters who inhabit a side of Atlanta that most residents would rather keep quiet.

Anne Rivers Siddons was reared just 20 miles from the big city. **Hills Town, King's Oak,** and **Homeplace** are all set in Georgia. Her **Peachtree Road** is a dark, hypnotic tale of the Atlanta Buckhead high society in the mid-20th century, when money and civil rights were the fuel on which the city ran.

In addition, Siddons' **Downtown** depicts Atlanta's last years of innocence: "Atlanta in the autumn of 1966 was a city being born, and the energy and promise of that lying-in sent out subterranean vibrations all over the just-stirring South, like underground shock waves—a call to those who could hear it best, the young. And they came, they came in droves, from small, sleeping towns and large, drowsing universities, from farms and industrial suburbs and backwaters so still that even the building firestorm of the civil rights movement had not yet rippled the surface."

And while he doesn't live in Atlanta, Tom Wolfe ruffled more than a few feathers with his 1998 tome **A Man in Full.** As Wolfe states in the book, Atlanta is a place "where your 'honor' *is* the thing you possess." However, more critics than not thought his depiction of the slums and socialites of Atlanta might do more harm than good in boosting the tourism economy here.

3

For International Visitors

Whether it's your first visit or your tenth, a trip to the United States may require an additional degree of planning. This chapter will provide you with essential information, helpful tips, and advice for the more common problems that some visitors encounter.

1 Preparing for Your Trip

ENTRY REQUIREMENTS

Check at any U.S. embassy or consulate for current information and requirements. You can also obtain a visa application and other information online at the **U.S. State Department's** website, at **www.travel.state.gov**.

VISAS The U.S. State Department has a **Visa Waiver Program** allowing citizens of certain countries to enter the United States without a visa for stays of up to 90 days. At press time these included Andorra, Australia, Austria, Belgium, Brunei, Denmark, Finland, France, Germany, Iceland, Ireland, Italy, Japan, Liechtenstein, Luxembourg, Monaco, the Netherlands, New Zealand, Norway, Portugal, San Marino, Singapore, Slovenia, Spain, Sweden, Switzerland, the United Kingdom, and Uruguay. Citizens of these countries need only a valid passport and a round-trip air or cruise ticket in their possession upon arrival. If they first enter the United States, they may also visit Mexico, Canada, Bermuda, and/or the Caribbean islands and return to the United States without a visa. Further information is available from any U.S. embassy or consulate. Canadian citizens may enter the United States without visas; they need only proof of residence.

Citizens of all other countries must have (1) a valid passport that expires at least 6 months later than the scheduled end of their visit to the United States, and (2) a tourist visa, which may be obtained without charge from any U.S. consulate.

To obtain a visa, the traveler must submit a completed application form (either in person or by mail) with a 1½-inch-square photo, and must demonstrate binding ties to a residence abroad. Usually you can obtain a visa at once or within 24 hours, but it may take longer during the summer rush from June through August. If you cannot go in person, contact the nearest U.S. embassy or consulate for directions on applying by mail. Your travel agent or airline office may also be able to provide you with visa applications and instructions. The U.S. consulate or embassy that issues your visa will determine whether you will be issued a multiple- or single-entry visa and any restrictions regarding the length of your stay.

British subjects can obtain up-to-date passport and visa information by calling the **U.S. Embassy Visa Information Line** (© 0891/200-290) or the **London Passport Office** (© 0990/210-410 for recorded information), or they can find the visa information on the U.S. Embassy Great Britain website at www.passport.gov.uk.

Irish citizens can obtain up-to-date passport and visa information through the **Embassy of USA Dublin,** 42 Elgin Rd., Dublin 4, Ireland (℃ **353/ 1-668-8777**), or check the visa page on the website at www.irigov.ie/ iveagh/services/passports/passport forms.htm.

Australian citizens can obtain up-to-date passport and visa information by calling the **U.S. Embassy Canberra,** Moonah Place, Yarralumla, ACT 2600 (℃ **02/6214-5600**), or check the website's visa page at www.usisaustralia.gov/ consular/niv.html.

Citizens of **New Zealand** can obtain up-to-date passport and visa information by calling the **U.S. Embassy New Zealand,** 29 Fitzherbert Terr., Thorndon, Wellington, New Zealand; (℃ **644/472-2068**), or get the information directly from the website at http://usembassy.org.nz.

MEDICAL REQUIREMENTS

Unless you're arriving from an area known to be suffering from an epidemic (particularly cholera or yellow fever), inoculations or vaccinations are not required for entry into the United States. If you have a medical condition that requires **syringe-administered medications,** carry a valid signed prescription from your physician—the Federal Aviation Administration (FAA) no longer allows airline passengers to pack syringes in their carry-on baggage without documented proof of medical need. If you have a disease that requires treatment with **narcotics,** you should also carry documented proof with you—smuggling narcotics aboard a plane is a serious offense that carries severe penalties in the U.S.

For **HIV-positive visitors,** requirements for entering the United States are somewhat vague and change frequently. According to the latest publication of *HIV and Immigrants: A Manual for AIDS Service Providers,* the Immigration and Naturalization Service (INS) doesn't require a medical exam for entry into the United States, but INS officials may stop individuals because they look sick or because they are carrying AIDS/HIV medicine.

If an HIV-positive noncitizen applies for a non-immigrant visa, the question on the application regarding communicable diseases is tricky no matter which way it's answered. If the applicant checks "no," INS may deny the visa on the grounds that the applicant committed fraud. If the applicant checks "yes" or if INS suspects the person is HIV-positive, it will deny the visa unless the applicant asks for a special waiver for visitors. This waiver is for people visiting the United States for a short time, to attend a conference, for instance, to visit close relatives, or to receive medical treatment. It can be a confusing situation. For further up-to-the-minute information, contact the Centers for Disease Control's **National Center for HIV** (℃ **404/332-4559;** www.hivatis.org) or the **Gay Men's Health Crisis** (℃ **212/367-1000;** www.gmhc.org).

DRIVER'S LICENSES   Foreign driver's licenses are mostly recognized in the U.S., although you may want to get an international driver's license if your home license is not written in English.

PASSPORT INFORMATION

Safeguard your passport in an inconspicuous, inaccessible place like a money belt. Make a copy of the critical pages, including the passport number, and store it in a safe place, separate from the passport itself. If you lose your passport, visit the nearest consulate of your native country as soon as possible for a replacement. Passport applications are downloadable from the Internet sites listed below.

Note that the International Civil Aviation Organization (ICAO) has recommended a policy requiring that *every* individual who travels by air have his or her own passport. In response, many countries are now requiring that children must be issued their own passport to travel internationally, whereas before, those under 16 or so may have been allowed to travel on a parent or guardian's passport.

FOR RESIDENTS OF CANADA

You can pick up a passport application at 1 of 28 regional passport offices or most travel agencies. As of December 11, 2001, Canadian children who travel must have their own passport. However, if you hold a valid Canadian passport issued before December 11, 2001, that bears the name of your child, the passport remains valid for you and your child until it expires. Passports cost C$85 for those 16 years and older (valid 5 years), C$35 children 3 to 15 (valid 5 years), and C$20, children under 3 (valid for 3 years). Applications, which must be accompanied by two identical passport-sized photographs and proof of Canadian citizenship, are available at travel agencies throughout Canada or from the central **Passport Office**, Department of Foreign Affairs and International Trade, Ottawa, ON K1A 0G3 (© **800/567-6868;** www. dfait-maeci.gc.ca/passport). Processing takes 5 to 10 days if you apply in person, or about 3 weeks by mail.

FOR RESIDENTS OF THE UNITED KINGDOM

To pick up an application for a standard 10-year passport (5-yr. for children under 16), visit your nearest passport office, major post office, or travel agency. You can also contact the **United Kingdom Passport Service** at © **0870/521-0410** or search its website at www.ukpa.gov.uk. Passports are £30 for adults and £16 for children under 16. Processing takes about 2 weeks.

FOR RESIDENTS OF IRELAND

You can apply for a 10-year passport, costing €57, at the **Passport Office,** Setanta Centre, Molesworth Street, Dublin 2 (© **01/671-1633;** www.irl gov.ie/iveagh). Those under age 18 and over 65 must apply for a €12 3-year passport. You can also apply at 1A South Mall, Cork (© **021/272-525**) or over the counter at most main post offices.

FOR RESIDENTS OF AUSTRALIA

You can pick up an application from your local post office or any branch of Passports Australia, but you must schedule an interview at the passport office to present your application materials. Call the **Australian Passport Information Service** at © **131-232,** or visit the government website at www.passports.gov.au. Passports for adults are A$144 and for those under 18 are A$72.

FOR RESIDENTS OF NEW ZEALAND

You can pick up a passport application at any New Zealand Passports Office or download it from their website. Contact the **Passports Office** at © **0800/225-050** in New Zealand or 04/474-8100, or log on to www.passports.govt.nz. Passports for adults are NZ$80 and for children under 16 NZ$40.

CUSTOMS
WHAT YOU CAN BRING IN

Every visitor more than 21 years of age may bring in, free of duty, the following: (1) 1 liter of wine or hard liquor; (2) 200 cigarettes, 100 cigars (but not from Cuba), or 3 pounds of smoking tobacco; and (3) $100 worth of gifts. These exemptions are offered to travelers who spend at least 72 hours in the United States and who have not claimed them within the preceding 6 months. It is altogether forbidden to bring into the country foodstuffs (particularly fruit, cooked meats, and canned goods) and plants (vegetables, seeds, tropical plants, and the like). Foreign tourists may bring in or take out up to $10,000 in U.S. or foreign currency with no formalities; larger sums must be declared to U.S. Customs on entering or leaving, which includes filing form CM 4790. For more specific information regarding U.S. Customs, contact your nearest U.S. embassy or consulate, or the **U.S. Customs** office (© **202/927-1770** or www.customs.ustreas.gov).

WHAT YOU CAN TAKE HOME

U.K. citizens returning from a non-EU country have a customs allowance of: 200 cigarettes; 50 cigars; 250g of smoking tobacco; 2 liters of still table wine; 1 liter of spirits or strong liqueurs (over 22% volume); 2 liters of fortified wine, sparkling wine or other liqueurs; 60cc (ml) perfume; 250cc (ml) of toilet water; and £145 worth of all other goods, including gifts and souvenirs. People under 17 cannot have the tobacco or alcohol allowance. For more information, contact HM Customs & Excise at © **0845/ 010-9000** (from outside the U.K., 020/8929-0152), or consult their website at www.hmce.gov.uk.

Canadian citizens who've been out of the country for over 48 hours may bring back C$200 worth of goods, and if you've been gone for 7 consecutive days or more, not counting your departure, the limit is C$750. The limit for alcohol is up to 1.5 liters of wine or 1.14 liters of liquor, or 24 12-ounce cans or bottles of beer; and up to 200 cigarettes, 50 cigars, or 200 grams of tobacco. You may not ship tobacco or alcohol, and you must be of legal age for your province to bring these items through Customs. For the helpful booklet *I Declare,* call the **Canada Customs and Review Agency** at © **800/461-9999** in Canada or 204/983-3500, or visit its website at www.ccra-adrc.gc.ca.

The duty-free allowance in **Australia** is A$400 or, for those under 18, A$200. Citizens can bring in 250 cigarettes or 250 grams of loose tobacco, and 1.125 liters of alcohol. If you're returning with valuables you already own, such as foreign-made cameras, you should file form B263. A helpful brochure available from Australian consulates or Customs offices is *Know Before You Go.* For more information, call the **Australian Customs Service** at © **1300/363-263,** or log on to www.customs.gov.au.

The duty-free allowance for **New Zealand** is NZ$700. Citizens over 17 can bring in 200 cigarettes, 50 cigars, or 250 grams of tobacco (or a mixture of all 3 if their combined weight doesn't exceed 250g); plus 4.5 liters of wine and beer, or 1.125 liters of liquor. New Zealand currency does not carry import or export restrictions. Fill out a certificate of export, listing the valuables you are taking out of the country; that way, you can bring them back without paying duty. Most questions are answered in a free pamphlet available at New Zealand consulates and Customs offices: *New Zealand Customs Guide for Travellers, Notice no. 4.* For more information, contact **New Zealand Customs,** The Customhouse, 17–21 Whitmore St., Box 2218, Wellington (© **04/473-6099** or 0800/ 428-786; www.customs.govt.nz).

HEALTH INSURANCE

Although it's not required of travelers, health insurance is highly recommended. Unlike many European countries, the United States does not usually offer free or low-cost medical care to its citizens or visitors. Doctors and hospitals are expensive, and in most cases will require advance payment or proof of coverage before they render their services. Some insurance policies can cover everything from the loss or theft of your baggage and trip cancellation to the guarantee of bail in case you're arrested. Good policies will also cover the costs of an accident, repatriation, or death. See "Insurance, Health & Safety" in chapter 2 for

---

> **Tips Before You Go**
>
> Be sure to keep a copy of all your travel papers separate from your wallet or purse, and leave a copy with someone at home should you need it faxed to you in an emergency.

---

more information. Packages such as **Europ Assistance's "Worldwide Healthcare Plan"** are sold by European automobile clubs and travel agencies at attractive rates. **Worldwide Assistance Services, Inc.** (© 800/821-2828; www.worldwideassistance.com) is the agent for Europ Assistance in the United States.

Though lack of health insurance may prevent you from being admitted to a hospital in nonemergencies, don't worry about being left on a street corner to die: the American way is to fix you now and bill the living daylights out of you later.

INSURANCE FOR BRITISH TRAVELERS Most big travel agents offer their own insurance and will probably try to sell you their package when you book a holiday. Think before you sign. **Britain's Consumers' Association** recommends that you insist on seeing the policy and reading the fine print before buying travel insurance. **The Association of British Insurers** (© 020/7600-3333; www.abi.org.uk) gives advice by phone and publishes *Holiday Insurance,* a free guide to policy provisions and prices. You might also shop around for better deals: Try **Columbus Direct** (© 020/7375-0011; www.columbusdirect.net).

INSURANCE FOR CANADIAN TRAVELERS Canadians should check with their provincial health plan offices or call **Health Canada** (© 613/957-2991; www.hc-sc.gc.ca) to find out the extent of their coverage and what documentation and receipts they must take home in case they are treated in the United States.

MONEY

CURRENCY The U.S. monetary system is very simple: The most common **bills** are the $1 (colloquially, a "buck"), $5, $10, and $20 denominations. There are also $2 bills (seldom encountered), $50 bills, and $100 bills (the last two are usually not welcome as payment for small purchases). All the paper money was recently redesigned, making the famous faces adorning them disproportionately large. The old-style bills are still legal tender.

There are seven denominations of coins: 1¢ (1 cent, or a penny); 5¢ (5 cents, or a nickel); 10¢ (10 cents, or a dime); 25¢ (25 cents, or a quarter); 50¢ (50 cents, or a half dollar); the new gold "Sacagawea" coin worth $1; and, prized by collectors, the rare, older silver dollar.

Note: The "foreign-exchange bureaus" so common in Europe are rare even at airports in the United States, and nonexistent outside major cities. It's best not to change foreign money (or traveler's checks denominated in a currency other than U.S. dollars) at a small-town bank, or even a branch in a big city; in fact, leave any currency other than U.S. dollars at home—it may prove a greater nuisance to you than it's worth.

TRAVELER'S CHECKS Though traveler's checks are widely accepted, make sure that they're denominated in U.S. dollars, as foreign-currency checks are often difficult to exchange. The three traveler's checks that are most widely recognized—and least likely to be denied—are **Visa, American Express,** and **Thomas Cook.** Be sure to record the numbers of the checks, and keep that information in a separate place in case they get lost or stolen. Most businesses are pretty good about taking traveler's checks, but you're better off cashing them in at a bank (in small amounts, of course) and paying in cash. Remember: you'll need identification, such as a driver's license or passport, to change a traveler's check.

CREDIT CARDS & ATMS Credit cards are the most widely used form of payment in the United States. The most popular are **Visa** (Barclaycard in Britain), **MasterCard** (EuroCard in Europe, Access in Britain, Chargex in Canada), **American Express, Diners Club, Discover,** and **Carte Blanche.** There are, however, a handful of stores and restaurants that do not take credit cards, so be sure to ask in advance. Most businesses display a sticker near their entrance to let you know which cards they accept. (*Note:* Businesses may require a minimum purchase, usually around $10, to use a credit card.)

It is strongly recommended that you bring at least one major credit card. Major credit cards—MasterCard, Visa, American Express—are accepted by most businesses, especially those where travel expenses are concerned (i.e. rental fees, reservations, etc.) You must have a credit or charge card to rent a car. Hotels and airlines usually require a credit-card imprint as a deposit against expenses, and in an emergency a credit card can be priceless.

You'll find **automated teller machines (ATMs)** on just about every block in almost every town, across the country. ATMs are linked to a network that most likely includes your bank at home. **Cirrus** (*C* 800/424-7787; www.mastercard.com) and **PLUS** (*C* 800/843-7587; www.visa. com) are the two most popular networks in the U.S.; call or check online for ATM locations at your destination. Some ATMs will allow you to draw U.S. currency against your bank and credit cards. Check with your bank before leaving home, and remember that you will need your personal identification number (PIN) to do so. Most accept Visa, MasterCard, and American Express, as well as ATM cards from other U.S. banks. Expect to be charged up to $3 per transaction, however, if you're not using your own bank's ATM.

One way around these fees is to ask for cash back at grocery stores that accept ATM cards and don't charge usage fees. Of course, you'll have to purchase something first.

ATM cards with major credit card backing, known as "debit cards," are now a commonly acceptable form of payment in most stores and restaurants. Debit cards draw money directly from your checking account. Some stores enable you to receive "cash back" on your debit-card purchases as well.

SIZE CONVERSION CHART

Women's Clothing

American	4	6	8	10	12	14	16
French	34	36	38	40	42	44	46
British	6	8	10	12	14	16	18

Women's Shoes

American	5	6	7	8	9	10
French	36	37	38	39	40	41
British	4	5	6	7	8	9

Men's Suits								
American	34	36	38	40	42	44	46	48
French	44	46	48	50	52	54	56	58
British	34	36	38	40	42	44	46	48

Men's Shirts							
American	14½	15	15 ½	16	16½	17	17½
French	37	38	39	41	42	43	44
British	14½	15	15½	16	16½	17	17½

Men's Shoes							
American	7	8	9	10	11	12	13
French	39½	41	42	43	44½	46	47
British	6	7	8	9	10	11	12

2 Getting to the U.S.

Hartsfield Atlanta International Airport (© **404/768-4100**), 10 miles south of downtown, is the world's largest and busiest passenger airport and transfer hub, accommodating 78 million passengers a year. It serves 186 U.S. cities with nonstop service.

Delta Air Lines (© **800/221-1212** or **www.delta.com** for reservations and flight information), which is based at Hartsfield, is the major carrier to Atlanta, connecting it to pretty much the entire country as well as 62 countries internationally. It carries 80% of the air passengers who come into Atlanta and serves over 350 international cities.

Other major carriers include **Airtran** (© 800/247-8726; www.airtran.com), **America West** (© 800/235-9292; www.americawest.com), **American Airlines** (© 800/433-7300; www.aa. com), **British Airways** (© 800/ 247-9297; www.british-airways.com), **Continental** (© 800/732-6887; www.flycontinental.com), **Japan Airlines** (© 800/525-3663; www.jal. com), **KLM** (© 800/374-7747; www.nwa.com), **Lufthansa** (© 800/ 645-3880; www.lufthansa-usa.com), **Northwest** (© 800/225-2525; www. nwa.com), **United Airlines** (© 800/ 241-6522; www.ual.com), and

USAirways (© 800/428-4322; www. usairways.com).

AIRLINE DISCOUNTS The smart traveler can find numerous ways to reduce the price of a plane ticket simply by taking time to shop around. For example, overseas visitors can take advantage of the APEX (Advance Purchase Excursion) reductions offered by all major U.S. and European carriers. For more money-saving airline advice, see "Getting There," in chapter 2. For the best rates, compare fares and be flexible with the dates and times of travel.

IMMIGRATION & CUSTOMS CLEARANCE Visitors arriving by air, no matter what the port of entry, should cultivate patience and resignation before setting foot on U.S. soil. Getting through immigration control can take as long as 2 hours on some days, especially on summer weekends, so be sure to carry this guidebook or something else to read. This is especially true in the aftermath of the September 11, 2001 terrorist attacks, when security clearances have been considerably beefed up at U.S. airports.

People traveling by air from Canada, Bermuda, and certain countries in the Caribbean can sometimes clear Customs and Immigration at the point of departure, which is much quicker.

3 Getting Around the U.S.

BY PLANE Some large airlines (for example, Northwest and Delta) offer travelers on their transatlantic or transpacific flights special discount tickets under the name **Visit USA,** allowing mostly one-way travel from one U.S. destination to another at very low prices. These discount tickets are not on sale in the United States and must be purchased abroad in conjunction with your international ticket. This system is the best, easiest, and fastest way to see the United States at low cost. You should obtain information well in advance from your travel agent or the office of the airline concerned, since the conditions attached to these discount tickets can be changed without advance notice.

BY TRAIN International visitors (excluding Canada) can also buy a **USA Railpass,** good for 15 or 30 days of unlimited travel on Amtrak (© **800/USA-RAIL;** www.amtrak. com). The pass is available through many foreign travel agents. Prices in 2002 for a 15-day pass were $295 off-peak, $440 peak; a 30-day pass costs $385 off-peak, $550 peak. With a foreign passport, you can also buy passes at some Amtrak offices in the United States, including locations in San Francisco, Los Angeles, Chicago, New York, Miami, Boston, and Washington, D.C. Reservations are generally required and should be made for each part of your trip as early as possible. Regional rail passes are also available. European travelers should note that the U.S. rail system is not as extensive as Europe's system, and many small towns lack access to national rail service.

BY BUS Although bus travel is often the most economical form of public transit for short hops between U.S. cities, it can also be slow and uncomfortable—certainly not an option for everyone (particularly when Amtrak, which is far more luxurious, offers similar rates). **Greyhound/Trailways** (© **800/231-2222;** www.greyhound. com), the sole nationwide bus line, offers an **International Ameripass** that must be purchased before coming to the United States, or by phone through the Greyhound International Office at the Port Authority Bus Terminal in New York City (© **212/ 971-0492**). The pass can be obtained from foreign travel agents or through Greyhound's website (order at least 21 days before your departure to the U.S.) and costs less than the domestic version. Passes in 2003 cost as follows: 4 days ($155), 7 days ($204), 10 days ($254), 15 days ($314), 21 days ($364), 30 days ($424), 45 days ($464), or 60 days ($574). You can get more info on the pass at the website, or by calling © **402/330-8552.** Special rates are available for seniors and students.

BY CAR Unless you plan to spend the bulk of your vacation time in a city where walking is the best and easiest way to get around (read: New York City or New Orleans), the most cost-effective, convenient, and comfortable way to travel around the United States is by car. The interstate highway system connects cities and towns all over the country; in addition to these high-speed, limited-access roadways, there's an extensive network of federal, state, and local highways and roads. Some of the national car-rental companies include **Alamo** (© 800/327-9633; www.goalamo. com), **Avis** (© 800/331-1212; www. avis.com), **Budget** (© 800/527-0700; www.budget.com), **Dollar** (© 800/ 800-4000; www.dollar.com), **Hertz** (© 800/654-3131; www.hertz.com), **National** (© 800/227-7368; www. nationalcar.com), and **Thrifty** (© 800/ 367-2277; www.thrifty.com).

If you plan to rent a car in the United States, you probably won't need the services of an additional automobile organization. If you're planning to buy or borrow a car, automobile-association membership is recommended. **AAA, the American Automobile Association** (© 800/222-4357), is the country's largest auto club and supplies its members with maps, insurance, and, most important, emergency road service. The cost of joining runs from $63 for singles to $87 for two members, but if you're a member of a foreign auto club with reciprocal arrangements, you can enjoy free AAA service in America. See "Getting There" in chapter 2 for more information.

 FAST FACTS: **For the International Traveler**

Automobile Organizations Auto clubs will supply maps, suggested routes, guidebooks, accident and bail-bond insurance, and emergency road service. The **American Automobile Association (AAA)** is the major auto club in the United States. If you belong to an auto club in your home country, inquire about AAA reciprocity before you leave. You may be able to join AAA even if you're not a member of a reciprocal club; to inquire, call AAA (© **800/222-4357**). AAA is actually an organization of regional auto clubs; so look under "AAA Automobile Club" in the White Pages of the telephone directory. AAA has a nationwide emergency road service telephone number (© **800/AAA-HELP**).

Business Hours Offices are usually open weekdays from 9am to 5pm. Banks are open weekdays from 9am to 3pm or later and sometimes Saturday mornings. Stores typically open between 9 and 10am and close between 5 and 6pm from Monday through Saturday. Stores in shopping complexes or malls tend to stay open late: until about 9pm on weekdays and weekends, and many malls and larger department stores are open on Sundays.

Currency & Currency Exchange See "Entry Requirements" and "Money" under "Preparing for Your Trip," earlier in this chapter.

Drinking Laws The legal age for purchase and consumption of alcoholic beverages is 21; proof of age is required and often requested at bars, nightclubs, and restaurants, so it's always a good idea to bring ID when you go out. Beer and wine often can be purchased in supermarkets, but liquor laws vary from state to state.

   Do not carry open containers of alcohol in your car or any public area that isn't zoned for alcohol consumption. The police can fine you on the spot. And nothing will ruin your trip faster than getting a citation for DUI ("driving under the influence"), so don't even think about driving while intoxicated.

Electricity Like Canada, the United States uses 110 to 120 volts AC (60 cycles), compared to 220 to 240 volts AC (50 cycles) in most of Europe, Australia, and New Zealand. If your small appliances use 220 to 240 volts, you'll need a 110-volt transformer and a plug adapter with two flat parallel pins to operate them here. Downward converters that change 220–240 volts to 110–120 volts are difficult to find in the United States, so bring one with you.

Embassies & Consulates All embassies are located in the nation's capital, Washington, D.C. Some consulates are located in major U.S. cities, and most nations have a mission to the United Nations in New York City. If your country isn't listed below, call for directory information in Washington, D.C. (© **202/555-1212**) or log on to **www.embassy.org/embassies**.

The embassy of **Australia** is located at 1601 Massachusetts Ave. NW, Washington, D.C. 20036 (© **202/797-3000**; www.austemb.org). There are consulates in New York, Honolulu, Houston, Los Angeles, and San Francisco.

The embassy of **Canada** is found at 501 Pennsylvania Ave. NW, Washington, D.C. 20001 (© **202/682-1740**; www.canadianembassy.org). Other Canadian consulates are in Buffalo (NY), Detroit, Los Angeles, New York, and Seattle.

The embassy of **Ireland** is situated at 2234 Massachusetts Ave. NW, Washington, D.C. 20008 (© **202/462-3939**; www.irelandemb.org). Irish consulates are found in Boston, Chicago, New York, and San Francisco.

The embassy of **Japan** is located at 2520 Massachusetts Ave. NW, Washington, D.C. 20008 (© **202/238-6700**; www.embjapan.org). Japanese consulates are located in Atlanta, Kansas City, San Francisco, and Washington D.C.

The embassy of **New Zealand** is found at 37 Observatory Circle NW, Washington, D.C. 20008 (© **202/328-4800**; www.nzemb.org). New Zealand consulates are in Los Angeles, Salt Lake City, San Francisco, and Seattle.

The embassy of the **United Kingdom** is situated at 3100 Massachusetts Ave. NW, Washington, D.C. 20008 (© **202/462-1340**; www.britainusa.com). Other British consulates are found in Atlanta, Boston, Chicago, Cleveland, Houston, Los Angeles, New York, San Francisco, and Seattle.

Emergencies Call © **911** to report a fire, call the police, or get an ambulance anywhere in the United States. This is a toll-free call. (No coins are required at public telephones.)

If you encounter serious problems, contact the **Traveler's Aid Society International** (© **202/546-1127**; www.travelersaid.org) to help direct you to a local branch. This nationwide, nonprofit, social-service organization geared to helping travelers in difficult straits offers services that might include reuniting families separated while traveling, providing food and/or shelter to people stranded without cash, or even emotional counseling. If you're in trouble, seek them out. Travelers Aid has an office at the Hartsfield airport near the baggage claim (© **404/766-4511**), which is open Monday to Friday. Because the office is staffed by volunteers, the hours are irregular. Travelers in need of assistance who find that location closed should call the downtown office at 828 W. Peachtree St., Suite 320 (© **404/817-7070**). This office is open Monday to Friday 8:30am to 5pm.

Gasoline (Petrol) Petrol is known as gasoline (or simply "gas") in the United States, and petrol stations are known as both gas stations and service stations. Gasoline costs about half as much here as it does in Europe (about $1.35 per gallon at press time), and taxes are already included in the printed price. One U.S. gallon equals 3.8 liters or .85 imperial gallons.

Holidays Banks, government offices, post offices, and many stores, restaurants, and museums are closed on the following legal national holidays: January 1 (New Year's Day), the third Monday in January (Martin Luther King, Jr. Day), the third Monday in February (Presidents' Day, Washington's Birthday), the last Monday in May (Memorial Day), July 4 (Independence Day), the first Monday in September (Labor Day), the second Monday in October (Columbus Day), November 11 (Veterans' Day/Armistice Day), the fourth Thursday in November (Thanksgiving Day), and December 25 (Christmas). Also, the Tuesday following the first Monday in November is Election Day and is a federal government holiday in presidential-election years (held every 4 years, and next in 2004).

Legal Aid If you are "pulled over" for a minor infraction (such as speeding), never attempt to pay the fine directly to a police officer; this could be construed as attempted bribery, a much more serious crime. Pay fines by mail, or directly into the hands of the clerk of the court. If accused of a more serious offense, say and do nothing before consulting a lawyer. Here, the burden is on the state to prove a person's guilt beyond a reasonable doubt, and everyone has the right to remain silent, whether he or she is suspected of a crime or actually arrested. Once arrested, a person can make one telephone call to a party of his or her choice. Call your embassy or consulate.

Mail If you aren't sure what your address will be in the United States, mail can be sent to you, in your name, c/o General Delivery at the main post office of the city or region where you expect to be. (Call ✆ **800/ 275-8777** for information on the nearest post office.) The addressee must pick up mail in person and must produce proof of identity (driver's license, passport, etc.). Most post offices will hold your mail for up to 1 month, and are open Monday to Friday from 8am to 6pm, and Saturday from 9am to 3pm.

Generally found at intersections, mailboxes are blue with a red-and-white stripe and carry the inscription, *U.S. Mail*. If your mail is addressed to a U.S. destination, don't forget to add the five-digit postal code (or ZIP code), after the two-letter abbreviation of the state to which the mail is addressed. This is essential for prompt delivery.

At press time, domestic postage rates were 23¢ for a postcard and 37¢ for a letter. For international mail, a first-class letter of up to one-half ounce costs 80¢ (60¢ to Canada and Mexico); a first-class postcard costs 70¢ (50¢ to Canada and Mexico); and a preprinted postal aerogramme costs 70¢.

Measurements See the chart on the inside front cover of this book for details on converting metric measurements to U.S. equivalents.

Safety See "The Safe Traveler" on p. 26.

Taxes The United States has no value-added tax (VAT) or other indirect tax at the national level. Every state, county, and city has the right to levy its own local tax on all purchases, including hotel and restaurant checks, airline tickets, and so on.

Sales tax in Atlanta is 7%. A total of 14% is paid by hotel and motel guests within the city of Atlanta and Fulton County. Of that tax, 7% is sales tax and 7% is room tax. Car rentals at Atlanta Hartsfield International are assessed 20% in taxes, but rentals in the metro area incur only the local sales tax.

Telephone, Telegraph, Telex, & Fax The telephone system in the United States is run by private corporations, so rates, especially for long-distance service and operator-assisted calls, can vary widely. Generally, hotel surcharges on long-distance and local calls are astronomical, so you're usually better off using a **public pay telephone,** which you'll find clearly marked in most public buildings and private establishments as well as on the street. Convenience grocery stores and gas stations always have them. Many convenience groceries and packaging services sell **prepaid calling cards** in denominations up to $50; these can be the least expensive way to call home. Many public phones at airports now accept American Express, MasterCard, and Visa credit cards. **Local calls** made from public pay phones in most locales cost either 25¢ or 35¢. Pay phones do not accept pennies, and few will take anything larger than a quarter.

You may want to look into leasing a cell-phone for the duration of your trip.

Most long-distance and international calls can be dialed directly from any phone. **For calls within the United States and to Canada,** dial 1 followed by the area code and the seven-digit number. **For other international calls,** dial 011 followed by the country code, city code, and the telephone number of the person you are calling.

Calls to area codes **800, 888,** and **877** are toll-free. However, calls to numbers in area codes **700** and **900** (chat lines, bulletin boards, "dating" services, and so on) can be very expensive—usually a charge of 95¢ to $3 or more per minute, and they sometimes have minimum charges that can run as high as $15 or more.

For **reversed-charge or collect calls,** and for person-to-person calls, dial 0 (zero, not the letter O) followed by the area code and number you want; an operator will then come on the line, and you should specify that you are calling collect, or person-to-person, or both. If your operator-assisted call is international, ask for the overseas operator.

For **local directory assistance** ("information"), dial 411; for long-distance information, dial 1, then the appropriate area code and 555-1212.

Telegraph and telex services are provided primarily by Western Union. You can bring your telegram into the nearest Western Union office (there are hundreds across the country) or dictate it over the phone (✆ **800/ 325-6000**). You can also telegraph money, or have it telegraphed to you, very quickly over the Western Union system, but this service can cost as much as 15 to 20 percent of the amount sent.

Most hotels have **fax machines** available for guest use (be sure to ask about the charge to use it). Many hotel rooms are even wired for guests' fax machines. A less expensive way to send and receive faxes may be at stores such as Mail Boxes Etc., a national chain of packing service shops. (Look in the Yellow Pages directory under "Packing Services.")

There are two kinds of telephone directories in the United States. The so-called **White Pages** list private households and business subscribers in alphabetical order. The inside front cover lists emergency numbers for police, fire, ambulance, the Coast Guard, poison-control center, crime-victims hot line, and so on. The first few pages will tell you how to make long-distance and international calls, complete with country codes and area codes. Government numbers are usually printed on blue paper within the White Pages. Printed on yellow paper, the so-called **Yellow Pages** list all local services, businesses, industries, and houses of worship according to activity with an index at the front or back. (Drugstores/pharmacies and restaurants are also listed by geographic location.) The Yellow Pages also include city plans or detailed area maps, postal ZIP codes, and public transportation routes.

Time The continental United States is divided into **four time zones:** eastern standard time (EST), central standard time (CST), mountain standard time (MST), and Pacific standard time (PST). Alaska and Hawaii have their own zones. For example, noon in New York City (EST) is 11am in Chicago (CST), 10am in Denver (MST), 9am in Los Angeles (PST), 8am in Anchorage (AST), and 7am in Honolulu (HST). Atlanta is on EST.

Daylight saving time is in effect from 1am on the first Sunday in April through 1am on the last Sunday in October, except in Arizona, Hawaii, part of Indiana, and Puerto Rico. Daylight saving time moves the clock 1 hour ahead of standard time.

Tipping Tips are a very important part of certain workers' salaries, so it's necessary to leave appropriate gratuities. In hotels, tip **bellhops** at least $1 per bag ($2–$3 if you have a lot of luggage) and tip the **chamber staff** $1 to $2 per day (more if you've left a disaster area for him or her to clean up). Tip the **doorman** or **concierge** only if he or she has provided you with some specific service (for example, calling a cab for you or obtaining difficult-to-get theater tickets). Tip the **valet-parking attendant** $1 every time you get your car.

In restaurants, bars, and nightclubs, tip **service staff** 15% to 20% of the check, tip **bartenders** 10% to 15%, tip **checkroom attendants** $1 per garment, and tip **valet-parking attendants** $1 per vehicle. Tip the **doorman** only if he has provided you with some specific service (such as calling a cab for you).

As for other service personnel, tip **cab drivers** 15% of the fare; tip **skycaps** at airports at least $1 per bag ($2–$3 if you have a lot of luggage); and tip **hairdressers** and **barbers** 15% to 20%.

Toilets You won't find public toilets or "restrooms" on the streets in most U.S. cities, but they can be found in hotel lobbies, bars, restaurants, museums, department stores, railway and bus stations, and service stations. Large hotels and fast-food restaurants are probably the best bet for good, clean facilities. If possible, avoid the toilets at parks and beaches, which tend to be dirty; some may be unsafe. Restaurants and bars in resorts or heavily visited areas may reserve their restrooms for patrons. Some establishments display a notice indicating this. You can ignore this sign or, better yet, avoid arguments by paying for a cup of coffee or a soft drink, which will qualify you as a patron.

4

Getting to Know Atlanta

The Atlanta metropolitan area is quite large and sprawling, but the city itself is compact, only 131 square miles. Most of the areas popular with visitors are inside the city limits.

1 Orientation

ARRIVING

Despite its size, **Hartsfield Atlanta International Airport** (© 404/768-4100) is well planned and easy to get around in, with six concourses, dozens of restaurants and retail shops, facilities for travelers with disabilities, car-rental desks, and banking and currency-exchange facilities. If you are confused by all the concourses, terminals, and trains, and need some help, look for 1 of the 10 **Hartsfield Host desks.** Friendly volunteers staff the desks and will help you with anything from finding your gate, to choosing the appropriate ground transportation, to locating the lost and found.

The airport has its own website, **www.atlanta-airport.com**, where you can check the status of flights for most major airlines, find maps showing how to get to and from the airport, check traffic conditions on the interstates leading to Hartsfield, and find a list of concessionaires and a list of emergency contacts. You'll also find an array of airport facts on the website. For example, there are more than 30,000 parking spaces—still not nearly enough.

The following major car-rental companies are represented at the airport, and they are reachable via their toll-free numbers. These include: **Avis** (© 800/331-1212), **Alamo** (© 800/327-9633), **Budget** (© 800/527-0700), **Dollar** (© 800/800-4000), **Hertz** (© 800/654-3131), and **Thrifty** (© 800/367-2277).

GETTING DOWNTOWN FROM THE AIRPORT

Hartsfield Atlanta International Airport is just 10 miles south of downtown, and there are several options for getting from the airport to your hotel. The cheapest, if your luggage is manageable, is to take **Atlanta's subway** (commonly referred to as "**MARTA**" because it's operated by the Metropolitan Atlanta Rapid Transit Authority), which stops right inside the airport. The fare is just $1.75. Almost all the major downtown and Buckhead hotels are close to MARTA rail stations. It should take you about 20 minutes to reach downtown, 35 minutes to reach Buckhead.

A taxi from the airport to a downtown hotel costs $25 for one passenger, $26 for two, and $30 for three. The ride should take about half an hour. To Midtown hotels, the fare is $28 for one passenger, $30 for two or more; to Buckhead hotels, the fare is $35 for one passenger, $36 for two or more.

Atlanta Airport Shuttle Vans (© 800/842-2770 or 404/524-3400) operate between the airport and most downtown, Midtown, and Buckhead hotels. They depart from the Delta baggage claim/ground transportation area in the South

---

Tips Art at the Airport

If your flight is delayed at Hartsfield Atlanta International Airport—and whose isn't?—make the most of it by checking out the airport's impressive public art installations. Although artwork is scattered throughout the buildings, the most stunning collection is on Concourse E, the international concourse. There, you'll find more than 70 mixed-media installations that capture various aspects of Southern culture.

Terminal. Reservations from the airport are not necessary, and you can catch one about every 20 to 25 minutes, in either direction, from 7am to 11pm, 7 days a week. To downtown and Midtown locations, the cost is $12 one-way, $20 round-trip; children under age 6 ride free. To Buckhead locations and the Emory University area in Decatur, the cost is $18 one-way, $28 round-trip; free for children under age 6. It's a well-organized system, with clearly marked destinations and helpful attendants on hand. Call **Atlanta Airport Northside Shuttle Vans,** a division of the same company (© **800/277-1165** or 770/952-1601), for information about transport to northside suburban locations. Door-to-door service to the Marietta and Roswell suburbs is available with 24-hour's notice. When you leave Atlanta, check with your hotel desk about departure times; for some hotels, reservations are required a day in advance.

If you're renting a car at the airport, it's easy to drive to your hotel. The airport is located off I-85, which merges with I-75 as you head toward downtown. Interstate-285, known as the Perimeter because it rings the city, is also accessible from I-85 about 3 miles south of Hartsfield.

2 Visitor Information

For information about hotels, restaurants, and attractions, contact the **Atlanta Convention & Visitors Bureau (ACVB),** 233 Peachtree St. NE, Suite 2000, Atlanta, GA 30303 (© **404/222-6688;** www.atlanta.com). Call or write in advance to obtain a copy of *Atlanta Now* (the official visitors' guide), a *Metro Atlanta Attractions Guide,* a map, a book of discounts, and a 2-month calendar of events.

In town, you can visit ACVB information centers at many locations. The best of the information centers is **Underground Atlanta,** 65 Upper Alabama St. (© **404/523-2311**). Open Monday to Saturday 10am to 6pm, Sunday noon to 6pm, this is the most comprehensive of all the ACVB centers. In addition to information about attractions, dining, shopping, and city tours, highlights at the Underground location include:

- An interactive exhibit on the city's cultural organizations. Visitors can access information on museums, plays, events, and concerts. The exhibit displays a photo, written description, and map for each subject or organization.
- AtlanTIX!, a ticket booth where visitors can purchase day-of-show half-price tickets to theater, dance events, and other live performances throughout the metro area.
- A display about Hartsfield Atlanta International Airport that includes a real Delta Air Lines cockpit connected by a live feed to the airport control tower.
- An exhibit demonstrating how to travel around the city.
- A film about Atlanta, shown in a new high-definition theater.

Tips Taxi Tip

Many Atlanta taxis, especially those that line up for passengers at the airport, are in notoriously bad shape, and a number of the drivers don't know the city well. Make sure the fares and zones are posted outside the cab, the driver's photo is displayed, and the taxi has a working meter. And ask if the driver accepts credit cards if you intend to use one. Better still, call ahead and have one of the more reputable companies have a taxi waiting for you when your flight comes in. Three of the best include: **Atlanta Lenox Taxi** (© 404/872-2600); **Buckhead Safety Cab** (© 404/233-1152); and **Atlanta Checker Cabs** (© 404/351-1111).

- Exhibits highlighting Atlanta's history, neighborhoods, and sports teams.
- City tour departures. **Gray Line** of Atlanta runs daily sightseeing tours out of the Underground center. No reservations necessary. Call © **800/965-6665** or 404/767-0594 for information.

Other information centers are located at **Lenox Square,** 3393 Peachtree Rd., open Tuesday to Saturday 11am to 5pm, and Sunday noon to 6pm (no phone); **Hartsfield-Atlanta International Airport,** near the car-rental booths between the north and south baggage claim areas and open Monday to Friday 9am to 9pm, Saturday 9am to 6pm, Sunday 12:30 to 6pm (no phone); and **Georgia World Congress Center,** 285 International Blvd., which operates only during GWCC conventions and has no phone.

The **Travelers Aid Society of Metropolitan Atlanta** is a private nonprofit agency providing help to travelers in difficulty. This might include assisting stranded travelers, providing crisis counseling, straightening out ticket mix-ups, or helping travelers with special needs.

Travelers Aid has an office at the airport near the baggage claim (© **404/766-4511**), which is open Monday to Friday. Because the office is staffed by volunteers, the hours are irregular. Travelers in need of assistance who find that location closed should call the office at 828 W. Peachtree St., Suite 320 (© **404/817-7070**). This office is open Monday to Friday 8:30am to 5pm.

3 City Layout

Atlanta is girded by a beltway called I-285, usually referred to as **the Perimeter.** As a tourist, you'll be spending most of your time within the confines of the Perimeter. Two interstate highways (I-75 and I-85) converge just above the airport and proceed north, forking off just northwest of Piedmont Park: I-75 goes northwest, I-85 northeast. When the highways meet and travel through downtown Atlanta, they're known as **the Downtown Connector.** A fourth interstate highway just below the downtown area, I-20, is an east–west artery that cuts all the way through Georgia and Atlanta, connecting South Carolina with Alabama. Georgia Highway 400 is a toll road connecting I-85 with the suburbs to the north. The cost is 50¢.

There's a joke that all directions in Atlanta begin with "Go to Peachtree . . . " That's because there are a few dozen Peachtrees—Peachtree Street, Lane, Road, Avenue, Circle, Drive, Plaza, and Way, not to mention West Peachtree Street, Peachtree Memorial Drive, Peachtree Battle Avenue, Peachtree Valley Road, and so on. So be sure to emphasize which Peachtree you're looking for when you ask for directions. **Peachtree Street** (which becomes **Peachtree Rd.** above Midtown and **Peachtree Industrial Blvd.** above Buckhead) is the backbone of Atlanta and its major north–south artery. It's possible, though time-consuming, to start out on Peachtree Street and travel all the way from downtown to beyond the Perimeter. Another main north–south thoroughfare is **Piedmont Avenue.** Peachtree is a two-way street, while Piedmont has two-way traffic above Fourteenth Street, but south-to-north only below Fourteenth Street. Major east–west streets include Memorial Drive, North Avenue, Ponce de Leon Avenue, Fourteenth Street, and, in Buckhead, East and West Paces Ferry Drives.

Because Atlanta just grew (and grew and grew) and wasn't planned out on a grid system, getting around the city by car can be confusing and frustrating, even for people who live here. Streets are often one-way downtown, or they change names, or are cut off by the interstate or the Chattahoochee River. Be sure to have a good map in hand if you are driving or if you venture much off the beaten path, and make sure your directions are clear. But if you do get lost, Atlantans—who are very friendly—are always eager to help visitors find their way.

ATLANTA NEIGHBORHOODS IN BRIEF

You can't really get the feel of a city until you understand the characteristics of its neighborhoods. Here's a brief rundown of Atlanta's diverse districts.

Downtown Atlanta's financial and business hub, this area of sleek skyscrapers includes the Peachtree Center hotel/convention center/trade mart/office-tower complex. Here, too: Underground Atlanta, a mix of shops, restaurants, and nightclubs fronted by a 138-foot light tower; the mammoth Georgia World Congress Center, one of the largest meeting and exhibition halls in the nation; the 71,500-seat Georgia Dome, home of the Atlanta Falcons and site of Super Bowl XXXIV; Philips Arena, home of the Atlanta Hawks and Atlanta Thrashers; CNN Center; Georgia-Pacific Center, housing the downtown branch of the High Museum of Art; Georgia State University; the golden-domed, century-old State Capitol, a major landmark; the 21-acre Centennial Olympic Park, the city's newest gathering place; Woodruff Park; and the SciTrek Museum.

Just south of downtown is Turner Field, home of the Atlanta Braves. In its previous incarnation, it was the 85,000-seat Olympic Stadium, but it was retrofitted as a baseball field and reopened in 1997. Also in the general area are Oakland Cemetery (it's mentioned in *Gone With the Wind,* and Margaret Mitchell is one of the many notables buried here), Grant Park, Zoo Atlanta and Cyclorama.

Unlike some big cities, Atlanta doesn't have a large population living in the downtown area, although it looks as if that is beginning to change. Currently, downtown consists primarily of businesses, hotels, restaurants, and sports venues, and it doesn't possess the round-the-clock big city excitement that can be found in New York City, for example. People are beginning to move into newly renovated lofts and other buildings, but there's still not a lot of activity in the central city after business hours. For that reason, it's wisest for visitors to stick to the hotel district and the sports venues, where most of the nighttime goings-on take place.

Sweet Auburn This traditionally African-American neighborhood, also called the **Martin Luther King, Jr., Historic District,** is just below downtown's central area.

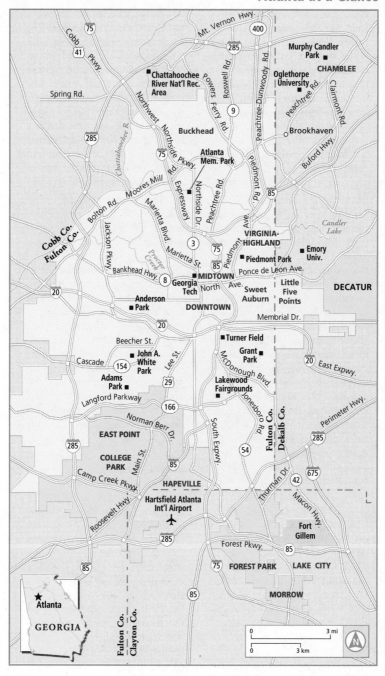

Under the auspices of the National Park Service, it was designated a park in 1980 to honor King, whose boyhood home, crypt, and church are located here. In spite of the yoke of segregation, affluent black businesspeople and professionals flourished here from the early part of the 20th century through the 1950s. Recently revitalized, today it's one of Atlanta's major sightseeing draws.

Midtown Though its boundaries have never been definitively decided, Midtown basically encompasses the area north of downtown from about Ponce de Leon Avenue to I-85. It includes Piedmont Park, the central city's major recreation area; the Woodruff Arts Center, home of the Atlanta Symphony Orchestra, the Alliance Theatre, and the High Museum of Art; the famed Fox Theatre, a 1920s Moorish-motif movie palace; the Atlanta Botanical Garden; Ansley Park, a 230-acre residential greenbelt area, designed at the turn of the century by Frederick Law Olmsted (of Central Park in New York fame); and Colony Square, an office/hotel/retail complex. AT&T, IBM, Bank of America, and BellSouth maintain corporate offices in Midtown.

Buckhead Named for an 1838 tavern called the Buck's Head, this is Atlanta's silk-stocking district—one of America's most beautiful and affluent communities. It begins about 6 miles north of downtown, just above I-85. Here, you'll find tree-shaded residential areas filled with magnificent mansions surrounded by verdant acreage, as well as many smaller middle-class homes, shops and boutiques (Lenox Square and Phipps Plaza, two exclusive shopping malls, are found here), superb restaurants, and first-class hotels. On weekends, the

bars and clubs in the center of Buckhead attract crowds of revelers. Buckhead is also a burgeoning business area, with most of its high-rise office buildings concentrated near Peachtree and Lenox roads. The area's major sightseeing attraction is the Atlanta History Center, centered on a Palladian villa designed by noted architect Phillip Schutze and surrounded by 32 woodland acres. The Greek Revival Governor's Mansion is also in Buckhead.

Virginia-Highland Every major American city has a district that claims kinship (however slight) with New York's Greenwich Village. In Atlanta, it's the Virginia-Highland section, so named for its central avenues, northeast of downtown. Here you'll find ethnic restaurants, antique shops, bookstores, sidewalk cafes, art galleries, lively bars and bistros, and browsable shops selling everything from gourmet gadgets and woodworking tools to ecologically correct clothing. The surrounding area is full of tree-lined streets with charming little cottages, many of them recently renovated.

Little Five Points Just below Virginia-Highland—and a funkier offshoot of it—Little Five Points offers a more offbeat ambience, attracting young and old members of the tie-dyed and pierced set. It is also the location of the Jimmy Carter Library/Carter Presidential Center, which opened in 1986 to house the correspondence and memorabilia of this Georgia-born president. The area's many Victorian homes make for an architecturally interesting stroll. The neighborhood is centered at the junction of Euclid and Moreland avenues. Don't confuse this with **Five Points,** which is a major downtown intersection.

West End & Cascade Road Southwest of town lies a booming area populated by well-to-do African-American singles and families. The historic West End, Atlanta's oldest neighborhood, is full of charming Victorian homes and is the gateway to the Cascade Road area. Here, you'll find the Wren's Nest, the former home of writer Joel Chandler Harris.

Decatur Founded in 1823 by Commodore Stephen Decatur, a dashing naval hero of the War of 1812 who died in a duel, this charming suburb centers on an old courthouse square. About a 15-minute drive east from downtown, Decatur is the scene of numerous annual events, festivals, and concerts, and it houses the sprawling DeKalb Farmers Market, an international food market that must be seen to be believed. Like Virginia-Highland and Little Five Points, Decatur weaves a splash of funky color and texture into Atlanta's tapestry of neighborhoods.

4 Getting Around

Even if you're here for just a few days, you'll get a pretty good feel for the layout of the city. Just remember that the main drag is **Peachtree Street** (becoming Peachtree Rd. to the north), and use it to get your bearings.

BY PUBLIC TRANSPORTATION

The **Metropolitan Atlanta Rapid Transit Authority (MARTA)** operates a rail (subway) and bus network, making it possible, though not always convenient, to reach just about any part of town by public transportation. While the system is fairly extensive within the city limits, outside the city (except for areas in DeKalb, Fulton, and Clayton counties) the service is quite limited. Even in some areas served by bus and rail lines, it's often necessary to walk a bit to a station or stop.

Cobb County, a suburban metro county that includes the city of Marietta, operates a bus system separate from MARTA. **Cobb Community Transit (CCT)** has five local and express routes that operate between Cobb and the Arts Center, Dunwoody, and H.E. Holmes MARTA stations. Transfers are free between CCT and MARTA. Call ✆ **770/427-4444** for information.

Beginning in the summer of 2003, the **Buckhead Area Transportation Management Association (BATMA)** is scheduled to begin operating free electric shuttle buses between the two MARTA rail stations in the area—Lenox and Buckhead—and the hotels, malls, and other businesses along Piedmont and Peachtree roads. At night and on weekends, the shuttles will run farther south on Peachtree Road to the entertainment district along Pharr and East Paces Ferry roads. Weekday routes are tentatively scheduled to operate from 7am to 11pm, while routes on Friday and Saturday will run until 2am. For more information, inquire at your hotel or visit **www.batma.org**.

MARTA RAPID RAIL

MARTA's rapid-rail (subway) service began in 1979. The stations are clean and modern, the service reliable. Although MARTA has a good safety record, there is the perception here—as in many big cities—that subway travel is less than safe. MARTA moves more than half a million people every day, and regular riders seem to have more confidence in the security of the trains and stations than infrequent riders do. Visitors should find the subway most pleasant during the day and during early evening hours when usage is heavy.

The major problem with MARTA is that not enough parts of the city are served by rail, which is much faster than travel by bus. Eventually, MARTA will have 45 stations, but currently the system includes only 40 stations. There are **two lines:** South–north trains (**orange lines** on the MARTA maps) travel between the airport and Doraville and North Springs; east–west trains (**blue** on the maps) travel between Indian Creek (east of Decatur) and Hamilton E. Holmes. They intersect at **Five Points Station** in downtown Atlanta, where you can transfer to another train for free. The system's two newest station additions—Sandy Springs and North Springs—were added in late 2000 to the north line that parallels Georgia Highway 400.

Fare is **$1.75** for any ride, payable in exact change (no pennies), tokens, or TransCards. A weekly **TransCard,** available at Ride Stores—in the Five Points, airport, Lenox, or Lindbergh stations—is good for unlimited bus and rail travel for 1 week and costs $13. A weekend pass, good Friday through Sunday, is $9.

MARTA trains generally arrive and depart every 8 to 10 minutes, 7 days a week from 5am to 1am. Free transfers between bus and rail are available when you board a bus or enter a rail station. Parking is free but limited at about half the rail stations. If you wish to park overnight, you must use the long-term secured parking available at the Doraville, Dunwoody, Medical Center, Lenox, Brookhaven, Lindbergh, North Springs, Sandy Springs, and College Park stations. Cost is $3 per day.

For MARTA schedule and route information, call © **404/848-4711** Monday to Friday from 6am to midnight, Saturday and Sunday from 8am to 10pm. Or visit the website at **http://itsmarta.com**. Printed schedules are available from racks at Five Points and several other stations; instructions are printed in English, French, Japanese, German, and Spanish. All stations and rail cars are fully accessible to disabled passengers.

BUSES

It's possible, but not always efficient, to get anywhere within the city limits by bus. The routes will deliver you to most major attractions and sightseeing stops, but travel can be slow and buses infrequent. MARTA buses operate on a 1,550-mile network of 150 routes, and the fare system is the same as described above for rail service. To find out what bus to take, call © **404/848-4711** for route information (same hours as listed above for rail information). You must have **exact change** ($1.75), a token, a valid transfer, or a TransCard. Special shuttle buses operate from downtown in conjunction with major stadium sports events and conventions; call the above number for details.

BY CAR

It's possible to reach most major Atlanta sights by transit system (MARTA), and public transportation is usually the best bet during sporting and entertainment events and conventions.

Traffic can be a nightmare, and the region's leaders are working hard to figure out what to do about it. Rush hours—roughly 6:30 to 9am and 3:30 to 6:30 or 7pm—can be vicious, especially when traveling into town in the morning or out of town in the afternoon on any of the interstates. The Downtown Connector (where I-75 and I-85 become one) is almost always congested, even during non-rush times, mostly because travelers on their way to points north, south, east, and west join the locals trying to make their way through the city. The area looks a lot like a pig trying to pass through a python. Atlanta drivers are generally courteous, but they tend to travel at breakneck speeds well above the posted limit, so it's wise to stay off the interstates during peak hours. Interstate-285, which circles the city and supports a lot of truck traffic, should be avoided if at all possible.

Georgia law requires the driver and front-seat passengers to wear seat belts while the car is in motion. Children age 4 and under must be buckled into safety seats in the rear, and children ages 5 to 12 must sit in the rear seat if the car is equipped with air bags.

Parking isn't a problem in Atlanta's outlying areas, but it's getting to be a headache downtown and in some commercial areas of Midtown and Buckhead. It can be especially scarce and expensive downtown during conventions and other major events. If you can't find a spot close to your destination, there's often parking available a block or two away, and it's likely to be cheaper.

If you drive, here are a few things to keep in mind:

CAR RENTAL

Renting a car in Atlanta will not be a problem. All of the major rental car companies maintain branch offices in the city.

Atlanta Rent-A-Car (© **404/344-1060**), a local independently owned company, has been serving Atlanta for over 20 years, and their rates are often lower than most. They have 20 metro locations, including one close to the airport, and provide free courtesy pickup anywhere in metro Atlanta.

If you pick up your rental car at Hartsfield-Atlanta International Airport, expect to pay a 10% government tax (which includes a 7% local sales tax) and a 10% airport tax. Elsewhere in the metro area, car rentals incur only the local sales tax, which can range from 5% to 7%.

Saving Money on a Rental Car   Car-rental rates vary even more than airline fares. The price you pay will depend on the size of the car, where and when you pick it up and drop it off, the length of the rental period, where and how far you drive it, whether you purchase insurance, and a host of other factors. A few key questions could save you hundreds of dollars. Here are some things to ask:

- Are weekend rates lower than weekday rates? Ask if the rate is the same for pickup Friday morning, for instance, as it is for Thursday night.
- Is a weekly rate cheaper than the daily rate? Even if you only need the car for 4 days, it may be cheaper to keep it for 5.
- Does the agency assess a drop-off charge if you don't return the car to the same location where you picked it up? Is it cheaper to pick up the car at the airport compared to a downtown location?
- Are special promotional rates available? If you see an advertised price in your local newspaper, be sure to ask for that specific rate; otherwise you may be charged the standard cost. Terms change constantly.
- Are discounts available for members of AARP, AAA, frequent flyer programs, or trade unions? If you belong to any of these organizations, you may be entitled to discounts of up to 30%.
- How much tax will be added to the rental bill? Local tax? State use tax?
- What is the cost of adding an additional driver's name to the contract?
- How many free miles are included in the price? Free mileage is often negotiable, depending on the length of your rental.
- How much does the rental company charge to refill your gas tank if you return with the tank less than full? Though most rental companies claim these prices are "competitive," fuel is almost always cheaper in town. Try to allow enough time to refuel the car yourself before returning it. Some

companies offer "refueling packages," in which you pay for an entire tank of gas up front. The price is usually fairly competitive with local gas prices, but you don't get credit for any gas remaining in the tank. If a stop at a gas station on the way to the airport will make you miss your plane, then by all means take advantage of the fuel purchase option. Otherwise, skip it.

Demystifying Renter's Insurance　Before you drive off in a rental car, be sure you're insured. Hasty assumptions about your personal auto insurance or a rental agency's additional coverage could end up costing you tens of thousands of dollars—even if you are involved in an accident that was clearly the fault of another driver.

If you already hold a **private auto insurance** policy, you are most likely covered in the United States for loss of or damage to a rental car, and liability in case of injury to any other party involved in an accident. Be sure to find out whether you are covered in the area you are visiting, whether your policy extends to all persons who will be driving the rental car, how much liability is covered in case an outside party is injured in an accident, and whether the type of vehicle you are renting is included under your contract. (Rental trucks, sport utility vehicles, and luxury vehicles such as Jaguars may not be covered.)

Most **major credit cards** provide some degree of coverage as well—provided they were used to pay for the rental. Terms vary widely, however, so be sure to call your credit card company directly before you rent.

If you are **uninsured,** your credit card provides primary coverage as long as you decline the rental agency's insurance. This means that the credit card will cover damage or theft of a rental car for the full cost of the vehicle. If you already have insurance, your credit card will provide secondary coverage—which basically covers your deductible.

Credit cards **will not cover liability,** or the cost of injury to an outside party and/or damage to an outside party's vehicle. If you do not hold an insurance policy, you may seriously want to consider purchasing additional liability insurance from your rental company. Be sure to check the terms, however: Some rental agencies only cover liability if the renter is not at fault; even then, the rental company's obligation varies from state to state.

Bear in mind that each credit card company has its own peculiarities. Most American Express Optima cards, for instance, do not provide any insurance. American Express does not cover vehicles valued at over $50,000 when new, luxury vehicles such as the Porsche, or vehicles built on a truck chassis. MasterCard does not provide coverage for loss, theft, or fire damage, and only covers collision if the rental period does not exceed 15 days. Call your own credit card company for details.

The basic insurance coverage offered by most car rental companies, known as the **Loss/Damage Waiver (LDW)** or **Collision Damage Waiver (CDW),** can cost as much as $20 per day. It usually covers the full value of the vehicle with no deductible if an outside party causes an accident or other damage to the rental car. In all states but California, you will probably be covered in case of theft as well. Liability coverage varies according to the company policy and state law, but the minimum is usually at least $15,000. If you are at fault in an accident, however, you will be covered for the full replacement value of the car but not for liability. Some states allow you to buy additional liability coverage for such cases. Most rental companies will require a police report in order to process any claims you file, but your private insurer will not be notified of the accident.

Package Deals   Many packages are available that include airfare, accommodations, and a rental car with unlimited mileage. Compare these prices with the cost of booking airline tickets and renting a car separately to see if these offers are good deals.

Arranging Car Rentals on the Web   Internet resources can make comparison shopping easier. **Microsoft Expedia** (www.expedia.com) and **Travelocity** (www.travelocity.com) help you compare prices and locate car-rental bargains from various companies nationwide. They will even make your reservation for you once you've found the best deal.

BY TAXI

Atlanta is not New York. It's not possible to step outside and hail a cab at all times, but there are always cabs waiting outside the airport, major hotels, Underground Atlanta, and most MARTA stations, except those found downtown. If a cab is not waiting at your MARTA rail stop, use the white assistance phone in the station and MARTA will call one for you.

Taxi fares are a bit complicated in Atlanta. Within the Downtown Zone, you pay a flat rate of $5 for one passenger, $1 for each additional rider. That's fine if you're going from one end of this extensive zone to the other; unfortunately, though, you pay the same rate if you only go 1 block.

There's also a flat rate for rides between downtown and the airport: $18 for one passenger, $10 each for two, $8 each for three or more, not to exceed $24. Between the airport and Midtown, the rate is $22 for one passenger, $25 for two or more. Between the airport and Buckhead, the rate is $28 for one, $30 for two or more. Within the Buckhead zone, there's a flat rate of $5 for one person, $1 for each additional person.

Outside these specified zones, Atlanta cabs charge a minimum $1.50 for the meter pull and first ⅙ mile, 20¢ for each additional ⅙ mile for the first passenger, and a flat rate of $1 for each additional passenger, adult or child. Waiting time is $15 per hour.

There are many taxi companies in town. If you need to call for a taxi, try **Atlanta Lenox Taxi** (© 404/872-2600), **Yellow Cabs** (© 404/521-0200), **Checker Cabs** (© 404/351-1111), or **Buckhead Safety Cab** (© 404/233-1152). If your destination lies outside of the zone system (which applies flat rates to trips within each zone), the meter won't start running until you get in the cab. A set flat rate is charged by these taxi companies for destinations within the zones. All accept cash and some accept credit cards.

If you have a complaint about taxi service, call the **Taxi Bureau** at © **404/658-7600.**

FAST FACTS: Atlanta

Airport   See "Getting There," in chapter 2.

American Express   The Buckhead office across from the Swissôtel near Lenox Square provides travel services and currency exchange (© **404/262-7561**).

Area Codes   In metro Atlanta, you must dial the area code (404, 770, or 678) and the seven-digit telephone number, even if you are calling a number within the same area code. It is not necessary to dial "1" before the area code when calling between communities within the Atlanta local calling area, even if they have different area codes.

Babysitters Most hotels will arrange babysitters for you. If yours doesn't, a highly recommended service is **A Friend of the Family** (℃ 770/725-2748), which has been in business 17 years. All of their sitters are carefully screened, and most are at least 21 years of age. On request, they will send someone who is trained in CPR. You can interview the sitter in advance on the phone. The rate is $10 to $12 per hour, with a 4-hour minimum, plus an agency fee of $25 per day. The agency fee must be paid by credit card; the sitters prefer cash. If you are staying in a hotel without free parking, you may be asked to pay for parking. Advance notice of 24 hours is appreciated but not required. A Friend of the Family also provides pet care and companions for adults. Office hours are Monday to Saturday 8am to 10pm, and Sunday 1pm to 10pm.

Buses See "Getting Around," earlier in this chapter.

Car Rentals See "Getting Around," earlier in this chapter.

Climate See "When to Go," in chapter 2.

Dentists **The Georgia Dental Association of Atlanta** (℃ 404/636-7553) offers a free referral service. They'll refer you to a dentist close to your hotel, or if need be, one who can accommodate special needs (for example, a dentist who does cosmetic work, speaks a foreign language, keeps emergency hours, or otherwise specializes). The service cannot match patients with dentists who offer services through specific insurance companies. Hours of operation are weekdays from 8am to 5pm. At other times, inquire at your hotel desk.

Doctors **The Medical Association of Atlanta** (℃ 404/881-1714), with more than 2,000 member physicians in town, runs a free referral service for every kind of medical specialty and subspecialty. Hours are Monday to Friday 9am to 4:30pm.

Promina Health Systems, a well-respected local consortium of physicians, hospitals, and clinics, operates its own referral service Monday to Friday 9am to 5:30pm (℃ 404/541-1111).

Emergencies To report a fire, summon the police, or procure an ambulance, simply dial ℃ 911. See also the listing for the **Travelers Aid Society of Metropolitan Atlanta** in "Visitor Information," earlier in this chapter.

Eyeglass Repair **Lenscrafters,** which has one location in the Lenox Square mall (℃ 404/239-0784) and another in the Around Lenox Shopping Center (south of Lenox Square, just behind Neiman-Marcus; ℃ 404/262-2020), offers 1-hour service on contacts and eyeglasses (including bifocals and trifocals), stocks a gigantic selection of frames (from designer to economy), provides on-premises eye examinations by independent doctors of optometry, maintains a complete contact-lens center, and gives discounts to seniors and college students. Check your phone book for other locations.

Hospitals/Emergency Rooms **Piedmont Hospital,** 1968 Peachtree Rd., just above Collier Road (℃ 404/605-3297), offers 24-hour full emergency-room service, as does **Grady Health Systems,** 35 Butler St., downtown (℃ 404/616-6200). For life-threatening medical emergencies, dial ℃ 911.

Liquor Laws No alcohol is served at bars, restaurants, or nightclubs between 4am and 12:30pm Sunday. Alcoholic beverages are not sold on Sunday in liquor stores, convenience stores, or grocery stores. The drinking age is 21.

Newspapers/Magazines The major newspaper in town is the *Atlanta Journal-Constitution.* Its "Weekend Preview" section, published every Friday, includes restaurant and movie reviews and highlights plays, festivals, live music, gallery openings, and other happenings for the weekend and the week ahead. You'll also find it helpful to pick up a current issue of *Atlanta* magazine when you're in town. And keep an eye out for *Creative Loafing,* an offbeat free publication available in shops, restaurants, and on the street; it offers lots of interesting information, including excellent restaurant reviews.

Pharmacies The **Kroger** supermarket chain (© **800/576-4377**) operates several pharmacies that are open 24 hours. Call the above number for the nearest location.

Poison Center Call © **404/616-9000.**

Police Call © **911** in an emergency. Call © **404/853-3434** for non-emergencies.

Post Office Open 24 hours a day, Atlanta's main post office is located not in the downtown area, but close to Hartsfield-Atlanta International Airport at 3900 Crown Rd., Atlanta, GA 30304 (© **404/765-7300**).

Road Conditions Call the **Georgia Department of Transportation** (© **404/635-6800**) for information about delays due to road construction.

Salons To some of us, a gifted hairdresser can be the most essential of services. Carey Carter and Mitchell Barnes of **Carter/Barnes Hair Artisans,** on the upper level of Phipps Plaza shopping mall (© **404/233-0047**), are among the best and best-known stylists in Atlanta (for men and women). Their work is often featured in well-regarded fashion magazines, and they regularly make the lists of top national salons. Their shop is in Buckhead, but their clients come from all over the southeast and other points around the country. Besides haircuts, color, and perms, there's also a full complement of salon and spa services—facials, manicures/pedicures, waxing, massage, extensive skin care, deep therapy for hands and feet, and full days of beauty services. Particularly fun is a makeup lesson with one of the makeup artists.

Two more excellent salons that are conveniently located and that serve both men and women include **Scott Cole Salon,** 2859 Piedmont Rd. NW (© **404/237-4970**); and **Van Michael Salon,** 39 W. Paces Ferry Rd. (© **404/237-4664**). In addition to the regular salon, Van Michael has a **New Talents** salon next door where you can get a lower-priced haircut from a stylist in training.

All of the above salons are quite popular, so try to book well in advance. It's sometimes possible to get an appointment on the spur of the moment, especially if you're willing to see one of the newer—but not necessarily less experienced—stylists.

Taxes Sales tax in Atlanta is 7%. A total of 14% is paid by hotel and motel guests within the city of Atlanta and Fulton County. Of that tax, 7% is sales tax and 7% is room tax. Car rentals at Atlanta Hartsfield International are assessed 20% in taxes, but rentals in the metro area incur only the local sales tax.

Taxis Call **Yellow Cabs** (℗ 404/521-0200), **Checker Cabs** (℗ 404/351-1111), **Atlanta Lenox Taxi** (℗ 404/872-2600), or **Buckhead Safety Cab** (℗ 404/233-1152) in Buckhead.

Tickets For tickets to almost all sports and performing arts events, call **Ticketmaster** (℗ **404/249-6400**) to charge by phone; a surcharge will be added to each ticket. The Ticketmaster surcharge ranges from $2.35 to $5.80 per ticket, depending on the event; there's an additional handling fee of $3.05 per order. Ticketmaster also has more than 100 locations throughout Georgia, including all Publix Supermarkets, where customers can purchase tickets in person, though they must be paid for in cash. To avoid the Ticketmaster surcharge, it's often possible to purchase tickets at the box office. If you are staying in a large hotel, the concierge service is often able to obtain tickets to even the most popular events.

Day-of-show half-price tickets are available at the AtlanTIX! ticket booth at the Atlanta Convention and Visitors Bureau in Underground Atlanta. Customers can look over the showboard to see what plays and other live performances have tickets available that day, purchase a voucher for the show, and pick up the ticket at the show's box office before curtain time. Vouchers must be paid for in person; phone sales are not available. AtlanTIX! is open Tuesday 11am to 3pm, Wednesday to Saturday 11am to 6pm, and Sunday noon to 3pm. Call ℗ **770/772-5572** for more information.

Time Call ℗ **770/455-7141**. Atlanta is on Eastern Standard Time (EST).

Transit Info To find out how to get from point A to point B via MARTA (bus and rail), dial ℗ **404/848-4711**.

Weather Call ℗ **770/455-7141**.

5

Where to Stay

Even in Hotlanta, sleep is inevitable. As a major convention city, metro Atlanta is capable of accommodating hoards of visitors. It has more than 88,000 rooms at 708 properties, including budget digs, bed-and-breakfast lodgings, and bastions of luxury. The choices listed below—offering good value in several different price brackets—are in the parts of the city that travelers frequent most often. If you have trouble finding a spot at these places, look to the suburbs. Nearly every chain is represented, and if you have a car and you're near one of the major interstates, getting into the city should be relatively simple, especially if you avoid rush hour.

Many preferential rates are available only when you reserve via toll-free reservation numbers or the Internet. That contact information is supplied in all applicable listings below.

Though many of the hotels are often full during the business week, they're usually not sold out on the weekend. Most of the major hotels that cater to business travelers, especially those downtown, offer reduced weekend rates. Also inquire about reduced-price packages (they may include extras such as meals, parking, theater tickets, and golf fees) and reduced rates for senior citizens, families, and active-duty military personnel. Although 100% occupancy is a rarity in Atlanta, it is a major convention city; booking well in advance assures you a room in the hotel of your choice. Keep in mind that hotel rates often increase during special events.

RATES The hotels below are classified first by area, then by price, using the following categories: **Very Expensive:** more than $200 per night; **Expensive:** $150 to $200; **Moderate:** $100 to $150; **Inexpensive:** less than $100. All rates are for double occupancy and are subject to change. They're rack rates, and if you ask about discounts and packages, or if you book through a travel agent, you can often do better than these posted rates. Any extras included in the rates (for example, breakfast or other meals) are listed for each property. A 14% tax will be added onto your hotel or motel bill within the city of Atlanta and Fulton County (7% sales tax plus 7% room tax); the rates listed below do not include that tax. If you have a car, be sure to consider the price of parking in the hotel garage at an average of $18 per overnight.

BED & BREAKFASTS Bed & Breakfast Atlanta, 1608 Briarcliff Rd. NE (© **800/967-3224** or 404/875-0525; www.bedandbreakfastatlanta.com), is a free professional reservation service that has been carefully screening facilities in the Atlanta area since 1979. Their list comprises more than 100 homes and inns; all accommodations offering private bathrooms. They include—among others—a turreted Queen Anne–style Victorian home with nine fireplaces near the Carter Library, a delightful honeymoon cottage with a Jacuzzi in "Miss Daisy's" Druid Hills, an elegant 1920s Tudor-style home in Buckhead, and a fully furnished garden cottage in

Ansley Park. They even have kosher homes on their roster. All rates include continental breakfast, in many cases extended considerably beyond the usual pastry and coffee. To make sure that you get a room in your top B&B choice, make sure you reserve as early as possible. Call during office hours, which are Monday to Friday from 9am to 5pm.

The rates run the gamut from $60 to $240 (the latter for a luxurious Buckhead guest cottage, on a 4-acre estate, that accommodates four people). Rates during special events may be higher. Weekly and monthly rates are available (in guesthouses and apartments) for long-term visitors. American Express, Diner's Club, MasterCard, and Visa are accepted.

1 Downtown

Downtown hotels primarily cater to the business/convention traveler, but there's plenty for tourists here too: CNN Center, Centennial Olympic Park, the Georgia Dome, and Philips Arena.

VERY EXPENSIVE

Hilton Atlanta ★★   One of Atlanta's top convention hotels—with 104,000 square feet of meeting and exhibit space—the Hilton is surprisingly upscale for a chain hotel. The rooms and bathrooms are very nice and quite large, and if you're going to stay in one of the downtown megahotels, this is a good choice. The rooms offer coffeemakers, minibars, and hair dryers, plus video checkout and account-review functions. Some of the suites have Murphy beds for extra guests. The Hilton's premier restaurant is Nikolai's Roof, a 30th-floor dining room offering spectacular skyline vistas. Multi-course prix-fixe French and Russian dinners are the specialty. A Point of View is the bar adjacent to Nikolai's Roof. Trader Vic's, a South Seas–Polynesian restaurant found at numerous Hiltons, offers its signature setting and potent rum drinks. The Garden Terrace, a pretty lobby-level eatery centered around a vast fountain, serves buffet meals at breakfast and lunch and Sunday champagne brunch. Adjoining it are the Cafe Express Deli (a 24-hr. facility) and Le Café, the Hilton's casual dining facility. Finally, there's the Bogart-and-Bergman–themed Casablanca Bar, whose big-screen TV attracts a sports-minded crowd.

255 Courtland St. (between Baker and Harris sts.), Atlanta, GA 30303. © **800/HILTONS** or 404/659-2000. Fax 404/524-0111. www.hilton.com. 1,224 units. Mon–Thurs $190–$245 double; Fri–Sun $99–$159 double, depending on the season; Tower rooms $255 double. Extra person $25. Children stay free in parents' room. AE, DC, DISC, MC, V. Valet parking $14; self-parking $12. MARTA: Peachtree Center. **Amenities:** 4 restaurants; 2 bars; 24-hr. deli; outdoor pool/sundeck; 4 outdoor tennis courts; 2 basketball courts; fitness center with jogging track; Jacuzzi; sauna; concierge; airport shuttle; business center; shops; limited room service. *In room:* A/C, TV, minibar, coffeemaker, hair dryer, video checkout.

Hyatt Regency Atlanta ★★   One of the city's major convention hotels, this Hyatt was designed in 1967 by famed Atlanta architect John Portman. With its innovative 23-story atrium lobby, it created quite a stir and was the prototype not only for future downtown hotels in the city, but also for hotel architecture throughout the United States. The hotel is connected to the Peachtree Center mall by a covered walkway.

The Hyatt accommodates guests not only in the original building, but in two later additions—the 24-story International Tower and the 22-story Ivy Tower. Rooms throughout feature plush modern furnishings. The comfortable bathrooms are equipped with hair dryers.

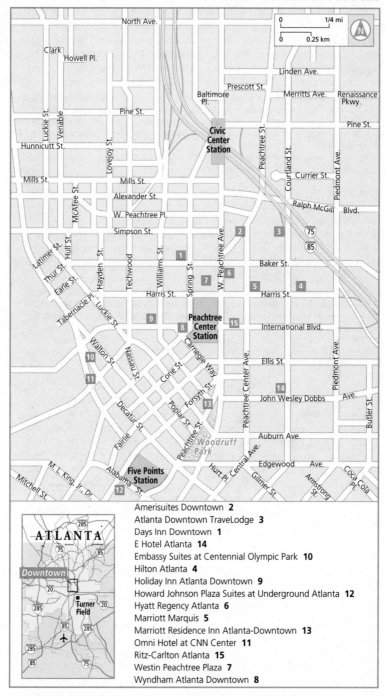

Amerisuites Downtown **2**
Atlanta Downtown TraveLodge **3**
Days Inn Downtown **1**
E Hotel Atlanta **14**
Embassy Suites at Centennial Olympic Park **10**
Hilton Atlanta **4**
Holiday Inn Atlanta Downtown **9**
Howard Johnson Plaza Suites at Underground Atlanta **12**
Hyatt Regency Atlanta **6**
Marriott Marquis **5**
Marriott Residence Inn Atlanta-Downtown **13**
Omni Hotel at CNN Center **11**
Ritz-Carlton Atlanta **15**
Westin Peachtree Plaza **7**
Wyndham Atlanta Downtown **8**

The main building's 22nd floor houses the Regency Club, and Business Plan rooms (equipped with personal work stations, in-room faxes, desk phones with computer jacks, and coffeemakers) are on the 21st floor. Business Plan guests get free local calls and other perks. The blue dome capping Polaris, the Hyatt's revolving rooftop restaurant, is a landmark on the city's skyline. Open for dinner, it features steak, seafood, decadent desserts, and spectacular views.

265 Peachtree St. NE (between Baker and Harris sts.), Atlanta, GA 30303. ⓒ 800/233-1234 or 404/577-1234. Fax 404/588-4137. www.hyatt.com. 1,264 units. $265 double (weekday rate); Business Plan $285. Extra person $25. Children under age 18 stay free in parents' room. Packages and promotional rates often available. AE, DC, DISC, MC, V. Valet parking $19. MARTA: Peachtree Center. **Amenities:** 3 restaurants; coffee cafe; bar; large outdoor pool; full health club in Peachtree Center ($15 per day); concierge; business center; limited room service; laundry service; multilingual staff. *In room:* A/C, TV/VCR, dataport in Business Plan rooms, minibar, coffeemaker in Business Plan rooms, hair dryer, iron, safe.

Marriott Marquis ★★★ A dramatic downtown landmark, the Marriott Marquis is a first-class megahotel designed by Atlanta's John Portman. Fronted by a vast fountain that looks like a flying saucer, it has a 50-story atrium lobby that is said to be the largest in the southeast. It's connected by covered walkway to shops in the Peachtree Center mall. The rooms are attractively decorated. The spiffy bathrooms have hair dryers and upscale complimentary toilet articles. Forty-two rooms are wheelchair accessible.

265 Peachtree Center Ave. (between Baker and Harris sts.), Atlanta, GA 30303. ⓒ 800/228-9290 or 404/521-0000. Fax 404/586-6299. www.marriott.com. 1,675 units. $230–$260 double; Concierge level $235 double. Extra person $20. Children under age 12 free. Packages available. AE, DC, DISC, MC, V. Parking $19 (self- or valet). MARTA: Peachtree Center. **Amenities:** 2 restaurants; sports bar; coffee shop; large swimming pool; full fitness center; Jacuzzi; concierge; airport shuttle; conference and banquet facilities; shops; unisex hairstylist; 24-hr. room service; Delta Air Lines desk. *In room:* A/C, TV, high-speed Internet access, fridge, coffeemaker, hair dryer, safe.

Omni Hotel at CNN Center ★★ *Kids* Recent renovations at The Omni brought about a complete personality change, taking out the blah sterile convention atmosphere and injecting class and sophistication. The Omni is all about location—especially if you're attending a sporting event. It adjoins the Georgia World Congress Center, Philips Arena, the Georgia Dome, and CNN Center, and is across from Centennial Olympic Park. Many of the rooms have balconies that overlook the bustle of the CNN Center atrium; the rest have views of Centennial Olympic Park or the downtown skyline. Kids receive a welcome gift, and the location of the Omni inside the CNN Center makes it easy to go down for a little shopping or to grab a bite to eat or just let the kids burn off steam. While these digs are comparable to the Embassy Suites just across the street, service here is just a tad better.

Most of the suites have huge living/dining areas with wet bars. If you're in Atlanta for a very special occasion and don't have a problem dropping $2,000 a night, ask for The Omni Suite. This three bedroom, four-bathroom, two-level suite extraordinaire is where media mogul Ted Turner stays when he is in town. A room search for Turner relics came up empty, however. Not even a forgotten workout video was to be found. A major $100 million expansion is currently underway that will add 593 rooms in a 24-story tower, to be completed by November 2003. Eleven rooms have been modified for visitors with disabilities. Signs around the hotel are written in Braille, and each guest room has a strobe fire alarm for deaf guests.

100 CNN Center (at Marietta St. and International Blvd.), Atlanta, GA 30335. ⓒ 800/THE-OMNI or 404/659-0000. Fax 404/659-1621. www.omnihotels.com. 470 units. $139–$314 double, depending on length of

stay; $775 1-bedroom suite; $2,000 3-bedroom suite. Children under age 18 stay free in parents' room. Weekend packages sometimes available; prices higher during special events. AE, DISC, MC, V. Valet parking $18. MARTA: Omni/Dome/GWCC. **Amenities:** Restaurant; privileges at nearby fitness center $10 a day; concierge; business center with secretarial services; conference and banquet facilities; salon; 24-hr. room service; laundry service. *In room:* A/C, TV, dataport, minibar, hair dryer.

Ritz-Carlton Atlanta ★★★ Without a doubt, this is Atlanta's finest downtown hotel. With Persian rugs strewn on marble floors, silk-tapestried and African mahogany-paneled walls hung with a collection of 18th- and 19th-century paintings, and valuable antiques throughout its public areas, it's hard to believe that the Ritz was built as late as 1984. The impeccable service also harks back to another, more gracious era; you'll be cosseted as never before. Elegant rooms, many with bay windows, are furnished with beautiful mahogany pieces (some have four-poster beds). Four rooms have been modified to be accessible to travelers with disabilities.

As at all Ritz-Carlton restaurants, dining at the Atlanta Grill downtown is a true culinary treat. Overlooking all the action along Peachtree Street, Atlanta Grill specializes in grilled game and seafood. Diners can count on the soothing sounds of live jazz in house every night. Offering Chef Peter Zampaglione's southern-inspired cuisine in a club-like, warm atmosphere, the Atlanta Grill is a popular choice for dining, even for folks who are not guests at the Ritz.

181 Peachtree St. NE (at Ellis St.; main entrance on Ellis), Atlanta, GA 30303. ℂ **800/241-3333** or 404/659-0400. Fax 404/688-0400. www.ritzcarlton.com. 444 units, including 22 suites. Fri–Sat $225–$325 double, based on availability; Sun–Thurs $310 double; Club $295 double; Club premium $475 double; $650 executive suite; Club suite $1,200, $1,500 Ritz-Carlton suite. AE, DC, DISC, MC, V. Parking $21 (valet only). MARTA: Peachtree Center. **Amenities:** Restaurant; fitness center; multilingual concierge staff; car-rental desk; limousine; business center; 24-hr. room service; babysitting can be arranged; laundry service. *In room:* A/C, TV/VCR, fax, dataport, minibar, coffeemaker, hair dryer.

Westin Peachtree Plaza ★★ You wouldn't expect that a 73-story, 1,000-room hotel could be described as cozy, but that adjective fits the Westin, which completed a $30 million renovation in 2000. The 300-square-foot rooms are both elegant and intimate, and floor-to-ceiling windows provide dramatic views of the city. The revolving Sun Dial Restaurant, on the 71st floor, offers sophisticated American fare and an impressive 360-degree view of the city skyline. The revolving bar, on the 73rd floor, is a good spot for cocktails and light fare. The Cafe restaurant, located in the atrium lobby, serves buffet and a la carte breakfasts. The Tivoli Coffee Bar is open daily for coffee, drinks, tea, sandwiches, and pastries. There's also the International Bar and the adjoining Sidewalk Cafe. Twenty-eight rooms are accessible to travelers with disabilities.

210 Peachtree St. NW (at International Blvd.), Atlanta, GA 30303. ℂ **800/228-3000** or 404/659-1400. Fax 404/589-7424. www.westin.com. 1,068 units. $199–$239 double; $350–$1,450 suite. Extra person $20. Children under age 18 free in parents' room. Inquire about packages. AE, DC, DISC, MC, V. Valet parking $20; no self-parking at this time. MARTA: Peachtree Center. **Amenities:** 2 restaurants; cafe; 2 bars; beautiful large pool (under a retractable skylight for year-round indoor/outdoor use); newly equipped health club; concierge; comprehensive business center; shopping gallery that connects with Macy's; 24-hr. room service. *In room:* A/C, TV, hair dryer, iron, safe.

EXPENSIVE

Embassy Suites at Centennial Olympic Park ★★ *Kids* This lovely all-suite hotel opened in 1999 on the edge of Centennial Olympic Park, Atlanta's most visible legacy of the 1996 Summer Games. The 21-acre park is now a lively venue for festivals, art markets, and concerts. The location is a good bet for tourists, conventioneers, and sports fans, since it's just across the street from the

> **Tips   Rooms and a View**
>
> For a bird's-eye view of the city, take a trip up to the top of the **Westin Peachtree Plaza**. You'll ride up 72 stories on a glass elevator to a viewing area with telescopes where you can get a 360-degree look at Atlanta and the surrounding area. On a clear day, you can see the foothills of the Appalachian Mountains. The attraction is open 10am to 11pm daily and costs $4 for adults, $2 for seniors and children. Call (C) **404/659-1400** for details.

Georgia World Congress Center, and within walking distance of MARTA, the CNN Center, the Philips Arena, and the Georgia Dome. Kids will love this location as it's just yards away from the fountains at Centennial Park, designed to allow visitors to run through them and get soaked from head to foot. What kid (or adult) wouldn't love that?

Each two-room standard suite is luxuriously decorated with contemporary furniture and includes a pullout sofa in the living room. Bathrooms, with Jacuzzi tubs and separate showers, are spacious and luxurious. Ask for a parkside room, which has a nice view of the park and the city skyline; there's no extra charge. The luxury suites, which have large private balconies overlooking the park, are huge and plush, perfect for business receptions or special occasions. Complimentary cooked-to-order breakfasts are served and prepared by Ruth's Chris Steak House, an on-premises restaurant, and there's a reception each evening that features complimentary drinks. Seventeen suites are accessible to travelers with disabilities.

267 Marietta St., Atlanta, GA 30313. (C) **404/223-2300.** Fax 404/223-0925. www.downtownembassysuites. citysearch.com. 321 suites. Mon–Thurs $119–$235 double; Fri–Sun starting at $109 double; $525–$1,500 luxury suite. Children under age 18 stay free in parents' room. Rates include full breakfast. Packages and weekend rates available; rates higher during special events. AE, DC, DISC, MC, V. Valet parking $18. MARTA: Omni/Dome/GWCC. **Amenities:** Restaurant; large outdoor pool with sundeck; health club with sauna and Jacuzzi; concierge; airport shuttle; business center and conference rooms; limited room service; dry cleaning and laundry services. *In room:* A/C, TV w/pay movies, microwave, fridge, coffeemaker, hair dryer, Internet access.

Wyndham Atlanta Downtown ✦   It took $49 million to renovate the old American Hotel, but the result is excellent—a small, upscale property with warmth and charm in a central downtown location. Reopened in June 1999, it's close to Peachtree Center and a short walk from Centennial Olympic Park, the Philips Arena, the CNN Center, and the Georgia World Congress Center. The rooms, which are traditionally decorated, are not huge, but they're nicely appointed. Some have views of Centennial Olympic Park, and 12 are accessible to travelers with disabilities.

Marble floors and countertops in the bathrooms lend a handsome touch. The oversize tubs are nice, though they aren't whirlpool. Wall-to-wall mirrors and soft lighting compliment one another. Guests will enjoy the Golden Door Spa toiletries endorsed by Wyndham at this location.

160 Spring St. (at International Blvd.), Atlanta, GA 30303. (C) **800/WYNDHAM [996-3426]** or 404/688-8600. www.wyndham.com. 312 units. $129–$299 double; $229–$379 suite; penthouse suites also available. Children under age 18 stay free in parents' rooms. Weekend rates often available; higher rates apply to special events. AE, DC, DISC, MC, V. Valet parking $17. MARTA: Peachtree Center. **Amenities:** Restaurant with adjoining bar; large outdoor heated pool; well-equipped health club; concierge; business center; conference

rooms; limited room service; massage; babysitting; laundry and dry cleaning service. *In room:* A/C, TV, dataport, coffeemaker, hair dryer, iron.

MODERATE

Amerisuites Downtown *Value* This property became part of the Amerisuites chain in the summer of 2000 and immediately underwent a $5 million renovation to gear it toward business travelers. Just a few blocks from downtown, it offers a lot for its price range. Rooms are large and nicely furnished and are a magnet for those in town on business, especially for extended stays. Five rooms have been modified to be accessible to travelers with disabilities. Complimentary deluxe continental breakfast buffet is served each morning.

330 Peachtree St. NE (between Baker St. and Ralph McGill Blvd.), Atlanta, GA 30308. © **800/362-5600** or 404/577-1980. Fax 404/688-3706. www.amerisuites.com. 94 suites. $109 double. Children age 16 and under stay free in parents' room. Rates include deluxe continental breakfast. Packages occasionally available. AE, DC, DISC, MC, V. Self-parking $10. MARTA: Peachtree Center or Civic Center. **Amenities:** Exercise room; business center; weekday dry cleaning and laundry service. *In room:* A/C, TV w/pay movies, dataport, a minikitchen including refrigerator, microwave, wet bar, and coffeemaker; hair dryer, iron.

Days Inn Atlanta Downtown This central Days Inn, which underwent an upgrade in 2001, allows visitors to stay in the heart of the business district at a moderate cost. Rooms on floors 3 to 10 have balconies, with views toward Midtown. Although you don't get all the luxury-hotel frills here, the accommodations are just fine. Guest rooms are a large and comfortable. Cherry furniture and a gold, green, and burgundy color scheme are classy. Bathrooms are separate from the vanity area, a plus for those traveling in packs and trying to get ready for dinner or an event all at the same time. Bathrooms are standard with shower/tub combination. Rooms all boast new slim-design (but not flat screen) televisions. Six rooms are wheelchair accessible. A hotel lounge open 5pm to midnight allows guests to view televised sporting events. Conference rooms are available. The new athletic center and large outdoor pool are a plus. This is a great choice for those in town to enjoy events at the Georgia Dome, Phillips Arena, Turner Field, and Centennial Olympic Park. Though the hotel's location in the heart of the business district makes it a great choice for folks in town on official business, rooms and facilities are also quite suitable for families.

300 Spring St. (at Baker St.), Atlanta, GA 30308. © **800/DAYS-INN** or 404/523-1144. Fax 404/577-8495. www.daysinn.com. 263 units. $69–$209 double (high end reflects special events). Extra person $10. Children under age 18 stay free in parents' room. Special weekend rates. AE, DC, DISC, MC, V. Self-parking $10. MARTA: Peachtree Center. **Amenities:** Restaurant; large outdoor pool; athletic center; conference rooms; 24-hr. room service; guest laundry. *In room:* A/C, TV, fridge, coffeemaker, microwave, hair dryer, safe.

Holiday Inn Atlanta Downtown ★★ This 11-story property offers appealing rooms that were renovated in the spring of 1999. This is one of the better set-ups for business accommodations at a rate that won't break you or your expense account. The hotel is adjacent to the Gift, Apparel, and Merchandise Marts, and Centennial Olympic Park, and it's 2 blocks from the CNN Center, Philips Arena, and the Georgia World Congress Center. Sixteen rooms are accessible to travelers with disabilities, eight of them with roll-in shower stalls.

101 International Blvd. (at Williams St.), Atlanta, GA 30303. © **800/535-0707** or 404/524-5555. Fax 404/221-0702. www.holiday-inn.com/atldowntown. 260 units. $79–$179 double. Rates range to $250 a night during major conventions. Extra person $10. Children age 18 and under stay free in parents' room. AE, DISC, MC, V. Self-parking $15, higher during special events. MARTA: Peachtree Center. **Amenities:** Restaurant; sports bar; nice-size outdoor pool/sundeck; a health club; Jacuzzi; concierge; a courtesy car (reserve in advance); conference rooms; a small business center with secretarial services; limited room service (during restaurant hours); dry cleaning and laundry service. *In room:* A/C, TV, coffeemaker, hair dryer, iron.

Howard Johnson Plaza Suites at Underground Atlanta ★ *Finds*   If huge, convention-oriented hotels turn you off, this may be just the place for you. Formerly the Suite Hotel Underground Atlanta, it's elegant and understated, and attracts a clientele that prefers the intimacy of a European-style hotel. Each suite has a small living room, a separate bedroom, and a marble bathroom, some with Jacuzzis. The entire suite is elegantly appointed with solid cherry furniture and modern prints. Many of the rooms have views of the downtown skyline. Seven rooms are accessible to travelers with disabilities.

The 16-story hotel was originally a 1918 office building to which 10 stories were added in 1990. It's on the top level of Underground Atlanta and within walking distance of the downtown business area and close to the main MARTA station, where all the lines converge, making it easy to travel to Midtown, Buckhead, and the airport.

54 Peachtree St. SW, Atlanta, GA 30303. © **404/223-5555.** Fax 404/223-0467. www.suitehotel.com. 156 units. $129 double; $189 king with Jacuzzi. Children under age 16 stay free in parents' suite. Packages available. AE, DC, DISC, MC, V. Valet parking $15; self-parking $9. MARTA: Five Points. **Amenities:** Restaurant; bar; access to nearby health club for $10; limited business center; limited room service; laundry service. *In room:* A/C, TV, fridge, microwave, coffeemaker, hair dryer, iron.

Marriott Residence Inn Atlanta-Downtown ★★ *Value*   This is the best deal downtown. It's close to all the action, the accommodations are nicely appointed studios or suites, and it's incredibly inexpensive—especially for an extended stay. The rooms, most of which are more like small apartments, all have queen-size beds and full kitchens outfitted with all the necessary equipment, with the exception of some of the smaller studios, which have kitchenettes. In addition to the complimentary breakfast, the hotel provides a light supper Monday, Tuesday, and Thursday, holds a cookout on Wednesday, and will even do your grocery shopping. And if the exercise room is too small, guests have complimentary access to the fitness center at the posh Marriott Marquis just a few blocks away. For a nice view of downtown, ask for one of the suites on the higher floors.

The building itself was constructed in 1928 and is listed on the National Register of Historic Places. Because it's an older building, the rooms are extremely quiet, and the high ceilings lend a feeling of spaciousness. As you pass through the marble lobby, be sure to look up at the ceiling. Painted by European artists when the building was new, the decoration has been restored to its original splendor.

134 Peachtree St. NW (1 block north of Woodruff Park), Atlanta, GA 30303. © **800/331-3131** or 404/522-0950. Fax 404/577-3235. www.marriott.com. Studios and 1-bedroom units start at $160 weekdays and $95 on weekends; 2-bedrooms from $240. Children under age 18 stay free in parents' room. Rates include deluxe continental breakfast. Rates are higher during special events. AE, DC, DISC, MC, V. Valet parking $19; self-parking $15. MARTA: Peachtree Center. **Amenities:** Small exercise room; coin-operated washers and dryers; same-day dry cleaning service; grocery shopping service. *In room:* A/C, TV, dataport, fully equipped kitchens in most rooms, kitchenettes in other rooms, hair dryer.

INEXPENSIVE

Atlanta Downtown TraveLodge *Kids* *Value*   Operated by the Clark family since 1964, this small but nicely kept TraveLodge offers an inexpensive alternative in the heart of downtown. All rooms are off an interior corridor and sport typical chain TraveLodge decor—nice but nothing out of the ordinary. The same goes for the bathrooms here. The Sleepybear Den Room, a guest room designed to accommodate families, includes a refrigerator and microwave, a VCR, and kid-themed movies. The new Business Class rooms offer well-lit work areas and

Kids Family-Friendly Hotels

Atlanta Downtown TraveLodge (p. 78)   What kid could resist the Sleepybear Den Room, a guest room designed to accommodate families, including a refrigerator and microwave, a VCR, and kid-themed movies?

Embassy Suites at Centennial Olympic Park (p. 75)   Kids will love this location, just yards away from Centennial Park, which is home to festivals, art markets, and concerts, plus fountains designed to allow visitors to run through them.

Four Seasons Hotel (p. 80)   Kids enjoy a special program that includes cookies and milk on check-in, a toiletries box with baby shampoo and a rubber duck, chocolates at nightly turndown, board games, and children's movie videos and video games.

Marriott Evergreen Conference Resort (p. 99)   Kids will love this "castle" nestled in a pine forest. The location is excellent for families who want to take advantage of all of Stone Mountain Park's activities.

Marriott Residence Inn Buckhead (p. 94)   This place not only has a swimming pool, but also boasts fully equipped kitchens—a potential money-saver when you're traveling with your family. Rates here include breakfast, and there are barbecue grills and picnic tables on the premises. It's like having your own Atlanta apartment, with parking at your door. The property also contains basketball, volleyball, and paddle-tennis courts, and guests can rent movies at the front desk.

Omni Hotel at CNN Center (p. 74)   Kids receive a welcome gift here, and the Omni's fabulous central location puts the kid-friendly attractions of the city at your fingertips.

Stone Mountain Park Inn (p. 99)   Located in Stone Mountain Park, this lovely inn is the perfect spot for families who want to take full advantage of the park's recreational opportunities. The inn itself has an outdoor pool, and in the park you can fish, boat, play miniature golf, bicycle, hike along wildlife trails, picnic, and more.

Summerfield Suites by Wyndham (p. 97)   All-suite hotels are almost always the most economical way to travel with a family, and this hotel is in an excellent location. An expanded continental breakfast is included in the rate, and there's also a fully equipped kitchen in each of the suites. There's a lovely pool on the premises, a barbecue grill on the patio, and VCRs in each room. A short walk down the street, there's a city park with a playground.

convenient access to e-mail while making phone calls. Business services include voice mail, modem hookups, fax, and copying. Three rooms are accessible to travelers with disabilities.

311 Courtland St. NE (between Baker St. and Ralph McGill Blvd.), Atlanta, GA 30303. ℂ **800/578-7878** or 404/659-4545. Fax 404/659-5934. www.travelodge.com. 71 units. $59–$109 double. Extra person $10. Children under 18 stay free in parents' room. Rates include continental breakfast. AE, DC, DISC, MC, V. Free parking. MARTA: Peachtree Center. **Amenities:** Outdoor pool; access to nearby Peachtree Center Athletic Club for

$14 a day or $33 for 3 days; concierge; secretarial services; babysitting; dry cleaning and laundry. *In room:* A/C, TV w/pay movies, fax, dataport, coffeemaker, hair dryer, safe; fridges available upon request.

E Hotel Atlanta   Formerly the Ramada Downtown Atlanta, this eight-story stucco building forms a courtyard around its swimming pool. Rooms here are nicely decorated with traditional cherrywood furniture. Because this is an older property, the rooms are a generous size, although the bathrooms are about what you'd expect for a chain. All but six rooms are accessible to travelers with disabilities; three have been modified to be especially comfortable for visitors with disabilities.

70 John Wesley Dobbs Ave. NE (at Courtland St.), Atlanta, GA 30303. © **800/2RAMADA** or 404/659-2660. Fax 404/524-5390. www.Ramada.com. 223 units. $89–$99 double. Extra person $10. Children under age 18 stay free in parents' room. AE, DC, DISC, MC, V. Free parking, subject to availability. MARTA: Peachtree Center. **Amenities:** Restaurant; use of nearby Phoenix Health Club; limited room service (during restaurant hours). *In room:* A/C, TV, dataports (some rooms); fridges, coffeemakers, and hair dryers are available on request.

2 Midtown

Travelers interested in the cultural highlights of Atlanta will appreciate a hotel in Midtown, home to the Woodruff Arts Center, the High Museum of Art, the Fox Theatre, and the Margaret Mitchell House. Joggers and other outdoor enthusiasts will like the proximity to Piedmont Park and the Atlanta Botanical Garden.

VERY EXPENSIVE

Four Seasons Hotel ★★★ *Kids*   This elegant hotel is the one to choose if you're looking for luxurious surroundings in the heart of Atlanta's cultural area. Built in 1991 as the Grand Hotel Atlanta, it was acquired in 1998 by Four Seasons, who immediately gave it a $65 million renovation. Service here is impeccable.

Accommodations are lavish and sophisticated, with large windows, upholstered lounge chairs and sofas, and handsome Beidermeier-style furnishings. The gorgeous marble bathrooms have huge tubs perfect for soaking and some have separate showers. Thirteen of the rooms have been modified to accommodate travelers with disabilities. Pets under 15 pounds are welcome and receive treats.

The hotel offers several services for children, including a gift upon arrival. Infant supplies are available. For older children, there is a variety of board and video games, movies, and books. Trips can be arranged to nearby attractions, such as the Center for Puppetry Arts, Children's Garden at the Atlanta Botanical Garden, World of Coca-Cola, and Fernbank Natural History Museum, which has an IMAX theater.

The Park 75 restaurant, open all day, offers New American cuisine, dependent on the freshest goods from the local markets, served in a modern atmosphere with Beidermeier furnishings and original oil paintings. Guests at the restaurant's Chef's Table dine in the heart of the kitchen, getting a close look at the chefs at work. The Park 75 Terrace offers a garden-like setting for lunch, afternoon tea, and cocktails, overlooking a three-story atrium. The Park 75 Lounge offers cocktails, light fare, and a wide selection of single-malt scotches; there's a pianist each night. Complimentary coffee is served from 6 to 8am each morning in the lobby.

75 Fourteenth St. (between Peachtree and West Peachtree sts.), Atlanta, GA 30309. © **800/332-3442** or 404/881-9898. Fax 404/873-4692. www.fourseasons.com. 244 units. $245 twin European; $500 suite; $2,500 presidential suite. Children under age 18 stay free in parents' room. Excellent weekend cultural packages available. AE, DC, DISC, MC, V. Valet parking $24. MARTA: Arts Center, Tenth Street. Pets under 15 lbs.

accepted. **Amenities:** Restaurant; Olympic-size indoor pool; health club and spa; Jacuzzi; sauna; concierge; business center with secretarial and translation service; laptop computer rental; 24-hr. room service; 24-hr. dry cleaning, laundry, and pressing. *In room:* A/C, TV, dataport, minibar, hair dryer, safe.

EXPENSIVE

The Georgian Terrace ⭐⭐ *Finds*   Listed on the National Register of Historic Places, the Georgian Terrace has seen its share of dignitaries and celebrities since it opened in 1911 as a luxury hotel. Clark Gable and Vivien Leigh stayed here in 1939 and attended the premiere party of *Gone With the Wind.* The hotel closed in 1981 after years of neglect, reopened in 1991 as an upscale apartment building, and has been in the process of being converted back to a hotel since 1997. The marble floors, soaring columns, and dramatic French windows hark back to the opulence and grandeur of a bygone era, but the rooms themselves are thoroughly modern.

The apartments have been turned into studios and one-, two-, and three-bedroom suites. Staying here is like having your own private apartment on Peachtree Street, convenient to all that Midtown has to offer. The Fox Theatre is right across the street. If you'd like a view of Stone Mountain, ask for a suite on the east side of the hotel. Breakfast is served in the original hotel lobby, and cocktails are served in the parlor.

Note: Although the suites have full-size kitchens, they lack pots and pans and have only enough dinnerware for two people. Call the front desk for additional accoutrements. If you're staying 30 days or longer, a more complete package of kitchen equipment is available. Also, most guests are inevitably puzzled about how to turn the shower on. If you can't figure it out, call the front desk.

659 Peachtree St. (just north of Ponce de Leon Ave.), Atlanta, GA 30308. ℂ 800/651-2316 or 404/897-1991. Fax 404/724-0642. www.thegeorgianterrace.com. 318 units. $149 double (studio); $149–$199 1-bedroom suite; $249–$299 2-bedroom suite; $349–$399 3-bedroom suite. Weekend packages available; reduced rates for stays of more than 30 days. AE, DC, DISC, MC, V. Valet parking $22; self-parking $14. MARTA: North Avenue. **Amenities:** 2 restaurants; heated junior Olympic rooftop swimming pool; fully equipped fitness center; children's amenities; concierge; airport shuttle; limousine service (when available) within a 3-mile radius; business center; conference and banquet rooms; limited room service; laundry service. *In room:* A/C, TV, dataport, kitchen, hair dryer, washer, dryer.

Marriott Suites ⭐   This all-suite hotel is a perfect choice for culture buffs, and its proximity to MARTA makes it easy to get to the rest of the city's attractions, too. Each spacious suite, attractively decorated in a warm, homey style, offers a king-size bed, and a full living room with a convertible sofa. Bedrooms are set off from living room areas by lace-curtained French doors. Each marble bathroom has a separate shower. Twelve rooms are accessible to travelers with disabilities.

35 Fourteenth St. NE (between Peachtree and W. Peachtree sts.), Atlanta, GA 30309. ℂ 800/228-9290 or 404/876-8888. Fax 404/876-7727. www.marriott.com. 254 suites. $109–$240 double. No extra-person charge. Discounted rates and packages may be available through the toll-free number. AE, DC, DISC, MC, V. Valet parking $12; self-parking $10. MARTA: Arts Center. **Amenities:** Bar; connecting indoor and outdoor

---

Tips **Hot Enough For You?**

Maybe you need to sip a *mojito* at Midtown's Four Seasons Hotel. The Park 75 Lounge serves up an icy concoction of rum, sugar, mint, lime, and tonic that's the perfect antidote to a steamy summer evening. OK, it costs about 10 bucks, a price that may make you sweat a bit at first, but you'll cool down by the time you finish the last of this classy beverage.

Midtown Accommodations

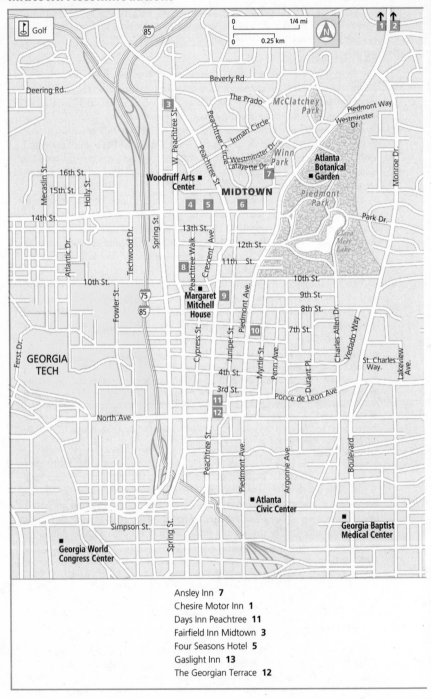

Golf

McClatchey Park

Winn Park

Piedmont Park

Clara Meer Lake

Woodruff Arts Center

MIDTOWN

Atlanta Botanical Garden

Margaret Mitchell House

GEORGIA TECH

Atlanta Civic Center

Georgia Baptist Medical Center

Georgia World Congress Center

Ansley Inn **7**
Chesire Motor Inn **1**
Days Inn Peachtree **11**
Fairfield Inn Midtown **3**
Four Seasons Hotel **5**
Gaslight Inn **13**
The Georgian Terrace **12**

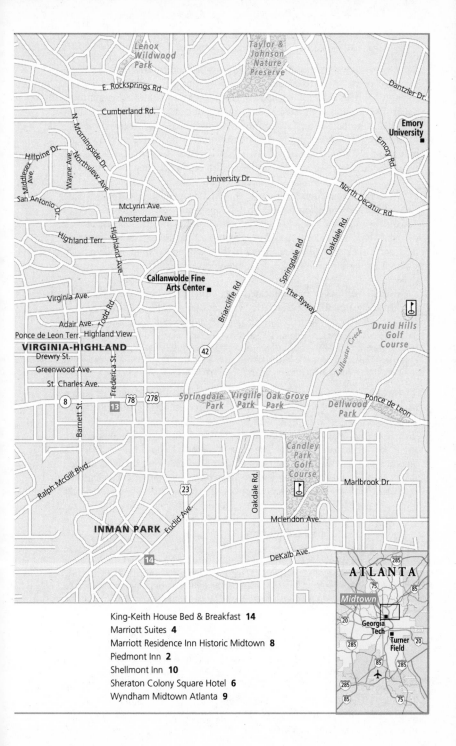

King-Keith House Bed & Breakfast **14**
Marriott Suites **4**
Marriott Residence Inn Historic Midtown **8**
Piedmont Inn **2**
Shellmont Inn **10**
Sheraton Colony Square Hotel **6**
Wyndham Midtown Atlanta **9**

swimming pools; health club; Jacuzzi; concierge; limited room service; laundry service and coin-operated laundry. *In room:* A/C, 2 TVs, dataport, fridge, coffeemaker, hair dryer, iron.

Shellmont Inn ⭐   This charming two-story Victorian mansion looks like a fairy-tale house, its exterior embellished with ribbons, bows, garlands, and shells. It has both a front porch and a small veranda out back, with wicker rocking chairs overlooking a flower garden and fishpond. The building, which dates to 1891, is on the National Register of Historic Places, and is a city landmark. Innkeepers Ed and Debbie McCord have done a superb job of restoration, meticulously researching original paint colors, stencil designs, woodwork, and period furnishings, and reproducing them with 100% accuracy.

There's a living room downstairs, and up the stairway (its landing graced by a five-paneled stained-glass window the McCords believe is an authentic Tiffany) are the four guest rooms. They have elegant queen-size beds (perhaps you'll have an Eastlake or a bed with a 6-foot oak headboard embellished with carved ribbons and bows), leaded-glass or bay windows, and Oriental rugs on pine floors. The carriage house offers a master bedroom with full modern bathroom. Most rooms have whirlpools, fully equipped kitchens, living rooms, and dressing area.

Breakfast consists of fresh-squeezed juice, fresh and dried fruits, an entrée (perhaps Belgian waffles or frittatas), cereal, and tea or coffee.

821 Piedmont Ave. NE (at Sixth St.), Atlanta, GA 30308. © **404/872-9290.** Fax 404/872-5379. www. shellmont.com. 4 units, plus carriage house. $150–$180 double in main house; $200–$275 double in carriage house. Extra person $25. Rates include full breakfast. AE, DC, DISC, MC, V. Free parking. MARTA: Midtown. Children age 12 and under allowed in the carriage house only. **Amenities:** The McCords live on the premises and offer all the services of a hotel concierge. *In room:* A/C, TV/VCR, dataport.

Sheraton Colony Square Hotel ⭐   This theatrically themed property is popular with entertainers playing at the Woodruff Arts Center just across the street. It was built in 1974, as an opulent anchor of the Colony Square complex (which includes a mini-mall of 20 shops and restaurants, including a copy shop, photo shop, post office, bank, drugstore, florist, and more). The hotel has hosted Frank Sinatra and Linda Ronstadt, not to mention presidents Reagan, Ford, Carter, Bush, and Clinton. For outdoor enthusiasts or those who like a daily run or walk outdoors, this hotel is the perfect choice since Piedmont Park is just a few blocks away. The hotel borders the lovely Ansley Park neighborhood. Also nearby are the High Museum of Art and the Atlanta Botanical Garden.

Rooms are quite plush and gorgeous.

188 Fourteenth St. NE (at Peachtree St.), Atlanta, GA 30361. © **800/325-3535** or 404/892-6000. Fax 404/872-9192. 467 units. $169 double; Club Level concierge floor $194 king; $495 king suite; Club Level concierge floor $194 double. Extra person $25. Children age 17 and under stay free in parents' room. AE, DC, DISC, MC, V. Valet parking $18; self-parking $16. MARTA: Arts Center. **Amenities:** Restaurant; nice-size outdoor pool; exercise room; concierge; airport shuttle; business services; limited room service. *In room:* A/C, TV, coffeemakers, hair dryer, iron.

Wyndham Midtown Atlanta ⭐   An 11-story redbrick building, the Wyndham is close to many Midtown cultural attractions, including the Margaret Mitchell House and Museum. It's also convenient to Georgia Tech, making it a favorite among visitors whose children are students there or who are attending Tech sporting events. It offers nicely appointed rooms that were spruced up in 2000. Each has a comfy armchair for enjoying a relaxing read. Suites feature separate sitting areas with sofas, extra TVs and phones, and refrigerators. Eight rooms are accessible to travelers with disabilities.

125 Tenth St. NE (just east of Peachtree St.), Atlanta, GA 30309. ℂ 800/WYNDHAM [996-3426] or 404/
873-4800. Fax 404/870-1530. 191 units. $109–$169 executive king; $149–$199 double; $178–$209 junior
suite. Extra person $10. Children stay free in parents' room. AE, DC, DISC, MC, V. Valet parking $14; self-
parking $12. MARTA: Midtown. **Amenities:** Restaurant; large heated indoor pool; 5,000-sq.-ft. fitness center
offering Nautilus equipment; Jacuzzi; courtesy van within a 3-mile radius (which includes Buckhead and
downtown); comprehensive business services; limited room service. *In room:* A/C, TV, dataport, coffeemaker,
hair dryer, iron.

MODERATE

Ansley Inn ✶   Occupying a 1907 yellow brick Tudor mansion, this former
estate of department-store magnate George Muse is located in Ansley Park, one
of the city's most beautiful residential areas. The rooms in the main house are
nicely decorated with antique pieces and mahogany four-poster beds. Several
rooms have oak floors, some adorned with Oriental rugs, and a few have lofty
cathedral ceilings and working fireplaces. One room is wheelchair-accessible.
The Ansley Room, on the third floor, offers a unique canopy bed (though rather
narrow) and an interestingly angled ceiling.

The rooms in what is called the corporate wing (actually just an addition out
back) are not nearly as charming. While this wing still has the same basic con-
veniences, the quarters resemble motel rooms. Choose one of these only if you
value privacy (each has a separate entrance).

Breakfast is served in a dining room furnished with a long English Chippen-
dale–style table and Empire sideboards. Guests enjoy hors d'oeuvres in the furnished living room, which boasts an 8-foot ceramic tile fireplace.

253 Fifteenth St. NE (at Lafayette Dr., between Piedmont Ave. and Peachtree St.), Atlanta, GA 30309. ℂ 800/
446-5416 or 404/872-9000. Fax 404/892-2318. www.ansleyinn.com. 22 units. $99–$149 double in corporate
wing; $139–$249 for rooms in the main house. Rates include full breakfast. AE, MC, V. Free parking. MARTA:
Arts Center. **Amenities:** Privileges are available at a nearby health club at no charge; concierge; limited room
service from local restaurants. *In room:* A/C, TV (some with VCRs), dataport, coffeemaker, hair dryer, iron.

Days Inn Peachtree ✶✶ *(Value)*   You'll realize that this Days Inn is not your
average chain motel branch from the moment you enter its charming lobby, outfitted with Persian rugs on Saltillo-tile floors and a brass chandelier suspended
from a lofty mahogany ceiling. Built as a fancy boardinghouse in 1925, it's right
across from the Fox Theatre, so it's a good choice if you're attending a performance there. All rooms, which are due for renovation in 2001, are nicely outfitted with traditional cherry wood furnishings; many have comfortable sofas or
upholstered recliners.

The five suites feature small refrigerators, pull-out sofas, two bathrooms, and
two televisions. Ask for a room on the top floor if you can; they're larger and
quieter. Pets are permitted, with advance notice and a $25 or $50 fee, depending on the size of the animal. Coffee is served in the lobby throughout the day.
Bridgetown Grill, a good Caribbean restaurant (p. 116), is next door.

683 Peachtree St. (between Third St. and Ponce de Leon Ave.), Atlanta, GA 30308. ℂ 800/329-7466 or 404/
874-9200. Fax 404/873-4245. www.daysinn.com. 139 units. $109 double; $139 suite. Extra person $10. Chil-
dren under age 18 stay free in parents' room. Rates include continental breakfast. Rates may be higher during conventions and special events. Weekend rates and packages available via the toll-free number; Super
Saver rate of $59 a night may be available if you reserve at least 30 days in advance. AE, DC, DISC, MC, V.
Self-parking $7. MARTA: North Avenue. Pets accepted with $25 or $50 fee and advance notice. **Amenities:**
Business center; conference room; coin-operated laundry. *In room:* A/C, TV, coffeemaker, hair dryer.

Marriott Residence Inn Historic Midtown ✶   Accommodations, which
underwent renovations in 1998, are studios or spacious suites with handsome oak
or mahogany furnishings—mostly antique reproductions, such as Chippendale-
style beds. Most rooms have balconies with French doors. There's not a whole lot

that's interesting to walk to, but you're not far from a MARTA station. Ten rooms are accessible to travelers with disabilities. Pets are allowed, with a $100 non-refundable fee.

The inn provides hot tea and coffee all day in the lobby, which is a nice touch. However, the complimentary dinners offered Monday through Thursday from 5:30 until 7:30pm sets this inn apart from others in the area. If the free food doesn't tempt your taste buds, you can opt for the complimentary grocery shopping service available Monday through Friday.

1041 W. Peachtree St. (at Eleventh St.), Atlanta, GA 30309. © 800/331-3131 or 404/872-8885. Fax 404/724-9218. www.marriott.com. 78 units. $124 studio; $134 1-bedroom suite; $159 2-bedroom suite. Rates include breakfast buffet. Rates higher during special events and reduced on weekends and for stays of several nights. AE, DC, DISC, MC, V. Free parking. MARTA: Midtown. Pets accepted for $100 fee. **Amenities:** Cocktail lounge; new exercise room; complimentary membership at the fitness center of the nearby Marriott Suites hotel; rooftop Jacuzzi; limited room service from local restaurants through "Take Out Taxi"; laundry service; coin-operated washers/dryers. In room: A/C, 2 TVs, fully-equipped kitchen, hair dryer.

INEXPENSIVE

Cheshire Motor Inn (Value)   This is the best kind of budget hotel, a small property run for decades by caring private owners who offer homelike hospitality and many personal touches. On attractively landscaped grounds, the Cheshire offers rooms that are nothing fancy, but are spacious and nicely kept. Many of the rooms have minibars, and half have pullout sofas, making this an especially good choice for families on a budget. Bathrooms here are clean but basic. This is one of the few centrally located hotels that allows pets. Another big plus is that a famous Atlanta restaurant, the Colonnade, is on the premises, serving authentic Southern food (p. 110). Cheshire Bridge Road is an odd mix of sleazy bars and second-hand furniture and antiques shops. Parts of the street are pretty weird, but the restaurant and motel are quite respectable.

1865 Cheshire Bridge Rd. NE (near the intersection of Piedmont Rd.), Atlanta, GA 30324. © 800/827-9628 or 404/872-9628. Fax 404/872-3035. 58 units. $73 double. Extra person $5. Children under age 12 stay free in parents' room. Rates may be higher during special events. AE, DC, DISC, MC, V. Free parking. MARTA: Bus No. 27 from Lindbergh Station, which is about a mile away. Pets accepted. In room: A/C, TV, minibars in most rooms.

Fairfield Inn Midtown   This is not the most charming spot in Atlanta, but it's reasonably priced, and a MARTA station, from which you can zip to the rest of the city, is about 4 blocks away. The rooms are standard motel decor with queen-size beds and average bathrooms, but seven have small, well-equipped kitchens with sink, refrigerator, microwave, and coffeemaker. Eight rooms are accessible to travelers with disabilities, and 22 rooms were converted to suites in 2001.

1470 Spring St. NW (at Nineteenth St.), Atlanta, GA 30309. © 404/872-5821. Fax 404/874-3602. www.day hospitalitygroup.com. 182 units. $84–$89 double; $94–$104 suite. Children age 12 and under are free. Rates include extended continental breakfast. AE, DC, DISC, MC, V. Free parking. MARTA: Arts Center. **Amenities:** Outdoor pool with sundeck; exercise room; complimentary shuttle within a 2-mile radius from 7am–11pm; conference room; takeout delivered from local restaurants; coin-operated laundry; dry cleaning. In room: A/C, TV, dataport, kitchen with fridge and coffeemaker in suites, hair dryer, iron.

Piedmont Inn   Poised on the border between Midtown and Buckhead, this former Comfort Inn is not in the most attractive location, but the price is right. The large rooms are furnished with king-size beds, desks, and recliners; suites offer full living rooms with pullout sofas, microwave ovens, and refrigerators. Business Executive rooms, at no extra charge, offer irons and ironing boards, hair dryers, and coffeemakers. Doughnuts, juice, tea, and coffee are served in a pleasant room off the lobby each morning, and coffee is available all day.

2115 Piedmont Rd. NE (between Lindbergh Dr. and Cheshire Bridge Rd.), Atlanta, GA 30324. ✆ **800/228-5150** or 404/876-4444. Fax 404/873-1007. www.comfortinn.com. 186 units. $62 double; $85 and up suites (for 5–8 people). Children age 12 and under stay free in parents' room. Rates may be higher during special events. AE, DC, DISC, MC, V. Free parking. MARTA: Lindbergh (about ¾ mile north; bus no. 31 stops at the door). **Amenities:** Small outdoor pool and sundeck. *In room:* A/C; coffeemaker, hair dryer, iron in Business Executive Rooms.

3 Buckhead

There's something for everyone in Buckhead—shoppers, foodies, history buffs, business travelers, and those looking for lively nighttime entertainment. It's the optimum hotel location. A word about dining: There are so many fine restaurants and nightspots in Buckhead that it's foolish to limit yourself to hotel fare. There are two notable exceptions—the Swissôtel and the Ritz-Carlton Buckhead, which have outstanding restaurants. You'll find these restaurants listed in chapter 6.

VERY EXPENSIVE

Grand Hyatt Atlanta ★   The towering Grand Hyatt Atlanta offers a winning combination of 18th-century American architecture and Japanese attention to aesthetic detail. Formerly the Hotel Nikko, the Grand Hyatt has retained much of its Japanese flavor and sensibility. The lobby overlooks a 9,000-square-foot garden with traditional plantings, rock formations, and splashing waterfalls created by noted Kyoto landscape architects. A collection of museum-quality Japanese art, spanning 4 centuries, is displayed throughout the hotel.

Rooms are furnished in 18th-century mahogany reproductions, with crane-motif headboards, fresh orchids, and Japanese prints in black lacquer frames providing an Oriental atmosphere. Every luxury is provided at this plush establishment. You'll even find an umbrella in your closet.

3300 Peachtree Rd. (just east of Piedmont Rd.), Atlanta, GA 30305. ✆ **800/233-1234** or 404/365-8100. Fax 404/233-5686. www.atlanta.hyatt.com. 437 units. Mon–Thurs $190–$240 double; Fri–Sun $145–$240 double; Mon–Fri only Regency Club floor $225–$300 double; $485–$3,500 suite. No more than 4 to a room. Children under age 16 stay free in parents' room. AE, DC, DISC, MC, V. Valet parking $17; self-parking $11. MARTA: Buckhead. **Amenities:** 2 restaurants; lovely outdoor pool and sundeck; fully equipped fitness center (with TVs and VCRs on the exercise bikes, Life Trim equipment, stair machines, aerobics videos, steam, and sauna); toys/activities for children; 24-hr. concierge; airport shuttle; complimentary town car within a 2-mile radius of the hotel; comprehensive business center; 24-hr. room service; massage; babysitting. *In room:* A/C, TV, fax, dataport, hair dryer.

J. W. Marriott Hotel Lenox ★★   This luxurious Marriott is a lovely property with an excellent location. Connected to the Lenox Square mall, across the street from MARTA, and within walking distance of the posh Phipps Plaza mall and many good restaurants, it's popular with business travelers and die-hard shoppers alike. Rooms are charmingly furnished with Chippendale-style mahogany pieces, and picture windows offer great views of Buckhead or the downtown skyline. Lavish marble bathrooms are equipped with scales, terrycloth robes, and hair dryers. Deluxe rooms have separate showers and bathtubs. Nineteen rooms have been modified for travelers with disabilities.

3300 Lenox Rd. NE (a few blocks east of Peachtree Rd. at E. Paces Ferry Rd.), Atlanta, GA 30326. ✆ **800/228-9290** or 404/262-3344. Fax 404/262-8689. www.marriott.com/marriott/atljw. 371 units. Mon–Thurs $220–$318 double or king; Fri–Sun $129–$189 double or king; $325 suite. Weekend packages available. AE, DC, DISC, MC, V. Valet parking $17; self-parking $12. MARTA: Lenox. **Amenities:** Restaurant; large indoor pool in a setting patterned after a Roman bath; full health club with Jacuzzi, steam, and sauna; concierge; car-rental desk; airport shuttle; full business center; 24-hr. room service, laundry service; 1-hr. dry cleaning. *In room:* A/C, TV/VCR, high-speed Internet access, minibar, fridge, coffeemaker, hair dryer, iron.

Buckhead Accommodations

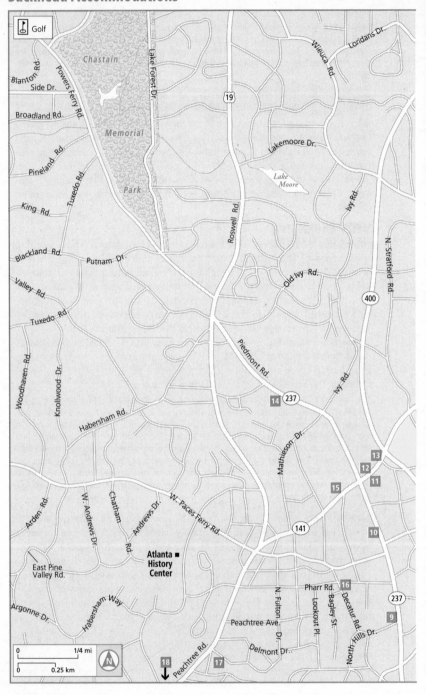

Golf

Chastain

Blanton Rd.
Side Dr.
Broadland Rd.
Powers Ferry Rd.
Lake Forest Dr.
Memorial
Pineland Rd.
Tuxedo Rd.
King Rd.
Park
Blackland Rd.
Putnam Dr.
Valley Rd.
Tuxedo Rd.
Woodhaven Rd.
Knollwood Dr.
Habersham Rd.
Arden Rd.
W. Andrews Dr.
Chatham Rd.
Andrews Dr.
W. Paces Ferry Rd.
East Pine
Valley Rd.
Atlanta
History
Center
Habersham Way
Argonne Dr.
Peachtree Ave.
N. Fulton Dr.
Delmont Dr.
Peachtree Rd.

19
Wieuca Rd.
Loridans Dr.
Lakemoore Dr.
Lake
Moore
Ivy Rd.
Roswell Rd.
N. Stratford Rd.
Old Ivy Rd.
400
Piedmont Rd.
Ivy Rd.
14 237
Mathieson Dr.
13
12
11
15
141
10
16
Pharr Rd.
Bagley St.
Decatur Rd.
Lookout Pl.
North Hills Dr.
237
9

0   1/4 mi
0   0.25 km

N

17
18

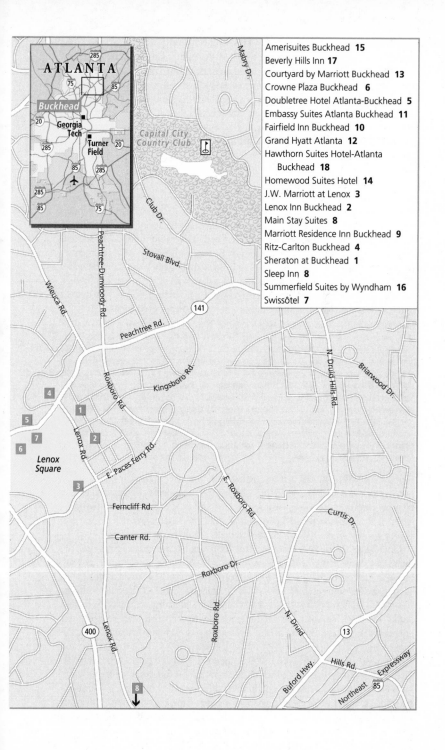

ATLANTA

Buckhead

Georgia Tech

Turner Field

Capital City Country Club

Amerisuites Buckhead **15**
Beverly Hills Inn **17**
Courtyard by Marriott Buckhead **13**
Crowne Plaza Buckhead **6**
Doubletree Hotel Atlanta-Buckhead **5**
Embassy Suites Atlanta Buckhead **11**
Fairfield Inn Buckhead **10**
Grand Hyatt Atlanta **12**
Hawthorn Suites Hotel-Atlanta
Buckhead **18**
Homewood Suites Hotel **14**
J.W. Marriott at Lenox **3**
Lenox Inn Buckhead **2**
Main Stay Suites **8**
Marriott Residence Inn Buckhead **9**
Ritz-Carlton Buckhead **4**
Sheraton at Buckhead **1**
Sleep Inn **8**
Summerfield Suites by Wyndham **16**
Swissôtel **7**

Lenox Square

Ritz-Carlton Buckhead ★★★   The Ritz-Carlton Buckhead is the Rolls Royce of Atlanta hotels. From the lobby to the public areas, which are graced with Regency and Georgian antiques and an outstanding collection of 18th- and 19th-century paintings and sculpture, every inch of this hotel bespeaks luxury. And the quality of service matches the sumptuous surroundings. The location is excellent—on the fringe of lovely neighborhoods, across the street from two upscale malls (Phipps Plaza and Lenox Square), and close to Buckhead's fine restaurants and nightspots. Many visiting celebrities, used to discreet elegance, choose to stay here. Even Atlantans looking for a special getaway check in on the weekends.

The rooms, all with large bay windows, were upgraded during a recent $5 million renovation, and are exquisitely decorated, with armoires, luxuriously upholstered sofas or armchairs, and marble-topped desks. Bathrooms contain the usual amenities you'd expect in a posh hotel. Twelve rooms are accessible to travelers with disabilities. Pets are accepted with a $250 nonrefundable deposit.

The Dining Room at the Ritz-Carlton Buckhead is one of Atlanta's premier restaurants (p. 121). The Lobby Lounge, with mahogany-paneled walls and a glowing fire, is the setting for afternoon English-style teas, which are hard to come by elsewhere in this city. A classical pianist plays here daily, a jazz quartet entertains in the evenings, and a martini menu is offered each night.

3434 Peachtree Rd. NE (at Lenox Rd.), Atlanta, GA 30326. © 800/241-3333 or 404/237-2700. Fax 404/239-0078. www.ritzcarlton.com. 553 units, including 29 suites. Mon–Thurs $255–$345 double; Fri–Sun $199–$319 double; Fri–Sun Club Level $345–$495 double (includes continental breakfast); $425–$1,500 presidential suite. Rollaway bed $30. Children under age 12 stay free in parents' room. Inquire about packages. AE, MC, V. Valet parking $22; self-parking $15. Pets are accepted with a $250 nonrefundable deposit. MARTA: Buckhead or Lenox. **Amenities:** 3 restaurants; wine bar; indoor pool; fitness center with aerobics and weight rooms, saunas, Jacuzzi, and sundeck; concierge; limousine on request; airport shuttle; shuttle when available to nearby malls; salon; 24-hr. room service; dry cleaning; laundry service; 1-hr. pressing on-premises. Babysitting and business services are available for a fee for Club Level guests. The Club Lounge, with 4 bay windows and comfortable living-room seating, also offers Club Level guests 5 complimentary meals or snacks, including continental breakfast, light lunch, afternoon tea, cocktails and hors d'oeuvres, and cordials and chocolates. *In room:* A/C, TV, high-speed Internet access, minibar, safe.

Swissôtel Atlanta ★★   If the Ritz-Carlton is the Rolls Royce of Atlanta hotels, the Swissôtel is the Ferrari. Its fresh Euromodern design makes it a favorite among trendsetters visiting the city, and its excellent location—in the heart of Buckhead between Lenox Square and the Atlanta Financial Center—makes it a top choice among business travelers and serious shoppers.

Opened in 1991 and renovated in 2000, the Zurich-based Swissôtel (it's owned by Swissair) added a new dimension to Atlanta's hotel scene. Its postmodern European architecture and interior spaces use Bauhaus elements, such as a pristine white-tile exterior with a graceful curve. Original works by renowned contemporary artists—Warhol, Rauschenberg, Chagall, Schnabel, Stella—grace public spaces. In fact, the hotel owns the second-largest private art collection in the Southeast. In the region, only the High Museum of Art has more works of art.

Rooms are sleekly furnished in Beidermeier-style maple pieces with black lacquer accents. Oversize desks include plug-ins for laptop computers and come with ergonomic chairs. Marble bathrooms offer cosmetic mirrors, TV speakers, hair dryers, and upscale, biodegradable toiletries. Especially nice are corner king rooms. Nineteen rooms are accessible to travelers with disabilities. Pets are allowed and are provided with a food bowl for a $75 nonrefundable fee.

The superb Palm restaurant is described on p. 126.

3391 Peachtree Rd. NE (between Lenox and Piedmont rds.), Atlanta, GA 30326. (C) **800/63-SWISS** or 404/ 365-0065. Fax 404/233-8786. www.swissotel.com. 365 units. $320–$335 double (depending on view), Club Level $390 double. Extra person $25. Children under age 17 stay free in parents' room. Weekend rates sometimes available. AE, DC, MC, V. Valet parking $17. MARTA: Buckhead. Pets allowed with $75 fee. **Amenities:** Restaurant; indoor lap pool; a small but nicely equipped health club offering exercise equipment, a sauna, a steam room, and a personal trainer; spa; concierge; complimentary shuttle to any destination in a 2-mile radius; airport shuttle; business center; unisex salon; 24-hr. room service; massage. *In room:* A/C, TV, minibar, coffeemaker, iron.

EXPENSIVE

Amerisuites Buckhead ✦   This is a rather plain-Jane all-suite hotel in a good location. It's not the best buy in the city, but you're paying for the convenience of being in the heart of Buckhead. The typical suite is not a true suite with a separate bedroom, but more like a studio or efficiency with the "bedroom" set off from the rest of the room by a low wall. There is a pullout couch for some extra sleeping space. The bathrooms are typical of most motels, but they do have hair dryers.

3242 Peachtree Rd. NE (at Piedmont Rd.), Atlanta, GA 30305. (C) **800/833-1516** or 404/869-6161. www. amerisuites.com. 172 suites. $119 and up double or king. Extra person $10. Children under age 18 stay free in parents' room. Rates include buffet breakfast weekdays, continental breakfast weekends. AE, DC, DISC, MC, V. Free parking. MARTA: Buckhead. **Amenities:** Small, heated outdoor pool; small exercise room on-site, and guests enjoy free privileges at a full-size health club next door; complimentary shuttle within a 3-mile radius; limited business center; on-site laundry and dry cleaning. *In room:* A/C, TV/VCR, dataport in most suites, minibar, fridge, coffeemaker, microwave.

Courtyard by Marriott Buckhead ✦✦ *Value*   Not your typical Courtyard property, this lovely hotel in a prime location provides a lot of bang for the buck. Can you say, "free valet parking"? It's a short walk to the Atlanta Financial Center, the Lenox Square and Phipps Plaza shopping malls, and a MARTA station, and it's close to everything that Buckhead has to offer.

Built in 1996, this full-service hotel is a favorite among business travelers, but it's a good choice for other travelers, too. The rooms are large and bright, and the suites—perfect for families in town for a few days—have a full-size pull-out couch. Some of the rooms are equipped with whirlpool tubs—in the room, not in the bathroom. Ask for one of the end rooms, which are a little larger than the others. Eight of the rooms are equipped for travelers with disabilities.

There are architects' drawings throughout, hence the name of the restaurant here—Atlanta Architects Grill and Bar. Be sure to seek out the rendering of the opulent Atlanta mansion owned by heavyweight world champion boxer Evander Holyfield, displayed in the restaurant.

3332 Peachtree Rd. NE (between Lenox and Piedmont rds.), Atlanta, GA 30326. (C) **800/321-2211** or 404/ 869-0818. Fax 404/869-0939. www.marriott.com. 181 units. Mon–Thurs $174 double, $224 suite; Fri–Sun $119 double, $179 suite. Children under age 18 stay free in parents' room. Rates may be higher during special events. AE, DC, DISC, MC, V. Free parking (self- and valet). MARTA: Buckhead. **Amenities:** Grill and bar; small heated indoor pool; small exercise room, and complimentary use of a nearby full-size health club; complimentary shuttle within a 1-mile radius; limited room service; laundry service; no-fee washers and dryers. *In room:* A/C, TV, fridge, microwave.

Crowne Plaza Buckhead ✦✦   Conveniently located near the Lenox Square mall and MARTA, this 11-story former Holiday Inn underwent a $14 million renovation in 2001. Though the prices did go up, so did the quality of this lovely hotel. All the rooms and public areas were completely transformed with the renovation. Guest rooms are new, with rich granite countertops, warm cherry wood, and beautiful luxury fabrics and duvets. All rooms are equipped with

The Vine That Ate the South

If you're visiting Georgia in the summer and traveling its interstate highways or country lanes, it's impossible to ignore the wild-looking vine growing along the roadside. That's kudzu, a frighteningly robust plant that upholsters billboards and fences, swallows up whole trees, and creeps eerily toward asphalt lanes, threatening everything in its path. It would surely blanket the pasturing cows if they stood still for a couple of days.

A native of the Far East, kudzu was introduced in the United States in the late 1800s, and became treasured as a porch vine whose prolific tendrils would shoot straight up at the rate of a foot a day, quickly covering a roof or trellis, providing welcome shade from the midday sun. It was touted as an excellent forage crop, and because it would grow almost anywhere, it was promoted as a means to control erosion.

By the turn of the century some horticulturists were having their doubts about kudzu, pointing out (to no avail) that the virtuous-seeming vine had some really bad manners. However, their warnings went unheeded, and the federal government continued to urge farmers to plant kudzu on worn-out farmland to keep it from washing away. It wasn't until the 1960s that the Soil Conservation Service stopped recommending its use. By then, the dense tangles had a lock on the landscape, not to mention barns and telephone poles.

Nobody's found a practical way to eradicate the stuff yet. Burning it won't work. Chemicals are impotent, unless each root and crown is hunted down relentlessly and sprayed and sprayed for years. And there are no natural predators, unless you count goats or other grazing animals—and there just aren't enough goats to go around. For now, the only thing for most of us to do is continue to hack away at the formidable vine and remember to close our windows at night.

those cloud-like pillow-topped mattresses that'll make you want to stay in bed all morning. Amenities include complimentary van transport within 3 miles of the hotel, an outdoor pool and sundeck, coin-operated laundry, and a business center.

Located in the heart of Buckhead, guests range from those in town for shopping at some of the finest stores in the country to those who appreciate the added benefits just for business travelers. This is a great choice for the frugal traveler who wants to be in the heart of the action, with access to the best nightlife in the city, without paying a fortune for a place to rest his or her head.

3777 Peachtree Rd. NE (between Lenox and Piedmont rds.), Atlanta, GA 30326. © **800/526-0247** or 404/264-1111. Fax 404/233-7061. www.holidayinn.com. 296 units. $146–$169 double on weekdays; $119–$199 double on weekends; $399 suite on weekdays; $245 suite on weekends. Extra person $20. Children under age 12 stay free in parents' room. AE, DC, DISC, MC, V. Valet parking $14. MARTA: Buckhead. **Amenities:** Restaurant; outdoor pool; health club; complimentary van transport within 3 miles of the hotel; business center; 24-hr. room service. *In room:* A/C, TV, high-speed Internet access, fridge in most rooms, coffeemaker, hair dryer.

Doubletree Hotel Atlanta-Buckhead ☆   Designed with the business traveler in mind and extensively renovated in 1999, this is also a good choice for pleasure travelers, since it's so convenient to Lenox Mall and Phipps Plaza. The comfortable guest rooms are outfitted with large desks in an ergonomic work center. The large rooms with king-size beds are especially desirable. All standard rooms have rich marble bathrooms with Neutrogena bath amenities and an armchair with ottoman for putting your feet up after you've shopped 'til you drop. Suites offer parlor rooms with spacious sitting areas, leather couches, and a full dining room ensemble for eight.

3340 Peachtree Rd. NE (between Lenox and Piedmont rds.), Atlanta, GA 30326. ℂ **800/833-TREE** or 404/231-1234. Fax 404/231-5236. www.doubletree.com. 229 units. Sun–Thurs $149–$249 double; Fri–Sat $124–$154 double. AE, DC, DISC, MC, V. Free parking. MARTA: Buckhead. **Amenities:** Restaurant; free use of nearby fitness center which offers exercise equipment, massage, steam, sauna, aerobics classes, childcare, basketball/racquetball courts, indoor track, and more; airport shuttle; free courtesy van within a 2-mile radius; limited room service. *In room:* A/C, TV, dataport, coffeemaker, hair dryer.

Embassy Suites Atlanta Buckhead ☆☆   This all-suite hotel stacks up well to the more expensive hotels in the same area. A favorite with business travelers, the suite arrangement is also ideal for families, and the location can't be beat, with Lenox Square, Phipps Plaza, and many fine restaurants within walking distance. The Buckhead MARTA station is less than a block away, so it's easy to connect quickly with other parts of the city and the airport.

Each elegantly appointed 800-square-foot, two-room suite has a queen-size, fold-out sofa. In addition to the bathroom with marble vanity and hair dryer, there is a sink in the separate bedroom. Although the entire hotel is accessible to travelers with disabilities (most of the participants in the wheelchair division of the Peachtree Road Race stay here), 10 of the suites are completely equipped for those with disabilities; 2 have roll-in showers.

Two popular bonuses: the complimentary cooked-to-order breakfast served in the atrium lobby, and complimentary cocktails each afternoon. Because almost everyone takes breakfast in the lobby, room service does not serve breakfast.

3285 Peachtree Rd. NW (1 block north of Piedmont Rd.), Atlanta, GA 30326. ℂ **800/362-2779** or 404/261-7733. Fax 404/262-0522. www.embassy-suites.com. 317 units. Mon–Thurs $184 double; Fri–Sun $129-$149 double. Children under age 18 stay free in parents' room. Prices include full breakfast. Rates may be higher during special events, lower during holidays and summer. AE, DC, DISC, MC, V. Valet parking $11; self-parking $8. MARTA: Buckhead. **Amenities:** Delicatessen with sandwiches to go; large outdoor pool; small indoor pool; small exercise room; Jacuzzi; sauna; pool table; concierge; courtesy van anywhere within a 1-mile radius; laundry and dry cleaning service, coin-operated laundry. *In room:* A/C, 2 TVs, fridge, microwave, coffeemaker, iron.

Hawthorn Suites Hotel-Atlanta Buckhead ☆   Located at the southern reaches of Buckhead, this is a convenient spot for anyone visiting Piedmont Hospital or the Shepherd Center. And although it's not in the heart of Buckhead, it's still close to many fine restaurants and shops, and a courtesy van will take you to anything within a 4-mile radius.

All the rooms are 600-square-foot, 1-room suites, remodeled and converted from corporate apartments in 1998. The suites are large, with queen-size beds, pullout sofas, and kitchens with coffeemakers and full-size refrigerators, making them good choices for an extended stay. Because it's an older building, all the suites are fairly quiet, and the bathrooms, though nothing special, are spacious. Monday through Thursday you can enjoy hot hors d'oeuvres and complimentary beer and wine in the lobby. All rooms are non-smoking. Four rooms are accessible to travelers with disabilities. Small pets are allowed with a $200 deposit, $100 of which can be refunded.

2030 Peachtree Rd. NW (just north of Collier Rd.), Atlanta, GA 30309. © **888/282-5432** or 404/352-3131. Fax 404/355-9902. www.hawthorn.com. 80 units. $159 double. Children under age 18 stay free in parents' room. Rates include full buffet breakfast. Good weekend discounts. AE, DC, DISC, MC, V. Free parking. MARTA: Lindbergh or Arts Center. Bus no. 23 from Arts Center stops in front of the hotel. Small pets are allowed with $200 deposit, $100 of which can be refunded. **Amenities:** Large heated outdoor pool; privileges at Shepherd Center fitness center for $5 fee; concierge; complimentary van within 4-mile radius; business services; room service delivery from neighboring restaurants; dry cleaning; coin-operated washers and dryers. *In room:* A/C, TV/VCR, kitchen with full-size fridge and coffeemaker, dataport.

Homewood Suites Hotel ★★ *(Value)*   This well-run suite hotel is an excellent value. Homewood is perfect for an extended business stay or a long weekend. The spacious one- and two-bedroom suites feel a lot like home, with pull-out sofas and large kitchen areas that include full-size appliances, plus coffeemakers, dishwashers, and toasters. The bathrooms are fairly standard. Some of the two-bedroom suites can easily sleep eight people.

The hotel is set back from a busy street, so all the rooms are quiet, with the nicest ones overlooking the pool and patio. Although you won't be within walking distance of most of the Buckhead attractions or the MARTA station, there is a courtesy van to take you to anything within a 3-mile radius. Four suites are accessible to travelers with disabilities. Pets are allowed with a $75 nonrefundable deposit.

In addition to a complimentary deluxe continental breakfast, there is an evening social Monday to Thursday with complimentary beer, wine, and light snacks or meals. About once a week, the social moves out to the patio for a cookout. If you're in the mood, you can even cook out yourself. There's no restaurant or room service, but delivery is available from several restaurants.

3566 Piedmont Rd. (between Peachtree and Roswell rds.), Atlanta, GA 30305. © **800/225-5466** or 404/365-0001. Fax 404/365-9888. www.homewood-suites.com. 92 suites. $129 double for 1-bedroom suite; $225 double for 2-bedroom suite. Children under age 18 stay free in parents' room. Rates include extended continental breakfast. Ask about special packages. AE, DC, DISC, MC, V. Free parking. MARTA: Buckhead. Bus no. 59 stops in front of hotel. Pets are allowed with a $75 nonrefundable deposit. **Amenities:** Small heated outdoor pool; small exercise room; concierge; business center; grocery shopping, video rental; coin-operated washers and dryers; small convenience store. One room is specially modified for travelers with disabilities. *In room:* A/C, 2 TVs/ VCR, dataports.

Marriott Residence Inn Buckhead ★★ *(Kids)*   This home-away-from-home was designed to meet the needs of travelers making extended visits, but it's great even if you're only spending a single night. It's like having your own apartment, with a private entrance and a large, fully equipped kitchen. It's in a good spot— near several excellent restaurants and not far from shopping and night life. Accommodations, which were redone in 1998, include comfortable living-room areas. About half the suites have working fireplaces, and during the winter, logs are available from the front desk. The most luxurious accommodations are duplex penthouses with vaulted ceilings, full dining-room/office areas, two bathrooms, and living-room fireplaces. Two rooms have been modified for travelers with disabilities. Pets are allowed, with a $125 nonrefundable deposit in studio suites, and a $150 deposit in penthouse suites.

The inn offers cocktail-hour parties on Monday, Tuesday, and Thursday from 5 to 7pm (free beer, wine, and hot and cold hors d'oeuvres); Wednesday, a complimentary full barbecue or buffet dinner is served.

2960 Piedmont Rd. NE (just south of Pharr Rd.), Atlanta, GA 30305. ☎ **800/331-3131** or 404/239-0677. Fax 404/262-9638. www.marriott.com. 136 suites. $140 studio suite (for up to 3); $180 penthouse suite (for up to 5). Reductions are available for stays of 7 nights or longer. AE, DC, DISC, MC, V. Free parking. MARTA: Bus no. 5 from Lindbergh Station; it stops at the corner of Pharr Rd. and Piedmont Rd., about half a block away. **Amenities:** Outdoor pool; basketball/volleyball/paddle-tennis courts; complimentary use of a well-equipped health club nearby (with every kind of workout equipment, Olympic indoor pool, an outdoor pool, jogging track, and tennis/racquetball/squash courts); Jacuzzi; free shuttle service within a 3-mile radius; coin-operated laundry. *In room:* A/C, TV.

Sheraton at Buckhead ☆   This is a lovely hotel that offers abundant services and facilities, plus a great location, close to MARTA, Lenox Square, Phipps Plaza, and many restaurants. It's not quite as fancy as other hotels in the area, but it's still very stylish. Rooms are furnished with French country and 18th-century-reproduction mahogany pieces, and some have four-poster or brass beds. Several have balconies, and rooms with king-size beds have plush armchairs with ottomans. Eleven rooms are accessible to travelers with disabilities.

3405 Lenox Rd. NE (between Peachtree and E. Paces Ferry rds.), Atlanta, GA 30326. ☎ **800/241-8260** or 404/261-9250. Fax 404/848-7391. www.sheraton.com. 369 units. $159 double; Club Level $179–$285 double. Extra person $20. Children under age 17 stay free in parents' room. AE, DC, DISC, MC, V. Self-parking $12. MARTA: Lenox. **Amenities:** Restaurant; outdoor swimming pool with waterfalls; health club; concierge; complimentary van within 3-mile radius; limited room service. *In room:* A/C, TV, dataport, coffeemaker, hair dryer, iron.

W Atlanta ☆☆   Pampering the modern business traveler is the goal of the helpful staff at this boutique hotel, which opened in February 1999. Though 20 minutes away from the shopping, dining, and nightlife of the famed Buckhead area, the W Atlanta is a convenient location if your plans include a trip to the World of Coca Cola or the IMAX Theater. Stark, light, and very chic, W Atlanta draws Atlanta's discerning business traveler with the many business-minded amenities and impeccable service. In fact, the service is tellingly named the Whatever/Whenever Service, and it offers just what it says. Where to dine in Buckhead? Any Braves tickets left for the game tonight? Ask and you shall receive.

Guest rooms offer a minimalist, boutique hotel ambience and stand well against the pricier Buckhead comparisons. Whether you're in town for work or play, slow down long enough to enjoy the Rainforest shower and Aveda bath products in every room, as well as the pillow-top mattresses with goose down comforters and pillows. Those planning an extended stay might want to request a room with a full kitchen.

111 Perimeter Center West, Atlanta, GA 30346. ☎ **770/396-6800.** Fax 770/399-5514. www.starwood.com/ whotels. 275 units. Deluxe king rooms start at $199; Suites with full kitchen $259. AE, DC, DISC, MC, V. Valet parking $13; self-park $4. MARTA: Dunwoody. **Amenities:** Restaurant, cafe; outdoor pool; health club; sauna; 24-hr. concierge; 24-hr. business center; 24-hr. room service; in-room massage; laundry service. *In room:* A/C, TV/VCR, dataport (high speed Internet access), full kitchen in some rooms, hair dryer, iron, safe.

MODERATE

Beverly Hills Inn ☆   Housed in a 1920s former apartment building, with forest green shutters and window awnings, this charming B&B is located on a tree-lined residential street. British owner/host Mit Amin offers warm hospitality to guests. This is a good spot for an extended stay, especially for families who prefer a neighborhood atmosphere to that of a commercial hotel. On the first floor is a parlor/library where a decanter of port is available all day. (You'll find a half-bottle of burgundy in your room upon arrival.) Another library is downstairs in the garden room, which has a sky-lit conservatory area filled with plants.

The spacious rooms are cheerful and attractive, decorated in a mix of antiques (many of them English pieces) and collectibles. Some have canopied beds. All are equipped with kitchenettes (the housekeeper does your dishes), and there's a private balcony through the French doors. A supermarket is within easy walking distance, should you want to cook in your room, but there are a number of good restaurants close by. Daily newspapers and local phone calls are complimentary. There's no elevator, so if stairs are a problem, reserve one of the six rooms on the ground floor.

65 Sheridan Dr. NE (just off Peachtree Rd.), Atlanta, GA 30305. © **800/331-8520** or 404/233-8520. Fax 404/233-8659. www.beverlyhillsinn.com. 18 units. $110–$130 1-bedroom suite; $130–$160 2-bedroom suite accommodating up to 4 people; $165 whirlpool suite; $120 designer suite. Extra person $10. Children under age 12 stay free in parents' room. Rates include deluxe continental breakfast. Discounts available for stays of a week or more. AE, DC, DISC, MC, V. Free parking. MARTA bus: no. 23 at the corner of Peachtree and Sheridan. Pets are allowed, with a $125 nonrefundable deposit in studio suites, and a $150 deposit in penthouse suites. **Amenities:** Complimentary membership privileges at a fully equipped health club nearby; fax machine and computer available; complimentary use of washer/dryer. *In room:* A/C, TV.

Fairfield Inn Buckhead   There's nothing fancy about the Fairfield Inn, except for its neighborhood. A stone's throw from several excellent restaurants and close to all that upscale Buckhead has to offer, this is an economical choice for business and leisure visitors who are more interested in location than luxury. Built in the late '90s, the large rooms are well-maintained and pleasant, with surprisingly high ceilings. The bathrooms are fairly standard, with the vanity and sink conveniently located outside the bathroom. The rooms near the elevators and ice machines can be a little noisy, so ask for one away from those locations. If you're in town for an extended stay, try to book one of the five suites, which have mini-fridges, microwaves, and wet bars.

3092 Piedmont Rd. NE (between Peachtree and E. Paces Ferry rds.), Atlanta, GA 30326. © **800/228-2800** or 404/846-0900. Fax 404/467-9878. www.fairfieldinn.com. 116 units. $79 double; $109 suite. Children under age 18 stay free in parents' room. Price includes expanded continental breakfast. AE, DC, DISC, MC, V. Free parking. MARTA bus: No. 5 from Lindbergh station. **Amenities:** Small indoor pool; Jacuzzi; coin-operated washers and dryers; overnight laundry service; dry-cleaning service. *In room:* A/C, TV. Suites have fridges and microwaves.

Lenox Inn Buckhead   If you want to spend more money on shopping than on a hotel room, the Lenox Inn is a great choice. It's a short walk to both the Lenox Square and Phipps Plaza malls, but it's also convenient to MARTA, the Atlanta Financial Center, and many excellent restaurants. Under the same ownership as the adjacent Sheraton (details above), and sharing all of its facilities, the hotel offers charming motel-style rooms with 18th-century-reproduction mahogany furnishings. Only one building has an elevator, so if stairs are a problem, either request that building or ask for a first-floor room. Three rooms are accessible to travelers with disabilities.

Guests gather in a cozy restaurant with a working fireplace for complimentary cocktails and hors d'oeuvres Monday to Saturday from 5:30 to 6:30pm.

3387 Lenox Rd. NE (between Peachtree and E. Paces Ferry rds.), Atlanta, GA 30326. © **800/821-0900** or 404/261-5500. Fax 404/261-6140. www.lenoxinnbuckhead.com. 180 units. $79–$149 double. Extra person $20. Children under age 18 stay free in parents' room. Rates include continental breakfast. AE, DC, DISC, MC, V. Free parking. MARTA: Lenox. **Amenities:** Large outdoor swimming pool; guests may use the Sheraton fitness center next door at no charge; airport shuttle, dry cleaning service. *In room:* A/C, TV.

Main Stay Suites   This all-suite hotel opened in March 2000, catering to business and leisure travelers who need a suite and are more interested in spending their money on Buckhead attractions than lodging. Each unit has a pullout sofa, an iron and ironing board, hair dryer, and a kitchen with full-size appliances. Studios have one TV; suites have two. Outdoor grills are available. A nice touch is the guest supply closet, where visitors can get replacement toiletries and towels whenever they want. The hotel shares an outdoor pool and fitness center with the adjacent Sleep Inn (see below), which is owned by the same hotelier. Five rooms are accessible to travelers with disabilities.

820 Sidney Marcus Blvd. (between Lenox and Piedmont rds.), Atlanta, GA 30324. (C) 800/660-6246 or 404/ 949-4820. Fax 404/949-4810. www.atlantabuckheadhotels.com. 80 suites. $109 studio; $119 1-bedroom suite; $199 2-bedroom suite. Extra person $5. Rates include continental breakfast. Rates lower for extended stays. AE, DC, DISC, MC, V. Free self-parking. MARTA: Lindbergh; bus no. 39 stops in front of hotel. **Amenities:** Access to outdoor pool and fitness center at the adjacent Sleep Inn; "Take-Out Taxi" service is available from several excellent restaurants in the area. Van service is complimentary within a 3-mile radius. *In room:* A/C, TV, kitchen, hair dryer, iron.

Summerfield Suites by Wyndham ⭐ *Kids* *Value*   This is a good choice if you're looking for a great Buckhead location at less than the usual Buckhead price. It's within walking distance of several fine restaurants (Pricci is across the street and the Atlanta Fish Market is a few blocks away), and close to Buckhead nightlife. There's also good shopping in the area, and a park nearby for the kids. Accommodations include spacious one- or two-bedroom suites with queen-size beds, and a separate living room. There is also a separate vanity/dressing area with a sink outside the bathroom. Six suites are equipped for travelers with disabilities. The complimentary full breakfast is served buffet-style in a bright room next to the lobby.

505 Pharr Rd. (about a block off Piedmont Rd.), Atlanta, GA 30305. (C) 800/833-4353 or 404/262-7880. Fax 404/262-3734. www.wyndham.com. 88 units. $99–$159 1-bedroom suite (for up to 3); $129–$189 2-bedroom suite (for up to 5). Rates include full breakfast. Weekend rates and summer packages available. AE, DISC, MC, V. Free parking. MARTA: Bus no. 5 from Lindbergh Station stops at the corner of Pharr Rd. and Piedmont Rd., about a block away. **Amenities:** Medium-size outdoor pool; small exercise room; Jacuzzi; complimentary shuttle service within a 3-mile radius of the property and to Lindbergh MARTA station; coin-operated laundry; 24-hr. convenience store. *In room:* A/C, TV/VCR, full kitchen with appliances, hair dryer.

INEXPENSIVE

Sleep Inn   This good value caters to business and leisure travelers. It's connected by a courtyard to Main Stay Suites (see above), which is owned by the same hoteliers. Attractively furnished business-class rooms include coffeemakers and fax. Guests can do their own laundry at no charge. Five rooms are accessible to travelers with disabilities.

There's a guest reception Monday to Thursday from 5 to 7:30pm, and a cookout each Wednesday evening.

800 Sidney Marcus Blvd. (between Lenox and Piedmont rds.), Atlanta, GA 30324. (C) 800/753-3746 or 404/ 949-4000. Fax 404/949-4010. www.atlantabuckheadhotels.com. 142 units. $89 double; $99 business class. Extra person $10. Children under age 18 stay free in parents' room. Rates include continental breakfast. Rates may be higher for special events. AE, DC, DISC, MC, V. Free self-parking. MARTA: Lindbergh; bus no. 39 stops in front of hotel. **Amenities:** Large outdoor pool; small fitness center with aerobic equipment and weights; van service within a 3-mile radius; business center; Take-Out Taxi service from area restaurants; laundry facilities. *In room:* A/C, TV, hair dryer, irons.

4 Virginia-Highland & Inman Park

Virginia-Highland is a marvelous choice for tourists—within easy walking distance of shops, galleries, and restaurants. The only problem is that, because it's mostly a residential area, there are few accommodations available. Nearby Inman Park, though not as convenient to attractions, is equally charming. You will find the following accommodations on the "Midtown Accommodations" map on p. 82.

EXPENSIVE

Gaslight Inn ★★   Owner Jim Moss has turned this charming, Craftsman-style 1913 house into a delightful B&B, with exquisitely decorated rooms and public areas. As its name implies, much of the inn is lit by flickering gaslight fixtures, and there are working fireplaces throughout. There are two downstairs parlors, a small, screened porch, and a comfortable den with cable TV, well-stocked bookcases, a baby grand piano, and a large selection of CDs and cassettes. Guests can breakfast on fruit, fresh-squeezed juice, muffins, and breads in the formal dining room or on the front porch furnished with antique wicker chairs and a swing.

The elegant English Suite—with a four-poster mahogany bed, a vast bathroom equipped with a steam bath and whirlpool, and a working fireplace—is perfect for a romantic getaway. The Ivy Cottage, a detached bungalow with a full kitchen (with washer/dryer) and living-room area, will remind you of Nantucket. And the Rose Room, with its lace draperies, working fireplace, and canopied four-poster bed, is another charmer. The other accommodations—some of them located in a 1904 house across the street—are equally lovely. The Terrace Suite, with two rooms with queen-size beds, even has a fully outfitted kitchen with dining area.

1001 St. Charles Ave. (between Frederica St. and N. Highland Ave.), Atlanta, GA 30306. © **404/876-1001.** Fax 404/876-1001. www.gaslightinn.com. 7 units. $95–$295 double. Rates include extensive continental breakfast. Higher rates apply to suites. AE, DC, DISC, MC, V. Some parking spaces behind house; street parking is not usually a problem. MARTA: Bus nos. 2 and 16 stop a block away. *In room:* A/C, TV (some with VCRs), dataport.

King-Keith House Bed and Breakfast   This 1890 home of hardware magnate George King is in Inman Park, a neighborhood of Victorian homes that is on the National Register of Historic Places. The lovely King-Keith home, in the Queen Anne style, boasts 12-foot ceilings and carved fireplaces, and a huge wraparound porch. Authentic period antiques add to the charm. The ambience is as warm as the hospitality.

Each room has a private bathroom, and beds range from double to king-size. Two of the rooms have a hall bathroom, but it is not shared. The large downstairs suite has a private entrance and a private sitting room with an extra twin bed. The one-room cottage, which is very spacious, has a king-size bed, sitting area, two-person Jacuzzi, and fireplace. Besides the parlor, there are several gathering places for guests: the large front porch, the upstairs porch, and the wicker-filled screened porch, which opens onto the garden.

Coffee is delivered to your room every morning, and the complete breakfast might include French toast, homemade pancakes, or eggs cooked to order. A nice touch is the small guest kitchen stocked with complimentary soft drinks, tea, bottled water, cookies, chips, and other snacks. The property is not far from the funky Little Five Points commercial district, the Martin Luther King, Jr. National Historic Site, the Jimmy Carter Presidential Library and Museum, and several restaurants. If you don't want to walk from the MARTA station, the hosts will pick you up with advance notice.

889 Edgewood Ave. NE (at Waverly Way), Atlanta, GA 30307. © **800/728-3879** or 404/688-7330. Fax 404/584-0730. www.kingkeith.com. 6 units, including a separate cottage. $90–$160 double. No charge for 2 or fewer infants or toddlers. Rates include full breakfast. AE, DISC, MC, V. Self-parking. MARTA: 2 blocks from Inman Park station. *In room:* A/C, TV.

5 Stone Mountain

Georgia's Stone Mountain Park, just 16 miles east of downtown Atlanta, is a recreation area with 3,200 acres of lakes and wooded parkland. It is, in itself, a major travel destination, visited by more than 4 million tourists annually. *Note:* There's a $6 parking fee upon entering the park.

EXPENSIVE

Marriott Evergreen Conference Resort *Kids*   Geared primarily to business groups, Evergreen is also a good choice for vacationing families who want to take advantage of the activities in Stone Mountain Park. A turreted stucco lakefront "castle" nestled in a fragrant pine forest, it has large, luxuriously appointed rooms with balconies. An 87-room expansion began late in 2000. Suites boast a lovely spacious bedroom. However, those who wind up on the uncomfortable pullout couch may be in for a restless night.

1 Lakeview Dr., Stone Mountain Park, Stone Mountain, GA 30086. © 770/879-9900. Fax 770/465-3264. www.evergreenresort.com. 249 units. Spring and summer $139–$189 double; fall and winter $129–$179 double; $225–$750 suite. No charge for extra person, but only 5 people in any room or suite. Children under age 18 stay free in parents' room. Inquire about packages. AE, DC, DISC, MC, V. Free parking. **Amenities:** Restaurant; Starbucks; indoor swimming pool; kiddie pool; large outdoor pool; 2 18-hole championship golf courses; 17 tennis courts (2 are lit); 24-hr. fitness center; Jacuzzi; concierge (who sells tickets to all park attractions); airport shuttle on request; full business/meeting facilities; 24-hr. room service. *In room:* A/C, TV, dataport, fridge, coffeemaker, hair dryer, iron.

INEXPENSIVE

Stone Mountain Park Inn *Kids* *Value*   This charming inn, which is across the street from the tennis venue built for the 1996 Olympics, is housed in a two-story, white-colonnaded brick building that wraps around a central courtyard. Rooms are lovely, featuring Chippendale-reproduction furnishings, and most have large vanity/dressing room areas and spacious parlors. Honeymoon suites offer king-size, four-poster beds. Almost all accommodations have courtyard-facing balconies or patios with rocking chairs. Five rooms are accessible to travelers with disabilities.

1058 Robert E. Lee Dr., Stone Mountain Park, Stone Mountain, GA 30086. © 770/469-3311. Fax 404/876-5009. 92 units. $129–$179 for 1 or 2 people (rates vary seasonally). Children under age 12 stay free in parents' room. Honeymoon, tennis, golf, and other packages available. AE, DC, MC, V. Free parking. **Amenities:** Restaurant; outdoor pool/sundeck in a woodsy setting; shuttle service; business service; coin-operated laundry. Tickets for all park attractions are sold at the inn. *In room:* A/C, TV.

A CAMPGROUND

Stone Mountain Park Campground   A large campground with sections for pop-ups, RVs, and tents, this is a great place to stay. Nestled in the woods, the area has many sites overlooking the lake, especially in the tent section. All sites have barbecue grills, and picnic tables are scattered throughout the area. Public facilities include a dining pavilion, playgrounds, laundries, and showers. The park's beach is close by, and the swimming pool is brand new. Pets are permitted if kept on a leash. This is a popular place, so be sure to call ahead. You may reserve a spot up to 90 days before you stay; all reservations must be made at least 1 week in advance.

Stone Mountain Park, P.O. Box 778, Stone Mountain, GA 30086. © 800/385-9807 or 770/498-5710. Fax 770/413-5082. $22 primitive tent site, $24 primitive lakeside tent site; $24 tent site with water and electricity, $28 lakeside tent site with water and electricity; $32 full hookup, $37 full lakeside hookup; $27–$32 for extra water and electricity. Rates cover 2 adults and 4 children; additional guests $2 per night. Children under age 12 stay free. AE, DISC, MC, V. Pets permitted.

6 Druid Hills/Emory University

Though not a happening section of town in terms of restaurants or attractions, this area, east of Midtown and Buckhead, offers good value for your hotel dollar. And if you have a car, the properties listed below are only about a 10-minute drive from the center of things.

MODERATE

Emory Inn This delightful hotel, owned by Emory University, is popular with visitors to Emory and the nearby Centers for Disease Control and Prevention. Rooms, furnished with early American–style knotty-pine pieces, are attractively decorated. Nine rooms are accessible to travelers with disabilities.

1641 Clifton Rd. NE (between Briarcliff and N. Decatur rds.), Atlanta, GA 30329. ⓒ 800/933-6679 or 404/712-6700. Fax 404/712-6701. www.emoryconferencecenter.com/emoryinn.asp. 107 units. $99–$135 double. AE, DC, DISC, MC, V. Free parking. MARTA bus: no. 6 Emory stops in front of the hotel. **Amenities:** Restaurant; outdoor pool; free use of a vast fitness complex on campus with a heated indoor pool, 12 lit tennis courts, basketball, indoor track, racquetball, and a full complement of Nautilus equipment; Jacuzzi; complimentary shuttle service to the Emory campus and hospital; airport shuttle on request, room service (during restaurant hours); coin-operated washers/dryers. *In room:* A/C, TV, coffeemaker, hair dryer, iron.

Executive Park Courtyard by Marriott This hotel is slightly outside the usual tourist areas, but it's close to town and convenient to I-85. Popular with business travelers, this is a limited-service, moderately priced lodging. But don't picture a Spartan, no-frills atmosphere. This property had a full facelift in 2001 and the results will be pleasing to newcomers as well as previous guests. Accommodations feature large desks and nice-size dressing-room areas. Suites have full pullout sofas and extra phones and TVs. Eight rooms are accessible to guests with disabilities.

1236 Executive Park Dr. (off N. Druid Hills Rd.), Atlanta, GA 30329. ⓒ 404/858-1827 or 404/728-0708. Fax 404/636-4019. www.courtyard.com. 145 units. $99 double; $119 suite. AE, DC, DISC, MC, V. Free parking. MARTA: Bus no. 8 from Brookhaven station. **Amenities:** Restaurant, bar; outdoor pool; exercise room; indoor Jacuzzi; airport shuttle service; limited room service, dry cleaning; coin-operated washers/dryers. *In room:* A/C, TV, dataport, coffeemaker, hair dryer.

7 Airport

There are more than three dozen hotels near the airport, most of them well-known chains. It's often convenient to stay near the airport, especially if you're flying out very early or in very late. Although most airport hotel guests are business travelers, it's not out of the question for leisure travelers to choose accommodations at the airport. Weekend rates are often very low, and many of the hotels offer free shuttles to the Airport MARTA station, making it easy to reach other parts of the city. Buckhead, for instance, is about 35 minutes away by MARTA rail. The hotels listed below are two of the finest, but there are several hotel and motel chains nearby.

EXPENSIVE

Hilton Atlanta Airport ⭐ Mercifully, this airport hotel is out of the normal flight pattern. That, and its triple-paned windows, makes it quieter than many hotels, especially the less expensive ones. (For the *very* quietest location, ask for a room with a city view.) The rooms, which were redone in 1999, are a good size, with tasteful, contemporary decor. They're outfitted with king-size beds or two doubles. The bathrooms have generous vanities. For an excellent value, ask for one of the Executive Corner rooms, which are only $20 more than the standard rooms. They're twice as big, though, and are spacious enough to accommodate a sofa and two easy chairs in the sitting area. The bathrooms have separate showers and garden tubs. The suites are quite large and luxurious. Twenty-five of the standard rooms have been modified for guests with disabilities.

1031 Virginia Ave. (at I-85 Exit 73A), Atlanta, GA 30354. © 800/HILTONS or 404/767-9000. Fax 404/768-0185. www.hilton.com. 503 units. $110–$189 double; $450–$550 suite. Rates may be lower during summer, higher during special events; weekend packages available. AE, DC, DISC, MC, V. Valet parking $6; self-parking $4. **Amenities:** 2 restaurants; sports bar; outdoor swimming pool; small indoor heated pool; lit tennis court; extremely large and well-equipped fitness center for a $6 fee (aerobics classes, personal trainers, massage available); Jacuzzi; 24-hr. concierge; complimentary airport shuttle; business center; salon; 24-hr. room service; laundry service. *In room:* A/C, TV, dataport, minibar, coffeemaker, hair dryer, iron.

Renaissance Concourse Hotel ★   If you're an airplane buff or just travel with one, this is the ticket. Built on the site of the old airport terminal in 1992, the Renaissance is literally on the edge of the runway. Half the rooms, in fact, face the runway, so you can step out on your balcony and watch the planes take off and land; on the other side, the rooms have views of the downtown skyline. Sounds noisy, but the soundproofing is more than adequate, and back in your room, you'd hardly know you were at the airport. The rooms themselves are luxuriously decorated, light, open, and quite large, even the bathrooms. Twenty rooms have been specially modified for travelers with disabilities; 19 have roll-in showers.

1 Hartsfield Center Parkway, Atlanta, GA 30354. © 800/HOTELS-1 or 404/209-9999. Fax 404/209-8934. www.renaissancehotels.com. 387 units. $169 double; $425 and up suite. Rates may be higher during special events; weekend packages available. AE, DC, DISC, MC, V. Valet parking $8; self-parking $4. **Amenities:** Restaurant; medium-size outdoor pool; indoor heated lap pool; fully equipped fitness center with steam rooms and sauna; Jacuzzi; 24-hr. concierge; complimentary airport shuttle; business center with audiovisual support and secretarial services; 24-hr. room service; laundry service. *In room:* A/C, TV, dataport, minibar, coffeemaker, hair dryer, iron.

8 South of Town

MODERATE

Seren-Be Bed and Breakfast Farm ★ *Finds*   Thirty-two miles south of Atlanta—amid rolling meadows, horse pastures, verdant woodlands, and fields of sage—Steve and Marie Nygren have created a retreat on 284 acres of farmland. Here, they offer warm Southern hospitality to visitors seeking a place to kick back and relax, a romantic getaway, or a family vacation that offers close encounters with farm animals. Visiting children are invited to play in a treehouse, pet the baby animals, feed the chickens, and otherwise participate in farm chores. Other activities include croquet, occasional hayrides, marshmallow roasts around a bonfire, fishing from a well-stocked lake, hiking along trails dotted with streams and waterfalls, moonlit canoe rides, and antiquing in the nearby town of Newnan.

In the 94-year-old house, a rustic recreation room with a working stone fireplace is comfortably furnished and equipped with games, books, puzzles, a TV, and videos. There are also many patios, porches, and gazebos where guests can gather or enjoy their privacy. In the dining room, which has lovely views of the surrounding countryside, you'll enjoy a hearty breakfast—perhaps cheese grits, baked ham, fresh eggs, fried green tomatoes, and biscuits.

The rooms—all with private bathroom, one with a Jacuzzi tub—are charming but unpretentious. Yours might have knotty-pine floors strewn with rag rugs, antique furnishings, a bed piled high with decorative pillows, or lace-curtained windows. The cottage has its own full kitchen, living room, front porch, and screened dining porch. One room has been modified for guests with disabilities.

The Nygrens are Atlanta restaurant royalty: Steve, now retired, was the founder of the successful Peasant group (including Mick's, City Grill, and others), while Marie is the daughter of Margaret Lupo, who established Mary Mac's Tearoom, a local institution.

10950 Hutcheson Ferry Rd., Palmetto, GA 30268. ℭ **770/463-2610.** Fax 770/463-4472. www.serenbe.com. 8 units. $140 double; $175 2-bedroom cottage. Rates include full farm breakfast. No credit cards. Free parking. Call ahead for directions. **Amenities:** Swimming pool with a water slide; exercise room with equipment; Jacuzzi; bicycle rental; conference room with multimedia equipment; massage; babysitting; communal kitchen and barbecue grill; unstocked refrigerator; fax and dataport available; complimentary washers and dryers. *In room:* A/C, coffeemaker, hair dryer and iron on request.

6

Where to Dine

It's sad to say, but not too many years ago, the famed Coca-Cola was about Atlanta's biggest contribution to gastronomy. Not today. In the last decade or so, the dining scene has exploded, and Atlanta has emerged as a sophisticated restaurant town where establishments have veered away from uninventive American fare and unauthentic down-home Southern cooking (happily, there are still lots of places to feast on *authentic* down-home Southern cooking).

Innovative chefs, who once left Atlanta for the great food capitals, have brought their expertise and ideas to the New South. As a result, there's now a little bit of everything available—from all around the world. You can munch on pierogi in East Atlanta, nibble fragrant basil rolls in Virginia-Highland, or dig into osso buco in Buckhead. There's French cuisine as authentic as any you'll find on the Left Bank, and Italian pasta that tastes like it came from Naples.

The Colonnade, Thelma's Kitchen, and Mary Mac's Tearoom, three bastions of tradition, still turn out some of the best Southern cooking you'll ever put in your mouth, but the current trend in many kitchens is to take heirloom recipes and give them a contemporary twist. So pork chops might be stuffed with eggplant and andouille sausage, collard greens sautéed and seasoned with balsamic vinegar, and comfy, familiar grits spiked with Stilton.

The audience for all these culinary concoctions is huge. Atlantans love to eat out, spending half their annual food budget on dining away from home. The debut of a new restaurant is more eagerly awaited than the opening of a new play, and Atlantans avidly peruse the local newspapers to find out about the hottest names in the food game.

Restaurants listed below are divided first by area, then by price, using the following guide: Very Expensive, more than $55 per person; Expensive, $35 to $55 per person; Moderate, $25 to $35 per person; Inexpensive, less than $25 per person.

I have listed valet parking where applicable.

1 Restaurants by Cuisine

AMERICAN

Blue Ridge Grill ✪ (Buckhead, $$$, p. 128)

Buckhead Diner (Buckhead, $$, p. 132)

George's Restaurant and Bar (Virginia-Highland/Inman Park, $, p. 139)

Houston's ✪ (Buckhead, $$, p. 133)

Mick's (Downtown, $, p. 106)

Murphy's (Virginia-Highland/Inman Park, $$, p. 136)

OK Café (Buckhead, $, p. 134)

Pano's & Paul's ✪✪✪ (Buckhead, $$$$, p. 126)

Key to Abbreviations: $$$$ = Very Expensive $$$ = Expensive $$ = Moderate $ = Inexpensive

Kyma ★★ (Buckhead, $$$$, p. 125)

ICE CREAM
Jake's Ice Cream & Sorbets (Midtown, $, p. 117)

ITALIAN
Abruzzi Ristorante ★★ (Buckhead, $$$$, p. 120)

Floataway Café ★★ (Decatur, $$$, p. 141)

Fratelli di Napoli (Buckhead, $$, p. 133)

Mondo Baking (Midtown, $, p. 118)

Pasta da Pulcinella ★ (Midtown, $$, p. 117)

Pasta Vino (Buckhead, $, p. 134)

Pastificio Cameli (East Atlanta, $, p. 140)

Pricci ★ (Buckhead, $$$, p. 131)

Sotto Sotto ★★ (Virginia-Highland/Inman Park, $$, p. 137)

Veni Vidi Vici ★★ (Midtown, $$$, p. 115)

MEDITERRANEAN
Anis Cafe and Bistro ★ (Buckhead, $$, p. 131)

The Dining Room ★★★ (Buckhead, $$$$, p. 121)

Eno ★★ (Midtown, $$$, p. 111)

MEXICAN
Raging Burrito (Decatur, $, p. 143)

Willy's Mexicana Grill ★ (Midtown, $, p. 119)

MODERN CLASSICAL
Seeger's ★★★ (Buckhead, $$$$, p. 127)

NORTHERN CALIFORNIAN
Woodfire Grill ★★ (Midtown, $$$, p. 115)

PIZZA
Athens Pizza (Decatur, $, p. 143)

Fellini's Pizza (Buckhead, $, p. 133)

Pasta Vino (Buckhead, $, p. 134)

REGIONAL AMERICAN
Harvest ★ (Virginia-Highland/Inman Park, $$$, p. 136)

SEAFOOD
Atlanta Fish Market ★ (Buckhead, $$$, p. 127)

Bone's ★★★ (Buckhead, $$$$, p. 120)

The Cabin ★ (Buckhead, $$$, p. 129)

Chops and The Lobster Bar ★★ (Buckhead, $$$$, p. 121)

The Palm ★ (Buckhead, $$$$, p. 126)

Prime ★★ (Buckhead, $$$$, p. 127)

SOUTHERN/REGIONAL
Colonnade ★ (Midtown, $$$, p. 110)

Mary Mac's Tea Room ★ (Midtown, $, p. 118)

Thelma's Kitchen ★ (Downtown, $, p. 109)

SOUTHWESTERN
Nava ★★ (Buckhead, $$$, p. 130)

Taqueria del Sol ★ (Midtown, $, p. 118)

SPANISH
La Fonda Latina (Buckhead, $, p. 134)

STEAK
Bone's ★★★ (Buckhead, $$$$, p. 120)

The Cabin ★ (Buckhead, $$$, p. 129)

Chops and The Lobster Bar ★★ (Buckhead, $$$$, p. 121)

The Palm ★ (Buckhead, $$$$, p. 126)

Prime ★★ (Buckhead, $$$$, p. 127)

SUSHI
Atlanta Fish Market ★ (Buckhead, $$$, p. 127)

Magic Fingers Sushi ★★ (Midtown, $$, p. 116)

Prime ★★ (Buckhead, $$$$, p. 127)

THAI

Surin of Thailand 🞰 (Virginia-
Highland/Inman Park, $$,
p. 138)

Tamarind Thai Cuisine 🞰🞰
(Midtown, $$$, p. 114)
Thai Chili 🞰 (Decatur, $$, p. 143)

2 Downtown

Your choices here range from the ultra-elegant City Grill to the world's largest
drive-in.

VERY EXPENSIVE

City Grill 🞰🞰🞰 CREATIVE AMERICAN   One of Atlanta's most opulent
restaurants, City Grill is *the* place for downtown power-lunchers and couples cel-
ebrating a special occasion. Located in the lavishly refurbished Hurt Building,
you enter the two-level restaurant through a marble-walled rotunda with a
rosette-and-gold-leaf-adorned dome. Downstairs, murals of misty pastoral scenes
adorn the walls, candelabra chandeliers glitter overhead, and floor-to-ceiling win-
dows are framed by gold draperies. The setting is quite grand, but the atmosphere
is more relaxed than you might expect.

Chef David Gross specializes in regional American fare with a few Southern
overtones. A recent menu included starters such as vanilla-scented scallops with
lobster slaw and blackberry vinaigrette. Main courses included jumbo lump blue
crab cakes with corn-smoked tomato coulis, and grilled duck with truffled
asparagus and fire-roasted shallot jus. City Grill's extensive cellar is stocked with
more than 400 wines (most of them French and Californian) in all price ranges,
with about 20 selections available by the glass.

50 Hurt Plaza (at Edgewood Ave.). ✆ 404/524-2489. Reservations recommended. Lunch items $9–$19; din-
ner 3-course prix-fixe menu $45; 4-course $55; and 5-course $65. AE, DC, MC, V. Mon–Fri 11:30am–2pm;
Mon–Sat 6–10pm. MARTA: Peachtree Center or Five Points.

EXPENSIVE

Mumbo Jumbo Bar & Grill 🞰🞰 CONTEMPORARY AMERICAN   Since
the day it opened, just before the Olympics, this energetic restaurant/bar/club
has been the place downtown to see and be seen. It is carpeted with beautiful
people, from the classic old art-filled bar out front to the sleek supper-club-like
restaurant in the back. This is one of the top spots for a happening happy hour
and late night dining. Chef Shaun Doty, former sous-chef at the Ritz-Carlton in
Buckhead, has created an eclectic array of seasonally influenced dishes, and the
menu is a treat to read over. Choices range from the braised short ribs with
radicchio and goat cheese to sautéed halibut with fennel salad. And there's a nod
here and there to the South—Mumbo Gumbo, a spicy stew of shrimp, crayfish,
sausage, and okra, is the signature starter. The wine list is as eclectic as the menu.
If you're looking for a sedate experience, try lunch or an early dinner. Things
crank up later in the evening with the arrival of the trendiest customers, and the
noise level in the restaurant can get uncomfortably high.

89 Park Place NE (at Woodruff Park). ✆ 404/523-0330. Reservations recommended. Lunch entrees $9–$18;
dinner main courses $18–$32. AE, DC, DISC, MC, V. Mon–Fri 11:30am–2:30pm, 5:30pm–around midnight. Bar
menu until 2am. Sat and Sun dinner only, 5:30–10:30 pm. MARTA: Peachtree Center.

INEXPENSIVE

Mick's *Kids* AMERICAN   Mick's is one of the best of the Underground restau-
rants, a two-story, turn-of-the-century–themed restaurant in Humbug Square.

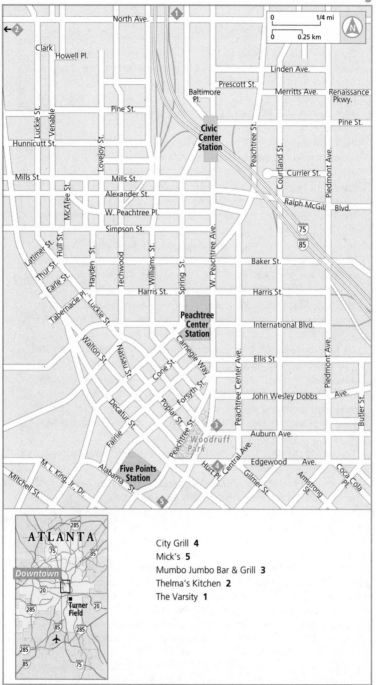

North Ave.

Clark
Howell Pl.

Linden Ave.

Prescott St.

Baltimore Pl.
Merritts Ave.
Renaissance Pkwy.

Pine St.

Pine St.

Luckie St.
Venable

Hunnicutt St.

Lovejoy St.

Civic Center Station

Peachtree St.

Courtland St.

Currier St.

Piedmont Ave.

Mills St.

McAfee St.

Mills St.

Alexander St.

W. Peachtree Pl.

Ralph McGill   Blvd.

Simpson St.

75
85

Latimer St.
Thur St.
Earle St.
Hull St.
Hayden St.
Techwood
Williams St.
Spring St.

Baker St.

Tabernacle Pl.
Luckie St.

Harris St.

W. Peachtree Ave.

Harris St.

Peachtree Center Station

International Blvd.

Walton St.

Carnegie Way

Nassau St.

Cone St.

Peachtree Center Ave.

Ellis St.

Piedmont Ave.

Butler St.

Decatur St.

Poplar St.
Forsyth St.

John Wesley Dobbs   Ave.

Fairlie

Peachtree St.

3

Woodruff Park

Auburn Ave.

M. L. King, Jr. Dr.

Alabama St.

Five Points Station

Hurt Pl.
Central Ave.

4

Edgewood   Ave.

Coca Cola Pl.

Mitchell St.

5

Gilmer St.

Armstrong St.

ATLANTA

285
75
85

Downtown

20

285
85
285

■ Turner Field

20

285

✈

285
85

75

City Grill **4**

Mick's **5**

Mumbo Jumbo Bar & Grill **3**

Thelma's Kitchen **2**

The Varsity **1**

Kids Family-Friendly Restaurants

Doc Chey's Noodle House (p. 138)   This casual neighborhood favorite has two special children's entrees, but there are several other rice and noodle dishes that would appeal to the younger set.

Heaping Bowl and Brew (p. 140)   If you're visiting Turner Field, Grant Park, or Zoo Atlanta, this casual restaurant, with its reasonably priced comfort food, is just a short drive away.

Fellini's Pizza (p. 133)   The New York–style pizza that Fellini's serves is a treat that will please everyone, and it's available by the slice. Salads are also superb, and you can sit outside if you choose.

Fratelli di Napoli (p. 133)   A big, bustling SoHo-like loft, Fratelli's bases its entire concept on feeding a family, offering big platters of food that serve two or three. It's sophisticated enough to interest the adults and friendly enough to welcome the kids.

Houston's (p. 133)   There are always lots of families in Houston's, where there's prime rib for the grown-ups, burgers for the kids, and reasonable prices that won't bust the budget. It's casual, but still a good place to take the family for a special occasion.

Mick's (p. 106)   This local chain serves the simple foods kids love at moderate prices. Even teenagers will like the retro-hip soda shop atmosphere.

OK Café (p. 134)   OK Café's classic comfort food and jukebox are sure to please kids of all ages.

Pasta Vino (p. 134)   Do kids like this place? One 3-year-old from the neighborhood insisted on having his birthday party here so he could have his favorite—a slice of white cheese pizza with pesto. There's plenty for parents too, including fresh veal, seafood, and excellent lasagna.

The Varsity (p. 109)   The greasy feasts at the world's largest drive-in restaurant are big kid-pleasers.

The Vortex (p. 119)   The flea market décor and big, juicy hamburgers at this wild bar and grill should satisfy any kid.

It's fronted by a gas-lit wraparound porch enclosed by black wrought-iron fencing, great for viewing indoor "street" action while sipping Pink Panty Pull Downs (vodka-spiked pink lemonade). The main dining room, done up in Victorian saloon red and black, has whitewashed brick walls hung with Early American patchwork quilts. Upstairs is a cozy bar. There's also cafe seating on both levels. There is often live entertainment of the talent show variety going on in Underground, which can make dining in the courtyard area extremely loud. If this is the case, be sure to ask for a table inside.

Mick's is best known for solid casual fare, from snacks to full meals, but the best bets are the hefty burgers or chicken grills, in various incarnations, accompanied by fries or pasta salad. Their delicious twist on fried green tomatoes with roasted red bell pepper sauce and crumbled goat cheese will dazzle your taste buds (my grandma can't even make them this good). Daily pasta specials and salads are good, and the portions are generous. The honey walnut chicken salad and salmon salad are especially popular. There's also a pretty good kids' menu, making this a favorite for families. Whatever you order, leave room for the rich, silky-smooth chocolate cream pie topped with whipped cream, one of the most sinful chocolate desserts in town.

Mick's has additional locations, including one in Midtown at 557 Peachtree St. (✆ **404/875-6425**), one near Peachtree Center at 229 Peachtree St. (✆ **404/ 688-6425**), one on the main level of Lenox Square mall (✆ **404/262-6425**), and one in Buckhead at 2110 Peachtree Rd. (✆ **404/351-6425**). Hours vary by location, but takeout is available at each.

In Underground Atlanta (at the corner of Pryor and Alabama sts.). ✆ 404/525-2825. Reservations not accepted. Main courses $6–$16. AE, DC, DISC, MC, V. Mon–Thurs 11am–10pm; Fri–Sat 11am–11pm; Sun noon–9pm. MARTA: Five Points.

Thelma's Kitchen ✪ SOUTHERN/REGIONAL   Tucked into a storefront across Marietta Street from Georgia Tech, Thelma's is not a fancy place, but it's where you want to head for a typical Southern meal—fast becoming an endangered species in this increasingly cosmopolitan city. There are plastic tablecloths on the tables, and the general ambience is that of a grade-school cafeteria. But this is fried chicken as it was meant to be. Not mass-produced stuff that's more crust than bird, but big meaty pieces with just the right seasoning in the crispy skin. Chicken is the most popular dish, but there's also country-fried steak, barbecued ribs, fried or baked fish, and Brunswick stew, as well as different daily specials. A typical meal of two pieces of white-meat fried chicken, two vegetables, and corn bread costs $9. On the high end is rib-eye steak for $12.

A fresh vegetable plate is $4 for three veggies and cornbread. You'll find the likes of collard greens, black-eyed peas, rutabagas, steamed carrots, green beans, okra, and other vegetables, depending on the season. Sweet-potato soufflé or macaroni and cheese (a vegetable in the South) are $1.75 each. For dessert, try the coconut pie or banana pudding. There are Southern-style breakfasts here, too.

768 Marietta St. NW (just north of Means St.). ✆ 404/688-5855. Everything except rib-eye steaks under $9.25. No credit cards. Mon–Fri 7:30am–4:30pm; Sat 8am–3pm. Take the Howell Mill bus from downtown.

The Varsity 🅺🅸🅳🆂 AMERICAN   Atlanta grew up around the Varsity, the world's largest drive-in restaurant, opened in 1928 by Frank Gordy and today run by his daughter Nancy Simms. This fast-food mecca's greasy feasts are an essential element of the Atlanta experience. A 150-foot stainless-steel counter is the hub of the operation, behind which red-shirted cooks and counterpeople rush out thousands of orders. It's a constant chorus of "What'll ya have? What'll ya have?" with customer responses translated into such esoteric orders as "walk a dog sideways, bag of rags" (a hot dog with onions on the side and potato chips). It takes 200 employees to process the ton of onions, 2,500 pounds of potatoes, 2 miles of hot dogs, and 300 gallons of chili consumed here by throngs of hungry customers each day. The Varsity's interior is spartan, with seating in large, windowed rooms with Formica tables. Big TVs are always on.

Order up a slaw dog or a couple of chili burgers (they're only 2 oz. each), with fries, onion rings, and a frosted orange (it's a creamy frozen orange drink). Barbecued pork, homemade chicken salad, and deviled-egg sandwiches are other options. And since none of this is health food (though it's all fresh and made from scratch), don't resist the fried apple or peach pie á la mode for dessert.

61 North Ave. (at Spring St.). ✆ 404/881-1706. Everything under $5. No credit cards. Sun–Thurs 9am–11:30pm; Fri–Sat 9am–12:30am. Closed Thanksgiving and Christmas. MARTA: North Ave.

3 Midtown

Midtown is becoming a hotbed of development, with new businesses, apartments, and restaurants springing up constantly. This is the theater district, and several restaurants in this part of town are good pre-theater choices.

VERY EXPENSIVE

Bacchanalia ★★★ CONTEMPORARY AMERICAN   When Bacchanalia abandoned the cozy warmth of its pleasantly informal Buckhead cottage for a former meatpacking plant on the outskirts of an industrial area, some fans were nervous that it wouldn't survive in its new locale. But the edgier, airier, more sophisticated space hits just the right note, plus the food is better than ever, and now Bacchanalia has spread the joy by opening for lunch as well as dinner.

Owner-chefs Anne Quatrano and Cliff Harrison, who consistently win reams of accolades, serve a prix-fixe menu at both meals—three courses at lunch, four at dinner, with ample, excellent options in each course. The emphasis here is on using locally produced natural and organic ingredients whenever possible, from farmstead cheeses to heirloom tomatoes to Georgia blackberries. Everything is absolutely the freshest, and perfectly prepared. The blue crab fritter appetizer with avocado, citrus, and Thai pepper essence is a signature dish, a plump, sweet all-lump crab cake that is not to be missed, regardless of whatever else you choose from the menu. Fish is done especially well, and you might find seared Virginia striped bass or a delicately sautéed turbot. The dinner menu will also include meat and game, and perhaps a pasta, such as the goat cheese raviolis that are often on the summer list. A long-time dessert favorite is the warm Valrhona chocolate cake with vanilla bean ice cream, a flourless concoction that oozes a puddle of richness from its gooey middle. The American wine list is overflowing with excellent choices, and there's a full bar now, too. Service is smooth and professional, but it's also warm, inviting, and remarkably free of attitude.

This is one of the best restaurants in town, and reservations are difficult to come by, especially on the weekend. Reservations are taken up to a month in advance, so when planning a trip to Atlanta, this should be one of the first phone calls you make. When you come to Bacchanalia, be sure to save time for browsing Star Provisions, the upscale cook's market on the premises. Stocked with excellent meats, seafood, cheeses, wine, pastries, tableware, cookbooks, and other cooking accessories, it's worth a separate trip.

1198 Howell Mill Rd. (just north of Fourteenth St.). ✆ 404/365-0410. Reservations essential. Lunch chef's tasting menu $48 without wine, $68 with wine; dinner 4-course prix-fixe menu $58 (does not include wine, which can be ordered separately). AE, DC, MC, V. Lunch Wed–Sat 11:30am–1:30pm; dinner Mon–Sat. 6–9:30pm. Closed Christmas Eve to New Year's Eve and 2 weeks in summer. MARTA: Midtown.

EXPENSIVE

Colonnade ★ SOUTHERN/REGIONAL   This Atlanta institution, established in 1927, offers authentic Southern specialties, without any newfangled twists. (Thank goodness.) It has an enormous local clientele of devoted regulars—many of whom look like they might enjoy a birthday greeting from Willard Scott any day—and some of the waitstaff have worked here for decades. The Colonnade is unpretentious and comfortable, with most of the seating at butcher-block tables in a large room. A cozy bar with a working fireplace is a nice place to sit if you have to wait for a table—and you probably will.

At lunch or dinner, you can order fresh turkey and dressing (they roast about a dozen a day), ham in redeye gravy, or roast leg of lamb, all served with a choice of two fresh vegetables (whipped potatoes, black-eyed peas, macaroni and cheese, sweet-potato soufflé, collard greens, fried okra, etc.). The fried chicken is some of the best in town—four huge pieces done the way Mama used to make it. The homemade yeast rolls and new whole wheat rolls will melt in your mouth. In addition to menu listings, there are economical blue-plate specials and fancier offerings ranging from corned beef and cabbage to frogs' legs. Fish is done exceptionally well. The portions are huge, and it's doubtful you'll have room for dessert. But if you decide to squeeze it in, the butterscotch meringue and banana pudding will satisfy any sweet tooth.

1879 Cheshire Bridge Rd. NE (between Wellborne Dr. and Manchester St.). © **404/874-5642.** Reservations not accepted. Lunch items $5–$16; dinner main courses $6–$29. No credit cards; personal checks accepted. Wed–Sat 11:30am–2:30pm; Mon–Thurs 5–9pm; Fri–Sat 5–10pm; Sun 11:30am–9pm. MARTA: Midtown.

Eno ★★ EUROPEAN/MEDITERRANEAN   Located in Midtown near several theaters and within walking distance of the Fox, Eno is the perfect place to stop for a pre- or post-theater dinner. It's actually two restaurants in one: a posh dining room for leisurely dinners, and a wine bar, where it's possible to feast on small plates and appetizers. There are two different menus for the two parts of Eno, and different wine lists, too. In the bar, the 100-odd selections are available by the taste, glass, or bottle, and in the dining room, nearly twice that number is available.

While dinner is a first-rate food and wine experience, the wine bar, with its more casual attitude, is a lot more fun, though you can easily snack and sip your way into a pretty hefty bill. The goodies range from a delectable butternut squash tortelli appetizer with brown butter and sage to whole roasted fish of the day with roasted fennel and potatoes and singed black olives. Regardless of which way you choose to dine, be sure to save room for the delicate fig and apple tart for dessert.

800 Peachtree St. (at the corner of Fifth St.). © **404/685-3191.** Reservations recommended for the dining room. Small plates and appetizers $5–$13; main courses $16–$25. AE, DC, DISC, MC. Tue–Fri 11:30am–4pm; Tue–Thurs 5:30–10pm; Fri–Sat 5:30–11pm; wine bar remains open between lunch and dinner. MARTA: North Ave.

South City Kitchen ★ CONTEMPORARY SOUTHERN   Fronted by a brick patio lined with pear trees, South City Kitchen is set in a converted two-story house. It's a bright space with light filtering through large windows, and a bustling exhibition kitchen serves as a visual focus. There's a lot of meeting and greeting here, and the place can be a little loud, but the crowd of well-dressed professionals (sometimes four and five deep at the small bar) seems to thrive on the buzz. If the weather's nice, try the patio, which is more sedate and a great people-watching spot.

The seasonally changing menu reflects widely varied Southern influences. If you're not in the mood for a full meal or want to do a little post-theater nosh-ing, this is a good destination. There are several options for light fare, such as the she-crab soup (a perennial favorite), and side dishes can be ordered a la carte. If you've never tried grits, this is a good time to take the plunge; the cheese-laced grits are exceptional.

Entrees are likely to range from jerk pork tenderloin to shrimp and scallops with garlic gravy over grits. A basket of freshly baked buttermilk biscuits and corn muffins accompanies all main courses. This is also a good stop for Sunday brunch, where you'll find everything from vanilla-buttermilk pancakes to a fried egg BLT. The wine list includes small signature acquisitions, plus about 20 wines available by the glass.

Dining in Midtown, Virginia-Highland & Little Five Points

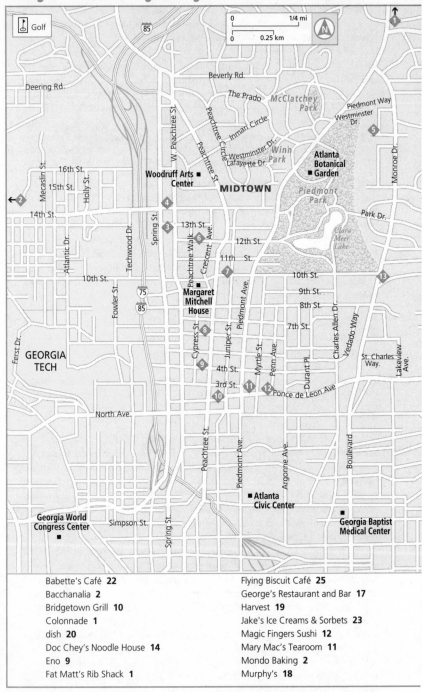

Babette's Café **22**
Bacchanalia **2**
Bridgetown Grill **10**
Colonnade **1**
dish **20**
Doc Chey's Noodle House **14**
Eno **9**
Fat Matt's Rib Shack **1**

Flying Biscuit Café **25**
George's Restaurant and Bar **17**
Harvest **19**
Jake's Ice Creams & Sorbets **23**
Magic Fingers Sushi **12**
Mary Mac's Tearoom **11**
Mondo Baking **2**
Murphy's **18**

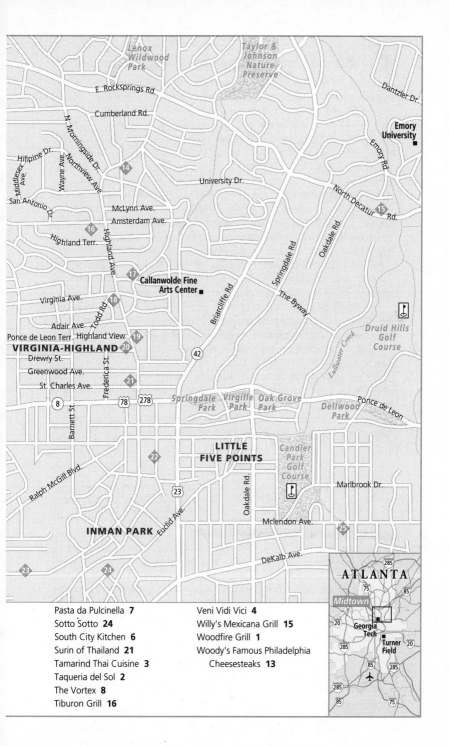

Pasta da Pulcinella **7**
Sotto Sotto **24**
South City Kitchen **6**
Surin of Thailand **21**
Tamarind Thai Cuisine **3**
Taqueria del Sol **2**
The Vortex **8**
Tiburon Grill **16**

Veni Vidi Vici **4**
Willy's Mexicana Grill **15**
Woodfire Grill **1**
Woody's Famous Philadelphia
  Cheesesteaks **13**

True Grits

In the South, a good ol' country breakfast isn't complete unless it includes grits. It's a staple here, kind of like potatoes are in the rest of the world, and we think everybody else is downright foolish for preferring hash browns or home fries to a heaven-sent bowl of buttered grits. Celestine Sibley, the late *Atlanta Journal-Constitution* columnist, called grits "nature's finest gift to mankind." And Celestine always told it like it was.

Grits are simply crushed kernels of dried corn. A trendier cousin, polenta, is the same thing, just more finely ground and cleaned of all traces of flour. If you've had grits and thought they were bland and tasteless, you probably just didn't have them prepared right. They can be yellow or white (usually white), but the best are stone ground and long-cooking (never instant), boiled with water and salt into a thick porridge and slathered with a big slab of real butter. If you want to expose yourself to ridicule—and ruin your grits—top them with sugar and milk, which is something akin to pouring gravy over a hot fudge sundae.

The beauty of grits is that they soak up flavors like a sponge, allowing them to travel easily from breakfast to dinner. Chicken broth or a little piece of country ham can transform a whole pot, and although many purists gnash their teeth at the thought, some folks cook their grits in milk or cream.

The best addition by far is a little cheese, which turns grits into the ultimate Southern comfort food. Sharp cheddar has been traditional for years, especially in a cheese grits casserole, but goat cheese added to grits transforms them into a tangy, creamy wonder, sinful and sophisticated enough dish to serve at a fancy dinner party.

1144 Crescent Ave. (between Eleventh and Fourteenth sts.). © **404/873-7358.** Reservations recommended. Lunch items $7.95–$13.95; brunch items $8.25–$14.95; dinner main courses $13.75–$20.95. AE, DC, MC, V. Daily 11am–3:30pm; Mon–Thurs 5–11pm; Fri–Sat 5pm–midnight; Sun 5–10pm. MARTA: Arts Center.

Tamarind Thai Cuisine ★★ *Finds* THAI   If you like Thai, you'll love Tamarind. And if you've never tried Thai food, this is the place to start. Tamarind is a serious, upscale restaurant, and the quality is higher than you'll find in most other Thai restaurants in the city. Located close to Georgia Tech, it's a favorite among the faculty there, and popular among others who appreciate excellent, authentically prepared ethnic cuisine.

Tamarind's is in an odd location—practically next to the downtown expressway—and the exterior doesn't give many clues about the delights that lurk within. But once inside, you'll find white tablecloths, fresh flowers, sophisticated decor, and impeccable service. It's a good choice for a romantic evening, business lunch, or pre-theater dinner.

The menu includes all the usual Thai standbys—pad-Thai, chicken-coconut milk soup, fresh basil rolls, curries, and so on—and even the most ordinary dishes are carefully prepared and artfully presented. If you try some of the more inventive dishes, you won't be disappointed. For instance, the *neua yang nam tok,* or "waterfall beef," consists of tender strips of steak marinated in tamarind and chile peppers and cooked with shallots, sesame seeds, and mint leaves. Keep in mind that Thai cuisine is designed to stimulate the five Thai taste senses: sweet, sour, neutral, salty, and hot. And they do mean hot. Tamarind doesn't skimp on the chiles, and many of their dishes are downright fiery. Be sure to pay attention to the "hotness guide" on the menu.

80 Fourteenth St. (at Spring St.). ℂ **404/873-4888**. Reservations recommended. Entrees $9.95–$26.95. AE, MC, V. Mon–Fri 11:30am–2:30pm; Mon–Thurs 5:30–10pm; Fri 5:30–11 pm; Sat 5–11pm; Sun 5–10pm. MARTA: Arts Center.

Veni Vidi Vici ★★ AUTHENTIC ITALIAN This elegant theater-district restaurant manages to create an intimate feeling in a 5,000-square-foot space. Cutting-edge design (handsome cherry wood wine cabinets, stenciled oak flooring, and sophisticated track lighting that replaces the glow of candles with a pinpoint splash of light on each table) complements the bustling exhibition rotisserie kitchen.

The specialties here are *piatti piccoli* (small plates, such as skewers of shrimp or prosciutto and pear, traditionally served with cocktails), fresh handmade pastas, and meat or seafood from the wood-fired rotisserie and grill. It's easy to make a meal of the piatti piccoli or other appetizers, but the pastas are so lovely it's a shame to pass them up. Especially good is the house specialty—linguine with plump Little Neck clams in a white or spicy red sauce. There are other excellent traditional dishes, such as risotto, osso buco, and veal scaloppine. The well-chosen wine list is almost 100% Italian.

41 Fourteenth St. (between W. Peachtree and Spring sts.). ℂ **404/875-8424**. Reservations recommended. *Piatti piccoli* $6.50; lunch items $9.95–$13.75; dinner pastas $12.50–$14.75; dinner main courses $15–$27. AE, DC, DISC, MC, V. Mon–Thurs 11:30am–11pm; Fri 11am–midnight; Sat 5pm–midnight; Sun 5–10pm. MARTA: Arts Center.

Woodfire Grill ★★ NORTHERN CALIFORNIAN For those of us who cried when Chef/Owner Michael Tuohy closed down Chefs Café . . . he's baaaaack. Woodfire Grill is his new baby, and it is one classy joint. Opened in August 2002, Woodfire is beautiful but a bit noisy. From the beautiful copper bar inside the entrance, the warm sights and sounds of Woodfire envelop diners, but the hard wood seats leave a little to be desired (pillows are available). The marble cheese-and-bread carving table is interesting. In fact, there is a resident cheese expert on staff here (no joke). Entering the dining room you'll find the wood-fired grill and rotisserie in plain view, providing dinner theater of sorts for diners whose tables are in the vicinity. Private dining is available.

Tuohy utilizes his West Coast connection and has dubbed Woodfire's cuisine "Northern Californian." Woodfire uses the freshest produce, much of which is organically grown. Meats, seafood, and artisan cheeses are also top quality. Especially popular is "Rocky the free-range chicken", served on a platter to share. The menu changes daily, so no matter how often you dine here, you'll always find something different. Tastes and small plates might include something as simple as a bowl of marinated olives or something more intriguing, such as organic squash blossoms stuffed with chevre, arugula, and zinfandel vinegar. The Maine lobster woodfire pizza with red onion, cream cheese, and capers is an excellent choice for one or two. Other entrees range from wood-grilled Carolina quail and spiced acorn squash to Columbia River sturgeon with sweet potato hash. Woodfire boasts quite an impressive wine list, most of which are available by the glass. An after dinner cheese service is available with three or five choices. The desserts are quite frou-frou, but you probably won't have room anyway.

1782 Cheshire Bridge Rd. © **404/347-9055.** www.woodfiregrill.com. Reservations recommended. Tastes and small plates $4–$11; pizzas $13–$18; entrees $18–$27; platters to share $28–$32. AE, DC, DISC, MC, V. Mon–Thurs 5:30–10:30pm; Fri–Sat 5:30–11pm. Complimentary valet parking. MARTA: Lindbergh.

MODERATE

Bridgetown Grill CARIBBEAN If you're going to a show at the Fox The-atre, this is a good place for a casual dinner. It's right across the street, and if you alert your waiter, they'll whisk you in and out in time for the show. There's not much fancy about Bridgetown. It has a laid-back attitude and decor reminiscent of the tropics, with reggae music, Haitian folk art, and a pleasant covered open-air porch. The thing to order here is spicy jerk chicken, served four different ways: in a burrito; grilled in a sandwich; as a main dish served with raspberry coulis (like all entrees, it comes with cucumber salad, black beans, and rice); or in a salad tossed with greens, cheese, and tropical fruit. Also worth trying are the guava–barbecued ribs and the sautéed chipotle shrimp. There's a full bar, but the house specialty is a frozen "mangorita" made with mango nectar. Very beachy.

There's another Bridgetown Grill in Buckhead at Piedmont Rd. (at Peachtree), © **404/266-1500;** one in Duluth (© **770/622-0212**); and another in Sandy Springs (© **770/394-1575**).

689 Peachtree St. NE (just north of Ponce De Leon Ave.). © **404/873-2996.** Reservations not accepted. Lunch items $4–$13; dinner main courses $8–$14. AE, DC, DISC, MC, V. Sun–Thurs 11am–10pm; Fri–Sat 11am–11pm. Dinner menu begins at 4pm. MARTA: North Avenue.

Magic Fingers Sushi ★★ SUSHI Though you'll hear this place referred to as M.F. Sushi, I wanted to give you the heads up as to what the M.F. stands for, just so you aren't shocked. Atlanta finally has a real live, honest-to-goodness sushi bar. Chef Chris Kinjo has worked his magic fingers all around the country, and his brother Alex takes care of greeting the guests as they enter this fusion fantasy. Whether you choose to sit at the sushi bar and keep a close eye on the action, or at one of the many tables, you'll be privy to a sushi menu unlike any you've ever seen. It's all there—sashimi from tuna to yellowtail, mackerel to eel. Don't wait until you're starving to show up here, though, because you might wait a while if it's crowded, especially on the weekends (typical Atlanta dining problem).

265 Ponce de Leon Ave. © **404/815-8844.** Reservations recommended. Nigiri sushi $.50–$10.50 for 2 pieces; rolls $4–$15. AE, D, MC, V. Mon–Fri 11:30am–2:30pm; Mon–Thurs 5:30–10:30pm; Fri–Sat 5:30–11:30pm. Valet parking. MARTA: North Ave.

One Midtown Kitchen ★ CONTEMPORARY AMERICAN You'll think you're in the heart of New York when you dine at renowned restaurateur Bob Amick's newest creation, both delicious and not too pricy (someone finally fig-ured it out). Even the chef, Kevin Reilly, is a New Yorker, and his menu ranges from the frou-frou to the very simple. Excellent choices would be grilled white salmon with bitter greens and fresh oranges or the wood-roasted striped bass with baby artichokes. Hugely popular is the "three from the garden" vegetable sampler that changes with the season. On this platter, the kitchen might tingle the taste buds with roasted cauliflower or baked artichokes. The restaurant also specializes in cold-water oysters accompanied by specialty sauces such as Peppar vodka Mignonette. The wine list is eclectic and affordable and the atmosphere is high energy—maybe the high spirits are left over from the restaurant's previous life as a swinging club. Located on the edge of Piedmont Park, One takes the cake when it comes to creativity in powder rooms (you'll see what I mean). This is becom-ing a fast favorite of locals, especially the younger crowd still working their way up the ladder to six figures. The late-night hours on weekends make this a great place for dining after clubbing.

559 Dutch Valley Rd. NE. © **404/892-4111**. Reservations recommended. Starters $5–$11; entrees $14–$19. AE, MC, V. Mon–Thurs 5:30pm–midnight; Fri–Sat 5:30pm–1am; Sun 11am-2:30pm and 5:30–10pm. Valet parking. MARTA: Midtown.

Pasta da Pulcinella ⭐ *Value* REGIONAL ITALIAN   Pasta da Pulcinella has been known for years as a humble hole-in-the-wall serving up great pasta at rock-bottom prices. Some things have changed since the restaurant moved into new digs. Tucked away in a charming but crowded cottage now, the interior is fancier, but still casual, with table service and a full bar. Prices are fancier, too, but they're still sensible. Though the lunch service was dropped following the move, it has since returned on weekdays only. What has stayed the same is a commitment to excellent pastas, made from scratch and beautifully presented with a surprising and innovative combination of flavors in each concoction.

The most popular dish is *tortelli di mele*—plump round pasta filled with sweet Italian sausage, browned Granny Smith apples, and parmesan, then topped with browned butter and sage. There are nightly entree specials each day, but your best bet is to stick with the pastas or risottos. There is a small selection of Italian wines that changes often. Pulcinella is near a number of theaters and is an easy pre-theater stop.

1123 Peachtree Walk (off Peachtree near Eleventh St.). © **404/876-1114**. Reservations accepted weekends for groups of 5 or more. Main courses $7.95–$10.95. MC, V. Lunch Mon–Fri 11:30am–2pm; dinner Sun–Thurs 5:30–10pm; Fri–Sat 5:30–11pm. MARTA: North Ave.

INEXPENSIVE

Fat Matt's Rib Shack BARBECUE   This blues and barbecue shack is a favorite among locals who like their ribs as smoky as their music. Don't expect much in the way of decor. This is truly a shack, where patrons order up at the counter, then sit elbow-to-elbow at plastic-topped tables while chowing down on pork ribs, barbecued chicken, or pulled pork sandwiches. There are sides of coleslaw, baked beans, and Brunswick stew—a Southern concoction that's a cross between a thick gravy and a thicker meat stew. Snack on an "appetizer" of peanuts in the shell, washed down with an ice-cold beer, while waiting for your order.

Live music—authentic blues by a variety of local and regional groups—starts every night around 8pm. People pack into the small space, and it's usually standing room only, especially on weekends, so come early if you want to see the show.

1811 Piedmont Rd. (a few blocks south of Cheshire Bridge Rd.). © **404/607-1622**. Reservations not accepted. Ribs and chicken $3.75–$16; chopped pork sandwiches $3.75. No credit cards. Mon–Thurs 11:30am–11:30pm; Fri–Sat 11:30am–12:30am; Sun 2–11:30pm. MARTA: Lindbergh.

Jake's Ice Cream & Sorbets ICE CREAM   Ice cream just doesn't get any better than this. Jake's has a true following in Atlanta and devoted fans will stand in line, outside, in the freezing cold and rain if that is what it takes to get the goods. Among the most popular flavors are Chocolate Slap Yo' Mama, the seasonal Honey Fig, the new White House cherry flavored ice cream, a delicious Tiramisu Su Sudio and the signature Brown Sugar Vanilla. Scoops are generous and can be enjoyed while lounging in one of a catacomb of small rooms, either on a couch or in overstuffed chairs by the fireplace. Jake's is also a good place to go for lunch, as the healthy menu includes great sandwiches, such as homemade chicken salad made with nonfat yogurt, honey, apples and pecans. Vegetarians—and those who eat like vegetarians on occasion - will likely enjoy the roasted peppers, goat cheese and Portobello mushroom sandwich.

676 Highland Ave. © **404/523-1830.** Mon–Thurs and Sun 11am–10pm; Fri–Sat 11am–11pm; lunch items $3.95–$7.95; MARTA: Five Points.

Mary Mac's Tea Room ⭐ SOUTHERN/REGIONAL   Mary Mac's is a colorful Atlanta institution, a bastion of classic Southern cuisine that has been patronized since 1945 by everyone from truck drivers to bank presidents. Jimmy Carter sometimes came by for lunch when he was governor. You'll find a glass of pencils on your table; check off menu items you desire (they change daily) and hand your selections to your server.

Now opening bright and early, customers can get a rib-sticking southern cooked breakfast featuring country ham, grits, and several omelet choices. Among the famous lunch and dinner entrees are fried chicken dredged in buttermilk and flour, country-fried steak, and chicken pan pie topped with thick giblet gravy. Steaks, chops, and burgers all come with a choice of side dishes, including expertly prepared fresh veggies. You might also select corn bread with *pot likker* (ham broth made with turnip greens), black-eyed peas, fried green tomatoes, whipped potatoes, fried okra, macaroni and cheese, or sweet-potato soufflé. Fresh-from-the-oven corn and yeast rolls are served with lunches; at night, there are hot cinnamon rolls, too. Desserts include peach cobbler and banana pudding—a favorite with locals. There's a full bar, but the drink of choice is sweet tea (sweetened ice tea). Mary Mac's can seat groups of up to 150.

224 Ponce de Leon Ave. NE (at Myrtle St.). © **404/876-1800.** Reservations accepted for more than 10. Breakfasts average $7; lunch $7–$15; dinner $9–$17. AE, MC, V. Mon–Sat 11am–8:30pm; Sun 11am–3pm. MARTA: North Ave.

Mondo Baking *Value* CREATIVE AMERICAN/ITALIAN/CAFE/BAKERY Mondo Baking is a casual retro-style cafe/dessert bakery with excellent coffee and an impressive array of periodicals for sale. It has built a solid customer base as a place with good food where you won't be hurried along even if you only come in to linger over a cup of coffee or browse the magazines (at least 200 different publications).

Everything is served with a creative twist, from the prosciutto and brie sandwich, studded with chopped dates and dressed with peppery arugula, to the lemon love bars. Bowing to less sophisticated tastes, there's PB&J or grilled cheese for the kids.

Breakfast Monday through Friday consists of breakfast sandwiches and fresh baked goods such as strawberry-lemon or plum-cardamom scones. Breakfast is bigger and better on Saturday, when it's served until noon. There's always a blue-plate special, homemade granola, and a vegetarian omelet variation—maybe with brie, roasted yellow peppers, and onions.

750 Huff Rd. NW. © **404/603-9995.** Breakfast $2.50–$5.75. Sandwiches $4.75–$6. AE, MC, V. Mon 8am–4pm; Tues–Fri 8am–5pm; Sat 9am–5pm. From I-75, take the 14th St. exit and head west to Howell Mill Rd. Turn right on Howell Mill. Mondo is a few blocks up on the left at the corner of Huff Rd.

Taqueria del Sol ⭐ SOUTHWESTERN   This is what fast food ought to be—fast and good, not to mention affordable. Taqueria del Sol resembles an extremely well-dressed taco stand, with inventive tacos, enchiladas, side dishes, soups, and chilis. You put together your own "plate," ordering as much or as little as you like. There is usually only one complete special for lunch and one or two for dinner; otherwise, you're on your own to come up with a creative combination. The lunch and dinner specials might include a southwestern interpretation of a southern dish, such as boneless fried chicken with ancho mashed potatoes, low country gravy, serrano chile sauce, and turnip greens.

But it's more fun to use your own imagination, picking a couple of tacos (the fish taco is a standout), an enchilada, and maybe a side of the addictive jalapeño cole slaw. There are 25 or so different kinds of beer to wash it all down, and a full bar. Don't expect table service, and do expect to wait during prime time, but the inconveniences are small, especially if you can snag a table on the covered patio.

1200-B Howell Mill Rd. NW. ℂ 404/352-5811. Lunch specials around $8; enchiladas $2.95, tacos $1.95, sides and soups $1.65–$1.95; dinner specials around $12. AE, MC, V. Mon–Fri 11am–2pm; Sat noon–3pm; Tues–Thurs 5:30–9pm; Fri–Sat 5:30–10pm. From I-75, take the 14th St. exit and head west to Howell Mill Rd. Turn right on Howell Mill. The restaurant is a few blocks up on the left, just before Huff Rd. MARTA: North Ave.

The Vortex *Kids* AMERICAN   The laughing skull logo should give you a clue that this is a wild little bar and grill with a big attitude. If you're easily offended, don't go. Or at least don't read the "stuff you really need to know" on the back of the menu, which, among other things, decrees the restaurant an Idiot-Free Zone and suggests you don't get a knot in your shorts if you aren't served within 5 minutes. There's all kinds of weird flea market stuff all over the walls, which should fascinate children, teenagers, and easily amused adults.

Attitude aside, this is the place to come for a big, fat, juicy chargrilled burger, one of the best in town. There's plenty here, too, for non-carnivores, including soups, generous sandwiches, and fresh salads. If you don't want a beef burger, you can substitute a turkey burger, chicken breast, veggie burger, or black bean burger for a nominal charge. There's a full bar, out-of-the-ordinary soft drinks, and more kinds of beer than you can imagine. There's another Vortex at 438 Moreland Ave., in Little Five Points (ℂ **404/688-1828**).

878 Peachtree St. NE. ℂ **404/875-1667**. Weekend brunch menu served Sat–Sun 11am–3pm $7–$9; sandwiches $3.95–$6.95; burgers $6–$8. AE, MC, V. Mon–Sat 11am–2am; Sun 11am–midnight. MARTA: Midtown.

Willy's Mexicana Grill ✦ MEXICAN   Voted Atlanta's best burritos, Willy's isn't exactly a place you'd take someone you really want to impress. However, if it's a close friend who doesn't judge you by the joints you hang out in, this is the place to go when you want a burrito. Almost like a Subway experience, you'll stand in line and direct the construction of your burrito as you first select the type of tortilla to hold it all together. Meat options include green mole chicken, grilled cilantro garlic steak, chipotle barbecue pork, grilled chicken, and even marinated tofu. Next, pile on the goodies, including rice, black beans, roasted peppers, and all your typical burrito toppings. Nachos, quesadillas, tacos . . . Willy's has the basic menu down. They also offer a few domestic and imported beers. Once you've got the goods, choose a booth along the brightly decorated wall or go outside where it's a bit less hectic. This place has the freshest salsa I've ever tasted, though it lacked the liquid to hold it all together. There are two more Willy's, located at 235 Peachtree St. NE (ℂ **404/524-0821**), and 4377 Roswell Rd. NE. (ℂ **404/252-2235**).

2074 N. Decatur Rd. ℂ **404/321-6060**. Burritos $4.90–$5.75. No credit cards. Mon–Sun 11am–10pm. Located on the square in Decatur by the courthouse.

Woody's Famous Philadelphia Cheesesteaks AMERICAN   Gourmet it ain't, but if you and the kids are all tuckered out from a romp in nearby Piedmont Park, walk on over to this casual little spot for lunch. It's barely bigger than a glorified hot dog stand, but serves up excellent Philly cheese steaks, Italian subs, Polish sausages, and hot dogs. The ordering line (there's no table service) often snakes all the way out the door, so arrive at off-peak hours or be prepared to wait. There are just five small booths inside, but the best place to sit on a nice day is the covered deck—perfect for enjoying an orange freeze or one of Woody's extra-thick, old-fashioned milkshakes.

981 Monroe Dr. NE (at Tenth St.). ℂ 404/876-1939. Hot dogs and sandwiches $2–$5. Cash only. Tues–Sat 11am–5pm. MARTA: North Ave.

4 Buckhead

Buckhead contains most of Atlanta's posh dining choices. Keep in mind that this is *the* area to dine, so plan in advance where you might like to go, so you can get your reservations made in time for your trip.

VERY EXPENSIVE

Abruzzi Ristorante ★★ ITALIAN   Situated in an unlikely spot—a strip shopping center with a hardware store on one side and a five-and-dime on the other—is one of the city's finest Italian restaurants. It's upscale, hearty, New York–Italian, both in ambience and cuisine. Owner Nico Petrucci himself is likely to greet you as a long-lost friend, and the rest of the staff will smother you with attention. You'll want to dress up and ask for one of the flower-decked banquettes, a perfect spot for a special occasion. It's also a great vantage point from which to watch all the goings-on in the main dining area.

Fresh pastas are a specialty, and all of them are excellent. If lobster fra diavolo is a special, don't pass it up. The Thursday night special is osso buco with saffron risotto, but if you call a day ahead, the chef will prepare it for you any day of the week. In fact, if you don't see exactly what you want on the menu, just ask. Special requests are seen as a challenge rather than an inconvenience, especially if there's a little advance notice. Traditional dessert favorites are tiramisu and rich New York–style cheesecake, but there's plenty more to choose from on the dessert cart. The award-winning selection of Italian wines is one of the best in the city. If Abruzzi is too much for your budget, try Pasta Vino (p. 134), an ultra-casual outpost run by Petrucci's son, Billy, in the same shopping center.

2355 Peachtree Rd. NE (in the Peachtree Battle Shopping Center at Peachtree Battle Ave.). ℂ 404/261-8186. Reservations recommended. Lunch items $12.50–$30; dinner main courses $14.50–$36.95. AE, DISC, MC, V. Mon–Fri 11:30am–2pm; Mon–Thurs 5:30–10pm; Fri–Sat 5:30–10:30pm. MARTA: Lenox or Buckhead.

Bone's ★★★ SEAFOOD/STEAK   Atlanta's best and most famous steakhouse, Bone's is a top power-lunch venue for the expense-account crowd, who are provided with notepads and phones at the midday meal. As many deals as steaks are cut here, and the place is rich with celebrity lore. When Bob Hope dined here, everyone respected his privacy until he rose to leave; then the entire dining room gave him a standing ovation. And during his presidency, George Bush came in for dinner one night, booking six surrounding tables for Secret Service men (they ate too). The setting is traditional masculine-clubby.

As noted for its seafood as for its steaks and chops, Bone's flies Maine lobsters in daily and serves fresh Gulf Coast crabmeat and shrimp. There is prime-aged, corn-fed Iowa beef, hand cut on the premises, always prepared exactly as ordered. Thick, juicy lamb chops are excellent alternatives to the beef. Lighter entrees are available at lunch, along with salads, sandwiches, and soups.

The wine gallery at Bone's houses over 500 selections; international in scope, it highlights French and Californian wines. Ultra-rich desserts include "Mountain-high Pie"—layers of chocolate chip, rum raisin, and vanilla ice cream.

3130 Piedmont Rd. NE (a half-block below Peachtree Rd.). ℂ 404/237-2663. Reservations essential. Lunch items $10.95–$34.95; dinner main courses $23.95–$45. AE, DC, DISC, MC, V. Mon–Fri 12–2:30pm; Sun–Thurs 5:30–10pm; Fri–Sat 5:30–11pm. Closed most major holidays. MARTA: Lindbergh.

Book your air, hotel, and transportation all in one place.

Hotel or hostel? Cruise or canoe? Car? Plane? Camel? Wherever you're going, visit Yahoo! Travel and get total control over your arrangements. Even choose your seat assignment. So. One hump or two? travel.yahoo.com

powered by **COMPAQ**

YAHOO!
Travel

Chops and The Lobster Bar ★★ SEAFOOD/STEAK   Apparently Chops, a popular Atlanta steakhouse, wasn't decadent enough. A few years ago, they added the Lobster Bar downstairs to the mix. Steaks are the specialty at Chops, but lobster and other seafood are available. Lobster is the main attraction in the Lobster Bar, but you can also order the steaks and chops from upstairs.

The steakhouse is an extremely elegant version of the clubby genre—definitely macho, but less so than its arch rival, Bone's (above). Still, this is power dining at its best and seats are much in demand, so reserve in advance. Tri-level seating is in comfortable upholstered armchairs or roomy banquettes. Meat entrees require a hefty wallet and a hearty appetite for the likes of a 24- or 48-ounce porterhouse steak, a 20-ounce New York strip, triple-cut loin lamb chops, salt and garlic crusted prime rib, and so on. There are traditional a la carte side dishes such as creamed spinach, jumbo asparagus hollandaise, cottage fries, or onion rings. You won't need dessert, which is just as well since they're nothing special. A large selection of wines is available, and at lunch, hefty sandwiches are an option.

The elegant Art Deco Lobster Bar is reminiscent of the Oyster Bar in New York's Grand Central Station. The menu is a blend of Chops' power steaks and seafood items, with new seafood additions. Lobster is prepared just about every way imaginable—lobster fingers, lobster cocktail, baked lobster oreganato, lobster bisque, fried lobster tail, steamed lobster. You get the picture. The star of the menu, though, is the crab lobster entree, one or two Maine 1-pounders prepared six different ways. For the purist, there is good old live Maine lobster (3–9 lb.), steamed and cracked. And for those who don't like lobster (what are you doing here, anyway?), there's a wide variety of impeccably prepared fish, shrimp, and crab. Stone crab claws are popular during winter months.

70 W. Paces Ferry Rd. (at Peachtree Rd.). (℃ **404/262-2675.** www.buckheadrestaurants.com. Reservations highly recommended. Lunch items $8.50–$14.95; dinner main courses $15.75–$45; market prices for lobster. AE, DC, DISC, MC, V. Mon–Fri 11:30am–2:30pm; Mon–Thurs 5:30–11pm; Fri–Sat 5:30pm–midnight; Sun 5:30–10pm. The Lobster Bar is open only for dinner, but large group lunches can be arranged. MARTA: Lindbergh.

The Dining Room ★★★ FRENCH/MEDITERRANEAN   For 11 years, The Dining Room was the domain of the nationally celebrated Guenter Seeger, and when he left to open his own restaurant, the hotel management launched an international search for a new chef.

Enter Bruno Menard—direct from a Ritz kitchen in Japan, where he adopted strong Asian techniques and flavors in his cooking, so much so that he wields stainless steel chopsticks in the kitchen. He's found his zone in Atlanta and in The Dining Room, where patrons come expecting a fantastic experience and never leave disappointed. From service to cuisine, it doesn't get much better than this. How about lamb loin coated in coffee grounds, or the squab and figs? Menard often pushes the envelope when concocting his culinary dreams, such as the Jordan almonds that he chops and uses as a topper for foie gras (yes, Jordan almonds are those candy movie theater almonds).

An impeccable cheese service is available, as well as a host of desserts, including a cart filled with chocolatier Good Ship Lollypop treats. Among the specialties is a Cuban chocolate tart—very rich but very worth it. Share the experience with a dining partner.

Service, of course, is impeccable, and the room is elegantly comfortable.

Buckhead Dining

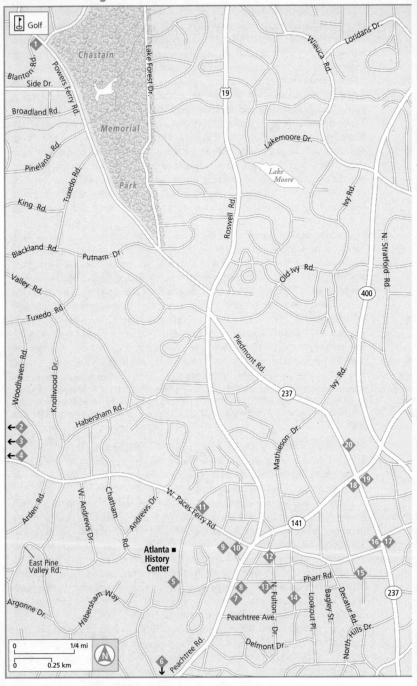

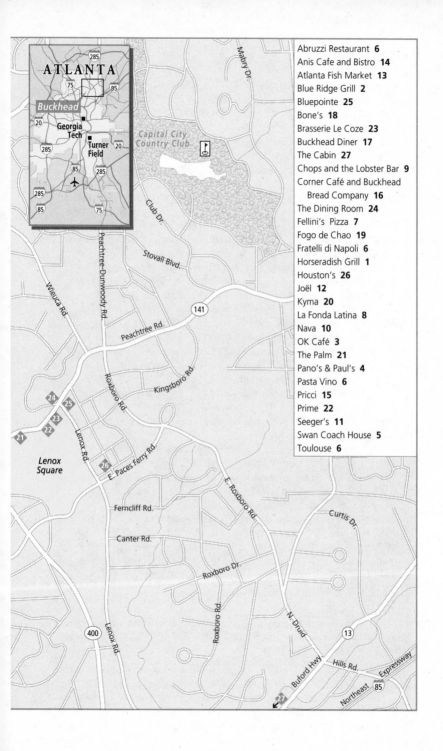

Abruzzi Restaurant **6**
Anis Cafe and Bistro **14**
Atlanta Fish Market **13**
Blue Ridge Grill **2**
Bluepointe **25**
Bone's **18**
Brasserie Le Coze **23**
Buckhead Diner **17**
The Cabin **27**
Chops and the Lobster Bar **9**
Corner Café and Buckhead
    Bread Company **16**
The Dining Room **24**
Fellini's Pizza **7**
Fogo de Chao **19**
Fratelli di Napoli **6**
Horseradish Grill **1**
Houston's **26**
Joël **12**
Kyma **20**
La Fonda Latina **8**
Nava **10**
OK Café **3**
The Palm **21**
Pano's & Paul's **4**
Pasta Vino **6**
Pricci **15**
Prime **22**
Seeger's **11**
Swan Coach House **5**
Toulouse **6**

Picnic Fare & Picnic Spots

There's plenty of opportunity to picnic in Atlanta, and loads of outdoor spots to spread your picnic blanket. Good bets include Piedmont Park in Midtown, Georgia's Stone Mountain Park, and Grant Park. And here are some places that can help you round up a great picnic lunch:

Alon's Bakery, 1394 N. Highland Ave. NE (© **404/872-6000**), has loads of delectable baked goods for a snack (some of the best pastries in town), and a variety of made-to-order sandwiches at reasonable prices. Try the garlic-roasted lamb or the Tuscany (goat cheese, arugula, roasted eggplant). There's also a selection of interesting, easily portable side dishes and salads.

The BREADGARDEN, 549–5 Amsterdam Ave. (© **404/875-1166**), is tucked away on a little dead-end street, but it's worth seeking out, especially if you want to picnic in nearby Piedmont Park. This shop started out as a retail bread store, but it now serves up sandwiches on its incomparable freshly baked breads. You can design your own sandwich, but it's hard to come up with anything better than the Mediterranean vegetarian—goat cheese, roasted red peppers, tomatoes, Kalamata olives, eggplant, and olive spread on whole grain bread.

In south Buckhead, the **Bread Market,** 1937 Peachtree Rd. NE (© **404/352-5252**), has a variety of baked goods and breads, entree salads, and sandwiches. There are always special lunch sandwiches in addition to the usual combinations.

Located adjacent to the Corner Café, the upscale **Buckhead Bread Company,** 3070 Piedmont Rd. (© **404/240-1978**), offers unusual sandwiches to go, as well as authentic French pastries that taste as good as they look.

In the heart of Buckhead, **EatZi's Market and Bakery,** 3221 Peachtree Rd. NE (just south of Piedmont Rd.; © **404/237-2266**), boasts that it has more than 1,800 daily choices to take home. Hard to believe, but this is a huge store dedicated to takeout, with everything from bread and wine to main dishes and desserts.

Located in an industrial area that is fast becoming a shopping and dining destination, **Mondo Baking,** 750 Huff Rd. NW. (© **404/603-9995**), may be off the beaten path, but it's worth seeking out for inventive sandwich combinations and delectable homemade pastries. They even make a kid-pleasing peanut butter and jelly.

At the Ritz-Carlton Buckhead, 3434 Peachtree Rd. NE (at Lenox Rd.). © **404/237-2700**. Reservations essential, and as far in advance as possible. Prix-fixe dinner $68 and $82. AE, DC, DISC, MC, V. Mon–Sat 6–9:30pm. MARTA: Lenox or Buckhead.

Fogo de Chao ★★ BRAZILIAN   Atlanta is very lucky to be one of only three cities with authentic Southern Brazilian–style *churrascaria* (grilled meats), the other two being in Houston and Chicago. Fogo has become one of the city's most popular restaurants, so don't even think about getting in at the last minute. No vegetarian would be caught dead in this place, as the highlights here are meat, meat, and more meat. From top sirloin, filet mignon, and pork ribs, to lamb, rumpsteak, and pork loin, Fogo de Chao seasons the meat selections to perfection before slow-roasting them over a flame to bring out each natural flavor. As you make your way to the 30-item salad bar—one of the best in the city, I might add—and enjoy your side dishes of black beans, fried yucca, garlic mashed potatoes, and cheese bread, the traditional "Gaucho" cooks and waiters will present the savory cuts of meat on skewers and slice them tableside. It's a one price fits all menu. You'd be hard pressed to find this dining experience anywhere else.

3101 Piedmont Rd. ✆ **404/266-9988.** Reservations highly recommended. Lunch is $22.50 per person; dinner is $41.50 per person. AE, DC, MC, V. Lunch Mon–Fri 11am–2pm; dinner Mon–Thurs 5–10pm; Fri–Sat 5–10:30pm. MARTA: Lindbergh.

Jöel ★★★ FRENCH   Joel Atunes is flying solo these days. Atunes, of The Dining Room at Ritz-Carlton Buckhead fame, is a Frenchman who trained in Nice under Paul Bocuse and went on to win his own accolades in Lyon, London, and Thailand. His experience as chef of a restaurant in the Oriental Hotel in Bangkok shaped his style, and his cuisine successfully strikes the chords of both East and West. His American debut has been stunning, and his solo venture in Atlanta is proving very successful. The highly anticipated 128-seat French brasserie with Mediterranean and Asian influences opened in late 2001. The restaurant includes a 65-seat tapas bar/lounge, two 16-seat private rooms, and Jöel patisserie, a gourmet takeout shop offering fresh pastries, sandwiches, and light meals. Designed by The Johnson Studio—creators of Canoe, Bluepointe, and Aria—Joel features a clean, sleek design featuring high windows and classic materials. The space is minimalist and contemporary, and color is used sparingly to give it a dramatic international feel. The 16-seat wine room has a glassed-in wall that holds 5,000 bottles of wine. As if that wasn't enough, Atunes boasts that he has the biggest piece of cooking equipment in the country—a 62-foot stainless steel stove, the longest in a standalone kitchen in the United States. Each of his 12 chefs focus on the preparation of three or four dishes from start to finish, and each has his or her own cooking area along the massive stove. Wow.

The restaurant's menu illustrates Antunes' extensive culinary experience in Paris, the South of France, Asia, and London. The menu is limited enough to keep your head from spinning, yet so varied that you don't feel cheated. Appetizers include sautéed snails with corn ravioli in truffle broth, and fresh oysters with horseradish sorbet. Entrees range from baked seabass with tomato lasagna and tapenade to roast guinea fowl with black olives served with polenta. Whatever you choose, you must save room for dessert or the after dinner cheese service. Especially tempting is the chocolate granite with chocolate streusel. Philippe Buttin, formerly of London's famed Mirabelle restaurant, compiled an impressive 300-selection international wine list with selections from Chile, Spain, France, Italy, Australia, New Zealand, South Africa, and the United States. An equally impressive reserve list is also available.

3290 Northside Parkway (Piazza at Paces). ✆ **404/233-3500.** Reservations recommended. Appetizers $7.25–$15.95; entrees $16.95–$29.75. AE, DC, MC, V. Breakfast Mon–Fri 7–9:30am; lunch Mon–Fri 11:30am–2pm; dinner Mon–Thu 5:30–10:30pm, Fri–Sat 5:30–11pm. MARTA: Midtown or Lindbergh.

Kyma ★★ GREEK   Fine Greek dining has finally arrived in Atlanta. Opened in 2002 as the newest addition to the Buckhead Life Restaurant Group, Kyma is absolutely stunning, with 16-foot solid marble columns weighing 55,000 pounds each, a ceiling lit by twinkling stars, a broken plate wall mosaic, and a fountain cascading over a marble display of iced fresh whole fish. The brainchild of BLRG founder and president Pano Karatassos, Kyma is a contemporary Greek seafood tavern unlike any other.

The predominantly Greek staff adds authenticity to the Kyma experience. Chef Pano I. Karatassos—son of the BLRG founder—led the menu development for Kyma. He loves French fundamentals and uses a clean technique, featuring spices, acidity, and finesse. Kyma will delight you with an innovative menu full of true Greek flavors, including mezedakia (assorted Greek appetizers), whole fresh fish flown in daily from Mediterranean waters, favorite spreads, and other traditional flavors. Mezedes are typically shared and enjoyed with ice cold Ouzo, a Greek liqueur flavored with anise. Try a combination tasting of appetizers to get the full range of flavors and textures, from traditional Greek red caviar mousse to roasted red pepper purée with feta cheese. Though you won't be able to pronounce anything on the menu, the waitstaff is used to the grunt and point method used by most non-Greek–speaking patrons. Choose your meat dish and sides seperately (sides serve two people). Sit back and enjoy this unique dining experience.

3085 Piedmont Rd. ✆ **404/262-0702.** Reservations required. Mezedes $3.75–$14; seafood entrees are priced by the pound ranging from $17–$32.50. AE, DC, MC, V. Mon–Fri 11am–11pm; Sat 5pm–midnight. MARTA: Lindbergh.

The Palm ⭐ *Value* SEAFOOD/STEAK New York's legendary purveyor of juicy prime steaks and succulent outsized lobsters—established in 1926 and still run by its founding family—also has a branch in Atlanta, and it's a beauty. Glossy oak floors, soft lighting, a lofty pressed-tin ceiling, potted palms, and tables spaced for power-lunch privacy create the classic Palm setting—a setting that would not be complete without the restaurant's signature "Wall of Fame," plastered with celebrity caricatures from Frank Sinatra to famous locals Jane Fonda and Ted Turner.

The expense account crowd is mostly from affluent Buckhead: folks looking for the kind of food served at Chops or Bone's (two premier steakhouses), but in a brasher, more boisterous setting. Food preparation is simple here (nothing drizzled or infused). The emphasis is on the freshest fish and seafood, and the highest-quality cuts of meat, all served up in satisfying hungry-man portions. The strip steak is huge and divine, done exactly to order. But the most popular entree is the lobster, a hefty critter weighing from 3 to 7 pounds. Other excellent choices are fluffy jumbo lump crab cakes and linguine with garlicky white clam sauce.

In Swissôtel, 3391 Peachtree Rd. (between Lenox and Piedmont rds., just south of Lenox Sq.). ✆ **404/814-1955.** Reservations recommended. Lunch items $9–$16; dinner main courses $16–$35. AE, DC, MC, V. Daily 11:30am–11pm. MARTA: Lenox or Buckhead.

Pano's & Paul's ⭐⭐⭐ AMERICAN/CONTINENTAL Well-heeled Atlantans consider this place, which has been on the scene since 1979, a kind of posh private club. And very posh it is, especially since a recent renovation turned it into a stylish Art Deco space that evokes 1940s sophistication. It's set in a shopping center just down the sidewalk from an Ace Hardware, but it's still one of the most special restaurants in town.

Everything is excellent, and the service is smooth as silk. Dinner might begin with smoked salmon, accompanied by a potato pancake and minced onions, and continue with crisply battered lobster tail with Chinese honey mustard (a signature dish). In season, the soft-shell crabs, lightly battered and sautéed crisp, are a succulent treat. If you don't see what you want on the menu, just ask; the staff will make every effort to prepare something that will tempt you. Desserts are as lush as the surroundings, and the wine list is excellent. A new 4-course prix-fixe menu is available Monday to Thursday featuring selections created daily by Chef Gary Donlick for $42.

1232 W. Paces Ferry Rd. (at Northside Pkwy., in the W. Paces Ferry Shopping Center). ✆ 404/261-3662. Reservations essential. Main courses $19–$37.50; prix-fixe $42. AE, DC, DISC, MC, V. Mon–Fri 6–10:30pm; Sat 5:30–11pm. MARTA: Lenox.

Prime ★★ SEAFOOD/STEAK/SUSHI   Don't be put off by the fact that this restaurant is located in a shopping mall. For one thing, it's in Lenox Square, *the* shopping mall of the Southeast. And what better finish to a shopping spree than a martini and a steak, or sushi? If you're going to indulge, you might as well go all the way. And this is an extremely indulgent place—a suave, hip interior with food to match. It's a steakhouse, but it's bright and contemporary rather than dark and clubby. Do start with a martini. The French say hard liquor spoils the meal, but hey, this isn't France and several specialty martinis are available. The sushi is the freshest you can get, the steaks are sublime and huge, and the seafood is stylish. At lunch you'll find lighter entrees, sandwiches, and a divine lobster salad with citrus vinaigrette (no mayo). Every Friday at happy hour, from 5 to 7pm, there's free sushi and live jazz in the atrium just outside the restaurant.

3393 Peachtree Rd. NE (upstairs at the main entrance to Lenox Sq.). ✆ 404/812-0555. Lunch items $6.95–$14.95; dinner main courses $16.95–$28.50. AE, DC, DISC, MC, V. Lunch Mon–Thurs 11:30am–2:30pm and dinner 5–10pm; Fri–Sat 11:30am–11pm and Sun 1–9pm. MARTA: Buckhead or Lenox.

Seeger's ★★★ MODERN CLASSICAL   Dinner at Seeger's has been one of the most sought-after reservations in town since the doors opened late in 1997. And for good reason. It is the domain of internationally-recognized Guenter Seeger, the high priest of Atlanta cuisine, who worked his magic for 12 award-winning years at The Dining Room in Buckhead's Ritz-Carlton. Set in a converted cottage, this restaurant is as much about theater as it is about food. The setting is sleek yet simple, an uncluttered background for an elegant dinner, beautifully prepared and presented. Each prix-fixe meal is a series of little treasures from the kitchen, and the menu changes daily. Seasonal truffle menus are sometimes available. The wines are excellent, and the service is smooth and pampering. If you choose the chef's menu, which is served at the "chef's table," you have the added pleasure of glimpsing the master and his team creating in the kitchen.

Though the dress code is not formal, they do recommend that gentlemen wear jackets.

111 W. Paces Ferry Rd. (between Peachtree Rd. and E. Andrews Dr.). ✆ 404/846-9779. Reservations essential. 5-course vegetarian menu $64; 5-course menu $69; 8-course chef's menu $85 (pairing wines $60 extra). AE, DC, MC, V. Mon–Sat 5:30–10pm. MARTA: Lenox.

EXPENSIVE

Atlanta Fish Market ★ SEAFOOD/SUSHI   It's hard to miss this place, and you really don't want to. It's a great mix of whimsy outside (there's a 65-foot copper fish standing on its tail out front) and serious seafood inside—some of the best you'll find anywhere. Like the Buckhead Diner (see below), the Atlanta Fish Market is simultaneously glitzy and informal. You'll want to dress up, but not too much. Housed in a brick building inspired by a 1920s Savannah train station, it has a dramatic interior with a soaring ceiling, plush leather booths, and distressed pine tables, and there's an enclosed porch that feels very beachy.

The menu is vast and the seafood is as fresh as it's possible to get. To some folks, seafood in the South means fried, and the fried dishes are okay, but the other preparations are exceptional. There are several daily specials and a list of at least a dozen fresh catch items that can be ordered charbroiled or Hong Kong–style,

A Buckhead Fish Tale

If you travel down Pharr Road in Buckhead, it's pretty hard not to notice the huge fish sculpture outside the Atlanta Fish Market, one of the city's finest seafood restaurants. The fish, which is perched on its swooped tail and appears to be about to leap over the restaurant, caused quite a commotion when it was first proposed. Although the restaurant was quite enthusiastic about its construction, many folks in the surrounding neighborhoods were not exactly hooked on the idea. Despite the protests, the project was approved, and the enormous creature, which resembles a cross between a salmon and a trout, was unveiled in late 1995. Here are some fish facts about a sculpture that, like it or not, is on its way to becoming an Atlanta landmark.

- The fish is about 65 feet high and weighs 50 tons.
- Measured from head to tail, it's 100 feet long, about the size of a large whale.
- It sports more than 600 copper scales, 3½ feet each, which will age to a patina over the years.
- Made of solid copper and steel, it is supported by a welded-iron infrastructure that is connected to a 35-foot-deep steel-and-concrete casing.
- Cost was in excess of $360,000.

spiked with soy, ginger, and scallions. There are steaks and chops, as well as a vast number of appetizers, many of which are nearly large enough for a meal. Desserts include chocolate toffee crunch pie drenched in caramel sauce and garnished with fresh fruit.

265 Pharr Rd. (between Peachtree Rd. and N. Fulton Dr.). ✆ **404/262-3165.** Reservations recommended. Sandwiches $8.25–$10.95; lunch and dinner entrees $13.95–$32.95 (most under $19). AE, DC, DISC, MC, V. Mon–Thurs 11am–11pm; Fri–Sat 11am–midnight; Sun 4–10pm. MARTA: Lenox.

Blue Ridge Grill ✮ TRADITIONAL AMERICAN   The Blue Ridge Grill's Adirondacks-style interior has the woodsy warmth of a national park lodge: stone pillars, weathered logs, and a soaring pine ceiling with massive heart pine beams salvaged from an old cotton mill. But this spot is as upscale as it is rustic, with antiques, original artwork, and cozy leather booths.

Blue Ridge Grill used to specialize in contemporary Southern cuisine, but the menu is vastly different now, with mostly traditional American fare such as steaks, chops, and seafood. The only remotely Southern items are collard greens and Georgia trout. As in many other restaurants these days, the emphasis is on two-fisted portions: a 22-ounce rib-eye, a 14-ounce veal chop, and huge sides of spinach, mashed potatoes, asparagus, and so on. ***Note:*** Driving here along West Paces Ferry Road, remember you're looking for Northside *Parkway,* not Northside *Drive,* which you'll pass first.

1261 W. Paces Ferry Rd. (at Northside Pkwy. in the Paces Ferry Plaza Shopping Center). ✆ **404/233-5030.** Reservations recommended. Lunch and brunch items $7.95–$19.95; dinner main courses $17.95–$29.95. AE, DC, DISC, MC, V. Sun–Fri 11:30am–2:30pm; Sun–Thurs 5:30–10pm; Fri and Sat 5:30–11pm. MARTA: Lenox.

Bluepointe ✮✮✮ ASIAN/CONTEMPORARY AMERICAN   At the corner of Peachtree and Lenox roads in the heart of upscale Buckhead is the newest member in the constellation of fine dining establishments that make up the locally owned and operated Buckhead Life Restaurants. (Others include Kyma, Pano's and Paul's, Nava, Veni Vidi Vici, Atlanta Fish Market, and Buckhead Diner, to name a few.) There's not a mediocre restaurant in the bunch, but Bluepointe, which opened in 2000, is easily the most exciting.

Part of its success comes from the setting itself, a dramatic, multi-level space with a flashy lounge and sushi bar, soaring ceilings, and a plush contemporary decor with Asian touches. There's a lot of energy and noise in the lounge/sushi bar in the "point" of the building, but it's possible to have a decent conversation in the restaurant portion of the establishment.

The specialty here is seafood, with Asian flavors that give the dishes a contemporary edge. Appetizers might include oysters or sushi, or perhaps lobster dumplings with toasted peanuts and radish sprouts for the more adventuresome. Menus change frequently, depending on what's fresh and available, but might include such stars as peanut-crusted grouper in Indian curry, or scallops with sushi rice cakes and passion fruit butter. There are also prime steaks and a delectable lobster; a house specialty is salt-crusted prime rib for two, which looks as if it could serve four people. There are also several sides served a la carte, such as wok-charred *choy sum,* or scallion and potato cake. Everything is beautifully presented, and the service is impeccable.

3455 Peachtree Rd. NE (at Lenox Rd.). ℭ 404/237-9070. Reservations necessary. Lunch entrees $9–$26.75; dinner main courses $17–$35. Mon–Fri 11am–2:30pm; Mon–Thurs 5:30–11pm; Fri–Sat 5:30pm–midnight; Sun 5:30–10pm. Complimentary valet parking. MARTA: Lenox or Buckhead.

Brasserie Le Coze ★★ TRADITIONAL FRENCH *Mon Dieu.* Is this Atlanta or the heart of St. Germain in Paris? Once inside Brasserie Le Coze, you'd swear you were in Paris, rather than in an outpost created by Maguy Le Coze and her late brother Gilbert, who built their reputations at Le Bernardin in New York. And this little bit of France lies in a shopping mall, no less. With small round tables and an abbreviated menu offering traditional French sandwiches, appetizers, and desserts, the restaurant's tiny mall-side cafe is the perfect spot to stop for a nibble of paté when shopping gets you down. The bar just inside is grand and cosmopolitan, all dark wood and brass and soft lights. The bright, mirror-lined main dining room, with its hand-painted tiles, posh banquettes, and staff in traditional vests and long aprons, is straight from Paris. All this would mean nothing if the cuisine failed to match the ambience, but it doesn't. It is very French—disciplined and bold while maintaining the casual bistro style.

Settle in with a bowl of mussels in an aromatic broth, or try the white bean soup with white truffle oil. A green salad and the crusty rolls would make this a full meal, but you'd be foolish not to go on to the incomparable herb-roasted chicken or the roast skate wing in brown butter caper sauce. The extensive, exceptional wine list will not disappoint, nor will the desserts, especially the warm, gooey chocolate cake.

3393 Peachtree Rd. NE (in the Lenox Square mall). ℭ **404/266-1440.** Reservations recommended. Lunch items $8–$16.50; dinner main courses $15.50–$32. AE, DC, MC, V. Main dining room Mon–Thurs 11:30am–2:30pm, 5:30–10pm; Fri 11:30am–3pm, 5:30–11pm; Sat 11:30am–3:30pm, 5:30–11pm. Bar and cafe open with a limited menu between lunch and dinner. MARTA: Lenox or Buckhead.

The Cabin ★ SEAFOOD/STEAK   Located in a 70-year-old log cabin slightly off the regular Buckhead track is a little mountain hideaway offering up aged Midwestern beef, Southern-style seafood, and wild game dishes. Southern style in this case does not mean deep-fried, but interesting and varied preparations of regional favorites. High marks go to the salmon (the preparation changes daily) and an interpretation of a South Carolina low-country boil crammed with lobster, shrimp, clams, and mussels. The rack of lamb and the cowboy steak (a 22-oz. bone-in rib-eye) are popular with the casually dressed Buckhead crowd that comes here in search of serious food.

The decor is Highlands cabin, complete with elk-antler chandeliers. The downstairs bar, with its stacked stone fireplace, is the more rustic of the two dining areas, and it's also where you'll find a selection of martinis, the specialty drink of the house. The Cabin also offers one of Atlanta's most extensive by-the-glass wine lists. Even though steaks and seafood are the main attractions, the Southern-style vegetables are a real treat, especially the creamed fresh corn and the bourbon-spiked mashed sweet potatoes.

2678 Buford Hwy. NE (north of Lenox Rd.). © **404/315-7676.** Reservations recommended. Lunch items $7.95–$11.95; dinner main courses $16.95–$33.95. AE, DC, DISC, MC, V. Mon–Fri 11:30am–2:30pm; Mon–Thurs 5:30–10pm; Fri–Sat 5:30–11pm. MARTA: Lindbergh.

Horseradish Grill ⭐ CONTEMPORARY SOUTHERN   This restaurant had a previous incarnation as the Red Barn Inn, and it still retains some of the rustic atmosphere: wood barn walls, a raftered pine ceiling, and a massive stone fireplace. Big windows overlook the restaurant's organic garden on one side, and Chastain Park on the other; patio seating is under ancient oaks. The view is lovely, whether you're inside or out, but pick the patio if you have a choice.

Chef Dave Berry, nominated as one of America's Rising Star Chefs by the James Beard House, emphasizes innovative but authentic Southern recipes, simply prepared. Ingredients are seasonal and regional: no salmon or lobster, no tomatoes in winter, no turnip greens in summer. Indulge yourself in the excellent specialties: spicy North Carolina barbecue on corncake, Georgia mountain trout, or hickory grilled double cut pork chop. The wine list is predominantly American, but there are international selections too. Oatmeal spice cake is the not-to-be-missed dessert. At lunch, there are sandwiches, small plates, and salads. The brunch menu is especially good. Try the sweet potato biscuit and eggs with sautéed spinach, grilled Andouille sausage, poached eggs and hollandaise, or the cold smoked Georgia mountain trout with crème fraîche, capers and chives.

4320 Powers Ferry Rd. (at Chastain Park). © **404/255-7277.** Reservations recommended. Lunch items $5–$14; dinner main courses $17–$25. AE, DC, DISC, MC, V. Mon–Fri 11:30am–2:30pm; Mon–Thurs 5:30–9pm; Fri–Sat 5–10pm; Sun 11am–2:30pm and 5–9pm. MARTA: Lenox.

Nava ⭐⭐ CONTEMPORARY SOUTHWESTERN   Nava's tri-level earth-toned interior is gorgeous—the work of architect Bill Johnson, who is known for creating fabulous settings. There's a bundled spruce ceiling beamed with tree trunks, a *kiva*-style fireplace, a copper-hooded exhibition kitchen, and a rustic and elegant decor rich with Southwestern and Native American art.

Don't come here expecting a beans and burritos Tex-Mex meal. This is truly inventive Southwestern cuisine, where you'll find enchiladas and tostadas and the like, but they're stuffed with such treats as rock shrimp and jalapeño honey mustard, or ancho-chile steak and portobello mushrooms. You can make a meal from the long list of starters, and it's an easy way to sample the creative menu. The mussels appetizer, dry roasted in a hot iron skillet and served in spicy chipotle broth, is a favorite among regulars. Save room for the banana quesadillas, served with warm caramel sauce—a great combination. Nava's extensive wine

list was composed to complement Southwestern dishes. There's also a large selection of tequilas, beers, and margaritas; the prickly pear margarita is a big seller.

3060 Peachtree Rd. (at W. Paces Ferry Rd.). © 404/240-1984. Reservations recommended. Lunch items
$7.95–$16.50; appetizers $5.50–$10.95; dinner main courses $14.50–$27.95. AE, DC, DISC, MC, V. Mon–Fri
11am–2:30pm; Mon–Thurs 5:30–11pm; Fri–Sat 5:30pm–midnight; Sun 5:30–10pm. MARTA: Lenox.

Pricci ⭐ REGIONAL ITALIAN   Pricci is strikingly glamorous, with part of
its drama stemming from an exhibition kitchen where a team of white-hatted
chefs is engaged in culinary frenzy around an oak-fired pizza oven. The decor is
also theatrical—Art Deco chrome and brass dividers, rich decorative woods,
cozy banquettes, and a snazzy bar. The downside is the noise; it's hard to escape
all the dining clatter.

Pricci's fare is hearty regional Italian cuisine: thin-crusted oak-fired pizzas;
pastas such as beef short-rib ravioli, osso buco with borlotti beans and gremo-
lata, and so on. The specialty of the house, which serves two, is an excellent
whole roasted fish with grilled asparagus. The lunch menu lists pastas, appetizer
pizzas, salads, and light entrees. A good value is the three-pasta tasting. The
award-winning wine list highlights every wine-producing region of Italy and features a good selection of grappas (an Italian brandy).

500 Pharr Rd. (at Maple Dr.). © 404/237-2941. Reservations recommended. Lunch $8.95–$14.95; pizzas,
pastas, risottos $8.50–$14.75; dinner entrees $13–$25. AE, DC, DISC, MC, V. Mon–Thurs 11am–11pm; Fri
11am–midnight; Sat 5pm–midnight; Sun 5–10pm. MARTA: Lenox.

Toulouse ⭐ _Finds_ CONTEMPORARY AMERICAN   The name is French,
but the cuisine is New American with influences from the south of France.
Toulouse is tucked away behind a strip of shops along Peachtree; it's a little hard
to spot, but you'll be glad you did. The neighborhood crowd, attired in anything
from blue jeans to black tie, likes to keep this place a secret, revealing it only to
friends and special visitors. It's casual and charming, a spacious loft with a large
wooden bar and an open kitchen in full view.

The menu changes seasonally, perhaps more often depending on the whims
of the chef, but you're likely to find some of the house specialties always available. A good bet is the plump roast chicken done to perfection in a wood-fired
oven, accompanied by arugula bread salad. Another favorite is the braised lamb
shank with a Kalamata olive–sweet pepper sauce and roasted vegetables. The
excellent wine list has lots of good values.

2293 Peachtree Rd. NE (south of Peachtree Battle Ave.). © 404/351-9533. Reservations recommended.
Main courses $12–$22. AE, DC, MC, V. Dinner served daily 5:30–10pm. MARTA: Lenox or Buckhead.

MODERATE

Anis Cafe and Bistro ⭐ _Value_ FRENCH/MEDITERRANEAN   In the midst
of pricey Buckhead, this unpretentious cafe serves up great food at the right
price. Set in a converted cottage on a side street, it's a perfect spot for a light
lunch or a dinner with a French accent. The specialties are Provençal versions of
healthy Mediterranean cuisine, and the atmosphere is reminiscent of that
region, especially if you're lucky enough to snag a table on the tree-shaded brick
patio. The key word here is _informal._ The service is sometimes maddeningly
casual, and occasionally there are glitches in the kitchen. But if you relax and
pretend you've been invited to a friend's house in the south of France, you won't
be disappointed.

Starters include Niçoise salad and warm focaccia toasts topped with tomatoes,
mozzarella, and fresh basil. The mussels, which are plump, plentiful, and almost

as good as those served at the pricier Brasserie Le Coze, make a full meal when paired with the goat cheese salad. The pasta with lemon chicken and roasted eggplant is a great entree choice, but so are the grilled lamb chops spiked with fresh thyme. There are also several specialty coffee drinks, including espresso over ice cream. The wine list is quite respectable, and there's a full bar.

2974 Grandview Ave. (1 block south of Pharr Rd.). ℂ 404/233-9889. Reservations suggested. Lunch $3.95–$13.95; dinner entrees $11.95–$18.95. AE, DC, MC, V. Mon–Sat 11:30am–2:30pm; Sun–Thurs 6–10pm; Fri–Sat 6–10:30pm. MARTA: Lenox.

Buckhead Diner AMERICAN   As sleek as a Thunderbird convertible, the exterior of this nouvelle diner glitters with neon tubing and chrome, and the posh interior conjures up images of the Orient Express. It's almost always crowded, so be prepared to wait at prime time; it's usually worth it—full of hustle and bustle and lots of fun.

Previously found cooking up Southwestern delights at Nava (p. 130), Kevin Rathbun is now executive chef of the Diner. Main courses are a mix of Mom and modern, some quite heavy on the calories (but who's counting?). Long-time favorites include the veal and wild mushroom meatloaf with celery mashed potatoes, and the thick BLT made with grilled salmon. There's something for everybody, from the Portobello mushroom melt on tomato-onion focaccia to the pan-roasted duck steak with baby bok choy. Many low-priced snacks, such as spicy shrimp dumplings or Dungeness crab cakes, make for fun grazing. If you order nothing else, be sure to get the homemade potato chips slathered with melted Maytag blue cheese—they're big enough for the table to share. You will not be too embarrassed to lick the plate. Desserts are great, ranging from peach bread pudding with Southern Comfort–flavored cream to a to-die-for chocolate-chip crème brûlée. All the breads are baked fresh daily at the Buckhead Bread Company (see below).

3073 Piedmont Rd. (at E. Paces Ferry Rd.). ℂ 404/262-3336. Snacks, sandwiches, salads $4.75–$16.95; lunch items $7.95–$15.95; dinner main courses $13.75–$22.95. AE, DC, DISC, MC, V. Mon–Sat 11am–midnight; Sun (including brunch) 10am–10pm. MARTA: Lenox.

Corner Café and Buckhead Bread Company ★ CAFE/BAKERY   This spot is a combination of an upscale cafe and gourmet bakery. The cafe portion is more casual and relaxed than the Buckhead Diner, its glitzy cousin across the street, but the food is still upscale. The menu is large and varied, with wonderful soups and hearty sandwiches. There are also interesting main-dish salads, including the long-time favorite, a chicken, egg, and tuna salad trio. About half the space is given over to a vast bakery (the Buckhead Bread Company) that displays many varieties of fresh-baked breads each day—everything from focaccia flavored with fresh rosemary and basil to honeyed eight-grain loaves studded with roasted sunflower seeds. The breads are used for the cafe sandwiches and are a major attraction. The gorgeous pastries have a French pedigree and will transport you to the Left Bank. It's possible to get something to go or pick out a pastry and have it served to you in the cafe or on the small patio with a cup of specialty coffee.

Weekday breakfast includes fresh-baked pastries, crepes, Belgian waffles, and traditional fare such as poached eggs with cheddar cheese grits. The weekend brunch is a busy time here and the menu is fancier, including a delicious dish composed of two pan-poached eggs with two Portobello mushrooms, and crispy prosciutto topped with a port wine glaze. The crème brûlée French toast is also quite delicious.

3070 Piedmont Rd. (at E. Paces Ferry Rd.). © **404/240-1978.** Sandwiches and main-dish salads $7.95–$11.25; brunch items $7.95–$13.95. AE, DC, DISC, MC, V. Mon–Sat 6:30am–5pm, Sun 8am–5p.m. MARTA: Lenox.

Fratelli di Napoli *Value Kids* ITALIAN AMERICAN   Grab a plate and sit down at the family dinner table in this upbeat, energetic establishment. Housed in a former warehouse on an odd little street filled with antiques shops and galleries, the place feels like a sunny loft in the middle of SoHo. It's noisy as the devil, so if that bothers you, ask for a table on the enclosed patio.

Service is friendly, presented traditional family style, with generous platters designed to serve two or three people. Many of the selections are available as half orders, but it's more fun to go for broke and share around the table. The menu is as huge as the portions, and everyone in the family (kids included) will be able to find something they can't live without. Specialties include tender-crisp fried calamari, and chicken di Napoli, a lightly breaded, sautéed chicken breast with fresh tomato and basil in balsamic vinaigrette. The shrimp fra diavolo, sautéed with hot pepper and tomato sauce, is quite good, especially when accompanied by hefty, chewy squares of focaccia. The desserts are forgettable, but who has room anyway? P.S. There's no pizza.

2101 Tula St. NW (in the Bennett St. complex behind Mick's restaurant). © **404/351-1533.** Reservations accepted for 6 or more. Main courses (which serve 2 or more) $12–$36. AE, DC, DISC, MC, V. Sun–Thurs 5–10pm; Fri–Sat 5–11pm.

Houston's ★ *Kids* AMERICAN   Part of an Atlanta-based group with restaurants throughout the country, Houston's serves up lavish portions of fresh, top-quality fare. It's always packed with people looking for an exciting but informal spot, with service as snappy as the food. There's almost always a wait, but you won't mind spending time on the front patio or in the bar. If you're in a rush, eat at the bar during lunch. The patio, across from Lenox Square, is a terrific people-watching spot.

Thick, hickory-grilled burgers are a specialty, as are the tender, meaty ribs, served with a choice of side dishes: skillet beans, fries, coleslaw, or couscous. The same fixings come with barbecued chicken. A lighter main course is the salad of sliced grilled chicken, tossed with chopped greens and julienned tortilla strips in a honey-lime vinaigrette, garnished with a light peanut sauce. For dessert, you can indulge in a huge, chewy brownie topped with vanilla ice cream and Kahlúa.

There are several locations around town, including one in Buckhead at 2166 Peachtree Rd. (at Colonial Homes Dr. in the Brookwood Square Shopping Center), © **404/351-2442.**

3321 Lenox Rd. (at E. Paces Ferry Rd.). © **404/237-7534.** Reservations not accepted; arrive at off-peak hours. Burgers and salads $7–$12; main courses $11–$28. AE, MC, V. Sun 11am–10:30pm; Mon–Sat 11am–11pm. MARTA: Lenox.

INEXPENSIVE

Fellini's Pizza *Kids* PIZZA   You won't get chèvre or cilantro on your pies here, but you will get traditional toppings like anchovies, Italian sausage, meatballs, pepperoni, fresh mushrooms, and onions piled on cheesy New York–style pies with thin, doughy crusts that exude the heavenly aroma of fresh-baked bread. Fellini's is a classic pizza joint, and a damn good one.

It's a wacky place, very atypical for Buckhead. Most of the seating is at tables on a large outdoor patio centered on a tiered fountain, with statues of angels and gargoyles. Because it fronts Peachtree Road, it's a great spot to sit and watch the city go by. When the heat is wilting, you can retreat to the funky, spare interior. Besides the pizzas, some of which are available by the slice, there are immense, well-stuffed calzones. The beer is always ice cold.

There are several additional locations; the most convenient for visitors are in Buckhead at 1991 Howell Mill Rd. (*©* **404/352-0799**), and in Midtown at 909 Ponce de Leon Ave. (*©* **404/873-3088**).

2809 Peachtree Rd. (at Rumson Rd.). *©* **404/266-0082**. Slice $1.45–$2.85; medium pie $8.50–$13.50, with additional toppings $1–$1.50 each; calzones $4.50–$5. No credit cards. Mon–Sat 11:30am–2am; Sun noon–midnight. MARTA: Lenox or Buckhead.

La Fonda Latina SPANISH   Funky and festive, La Fonda is a brightly painted little hole-in-the-wall consisting of a small interior dining area with an open kitchen, a covered outdoor patio, and an open-air rooftop patio with seating in wooden booths amid lots of plants. Outdoor areas are heated in winter and cooled by large fans in summer.

The food is both fresh and refreshingly authentic. You might simply order up a bottle of *vino blanco* and a delicious *ensalada mixta* (tuna, black olives, lettuce, onions, and peppers in a classic vinaigrette that you can soak up with Cuban bread). There are several different kinds of quesadillas, and three types of paella—traditional, seafood, and vegetarian. The Latin sandwiches are served on crusty Cuban bread, and the chicken is nicely grilled and served with rice and beans. Try a creamy, homemade flan for dessert.

Note: La Fonda has two other locations; the most convenient for visitors is in Little Five Points at 1150B Euclid Ave., off Colquitt Avenue (*©* **404/577-8317**).

2813 Peachtree Rd. NE (between Rumson Rd. and Sheridan Dr.). *©* **404/816-8311**. Main courses $5.50–$8.95. V, MC Sun 12:30–11pm; Mon–Thurs 11:30am–11pm; Fri–Sat 11:30am–midnight. MARTA: Lenox or Buckhead.

OK Café *Kids* AMERICAN   The specialties here are down-home classics served in a simple setting of leather booths at old-style Formica tables, a juke-box stocked with oldies, and waiters in white diner uniforms. There's a witty sculpture of a money tree in the dining room—perhaps to pay homage to the moneyed crowd, which comes here for updated comfort food. It's a good spot to bring the whole family, especially if you have kids who turn their noses up at anything more complex than mashed potatoes.

The place is full of memories of Mom: blue-plate specials such as meatloaf, pot roast, and roast turkey with corn-bread dressing, all served with corn muffins and two side dishes—the best of which is a six-cheese macaroni. Sandwiches, burgers, salads, and thick, old-fashioned shakes are other options. OK Café is also known for country-style breakfasts and brunches. Takeout is available.

1284 W. Paces Ferry Rd. NW (at Northside Pkwy., in the W. Paces Ferry Shopping Center). *©* **404/233-2888**. Reservations not accepted. Burgers, salads, and sandwiches $5.25–$7.95; lunch $8.95–$10.95; dinner $9.95–$11.95. AE, DC, DISC, MC, V. Sun–Thurs 7am–11pm; Fri–Sat 7am–midnight; takeout daily 11am–10pm. MARTA: Lenox.

Pasta Vino *Kids* ITALIAN/PIZZA   This may not be the very best Italian restaurant in town, but the combination of high quality and low prices makes it a favorite neighborhood stop. Billy Petrucci runs this little trattoria, and his father, Nico, runs the chic, upscale Abruzzi in the same shopping center. It's a great choice when you want good food but don't want to dress up and go "out."

The yeasty, chewy pizzas, most of which are available by the slice, are as good as they come. Seafood and veal, served with a side of pasta marina, are done especially well. And the mussels appetizer is large enough for an entree. The best traditional Italian dish on the menu is the lasagna, made with the tenderest of noodles, a little ground beef, delicate béchamel and tomato sauces, and lots of mozzarella. It's worth twice the price. The eggplant lasagna is even better. The house salad is made with boring iceberg lettuce, so choose the huge Caesar instead and split it. The wine is limited to the house variety—one white, one red—but they're not bad. This place is extremely kid-friendly and usually filled with families from the local, well-heeled neighborhood. The patio is a great spot in summer.

2391 Peachtree Rd. NE (in the Peachtree Battle Promenade at Peachtree Battle Ave.). ℂ 404/231-4946. Reservations not accepted. Pizzas $10.75–$18; pastas $7.50–$10.25; subs $5.75–$6.75; main courses $8.95–$11.75. No credit cards. Mon–Sat 11am–2pm; Mon–Thu 5–9pm; Fri–Sat 5pm–10pm; Sun 5–9pm. MARTA: Lenox or Buckhead.

Swan Coach House *Finds* AMERICAN   If you visit the Atlanta History Center in Buckhead (p. 147), this delightful restaurant is a great lunch option. It is a genteel spot with a "ladies' lunch" ambience, and the menu mirrors the setting, featuring fare such as salmon croquettes with cucumber relish and Dijon dill sauce. There's even a 1950s-style congealed salad on the list. The best choice, which has been on the menu for 30 years, is the Swan's Favorite: chicken salad in pastry timbales served with cheese straws and creamy frozen fruit salad. For dessert, order the French silk swan—a meringue base filled with chocolate mousse and covered with whipped cream and slivered almonds. There's a full bar.

Note: You don't have to visit the History Center to dine here; it has a separate entrance. A gift shop and art gallery adjoin the dining room.

3130 Slaton Dr. NW (at the Atlanta History Center). ℂ 404/261-0636. Reservations accepted Mon–Thurs for 6 or more, Fri–Sat for 10 or more. Main courses $7.25–$9.95. AE, MC, V. Mon–Sat 11am–2:30pm. Closed New Year's Day, Memorial Day, July 4, Labor Day, Thanksgiving, and Christmas. MARTA: Lindbergh.

5 Virginia-Highland/Inman Park

Make a meal in this charming district the occasion to see a non-touristy part of Atlanta. Come a little early, so you can browse in the area's great little shops and galleries. (For a map with Virginia-Highland and Inman Park restaurants, see "Dining in Midtown, Virginia-Highland & Little Five Points," on p. 112)

EXPENSIVE

dish ★★ CONTEMPORARY AMERICAN   This has been a hot spot for several years, and the 1- to 2-hour wait reflects its continuing popularity. Is it worth it? You bet. Set in a converted gas station in the midst of other trendy restaurants, dish's decor is as whimsical and stylish as its menu. There are "tastes" at the top of the list—small appetizers such as crisp packages of asparagus, sweet peppers, Portobello mushroom, and fontina cheese; more substantial starters such as a crab cake with mango-citrus vinaigrette; and an intriguing endive, grilled pear, and Gorgonzola salad. The excellent main dishes might include tender pan-seared skate wing or a grilled prosciutto-wrapped pork fillet. The desserts are delectable but *way* too tiny, so don't get talked into sharing.

How to beat the hour-plus wait? Tables are most plentiful during warm weather when the patio is open and the tiny restaurant's capacity nearly doubles. Arrive at 5:30pm or put your name on the waiting list and stroll around the neighborhood.

870 N. Highland Ave. (at Drewry St.). ℂ 404/897-3463. Reservations for 5 or more. Main courses $15–$25. AE, DC, MC, V. Sun–Thurs 5:30–10pm; Fri–Sat 5:30–11pm. MARTA: North Ave.

Harvest ✦ REGIONAL AMERICAN   A lovely restaurant set in an old two-story frame house with fireplaces and hardwood floors, Harvest is a favorite in a neighborhood filled with eateries. The menu reflects what's fresh and seasonal, so it changes frequently. There are a few favorites, however, that usually make the list. Try the sun-dried tomato Caesar for starters if you find it. Fish is always nicely done, especially the pumpkin seed-crusted halibut with salsa verde and ancho chile mashed potatoes. Light entrees and sandwiches are available at lunch, and brunch dishes include the excellent Low Country cheese grits with shrimp and sausage. There's a small, pleasant bar upstairs if you have to wait for a table.

853 N. Highland Ave. (at Briarcliff Place). ℭ 404/876-8244. Dinner reservations accepted Sun–Thurs; reservations for 6 or more Fri–Sat, but names are accepted for the waiting list at 6:30pm. Lunch items $7–$11; brunch items $7–$9; dinner main courses $15–$25. AE, DC, MC, V. Mon–Fri 11:30am–2:30pm; Sun 11am–2pm; Sun–Thurs 5:30–10pm; Fri–Sat 5:30–11pm. MARTA: North Ave.

MODERATE

Babette's Café ✦✦ EUROPEAN PROVINCIAL   Owner-chef Marla Adams has put together a menu that's decidedly anti-haute cuisine, full of excellent interpretations of comfy, everyday provincial dishes. The crowd is full of loyal locals, and the French farmhouse ambience matches the fare.

Start off with the mussel appetizer, and don't let the offbeat combination of ingredients scare you off. Bivalves are Adams's specialty, and this unusual dish, steamed mussels with white wine, strawberries, and serrano peppers, is excellent. The restaurant has some of the best mussels in town. A long-time favorite entree—grilled lamb loin chops with red-wine reduction and shoestring potatoes—is kept on the menu by popular demand. Ditto the grilled Portobello tortellini in brown butter sauce and the beef tenderloin with Gorgonzola sauce and spicy onion rings. The best dessert in the house is the chocolate bread pudding with banana ice cream.

Most of the selections from the reasonably priced wine list are available by the glass, part of Adams's strategy to encourage customers to sample different wines. There are special prix-fixe dinners held each season, the most famous of which is at New Year's and is a re-creation of the food and wine from the book *Babette's Feast,* for which the restaurant is named. Babette's is a great place to stop after a visit to the Carter Center, which is just around the corner.

573 N. Highland Ave. (just north of Freedom Pkwy.). ℭ 404/523-9121. Reservations recommended; reservations required for wine dinners held once a season. Brunch items $6.25–$11; main courses $12–$21.50; seasonal wine dinners $65–$85. AE, DC, DISC, MC, V. Tues–Sat 6–10pm; Sun 10:30am–2pm, 5–9pm. MARTA: North Ave.

Murphy's AMERICAN   Murphy's, originally a wine-and-cheese shop that evolved into a restaurant and bakery, today comprises a cozy warren of rooms and is one of the most popular places for brunch. Its interior is charming and inn-like, with the French doors flung open and the area cooled by ceiling fans in nice weather. Up front is the bakery/wine shop, with glass display cases overflowing with pastries, crusty fresh-baked breads, and luscious desserts. Murphy's is a popular destination for the surrounding neighborhood, which is full of young professionals who like casual dining. This is a good stop if you're exploring the Virginia-Highland area; if there's a wait, you can kill some time in the nearby shops.

At dinner, you'll find a variety of entrees, such as sautéed rainbow trout with mashed potatoes, spinach, and garlic-butter sauce. The hefty sandwiches are always winners, and there's a selection of pastas and salads. Brunch includes egg dishes, breads, waffles, pancakes, salads, and sandwiches.

Outdoor Dining

Food always seems to taste better outdoors, and Atlanta's temperate climate makes alfresco dining possible 6 to 8 months out of the year. It's true that there are always some stifling midsummer days, but things usually cool off enough in the evening to make outdoor dining quite pleasant. And many of these places heat their patios during the winter, closing them only on the most frigid days. Here are a few prime spots.

Anis Cafe and Bistro (p. 131): This tree-shaded spot outside a converted Buckhead bungalow is reminiscent of a terrace in the south of France. You can imagine you're in Provence.

Canoe (p. 140): Lovely gardens surround the covered terrace on the banks of the Chattahoochee River for a perfect setting. Wear your best Ralph Lauren outfit.

dish (p. 135): In trendy Virginia-Highland, this is one of the most popular patios in town, even though it fronts busy North Highland Avenue.

Fellini's Pizza (p. 133): Have a beer or a slice of pizza, and watch the world sail down Peachtree Road.

George's Restaurant and Bar (p. 139): There are only a few tables outside this plain neighborhood tavern, but it's in the heart of trendy Virginia-Highland, prime people-watching territory.

Horseradish Grill (p. 130): If you're looking for a place to propose, this is it. A candle-lit patio is set under ancient oaks and overlooks lovely Chastain Park.

Nava (p. 130): Located at the busy intersection of Peachtree and West Paces Ferry roads, but comfortably away from the street, the lovely brick terrace is a great perch from which to watch all the Buckhead activity while sipping margaritas and nibbling appetizers.

South City Kitchen (p. 111): There's limited seating outside this converted Midtown house, but it's a perfect spot to watch the comings and goings of all the beautiful young people who dine here.

Tiburon Grille (p. 138): There's lots of competition for a place on the covered terrace of this neighborhood restaurant smack in the middle of Virginia-Highland, so arrive early.

If you've eaten elsewhere, Murphy's is a perfect destination for dessert and coffee, which for some reason is otherwise hard to find in this area.

997 Virginia Ave. NE (at N. Highland Ave.). ✆ 404/872-0904. Reservations not accepted. Lunch, brunch, and breakfast items $8–$13; dinner main courses $8.95–$19.95. AE, DC, DISC, MC, V. Sun 8am–10pm; Mon–Thurs 11am–10pm; Fri 11am–midnight; Sat 8am–midnight. MARTA: North Ave.

Sotto Sotto ⭐⭐ NORTHERN ITALIAN Sotto Sotto means "hush hush" in Italian. How ironic. The food is divine here, but the noise is unbearable. It seems that half of Atlanta has discovered that this is the place of the moment and has tried to wedge into the tiny restaurant on the same night, at the same time. It's an energetic crowd, and they all appear quite content to shout at each other over their seafood risotto. If this is your kind of scene, then by all means go. You may have to wait to be seated even if you have a reservation, but it's worth it. But if you're looking for a quiet, romantic spot, forget it.

That's the bad news. The good news is the wood-roasted fish, Sotto Sotto's specialty (the chef fillets it tableside), the meltingly tender homemade pastas, the creamy risottos, the inventive appetizers, the attentive service, and the small but tempting selection of desserts. The unbelievably rich chocolate soup (yes, soup) of dark Belgian chocolate with hazelnut whipped cream and sugar croutons will make you swoon. The bartender makes a top-notch martini, and the 100-percent-Italian wine list is extensive, with several excellent selections by the glass.

313 N. Highland Ave. (at Elizabeth St.). © **404/523-6678**. Reservations recommended. Entrees $14–$22. AE, DC, MC, V. Mon–Thurs 5:30–11pm; Fri–Sat 5:30–midnight. Valet parking. MARTA: North Ave.

Surin of Thailand ⭐ THAI   This charming Thai restaurant opened in 1991 to big crowds, and it has continued to enjoy hearty acclaim. The place is full of neighborhood regulars and suburbanites looking for consistent Asian cooking in an upbeat, contemporary setting—bare oak floors, candlelit tables covered in royal blue linen cloths, and cheerful yellow walls.

The same menu is offered throughout the day, with specials at both meals. The fresh basil rolls are some of the best around, but another appetizer favorite is chef Surin Techarukpong's exquisite deep-fried edible "baskets" filled with shrimp, chicken, and corn, served with a piquant vinegar-chili-peanut sauce. Entrees range from seafood dishes to traditional noodles and curry. If it's on the specials menu, opt for *neur nam tok*—strips of grilled beef tenderloin seasoned with lime, hot serrano chile peppers, fresh basil, fish sauce, and green onion; it's eaten rolled in cabbage leaves. For a cool finale, try the creamy homemade coconut ice cream or one of the mango, green tea, or ginger versions.

On weekends, arrive early or late to avoid a wait, and try for a table in the window or along the wall. Try to avoid seating in the small back rooms; the main dining area is noisy and crowded but much more fun.

810 N. Highland Ave. (at Greenwood Ave.). © **404/892-7789**. Reservations not accepted. Lunch items $5.95–$6.50; dinner main courses $6.95–$14.95. AE, DC, DISC, MC, V. Mon–Fri 11:30am–11:30pm; Sat noon–11:30pm; Sun noon–10:30pm. MARTA: North Ave.

Tiburon Grille *Finds* CONTEMPORARY AMERICAN   This little restaurant in the heart of Virginia-Highland is a neighborhood favorite, even though the kitchen can be uneven at times. Despite the fact that it opened in the mid-1990s, the interior, with its distressed walls and old wood floors, makes it look as if this has been a gathering spot for decades. There's a full-service bar and a covered terrace that fills up fast on balmy evenings.

There's a little of everything on the menu, from Asian to Mediterranean to traditional Southern. The portions are large, and the dishes offer a variety of distinct but complementary flavors. The menu changes seasonally, but there are three specialties nearly always on the list: sesame-seared ahi tuna, Georgia shrimp over Stilton grits, and Asian spring rolls. The wine list is reasonably priced and well chosen.

1190B N. Highland Ave. (at Amsterdam Ave., behind the post office). © **404/892-2393**. Reservations recommended. Main courses $9.50–$25. AE, DC, DISC, MC, V. Mon–Thurs 6–10pm; Fri–Sat 6–11pm; Sun 6–9pm. MARTA: North Ave.

INEXPENSIVE

Doc Chey's Noodle House *Kids* ASIAN   This may not be the most authentic noodle house in the city, but it's a neighborhood standby that won't let you down if you're looking for a good, inexpensive meal. It's kid-friendly, too, and offers two children's meals (Chinese chicken soup or chicken, carrots, and broccoli over rice) that should please finicky little eaters. The rest of us have a lot to choose from: fragrant basil rolls, Chinese scallion pancakes, soup bowls, noodle bowls, rice bowls and salads, each with a Thai, Chinese, Japanese, or Vietnamese accent. You can ask for most of them to be prepared vegetarian style. The decor is nothing fancy, but the patio's large and pleasant, the Asian beer is cold, and at these prices, there's not much to complain about.

There's another Doc Chey's in Emory Village near Emory University, 1556 N. Decatur Rd. (© **404/378-8188**). The hours are slightly different.

1424 N. Highland Ave. (at University Dr.). © **404/888-0777**. Main dishes $4–$8. AE, DISC, MC, V. Mon 5:30am–10pm; Sun and Tues–Thurs 11:30am–10pm; Fri–Sat 11am–11pm. MARTA: North Ave.

Flying Biscuit Cafe ★ *Finds* CREATIVE AMERICAN   This totally unpretentious neighborhood hangout has got the best biscuits in town, but that's not all that makes folks willing to wait up to an hour and a half for a table. A cozied-up storefront near the funky Little Five Points area, it's got an around-the-clock breakfast menu that will get you over the worst day-after-the-night-before and an assortment of dishes that are best described as comfort food for the granola crowd.

Orange-scented French toast with raspberry sauce and honey crème anglaise is hard to beat for breakfast, especially when accompanied by homemade turkey and sage sausage. But the aptly named Love Cakes, a mix of black bean and cornmeal, sautéed and topped with tomatillo salsa, sour cream, feta, and raw onion spears, will steal your heart away. Though there's a vegetarian slant to the menu, there's plenty to please carnivores, from turkey meatloaf, thick-sliced and grilled, to the ever-changing warm chicken salad atop organic field greens. There are nightly chicken, seafood, and pasta specials, too. You can get a cup of coffee while you wait outside for your table, but to avoid the serious crowds, come on a weekday or in the early afternoon. If you have any sullen teenagers in your party, they'll think you're really cool for bringing them here. They recently added a second location in Midtown at 1001 Piedmont Ave. (© **404/874-8887**).

1655 McLendon Ave. (at Clifton Rd.). © **404/687-8888**. Reservations not accepted. Breakfast $4.95–$8.95; main courses $5.95–$14.95. AE, MC, V. Sun–Thurs 9am–10pm; Fri–Sat 9am–10:30pm. MARTA: Midtown.

George's Restaurant and Bar *Value* AMERICAN   Smack in the middle of trendy Virginia-Highland, surrounded by chic boutiques and cafes, is a comfy old neighborhood tavern—nearly a juke joint—that's managed so far to buck the gentrification sweep. This place, which has been operated by George Najour and his family for 40 years, is not trendy, so don't expect wild mushroom risotto or seared tuna. But its solid bar fare—burgers, sandwiches, fries, and the like—and the unpretentious attitude can be a relief if you've overdosed on Yuppiedom. George passed away in late 2002 and his son continues to run the place.

Good bets are the substantial homemade black bean soup, the Greek salad, and the crispy onion rings—even better than the Varsity's. When you order a burger, be sure to specify how you want it done. The charbroiled chicken salad, chunks of tender breast atop mixed greens, is another decent alternative. The place is thick with neighborhood regulars and is home to a couple of book discussion groups, which meet there regularly. On a sunny day, grab a table on the sidewalk out front; it's a great place for watching the world (and some unusual folks) go by.

1040 North Highland Ave. NE (near Virginia Ave. intersection). © **404/892-3648**. Main courses $3.95–$6.95. AE, MC, V. Mon–Sat 10:30am–midnight; Sun 12:30–9pm. MARTA: North Ave.

6 East Atlanta

East Atlanta is a little bit out of the loop for most tourists, but the emerging commercial area around Flat Shoals and Glenwood avenues is worth a trip if you're looking for a nontouristy scene that's a little adventuresome. There are several shops, a coffeehouse, a couple of bars, a pizza parlor (great pies), and a handful of restaurants. Two of the best are listed here. East Atlanta is not hard to find, and it's not too far from Turner Field, the zoo, and the Cyclorama.

INEXPENSIVE

Heaping Bowl and Brew _Kids_ ECLECTIC   When Todd Semrau moved into this transitional neighborhood a few years ago, he lamented the fact that there was no place to go for a good meal and a beer. Recognizing the potential, Semrau opened this modest but sassy little storefront restaurant with the hope of attracting neighborhood singles and families. It quickly caught the attention of in-town and suburban folks who don't mind venturing off the beaten track for simple but interesting fare at the right price. Semrau's restaurant was the first new venture to attract people from outside the neighborhood, and he gets a lot of the credit for beginning the East Atlanta commercial renaissance. This place offers some diversity in a growing area of the city.

The big attractions here are the Heaping Bowls, hearty one-dish meals: a stew of greens and beans in an Italian herb broth; chicken and noodles; or comfy cheese-and-potato-filled pierogi with sausage, brown butter, sage, and mushrooms, to name three of the perennial favorites. The menu changes with the seasons, and there are several specials each day. There's a full bar, including Guinness on tap and a good selection of micro-brewed beers. For brunch, try the Hungry Bear, a wrap with eggs, chicken, and bacon, accompanied by home fries.

469 Flat Shoals Ave. ℂ **404/523-8030.** Heaping Bowls $3.95–$10.95; brunch entrees $5.95–$8.95. AE, MC, V. Mon–Wed 11am–11pm; Thur–Sat 11am–midnight; Sun 11am–10pm. Take I-20 east to the Moreland Ave. exit. Go south on Moreland 1 block, turn left on McPherson Ave., then right on Flat Shoals.

Pastificio Cameli _Value_ ITALIAN   Pastificio Cameli is a cut above what is typical for East Atlanta both in style and substance. The exposed stone walls and soft lighting make a nice setting, romantic enough for an intimate dinner, but casual just the same. The homemade pastas are exceptional for a small neighborhood restaurant, and you'll be happy with just about anything on the list. Especially good is the tender ricotta, spinach, and Gorgonzola-filled ravioli topped with a diced tomato sauce. The entrees are more hit and miss, but the wine selection is decent and affordable, with several possibilities available by the glass. The deck out back is a good choice if you have kids along.

1263 Glenwood Ave. SE (½ block east of Moreland Ave.). ℂ **404/622-9926.** Reservations not accepted. Pastas $9.75–$11.95; entrees $13.95–$16.95. AE, DISC, MC, V. Sun and Tues–Thurs 5pm–10pm; Fri–Sat 5pm–10:30pm. MARTA: Inman Park and bus no. 107 or 34.

7 Vinings

MODERATE

Canoe ★★ CONTEMPORARY AMERICAN   Canoe's cuisine is exceptional and the setting is divine—a picturesque spot on the Chattahoochee River, surrounded by heavenly gardens. The interior is ultra-upscale boathouse, with polished wood, classy fabrics, and fun, sophisticated metalwork. (Wrought-iron kudzu vines trail through the dining room.) The canoe motif is everywhere; there's even a canoe-shaped phone booth.

The menu is American, with Asian accents. Dinner might start with the roasted rabbit spring rolls with fig barbecue glaze. The pastas and risottos are innovative, to say the least. If it's available, try the slow-roasted rabbit with Swiss chard–country bacon ravioli and candied garlic glaze. Any of the fish are good, but for a regional dish with a twist, try the seared Carolina trout with citrus brown butter sauce. The excellent wine list is encyclopedic, even including a few organic wines. If the weather is good, ask for a table on the large, canopied patio.

4199 Paces Ferry Rd. NW (at the Chattahoochee River), in Vinings. ℭ 770/432-2663. Reservations essential on weekends. Lunch items $6.95–$14.95; brunch items $8.95–$14.95; dinner main courses $16.25–$22.50. AE, DC, DISC, MC, V. Mon–Fri 11:30am–2:30pm; Sun 10:30am–2:30pm; Sun–Thurs 5:30–10pm; Fri–Sat 5:30–11pm.

8 Decatur

EXPENSIVE

Floataway Café ★★ COUNTRY FRENCH/ITALIAN   Tucked away on a secluded industrial street in a renovated warehouse near Emory University, the Floataway Café is not easy to find. But people have been flocking to it since it opened in May 1998, the second venture by Anne Quatrano and Clifford Harrison of the renowned Bacchanalia in Midtown. The restaurant and menu here are less formal, but the food is the same high quality.

The menu changes daily, with an emphasis on local organic produce and other fresh and unusual ingredients. You'll find succulent wood-grilled or roasted meats and seafood, homemade pastas, even a couple of pizzas—all inventively prepared. One favorite is a house specialty: grilled steak with pommes frites and red wine shallot butter. You can make a meal of the starters; ricotta-stuffed sautéed squash blossoms and prosciutto with Georgia figs are two that shouldn't be passed up if they're available. The wine list has an international slant and is chosen to go well with food.

The only drawback to the place is that it can be as loud as a working warehouse. Ask for a table away from the bar, which can be quite boisterous.

1123 Zonolite Rd., Suite 15 in Decatur (west of the intersection of Johnson and Briarcliff rds.). ℭ 404/892-1414. Reservations essential. Main courses $14–$28. AE, DC, MC, V. Tues–Sat 5–10pm.

Watershed ★ CONTEMPORARY AMERICAN   When executive chef Scott Peacock left the highly successful Horseradish Grill a few years ago, who would have thought that he'd land in a sandwich shop housed in a former gas station in Decatur? Oh, OK, it's better than it sounds. Owned in part by Emily Saliers, one of the Indigo Girls, and carrying the same name as one of that group's songs, Watershed works on several levels—hip restaurant, wine bar, and retail store featuring wine, cookbooks, kitchen-related items, and other gifty little things. It's all in a bright, airy retro-style space whose industrial feel is softened by its pastel decor.

There are three or four entrees on the lunch menu, but sandwiches are the thing here—highly inventive and served on a variety of buttered, toasted breads. Two standouts include the sandwich with bosc pear, Maytag blue cheese, applewood smoked bacon, toasted walnuts, and arugula; and the white-truffle chicken salad with sultanas and pine nuts. Oh, yes, and you can't ignore the tangy but comforting pimento cheese made with extra sharp cheddar. At dinner, more entrees are added to the seasonal list of sandwiches, sides, and soups. You might find a whole roasted trout with garlic and lemon, or tender braised pork over creamy polenta. Tuesday night is fried chicken night, so arrive early to avoid

Cheesecake Fit for a President

Sweet potatoes are a staple in many southern homes and they find their way into recipes that never cease to surprise me. From sweet potato casserole and sweet potato pie to the popular sweet potato biscuits served during brunch at the Horseradish Grill, this tasty tuber is very versatile. But there is one Atlanta treat that does true justice to this spectacular spud: Sweet Auburn Bread Company's sweet potato cheesecake. The creation of Atlanta chef Sonya Jones, this sweet treat is known far and wide. In fact, former President Bill Clinton even stopped by the market while in town one day to try it for himself. Let's just say he didn't let any go to waste.

Trained at the Culinary Institute of America in Hyde Park, New York, Jones grew up in the restaurant business watching every move her mother made around the kitchen. She fell in love with baking. After graduating from the CIA she went on to share her culinary talents as a baking and pastry chef instructor at a local technical college. Soon she had opened her own bakery and was turning out pound cakes, buttermilk and lemon chess pies, even cakes made from towers of Krispy Kreme doughnuts. But it was in 1998 that her name would become synonymous with the famed sweet potato cheesecake. "I wanted to come up with something really southern and yet gourmet," she said of the smooth sweet pie resting atop a pound cake crust. The cheesecake has been featured in numerous magazines and newspapers and even on the Food Network. Now her goods are available in 22 Starbucks coffee shops around Atlanta, 2 of which are owned by Magic Johnson.

Formerly housed in the Sweet Auburn Curb Market, her bakery is now located at 2457 Martin Luther King, Jr. Drive SW, Suite J, in the same neighborhood where she grew up and learned to love baking as a young girl. She has reduced the retail hours to Fridays and Saturdays only, but special orders and pick up times are available by calling ⓒ **404/696-5676.**

a long wait. The wine list is extensive and well chosen, and the desserts, from the chocolate almond macaroon to the organic Georgia pecan tart, are scrumptious. Watershed recently began opening on Sundays for brunch.

406 W. Ponce de Leon Ave. (just west of the Decatur Sq.). ⓒ **404/378-4900.** Reservations for parties of 8 or more. Sandwiches and salads $7–$9; lunch entrees $8–$12; dinner entrees $12–$18. AE, MC, V. Mon–Sat 11am–10pm. Sunday brunch 10am–3pm.

MODERATE

Brick Store Pub ECLECTIC   On the square in Decatur, this pub has Olde World charm without being dark and gloomy. Featuring the most eclectic beer menu available in the Atlanta market, many patrons come here for the drink as much as for the equally diverse food. Starters include such treats as baked Brie or roasted red pepper hummus with warm pita points. Pierogi Primavera is another popular item, as are the potato wedge fries with lots of salt and vinegar. Each of the 16 draughts—from Germany, England and even the Czech Republic—is served in its own special glass. In addition, the 62 bottled beers might make it difficult for you to make a decision. Brick Store also offers 26 single malt scotches, 9 Irish whiskeys, and 8 small batch bourbons.

Choose to sit around the horseshoe bar for a real pub experience or at one of several tables outdoors. There are several great shops in the area for some before- or after-dinner shopping, as well as a coffee shop and a new ice cream shop.

125 E. Court St. (on the square), Decatur. ℭ **404/687-0990**. Salads, sandwiches, and burgers $2.75–$6.25; dinner entrees $6–$8. Monday 11am–1am; Tues–Sat 11am–2am; Sun 12–10pm.

Thai Chili ⭐ THAI   Owner Robert Khankiew, who was a chef at several other local Thai restaurants, has been packing people in since he and his family opened the doors of this friendly restaurant. The dishes are authentic, the flavoring bold, and the dining room casual yet polished (tablecloths, soft lighting).

Start off with traditional basil rolls with plum sauce, or try the *namsod*—minced pork with chiles, ginger, onion, and lime juice, which you roll up in a cabbage leaf. The spicy basil lamb (charbroiled chops with mushroom and onions) is succulent and exceptional, and the curries are quite good. When in doubt, stick with the daily specials or the chef's special section of the menu; all are good bets. There is no children's menu, but the restaurant is very child-friendly. You're likely to wait if you arrive without a reservation on the weekend.

2169 Briarcliff Rd. NE (at LaVista Rd. in the BriarVista Shopping Center). ℭ **404/315-6750**. Reservations recommended for dinner. Lunch items $6.75–$10.95; dinner main courses $8.25–$19.95. AE, DISC, MC, V. Mon–Fri 11am–2:30pm; Sun–Thurs 5–10pm; Fri–Sat 5–11pm.

INEXPENSIVE

Athens Pizza *Value* GREEK/PIZZA   Who says pizza has to have an Italian pedigree? The Papadopoulos family migrated here more than 20 years ago from Connecticut, and they've been serving up Greek specialties and their interpretation of pizza ever since. Their restaurant draws a large number of families and Emory University students from the surrounding area. The interior is ultra-casual, with Naugahyde booths and Formica-topped tables, and you'll be welcome in shorts or jeans.

There's quite a variety of Greek dishes, from gyros to pastitsio to rotisserie-cooked lamb. Portions are generous, prices are reasonable, and everything is authentic. It's home-style rather than fancy—exactly what you would get if the Papadopouloses invited you over for dinner. The signature creation is the pizza, and if you've never had it Greek style, it's worth a try. It has a thick, yeasty crust and comes in several varieties, but the best is the vegetarian special, with fresh tomatoes, onions, sweet green peppers, Kalamata olives, and a generous portion of feta cheese. A good ending is the honey-soaked baklava.

Note: There are several Athens Pizza restaurants and Athens Pizza Express takeout stores around town. Check your phone book for other locations.

1341 Clairmont Rd. (at N. Decatur Rd.), Decatur. ℭ **404/636-1100**. Pizzas $4.70–$17.95; main courses $3.70–$7.95. AE, DC, DISC, MC, V. Sun–Thurs 11am–11pm; Fri–Sat 11am–midnight.

Raging Burrito MEXICAN   When you're on the square in Decatur (and even when you're not) and have a craving for some out-of-the-ordinary taqueria fare, the Raging Burrito is the place to go. From a BBQ chicken burrito with caramelized onions and cilantro to the Sydney Salad Burrito with fresh guac or feta, Raging is sure to satisfy even the biggest hunger pangs. Choose flour, wheat, spinach, or sun-dried tomato tortillas to build your dream burrito. Chase down the chow with any of 38 tequilas offered here and you might be hanging around at an outside table for a while. Nachos, quesadillas, and vegetarian chili are also popular menu items. They offer a Sunday brunch. There is a second Raging Burrito located on Piedmont Avenue in Midtown.

141 Sycamore St. (on the square), Decatur. *©* **404/377-3311**. Burritos $4–$7.75. Sun–Thurs 11am–11pm; Fri–Sat 11am–midnight; Sunday brunch 11am–3pm.

9 Doraville

MODERATE

Little Szechuan CHINESE   Little Szechuan is a perennial favorite among the ethnic restaurants that now line Buford Highway in northeast Atlanta. It's nothing fancy, but the price is right. Most of the patrons are Chinese or regulars who make it a point to seek out good ethnic food. Two Chinese restaurant clichés are pointedly absent: egg rolls and fortune cookies. When you're seated, you'll be given a small bowl of spicy sprouts to munch on while you peruse the extensive menu. And when your check arrives at the end of the meal, it will be accompanied by a piece of fresh, seasonal fruit, perhaps a slice of watermelon.

The potstickers are good for a starter, but there's also fried soft-shell crab and steamed or fried Chinese sliced roll. The standout entree is also the most expensive: fresh steamed red snapper with black bean sauce. It's best when you request it spiced up a little. (Even though the name of the restaurant would suggest otherwise, not everything on the menu is spicy Szechuan-style Chinese.) An excellent side would be the stir-fried string beans or sautéed sweet pea leaves. The wine selection is extremely limited (and the red wine has been known to arrive slightly chilled) so it's best to forget it and have an ice-cold Tsing-Tao beer.

5091-C Buford Highway (just north of Shallowford Rd. in Northwoods Plaza), Doraville. *©* **770/451-0192**. Lunch combination plates $4.65–$6.75; dinner entrees $7.25–$19.95. MC, V. Wed–Mon 11:30am–2:30pm, 5pm–9:30pm.

What to See & Do in Atlanta

People used to say Atlanta was a great place to live, but you wouldn't want to visit. Not anymore. In fact, because of traffic and some other major pains in this city, some say just the opposite—give me a weekend in Atlanta and let me live elsewhere. Oh well, to each his own. A lot has happened since Atlanta's humble beginnings as a railroad depot, and the city is rich in historic sites—Civil War sites, landmarks of the civil rights movement, and monuments (such as World of Coca-Cola) to the businesses that have energized the city's development. And all those elements that make Atlanta a great place to live are here for visitors, too. You can take a stroll through a world-class botanical garden, picnic in a scenic park, raft down a river, visit a major art museum, splash through the Olympic ring fountains, take in an enchanting puppet show, and more.

MARTA stops near attractions are listed where applicable. If you need bus-routing information, call © **404/ 848-4711.**

SUGGESTED ITINERARIES

If You Have 1 Day

Head up to Buckhead and visit the **Atlanta History Center.** It will give you a good overview of the city's history and make the rest of your visit a richer experience. Especially noteworthy at the center is a tour of the **Tullie Smith Farm,** once an authentic, antebellum working plantation (and decidedly un-Tara-like) that was moved here from outside Atlanta. Have lunch at one of the many upscale Buckhead restaurants, then take a drive through the lovely surrounding neighborhoods. In the afternoon, head downtown for a tour of the **CNN studios,** then walk across the street to **Centennial Olympic Park,** the gathering place during the Olympic Games. Early in the evening, visit the shops and galleries in the Virginia-Highland neighborhood, then have dinner at one of the many restaurants there. Later, have a nightcap in a cafe or bar along North Highland Avenue.

If You Have 2 Days

Follow the suggestions above on the first day. On the second day, get up early, go over to Auburn Avenue (see the walking tour in chapter 8), and visit the **Martin Luther King, Jr., National Historic Site** and surrounding neighborhood. In the afternoon, head over to Grant Park and see **Atlanta Cyclorama** and/or visit the pandas at **Zoo Atlanta.** If you have time, head to **Underground Atlanta** and take a tour of **World of Coca-Cola.**

If You Have 3 Days

On your first 2 days, see as many of the sights described above as a comfortable pace allows. If the weather is nice on the morning of your last day, nothing could be better than spending a day at Georgia's **Stone Mountain Park** and its new feature **Crossroads,** a re-created 1870s

Southern town. In summer, be sure to stay late and see the laser show.

If it's cold or rainy, plan a morning tour of the **Carter Library and Museum,** then take in the **Margaret Mitchell House.** If you're traveling with kids, spend the day at the **Center for Puppetry Arts** or the **Fernbank Museum of Natural History.**

If You Have 4 Days or More

Take it easy. Over the first 4 days, juggle the above suggestions as you see fit. On the fifth day, if you have children in tow, tour **Turner Field** or take them to the children's garden at the **Atlanta Botanical Garden.** Civil War buffs should take in the **Kennesaw Civil War Museum** and **Kennesaw Mountain/National Battlefield Park** (both can be done in 1 day). If none of the above interests you, take in the latest exhibition at the **High Museum of Art,** then stroll through **Oakland Cemetery** in the afternoon.

1 The Top Attractions

The APEX (African-American Panoramic Experience) Museum   This museum chronicles the history of Sweet Auburn, once Atlanta's foremost black residential and business district, and serves as a national African-American museum and cultural center. In the museum's Trolley Car Theater, a replica of a turn-of-the-century tram that ran on Auburn Avenue, you can view a 12-minute multimedia presentation, *Sweet Auburn: Street of Pride,* that acquaints visitors with the area's history. Sweet Auburn history is also represented in tableaux such as a replica of an Auburn Avenue barbershop and a re-creation of the 1920s-era Yates & Milton's Drugstore (Atlanta's first black pharmacy), featuring some original furnishings. There are interactive displays for children. Inquire about special events and workshops taking place during your visit to Atlanta.

Across the street from the APEX Museum, at 100 Auburn Ave., is **Herndon Plaza,** where you can see a permanent exhibit on the Herndon family (former slave Alonzo F. Herndon founded the Atlanta Life Insurance Company) and changing shows of the works of African-American artists.

135 Auburn Ave. (at Courtland St.). ✆ **404/521-2739**. www.apexmuseum.org. Admission $3 adults, $2 seniors and students, free for children under age 4. Tues–Sat 10am–5pm; also Sun 1–5pm in Feb and June–Aug. Closed Thanksgiving, Christmas, and New Year's Day. MARTA: Bus no. 3 from the Five Points MARTA station.

Atlanta Botanical Garden   This delightful botanical garden, occupying 30 acres in Piedmont Park, saw the addition of the $4.8 million 25,000-square-foot Fuqua Orchid Center and the Dorothy Chapman Fuqua Conservatory in 2002. For the first time ever, a collection of rare high-elevation orchids, which flourish in the cool, humid mountains in South America, are being grown in the warm Southeast. Typically, one would have to go to San Francisco or Seattle to see such plants. This is part two of a three-part expansion project at the gardens. A children's garden opened in 1999 and the final phase—a new education center—is currently being constructed.

Another main section highlights plants that flourish in North Georgia's extended growing season. Displays in this area include a rock garden, a dwarf conifer garden, an English knot herb garden, a tranquil moon-gated Japanese garden, a rose garden, and annual and perennial displays. The delightful children's garden, with its wonderful climbing structures and whimsical sculptured fountains, has become a hot spot for young families. Lunch is served April through October, Tuesday to Sunday, on Lanier Terrace, overlooking the Rose Garden.

Another section of the garden consists of two wooded areas. The 5-acre Upper Woodland features a paved path, a fern glade, camellia and hosta gardens, gurgling streams, beautiful statuary, and a habitat designed to show visitors how to attract wildlife to their own backyards. Still more rustic is Storza Woods, 15 acres of natural woodlands and one of the few remaining hardwood forests in the city. Even though its path is unpaved, it makes for an easy and interesting walk.

Most exciting is the 16,000-square-foot, glass-walled Dorothy Chapman Fuqua Conservatory, housing rare and endangered tropical and desert plants—and a fascinating exhibit of poison dart frogs (more about them later). With acres of irreplaceable rainforest being bulldozed every minute, the technology-threatened plant species inside seem all the more special. Approached via an arbored promenade and fronted by a water lily pond, the conservatory has a revolving globe outside its entrance showing the many global regions where plant life is endangered.

The focal point of the conservatory is the misty Tropical Rotunda, housing fern collections, cycads (the most primitive seed-bearing plants known), epiphytes (plants that don't require soil to grow), gorgeous orchids, carnivorous plants, a wide variety of begonias, and towering tropical palms. It's a lush and humid jungle, with brightly hued tropical birds warbling overhead, a splashing waterfall, and winding pathways lined with fragrant hibiscus, ginger, and flowering jasmine vines. Of special interest is a double coconut palm from the Seychelles, growing from the largest and heaviest seed in the plant kingdom. Its first 12-foot leaves have already begun to grow, but it will be 100 years before the tree reaches its full height.

In the midst of all this is an intriguing exhibit of Central and South American poison dart frogs—small, active ground dwellers in unbelievably bright colors (yellow, orange, lime green, cobalt blue) and vivid patterns. About 12 species are exhibited in 3 large terrariums filled with tropical rain-forest plants and designed to simulate the climates in the frogs' native lands. The exhibit is a big hit with visiting children.

The arid Desert House displays Madagascan succulents, such as a unique family of spiny plants called *Didieriaceae*. Here, too, are "living stones" (desert succulents that nature designed to look like pebbles to protect them from being eaten by animals), tree aloes, caudici-forms (with swollen stems and roots for storing water), and conifers from Africa. Adjoining is an area for special exhibits.

The building also houses an orangery of tropical mango, papaya, star fruit, lychee, coffee, and citrus trees. A 1996 addition was an "Olympic" olive tree presented by Greece in honor of the Centennial Olympic Games.

There are flower shows throughout the year, along with lectures and other activities. Call to find out what's scheduled during your stay. A marvelous gift shop is on the premises; your purchases help support the garden.

1345 Piedmont Ave. NW (adjacent to Piedmont Park at Piedmont Ave. and the Prado). (C) 404/876-5859. www.atlantabotanicalgarden.org. Admission $10 adults, $7 seniors, $5 students with ID; free for children under age 3. Free every Thurs 3pm–closing. A $2 taped audio tour is available in 5 languages. Tues–Sun 9am–6pm, until 7pm during daylight saving time. The Conservatory, Orchid Center, and Gift Shop open at 10 a.m. The gardens are closed every Mon except Mon holidays. All areas accessible to visitors with disabilities. Free parking. MARTA: Bus no. 36 from the Arts Center Station Tues–Sat; bus no. 31 from Five Points or Lindbergh stations on Sunday.

Atlanta History Center ★★★   The Atlanta History Center chronicles the past of Georgia and the Southeast, as well as the city of Atlanta. The Center maintains a vast collection of photographs, maps, books, newspaper accounts, furnishings, Civil War artifacts, and decorative arts. It occupies 32 woodland acres, with self-guided walking trails and 5 gardens. Plan to spend the better part of a day here. And call ahead, or inquire on the premises, about lectures, films, festivals, and other events that take place here on a regular basis; activities range from sheep-shearing demonstrations to decorative arts forums. When you call, also check on house-tour times for the day of your visit (house-tours are described below). The Swan Coach House is a delightful restaurant on the premises (p. 135).

Note: House-tour tickets are limited and can only be purchased on the day of your visit. Arrive early to avoid disappointment.

Begin your visit at the **Atlanta History Museum.** This is where you can buy tickets and get information about historic house tours (see below) and other activities. The museum is the single best place to go for a cultural record of the city and the South. The museum's major permanent exhibit, "Metropolitan Frontiers: Atlanta, 1835–2000," traces Atlanta's history from the days of Native Americans and rural pioneer settlements to the present day. Displays, enhanced by hands-on discovery areas and informative videos, feature hundreds of photographs, documents, and artifacts. Included are an entire 1890s shotgun house, a fire engine that was used in Atlanta's great fire of 1917 (when 50 city blocks were ravaged by flames), a rare 1920 Hanson Six touring car; and a model of Atlanta's most complex interstate intersection, known locally as "Spaghetti Junction."

Also on the center's grounds is the **Swan House,** the 1928 estate of Edward Hamilton Inman, scion of an old Atlanta family. The house and gardens were designed by renowned architect Philip Trammell Shutze and are considered his finest residential work. The house is interesting not only architecturally but for its eclectic contents and furnishings, which comprise a veritable museum of decorative arts. It's also a fascinating glimpse into the lifestyle enjoyed by upper-crust Atlantans in the early 20th century.

Swan House is fronted by a classical colonnaded porte cochére, leading to a circular entrance hall with Ionic columns and a dramatic floating stairway. The formal gardens include terraced lawns and waterfalls, retaining walls with recessed ivy arches, and fountain statuary. In the entrance hall, you'll notice that the fanlight over the door centers on a swan, announcing the theme of the house. In fact, there is supposed to be at least one swan emblem or decoration in each room—see if you can find them.

Tullie Smith Farm gives a sense of the life of Georgia's mid–19th-century farmers. A two-story "plantation-plain" house built in the early 1840s, it was brought here along with period outbuildings in 1972. This was no Tara-like colonnaded mansion—just an everyday farmhouse whose occupants lived in rustic simplicity. Costumed docents give tours throughout the day, and there are frequent demonstrations of 19th-century farm activities.

A bedroom has a rope bed with a feather mattress and a crib that was always occupied by the youngest baby. Here, a docent will demonstrate how to use a spinning wheel. The basket of pomander balls was typical—the 19th-century answer to today's air fresheners.

In a back room, there are weaving demonstrations. During cooler months, demonstrations of 19th-century hearth cookery take place in the whitewashed kitchen, where herbs hang from the rafters. Additional outbuildings are a barn, corncrib, root cellar, blacksmith shop, and smokehouse. The gardens and grounds are authentic to the period.

Fun Fact **Did You Know?**

- Atlanta has 100 streets with the name Peachtree.
- Georgia's major agricultural crop is peanuts, not peaches.
- Atlanta's earliest streetlights burned whale oil.
- The world's largest bas-relief sculpture (Stone Mountain—90 ft. × 190 ft.) and the world's largest painting (*Cyclorama,* using 20,000 sq. ft. of canvas) are in Atlanta.
- Georgia Tech's Yellow Jackets set a world record football score in 1916: 222 to 0 (they were the zero).
- Because it has received over $250 million from Coca-Cola, Emory University is known as "Coca-Cola U."
- *Fortune* magazine consistently rates Atlanta one of the nation's best places to do business.
- Not a single scene from the movie *Gone With the Wind* was filmed in Georgia, though a few bushels of Georgia red clay were transported to the Hollywood set to add verisimilitude.
- Hartsfield is the country's busiest airport and is consistently ranked among the best airports in the world. Eighty percent of the U.S. population is within a 2-hour flight of Atlanta.

Leave some time to stroll the gardens, most notably the forested mile-long **Swan Woods Trail.** It includes plants native to Georgia, and the Garden for Peace, where you will see a sculpture by noted Soviet artist Georgi Dzhaparidze and Atlanta artist Hans Godo Frabel.

130 W. Paces Ferry Rd. (at Slaton Dr.). © **404/814-4000.** www.atlantahistorycenter.com. Admission $12 adults, $10 seniors and students age 18 or older, $7 children age 4–17, free for under age 3. General admission is all-inclusive. Mon–Sat 10am–5:30pm; Sun and some holidays noon–5:30pm. Ticket sales stop at 4:30pm. Closed Thanksgiving, Christmas Eve, Christmas, and New Year's Day. MARTA: Take MARTA rail to Lenox station; from there take bus no. 23 to Peachtree St. and W. Paces Ferry Rd., then walk 3 blocks west on the latter.

Birth Home of Martin Luther King, Jr ★★   Martin Luther King, Jr. was born in this two-story Queen Anne–style house on January 15, 1929, the oldest son of a Baptist minister and an elementary school music teacher. His childhood was a normal one. He preferred playing baseball to piano lessons, liked to play board games, and got a kick out of tearing the heads off his older sister's dolls (nonviolence came later). To quote his sister, Christine King Farris, "My brother was no saint ordained at birth, instead he was an average and ordinary man, called by . . . God . . . to perform extraordinary deeds."

King lived here through the age of 12, then moved with his family to a house a few blocks away. A visit provides many insights into the formative influences on one of the greatest leaders of our time. The Rev. A. D. Williams, King's maternal grandfather and pastor of Ebenezer Baptist Church, bought the house in 1909. Reverend Williams was active not only in the church, but in the community and in early manifestations of the civil rights movement. He was a charter member of Atlanta's NAACP and led a series of black registration and voting drives as far back as 1917. He was instrumental in getting black officers on the

Atlanta police force. Martin Luther King, Sr. moved in on Thanksgiving Day, 1926, when he married Williams's daughter Alberta. When Reverend Williams died in 1931, King became head of the household and took over Williams's pulpit at Ebenezer Church.

The King family retained ownership of the house at 501 Auburn even after they moved away. King's younger brother, Alfred Daniel, lived here with his family from 1954 to 1963. In 1971, King's mother deeded the home to the Martin Luther King, Jr. Center. It has since been restored to its appearance during the years of King's boyhood. The furnishings are all originals or similar period reproductions, and some personal items belonging to the family are on display. Christine was actively involved in the restoration, providing a wealth of detail about the former appearance of the house, as well as anecdotal material about life in the King family.

Tours of the house, conducted by National Park rangers, begin in the downstairs parlor, where you'll see family photographs showing Martin Luther as a child. The parlor was used for choir practice, for the dreaded piano lessons, and as a rec room where the family gathered around the radio to listen to shows like "The Shadow." In the dining room, world events were regularly discussed over meals, and every Sunday, before dinner, each child was required to recite a newly learned Bible verse from memory. You'll also see the coal cellar (stoking coal was one of King's childhood chores); the children's play area; the upstairs bedroom of King's parents in which Christine, King, and Alfred Daniel were born; Reverend Williams's den, where the family gathered for nightly Bible study; the bedroom King shared with his brother ("always in disarray," says Christine); and Christine's bedroom.

Note: In summer, especially, tickets often run out early; for your best chance to tour the home, arrive at 9am.

501 Auburn Ave. ⓒ 404/331-6922. www.nps.gov/malu. Free admission. Tickets are available at the National Park Service Visitors Center, 450 Auburn Ave. Tours depart from Fire Station No. 6 (at Boulevard and Auburn Ave.) about every 30 min. in summer, every hour the rest of the year. Daily 9am–5pm. Closed Thanksgiving, Christmas, and New Year's Day. From I-75/85 south, exit at Freedom Parkway/Carter Center (248C). Turn right at first stoplight onto Boulevard. Follow signs to Martin Luther King, Jr., National Historic Site. MARTA: King Memorial Station is about 8 blocks away, or take bus no. 3 east from the Five Points Station.

Centennial Olympic Park ★★★   Centennial Olympic Park, one of the most enduring legacies of the 1996 Olympic Games, is a living monument to the city's memories—both good and bad—of that seminal event. Conceived as a town square, it represents the heart of the Olympic effort, the site where everyone flocked to celebrate the games. And when the games resumed after the bombing in the park that claimed two lives, it was where people gathered to try to revive the Olympic spirit.

A 21-acre swath of green space and bricks, the park was carved out of a blighted downtown area. It was closed after the games, redesigned for permanent use, then reopened in 1998. Once again the universal gathering place it was intended to be, it's an oasis of rolling lawns crisscrossed by brick pathways and punctuated by artwork, rock gardens, pools, and fountains. There are usually a few free events each month—festivals, artists' markets, concerts, and other performances. Call for a complete listing of happenings.

If you're visiting the park on your own, and not coming for a specific event, your first stop should be the visitor center on International Boulevard, in the southwest corner of the park, across from the CNN Center. Here, you'll find

Baker St.

Park Offices

Tribute to Georgia Agriculture

Two Garden Pavilions

The Quilt of Nations

The Quilt of Olympic Spirit

Androgyne Planet

The Quilt of Origins

The Belvedere

The Quilt of Remembrance

The Quilt of Dreams

Centennial Tree

The Game Board

The Allen Family Tribute

Fountain of Rings

Visitors Center

Luckie St.

Techwood Drive

International Blvd.

Marietta St.

Southern Co. Amphitheater

Techwood St.

ATLANTA

285

75

85

Centennial Olympic Park

20

285

Turner Field

20

85

285

285

85

75

Moments **In the Spotlight**

If you get to the CNN Center at the right time of day, you can get yourself on national television by being in the audience of "Talk Back Live," CNN's live talk show (3–4pm) that encourages the audience to give opinions on a topic of the day. Be sure to call home and get someone to tape the show; the audience is in front of the camera much of the time.

---

information about the park, and if you bought a $35 commemorative brick, someone will help you locate it among the nearly 500,000 engraved bricks that were used to pave the plaza and walkways. Even if you didn't buy a brick, it's fun to wander around and read the names and messages (some pretty intriguing) engraved on them. You'll find names from around the world.

The best part of the park is the fountain in the shape of five interlocking Olympic Rings. It's the central focus of a vast paved plaza bordered by 23 flags honoring all the host countries of the modern Games. If you're here in summer, you and the kids can frolic in the fountain (wear shirts and shoes, please), a good way to cool off in the sizzling Southern heat. Don't be shy. Just about everybody in Atlanta has done this at one time or another. If getting drenched is not your thing, you can still enjoy one of the concerts put on by the fountains. Seven songs are programmed to play during timed sequential water and light displays. The water jets, which normally shoot 12 feet into the air, can reach 35 feet during special effects.

Located along the east border are the Quilt Plazas, five plazas of contrasting bricks that tell the story of the Centennial Olympic Games. The best "quilt" is also the most moving. Titled the Quilt of Remembrance, it pays homage to the bombing victims and contains colored marble from five continents. Be sure to read the inscriptions on its borders.

285 International Blvd. NW (at Techwood Dr.). © **404/222-PARK (7275).** www.gwcc.com/parkinfo.htm. Free admission. Daily 7am–11pm. MARTA: Omni/Dome/GWCC or Peachtree Center.

CNN Studio Tour ★★★ This tour of the world's largest newsgathering organization is lots of fun, and a uniquely Atlanta experience. The CNN Center is headquarters for CNN, CNN International, and Headline News. During 40-minute guided walking tours, visitors get a behind-the-scenes look at the high-tech world of 24-hour TV network news in action. You'll find the tour desk in the main lobby near the base of an eight-story escalator. While you're waiting for the tour to begin, you can have a videotape made of yourself reading the day's top stories from behind a CNN anchor desk.

The tour starts in an exhibit area where you'll find timelines covering the history of CNN and Turner Broadcasting, interactive kiosks where you can surf the CNN websites or access clips from the top 100 stories that CNN has covered, memorabilia from some of those events, and a journalism ethics display. A theater that re-creates CNN's main control room allows you to experience the behind-the-scenes elements of a news broadcast.

Next, you'll enter a special effects studio and get a glimpse of the technology that goes into the production of global news. Here you'll discover the magic of a high-tech Blue Chromakey system (it's what's used to broadcast that big map behind the weather folks), see how on-air graphics are made, and learn the secrets of the TelePrompTer.

On another level, visitors get a bird's-eye view of the main CNN newsroom from a glass-walled observation station. You'll see the hustle and bustle of writers composing news scripts. If a live broadcast is in progress—and chances are good that one will be—you can see CNN newscasters at work. Tour guides are knowledgeable and can answer virtually any question.

The longer, more extensive VIP tour allows visitors to actually step out onto the main CNN newsroom floor and explore production areas not normally accessible to the public.

After your visit, stop by the Turner Store, which carries network-logo clothing and gift items, along with MGM movie memorabilia. For sports fans, there's the Braves Clubhouse store, featuring the Atlanta Braves logo on every item you can imagine. There are several restaurants and numerous fast-food outlets in the atrium of the CNN Center, as well as a few shops. Keep in mind that this tour includes quite of bit of walking and a very steep escalator ride, which carries you to great heights to begin the tour. Those afraid of heights might want to consider skipping the tour.

CNN Center, Marietta St. (at Techwood Dr.). (℃) **404/827-2300** or 877/4CNN-TOUR. www.cnn.com/studiotour. Admission $8 adults, $6 seniors, $5 children age 6–12. Children under age 6 not permitted. A more in-depth, 70-min. VIP tour costs $25 (includes standard admission price). **Note:** Reservations are recommended, but some tickets are available on a first-come, first-served basis on the day of the tour and go on sale at 8:30am. Tours are given daily every 20 minutes 9am–5pm. Arrive early for the tour you wish to take, since most tours sell out. Closed Easter, Thanksgiving, and Christmas Day. Free tickets are available for "Talk Back Live," a live interactive talk show on CNN. The show airs 3–4pm weekdays, and tickets can be reserved by calling (℃) **800/410-4266.** MARTA: Omni/Dome/GWCC. Many parking lots around the building.

Atlanta Cyclorama & Civil War Museum ★★   Though it sounds like something out of Disney World, this Cyclorama was created in the 1880s, and the concept—a huge, 360-degree three-dimensional cylindrical painting viewed from a rotating platform—dates back to a century earlier. Cycloramas were the rage of 18th- and 19th-century Europe, Russia, Japan, and later, the United States, depicting subject matter ranging from the splendors of Pompeii to Napoleonic battles. Enhanced by multimedia effects and faux terrain extending 30 feet from the painting into the foreground, they were the forerunners of newsreels, travelogues, and TV war coverage.

The one you'll see here—a 42-foot-high cylindrical oil painting, 358 feet in circumference (on about 16,000 sq. ft. of canvas)—depicts the events of the Battle of Atlanta, on July 22 1864, in meticulous detail. It took 11 eastern European artists, working in the United States in the studio of William Wehner, 22 months to complete the project.

For 21st-century tourists, the concept itself is as interesting as the action depicted, and the restoration is incredibly impressive. Though painted on fine Belgian linen in the painstaking style of the 19th-century art academies, the work suffered in moves from city to city, and later (when motion-picture epics made cycloramas passé) from neglect. Well-intentioned but incompetent attempts at restoration caused further damage. In the 1970s, a severe storm waterlogged the painting, causing seemingly irreversible damage.

But Mayor Maynard Jackson recognized the historic and artistic importance of Cyclorama; under his auspices, $11 million was raised for its restoration. It took 2½ years for renowned conservator Gustav Berger and his crew to repair the damaged work, a process that included mending more than 700 rips in the canvas. In the auditorium itself, the Cyclorama viewing is preceded by a 14-minute film about the Battle of Atlanta. The total program lasts about 35 minutes.

The fascinating story of Cyclorama's development and restoration is related in a video format near the auditorium entrance. Cyclorama's central theme is Gen. John B. Hood's desperate attempt to halt Sherman's inexorable advance into the city. Comprehensively narrated, and complete with music and sound effects, including galloping horses and cannon fire, it vividly depicts the troop movements and battles on the day in which the Confederates lost 8,000 men, and the Yankees lost 3,722. A figure highlighted far beyond his historic importance is Gen. John A. Logan of the Federal Army of Tennessee (who commissioned the painting at a cost of $42,000 as a campaign move in his bid for the vice presidency). He's shown gloriously galloping into the fray, bravely exposing himself and his men to enemy fire. The work was originally called *Logan's Great Battle*.

The building housing Cyclorama also comprises a museum of related artifacts, the most important being the steam locomotive *Texas* from the 1862 Great Locomotive Chase. Other exhibits include displays of Civil War arms and artillery, Civil War–themed paintings, portraits of Confederate and Union leaders, "life in camp" artifacts and photographs, and uniforms. You'll need about an hour and a half to see the museum in full if you visit both floors.

Note: No video cameras are allowed inside the Cyclorama auditorium.

800 Cherokee Ave. (in Grant Park). (✆ **404/658-7625**. www.bcaatlanta.org. Admission $6 adults, $5 seniors, $4 children age 6–12; free for under age 6. Daily June to Labor Day 9:20am–5:30pm; the day after Labor Day to May 31, 9:20am–4:30pm. Shows begin every half hour starting at 9:30am. Closed Thanksgiving, Christmas, New Year's Day, and Martin Luther King Day. MARTA: Bus no. 105 from the West End station. By car, take I-20 East from downtown to Exit 59A.

Ebenezer Baptist Church   Founded in 1886, Ebenezer was a spiritual center of the civil rights movement from 1960 to 1968, when Martin Luther King, Jr. served as co-pastor. His grandfather, the Rev. A. D. Williams, dedicated the church to "the advancement of black people and every righteous and social movement." His son-in-law and successor, Martin Luther King, Sr., worked for voting rights and other aspects of black civil and social advancement, following Williams's activist example. Later, Martin Luther King, Jr. would join his ancestors in pursuing justice for African Americans. The congregation has built a new sanctuary directly across the street, but the older building, where Martin Luther King, Jr. preached, continues to be open to the public. Short but informative tours of the sanctuary, conducted by members of the Ebenezer congregation, are given Monday to Friday 9am to 4pm, Saturday 9am to 2pm, and Sunday 2 to 4pm. One of the best things to do is attend a Sunday morning worship service in the new sanctuary. The public is welcome—and you'll realize just *how* welcome when the members of the congregation leave their seats at the beginning of the service to shake the hands of as many visitors as possible. It's a living testimonial to all that the church's most famous son stood for. Sunday services are at 7:45am and 10:45am. The sanctuary is usually packed, so it's a good idea to arrive well ahead of time. Groups of 6 or more should call the church office at (✆ **404/688-7263** to make reservations. An ecumenical service also takes place here every year during King week.

407–413 Auburn Ave. NE. (✆ **404/688-5001** or 404/688-7263. Free admission (donations appreciated). Mon–Sat 9am–5pm; Sun 2–4pm. From I-75/85 south, exit at Freedom Parkway/Carter Center. Turn right at first stoplight onto Boulevard. Follow signs to Martin Luther King, Jr., National Historic Site. MARTA: King Memorial Station is about 8 blocks away; you can also take a no. 3 bus from the Five Points Station.

Fernbank Museum of Natural History   The largest museum of natural sciences in the Southeast, this architecturally stunning facility borders 65 acres of pristine forest. The building, which nearly eclipses the attractions inside, centers on a soaring three-story, sky-lit Great Hall—an Italianate brick atrium with spiral staircases, lofty columns, and windows revealing the woodlands beyond. Architect Graham Gund has achieved a marvelous integration of interior/exterior space. Look closely at the museum floors, where ancient fossil remains from the late Jurassic period are embedded.

When the Great Hall was designed, it was meant to one day be the home of a large-scale permanent dinosaur exhibition, and in 2000, Fernbank became the only place in the world to display a complete mounted skeleton of *Argentinosaurus,* the largest dinosaur ever found. The dramatic permanent exhibit, "Giants of the Mesozoic," features the 90-foot-long plant-eater as it defends its nest of eggs against the 45-foot-long *Giganotosaurus,* the largest meat-eater ever classified. Hovering above in the 86-foot-tall Great Hall are two flying *pterosaurs.* Dinosaurs just don't get any bigger than this, and it's a little hair-raising to walk into the hall and see these beasts towering over the tiny humans below.

There are several other permanent exhibits, including "A Walk Through Time in Georgia," which uses the state as a microcosm to tell the story of the earth's development through time and the chronology of life upon it. Eighteen galleries here re-create landform regions from the rolling pine-forested foothills of the Piedmont Plateau to the mossy Okefenokee Swamp, from the Cumberland Plateau (where you can walk through a typical "limestone cavern") to the marshy Coast and Barrier Islands. Exhibits are enhanced by creative films and videos, informational audiophones, interactive computers, sound effects, and old-fashioned field guides—not to mention more than 1,500 fabricated plants and mounted specimens of birds and animals. Visitors travel back 15 billion years to experience the origins of the universe (the Big Bang) and the formation of galaxies and solar systems, and into the future to consider the fate of our planet.

"Sensing Nature" tantalizes each of your senses with hands-on exhibits that explore how we experience the natural world. The room bristles with computers, colored lights, and mirrors, and you can step into a life-size kaleidoscope, play with perspective, gaze into infinity, see physical evidence of sound waves, and mix colors on a computer.

The "Children's Discovery Room," which is open daily June through August and on a limited basis during the school year, includes Fantasy Forest, a colorful play area designed for preschoolers (ages 3–5), where kids can become bees and pollinate flowers, climb a tree house, walk through a swamp, and play at being farmers. The state-shaped Georgia Adventure is a similar discovery room for ages 6 to 10.

While you're here, be sure to catch a stunning IMAX film (buy tickets as soon as you enter the museum; they sometimes sell out). The immense IMAX screen—5 stories high and 72 feet wide—puts you right in the middle of all the action.

Other museum attractions include a wetlands exhibit, a dramatically colorful living coral reef aquarium, a unique shell display, a gemstone collection, and the McClatchey Collection of jewelry and textiles from the old Silk Road countries. A museum store is stocked with entertaining and educational gifts and books, and there's a restaurant with arched windows overlooking Fernbank Forest, as well as outdoor patio seating. See p. 225 for a description of the adult-geared Martini & IMAX Friday nights.

767 Clifton Rd. NE (off Ponce de Leon Ave.). ℂ **404/370-0960** for information, 404/929-6400 for tickets. www.fernbank.edu/museum. Admission $12 adults ($17 includes an IMAX Theater ticket), $11 seniors and students ($15 includes an IMAX Theater ticket), $10 children ages 2–12 ($13 includes IMAX Theater ticket); children age 2 and under free. IMAX Theater admission alone $10 adults, $9 seniors and students, $8

children ages 2–12, free for children under 2. Mon–Sat 10am–5pm; Sun noon–5pm. The IMAX Theater is open until 10pm on Fri nights, Jan–Nov, for Martinis and IMAX. Closed Thanksgiving and Christmas.

Fox Theatre Originally conceived as a Shriners' temple in 1916, this lavish, block-long Moorish-Egyptian fantasyland ended up as a movie theater when the Shriners realized that their grandiose plan had far exceeded their budget. In 1927, they sold the temple to movie magnate William Fox, who created a peerless pleasure palace. French architect Oliver J. Vinour designed the building, using design motifs of the Middle East, including replicas of art and furnishings from King Tut's tomb.

Atlanta's new theater opened in 1929 as a masterpiece of Eastern splendor, its Moorish facade, onion domes, and minarets in exotic contrast to the surrounding Victorian boardinghouses. A brass-trimmed marble kiosk imported from Italy served as a ticket booth. The 140-foot entrance arcade led to a lushly carpeted lobby with blue-tiled goldfish pools. The auditorium was an Arabian courtyard under a twinkling starlit sky that could, with state-of-the-art technology, be transformed to a sky at sunrise or sunset. A striped Bedouin canopy sheltered the balcony, and sequin- and rhinestone-studded stage curtains depicted mosques and Moorish horsemen.

As the show began, a gigantic gilded 3,610-pipe Möller organ rose majestically from its vault, its rich chords accompanied by a full orchestra. A medley of popular songs, cartoons, a follow-the-bouncing-ball sing-along, a stage-show extravaganza by a bevy of Rockette-like chorines called the Fanchon and Marco Sunkist Beauties, and a newsreel preceded every main feature. At night, there were dances in the Egyptian Ballroom, designed to replicate Ramses' temple. And even the men's lounge was exotically appointed with hieroglyphic adornments, winged scarab-motif friezes, bas-reliefs of royal figures, and throne chairs.

Unfortunately, the Fox's opening coincided with the Great Depression, and it proved impossible to maintain its opulence. In 1932, the company declared bankruptcy and closed its doors. The theater reopened 3 years later for occasional concerts. By the 1940s, it was a successful concern once more, and in 1947, the Metropolitan Opera began performing here for a week each year—an offering which lasted 2 decades. An oversize panoramic screen was installed in the 1950s, along with a 26-speaker stereo system. But like monumental movie palaces nationwide, the Fox inevitably declined in the age of television. In 1975, its doors were padlocked once again.

An organization of concerned citizens calling themselves Atlanta Landmarks raised $1.8 million and saved the Fox from the wrecking ball in 1978, foiling Southern Bell's plans to purchase and demolish it to make way for a regional headquarters building. Ever since, it's been a thriving entity, featuring Broadway shows, headliners, dance companies, and comedy stars. Best of all, the theater has been restored to its former glory, its fabulous furnishings and fixtures all refurbished or replaced with replicas.

You cannot explore the building on your own, so call to find out when you can take a tour, or come to see a performance in the theater.

660 Peachtree St. NE (at Ponce de Leon Ave.). © **404/817-8700** for box office, 404/876-2041 for tours. Tours $5 adults, $3 seniors and students. The Atlanta Preservation Center conducts walking tours of the Fox Theatre and the surrounding area Mon, Thurs, and Sat. Call to verify tour times before you go as production rehearsals occasionally cancel out tours. MARTA: North Ave.

Georgia's Stone Mountain Park ★ *Kids* A monolithic gray granite outcropping (the world's largest), carved with a massive monument to the Confederacy, Stone Mountain is a distinctive landmark on Atlanta's horizon and the

Margaret & Morrison

Lucy   10:35

Georgia's Stone Mountain Park

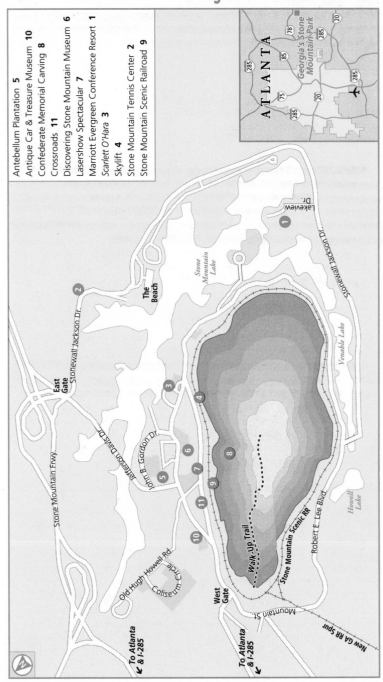

Antebellum Plantation **5**
Antique Car & Treasure Museum **10**
Confederate Memorial Carving **8**
Crossroads **11**
Discovering Stone Mountain Museum **6**
Lasershow Spectacular **7**
Marriott Evergreen Conference Resort **1**
Scarlett O'Hara **3**
Skylift **4**
Stone Mountain Tennis Center **2**
Stone Mountain Scenic Railroad **9**

ATLANTA

Georgia's Stone
Mountain Park

Stone
Mountain
Lake

Venable Lake

Howell
Lake

Lakeview Dr.

Stonewall Jackson Dr.

The
Beach

East
Gate

Stone Mountain Frwy

Jefferson Davis Dr.

John B. Gordon Dr.

Old Hugh Howell Rd.

Coliseum Cir.

West
Gate

Walk-Up Trail

Stone Mountain Scenic RR

Robert E. Lee Blvd.

Mountain St.

New GA RR Spur

To Atlanta
& I-285

To Atlanta
& I-285

focal point of its major recreation area, which includes 3,200 acres of lakes and beautiful wooded parkland. It's Georgia's number-one tourist attraction and 1 of the 10 most-visited paid attractions in the United States.

Stone Mountain itself was formed about 300 million years ago, when intense heat and pressure caused molten material just below the earth's surface to push upward. That material cooled slowly (it took 100 million years) and formed compact, uniform crystals. Initially, a 2-mile thick overlay of the earth's surface covered the hardened granite, but over the next 200 million years, that layer eroded, exposing the mountain we see today. The dome-shaped rock rises 1,683 feet above sea level and covers 583 acres. Half of Georgia and part of North Carolina rest on the mountain's base.

Although the best view of the mountain is from below, the vistas from the top are spectacular. Visitors who are part mountain goat can take a walking trail up and down its moss-covered slopes, especially lovely in spring when they're blanketed in wildflowers. Or you can ride the **Skylift** to the top, where you'll find an incredible view of Atlanta and the Appalachian Mountains. The best approach is to take the cable car up, then walk back down.

A highlight at Stone Mountain is the **Lasershow Spectacular,** an astonishing display of laser lights and fireworks with animation and music. The brilliant laser beams are projected on the mountain's north face, a natural one million-square-foot screen. The show begins in March, when it can be seen on Saturdays at 8:30pm. From Memorial Day Weekend through Labor Day, the show takes place each night at 9:30pm; after Labor Day, it can be seen at 8:30pm Saturdays only, through October. Bring a picnic supper and arrive early to get a good spot on the lawn at the base of the mountain.

It's a good idea to make your first stop the **Discovering Stone Mountain Museum** to get some perspective on the mountain's history. Exhibits take you through an intriguing chronological journey from the area's past into its present.

Other major park attractions include the **Stone Mountain Scenic Railroad,** an open-air train that chugs around the 5-mile base of Stone Mountain. The ride takes 40 minutes and includes a live "train robbery" skit. Trains depart from Railroad Depot, an old-fashioned train station, where there's a restaurant with all the fixings for a fried chicken picnic, just in case you forgot to bring your own.

(**Fun Fact**   **The Face of a Mountain**

Over half a century in the making, Stone Mountain's neoclassic carving—90 feet high and 190 feet wide—is the world's largest bas-relief sculpture. Originally conceived by Gutzon Borglum, it depicts Confederate leaders Jefferson Davis, Robert E. Lee, and Stonewall Jackson galloping on horseback throughout eternity. Borglum started work on the mountain sculpture in 1923 but abandoned it after 10 years due to insurmountable technical problems and rifts with its sponsors. (He went on to South Dakota, where he gained fame carving Mount Rushmore.) No sign of his work remains at Stone Mountain, but it was his vision that inspired the project. Augustus Lukeman took over in 1925, but 3 years later, the work still far from complete, the family that owned the mountain lost patience and reclaimed the property. It wasn't until 1963, after the state purchased the mountain and surrounding property for a park, that work resumed under Walter Kirtland Hancock and Roy Faulkner. It was completed in 1970.

The *Scarlett O'Hara,* a paddlewheel riverboat, cruises the 363-acre Stone Mountain Lake.

The **Antique Car and Treasure Museum** is a jumble of old radios, jukeboxes, working nickelodeons, pianos, Lionel trains, carousel horses, and clocks, along with classic cars.

Visitors can now travel back in time thanks to a new $30 million attraction at the park called **Crossroads** ✦, which opened in May 2002. At Crossroads, you can explore an 1870s rural Southern town, complete with a cast of authentically costumed characters who sing, play instruments, tell stories, and demonstrate crafts such as glass blowing, candle-making and blacksmithing. In addition to the town's quirky and talented characters, other special treats include a grist mill and bakery and a general store with candy and ice cream production facilities. A boarding-house restaurant offers up tasty Southern cuisine, from chicken and dumplings to fried catfish. If you plan to eat, you might want to stop by and add your name to the list before you explore the town, as there is often a wait. The town's centerpiece is the Tall Tales of the South theater, where visitors use special glasses to view a 3-D film with 4-D (yes, 4) special effects. The frog's tongue, which stretches into the movie audience from its perch on a swamp log, is just one of the surprises the experience offers. Small children might not enjoy the film, as some of the effects are a bit unnerving. Another part of the attraction is The Great Barn, a hit with children and adults. Join in the fun as you help "harvest" fruit and vegetables throughout this multi-level foam factory to rack up points for your team.

The 19-building **Antebellum Plantation** offers self-guided tours assisted by hosts in period dress at each structure. Highlights include an authentic 1830s country store; the 1845 Kingston House (it represents a typical overseer's house); the clapboard slave cabins; the 1790s Thornton House, elegant home of a large landowner; the smokehouse and well; a doctor's office; a barn, a coach house, and crop-storage cribs; a privy; a cook house; and the 1850 neoclassical Tara-like Dickey House. The grounds also contain formal gardens and a kitchen garden. It takes at least an hour to tour the entire complex. Often (especially in summer) there are Civil War reenactments, crafts and cooking demonstrations, storytellers, and balladeers on the premises. Children will enjoy getting up close and personal with the critters at Grandpa's Farm at The Plantation, featuring domesticated farm animals, including pigs and goats.

Additional activities: golf (on top-rated courses designed by Robert Trent Jones and John LaFoy), miniature golf, 15 tennis courts, a sizable stretch of sandy lakefront beach with 4 water slides, carillon concerts, rowboats and paddleboats, bicycle rental, fishing, hiking, picnicking, and more.

Stone Mountain is one of the most beautiful parks in the nation. Consider spending a few days of your trip here; it's a great place for a romantic getaway or a family vacation. On-site accommodations are detailed in chapter 5. If you can only spare a day, it's an easy drive (about 30 min.) from downtown.

U.S. Highway 78E, Stone Mountain, GA (16 miles east of downtown Atlanta). ℂ 800/317-2006 outside metropolitan Atlanta, or 770/498-5690. www.stonemountainpark.com. A ticket for all major attractions is $19 adults, $15 children age 3–11. Year-round gates open 6am–midnight. Major attractions open fall and winter 10am–5pm; spring and summer 10am–8pm. Parking charge $7 a day (one-time-only charge if you stay on the grounds) or $30 for 12-month pass. Attractions only are closed Christmas Eve and Christmas Day; park is open. Take MARTA to the Avondale station, where you can transfer to a bus to Stone Mountain Village. The park is 4 blocks from the village.

High Museum of Art   Designed by architect Richard Meier, this facility—part of the Woodruff Arts Center complex—is itself a work of art. A dazzling white porcelain–tiled building with an equally pristine white interior (the *New York Times* jokingly cautioned that visitors risk snow blindness on a sunny day), it houses four floors of galleries connected by semicircular pedestrian ramps girding a spacious, sun-filled, four-story atrium. It's a lovely building and a favorable setting in which to view art. However, the High has outgrown its space and details of a multimillion-dollar building expansion program were released in mid-2002. Groundbreaking is planned for spring 2003 with the new 177,000-square-foot addition to open in early 2005. The addition will include additional gallery space for the museum's permanent collection, enlarged special exhibit space, and a new restaurant, coffee bar, and retail shop.

The permanent collection includes more than 10,000 pieces, among them a significant group of 19th- and 20th-century American paintings. It features Hudson River School artists such as Thomas Cole and Frederic Church, as well as works by Thomas Sully, John Singer Sargent, and William Harnett. The Virginia Carroll Crawford Collection of American Decorative Arts comprehensively documents decorative arts styles from 1825 to 1917. The Samuel H. Kress Foundation collection includes Italian paintings and sculpture from the 14th through the 18th century. The Uhry Print Collection contains important works by French impressionists and post-impressionists, German expressionists, and American 20th-century artists. Also notable are collections of sub-Saharan African art, a folk art collection, and works by noted 19th- and 20th-century American and European photographers.

In addition to the permanent collection, which is shown on a rotating basis, the museum hosts a number of major traveling exhibitions each year, complemented by films, lectures, workshops, gallery talks, concerts, and other cultural events. Inquire at the desk about happenings during your stay, and call in advance to inquire about the free guided gallery tours of the High's permanent collection offered every Wednesday and Sunday at 1pm.

The museum has a wonderful gift shop with an impressive stock of art books, prints, and interesting art-oriented objects. There's also an excellent cafe run by Alon's, which has two other locations in town. It's a delightful space, accented with the same colors as the Calder mobile that is visible just outside the big glass windows. The cafe serves up sandwiches, soups, pastries, and desserts, fresh juice, tea, and specialty coffees. It's open Monday through Friday 9am to 5pm, Saturday 10am to 5pm, and Sunday noon to 5pm. You don't have to enter the museum to get to the cafe.

1280 Peachtree St. NE (at Sixteenth St.). ✆ **404/733-HIGH.** www.high.org. Admission $8 adults, $6 seniors and students with ID, $4 children age 6–17; free for children under age 6. Fees subject to change for special exhibitions. Tues–Sat 10am–5pm; Sun noon–5pm. Closed July 4th, Thanksgiving, Christmas, and New Year's Day. MARTA: Arts Center. (A covered walkway links the station to the museum.) Parking is available on 15th Street or in the parking garage across from the museum.

Jimmy Carter Library and Museum   Set on 30 acres of gardens, lakes, and waterfalls, this impressive presidential library houses some 27 million pages of documents, memoranda, and correspondence from Jimmy Carter's White House years. There are also 1½ million photographs and hundreds of hours of audio- and videotapes. The library's hilltop site is a historic one; it was from this spot that Sherman watched the Battle of Atlanta.

In the facility's extensive museum, you'll find an exact replica of the Oval Office during Carter's presidency, an exhibit enhanced by a recording of Carter speaking about his experiences in that office. A large display of "gifts of state" runs the gamut from a Dresden figurine of George and Martha Washington (a gift from Ireland) to a carpet from the Shah of Iran. You'll see the table setting used when the Carters entertained Chinese Vice Premier Deng Xiaoping and his wife in the State Dining Room; a video of artists such as the late pianist Vladimir Horowitz performing in the East Room; campaign memorabilia; and a large display devoted to the activities of Rosalynn Carter.

Other exhibits focus on Carter's support of human rights (there's a letter from Soviet dissident Andrei Sakharov and Carter's reply); his boyhood days (his sixth-grade report card and a photo of the Plains High basketball team are two of the items on display); and his pre-presidential life as a peanut farmer, governor, and state senator.

There are informative videos throughout, including an interactive "town meeting" format in which visitors can ask Carter questions on subjects ranging from world affairs to his personal life. And a most interesting participatory video lets you choose your response to a terrorist crisis and learn the probable consequences of your choice. The whole tour is self-guided, so you can go at your own pace.

Consider having lunch here. There's an excellent cafeteria, run by one of the city's top catering companies, with patio seating overlooking a Japanese garden and pond. Or if you're still in a political mode, stop by nearby **Manuel's Tavern,** a local pub at 602 N. Highland Ave. that's popular with journalists and politicians. President Carter stops in occasionally, too.

441 Freedom Pkwy. (Exit 248-C off I-75/85). ℂ **404/331-3942** or 404/331-0296. http://carterlibrary.galileo. peachnet.edu. Admission $5 adults, $4 seniors over 55; free for children age 16 and under. Mon–Sat 9am–4:45pm; Sun noon–4:45pm. Closed New Year's Day, Thanksgiving, Christmas.

Margaret Mitchell House and Museum (Birthplace of *Gone With the Wind*) ⭐

Six decades after it was first published, *Gone With the Wind* continues to fascinate people around the world. But until this attraction opened in 1997, after a 10-year effort to preserve the house from demolition, disappointed pilgrims found precious little evidence here of the famous book or its author. Now the house and museum are a must-see for visiting *GWTW* fans.

It's rather surprising that it took so long for restoration efforts to get under way on the dilapidated Tudor-revival apartment house where Margaret Mitchell wrote most of her epic novel and lived with her husband, John Marsh, from 1925 to 1932. The structure was built as a single-family dwelling in 1899, then moved to the back of the lot in 1913 and converted into a 10-unit apartment building 6 years later. It remained an apartment building until 1979, when it was abandoned and eventually boarded up. When the newlyweds moved in, they called it "The Dump"; it was not an affectionate nickname. According to a friend of Mitchell's, she disliked living there (finances left few alternatives) and would probably be offended by the notion of its restoration. But the house has been attracting its share of visitors—from all 50 states and more than 70 foreign countries.

The building includes a re-creation of Mitchell's first-floor apartment and exhibits telling the complex story of the famous novelist. Guided tours, which last an hour to an hour-and-a-half, begin in the visitors center, where guests see a 17-minute film titled "It May Not Be Tara," featuring an overview of Mitchell's life and interviews with some of her friends and family members. Also in the theater is an exhibition of photos taken of Mitchell in her teens and 20s. The tour of the house includes a visit to the Mitchell-Marsh apartment, which is furnished much as it was during their stay there. Mitchell wrote much of her

Searching for Margaret Mitchell

More than 6 decades after Margaret Mitchell published *Gone With the Wind,* the novel continues to attract new fans and fascinate people around the world. And thousands of them come to Atlanta each year, looking for some trace of Tara or the woman who wrote about it.

Well, Tara doesn't exist, no matter how much the book and movie brought it to life for us. The white-columned mansion we equate with Tara was more the product of Hollywood's fancy than of Mitchell's imagination. She begged filmmakers to represent the house as she envisioned it—a plain structure without columns—which was far closer to the reality of a working plantation than the image that's been perpetuated.

Until the Margaret Mitchell House and Museum opened in 1997, evidence of Mitchell herself was nearly as elusive as the fictional Tara. An extremely private person, she left a will stipulating that her papers and manuscripts be burned upon her death. Only a portion of the manuscript of *Gone With the Wind* was spared, enough to prove that Mitchell was its author. And several places where she lived fell victim to development or were destroyed in 1917, when a second great fire swept the city.

Still, it's possible to walk the streets of Atlanta and find traces of the famous author, either by viewing exhibits honoring her or by retracing some of her steps.

- **1401 Peachtree St.** The house is gone, but a plaque commemorates the site of the home where Mitchell spent her adolescence. She ordered that it be torn down after her death, possibly because she wasn't happy there. Her mother's dream house, it was a white, two-story Colonial Revival with Doric columns.
- **Margaret Mitchell House and Museum,** 990 Peachtree St. (at Tenth St.; ✆ **404/249-7015**). In 1925, newlywed Mitchell and her husband, John Marsh, moved into Apt. 1 on the bottom floor of this building, and it's where they lived until 1932. It was in "The Dump," as she called it, that Mitchell wrote much of her novel. MARTA: Midtown.
- **Georgian Terrace,** 659 Peachtree St. It was in this former hotel in 1921 that debutante Mitchell shocked polite society by performing an Apache dance—all the rage in Paris—with her partner at a charity ball. As a result, she was blackballed from the Junior League. Years later, when the Junior League held a costume ball the night before the world premiere of *Gone With the Wind,* Mitchell declined their invitation to be guest of honor. It was also here that Mitchell handed over her manuscript to Harold Latham, an editor for Macmillan. MARTA: North Avenue.
- **Margaret Mitchell Square,** intersection of Peachtree and Forsyth streets and Carnegie Way. It's possible to walk right by this spot and not even know that you've just passed one of the few public memorials to Atlanta's most famous author, which is probably just the way Mitchell would have preferred it. (Friends and acquaintances say she would have disliked the idea of a monument to her life.) The understated square contains a fountain, an inscription, and a sculpture symbolizing the columns of Tara. One block away is the famous

intersection known as Five Points, which Mitchell referred to in her book. MARTA: Peachtree Center.

Across the street from the square is the **Atlanta-Fulton Public Library** (© **404/730-1700**), which has a permanent Margaret Mitchell exhibit on its third floor. Among the interesting memorabilia, you'll find numerous photographs, a facsimile copy of one of the pages of the original manuscript and her library card. The library also possesses Mitchell's personal literary collection, including the books she used to research *Gone With the Wind*, her typewriter, and her Pulitzer Prize. If you sign the guest book at the exhibit, look back through its previous pages. You'll be astounded at the number of people from foreign countries who have visited the display. This is the site of an earlier building, the Carnegie Library, where Mitchell did much of her research. Her father was one of the founders of the library, and in the years after his death, Mitchell made many contributions in his name. The Carnegie Library was razed in 1977 to make way for the present building. Open Monday 9am to 6pm, Tuesday to Thursday 9am to 8pm, Friday and Saturday from 9am to 6pm, and Sunday from 2 to 6pm. MARTA: Peachtree Center.

Across Peachtree Street is the rose granite **Georgia-Pacific Building,** built on the site of the Loew's Grand Theatre, where *Gone With the Wind* had its premiere on December 15, 1939. The theater burned in 1979, but there's an inscription to the right of the main entrance to the current building. See if you can find the misspelling. MARTA: Peachtree Center.

• **Accident scene,** Peachtree and Thirteenth streets. On August 11, 1949, Mitchell and her husband were crossing the street to attend a play. She darted into the path of a taxi rounding the curve, was struck, and died 5 days later.

• **Gravesite,** 240 Oakland Ave. SE. Mitchell was laid to rest in Oakland Cemetery on August 17, 1949. Only 300 guests were allowed to attend, but after the service, fans invaded the cemetery, many taking funeral flowers as souvenirs. The cemetery (© **404/688-2107**), which is an interesting place in and of itself, is open daily from dawn to dusk. Admission is free, and a map of famous graves is available for a small fee at the cemetery office Monday to Saturday from 9am to 5pm, and Sunday 1 to 5pm. MARTA: King Memorial.

• **Atlanta History Center,** 730 W. Paces Ferry Rd. (© **404/814-4000**). For a look at what plantation life was really like, visit the Tullie Smith Farm on the grounds of the history center. The house itself, built in 1845 and moved here in 1972, is a plain, columnless two-story building, typical of an antebellum working plantation in North Georgia. In addition, a popular exhibit, "Disputed Territories: *Gone With the Wind* and Southern Myths," contrasts images from the famous book and movie with historical evidence.

For more information, read *Looking for Tara*, a small but informative guidebook to Margaret Mitchell's Atlanta. It's written by Don O'Briant and is available in local bookstores.

novel in the front room, seated at a typewriter and desk below the beveled glass windows in the small corner alcove. Like most writers, she preferred to keep her literary efforts private and would throw a towel over her typewriter when friends dropped in—which was often.

The museum contains movie memorabilia and chronicles the making of the movie, its premiere in Atlanta, and the impact that the book and movie had on society. The tour concludes in the museum shop, which includes a variety of *GWTW* collectibles and memorabilia.

If you finish your tour around mealtime and you're ready for a real change of pace, walk a few blocks south on Peachtree to the Vortex, a rowdy burger joint and bar that serves some of the best hamburgers in town. (Details on the restaurant are on p. 119.)

990 Peachtree St. (at Tenth St.). © 404/249-7015. www.gwtw.org. Admission $12 adults, $9 seniors and students, $5 children age 6–17; free for children under age 6. Daily 9:30am–5pm. Closed Thanksgiving, Christmas Eve, Christmas, and New Year's Day. Free parking. MARTA: Midtown.

Martin Luther King, Jr. Center for Nonviolent Social Change   Martin Luther King, Jr.'s commitment to nonviolent social change lives on at this memorial and educational center. A nongovernmental member of the United Nations, the center works with government agencies and the private sector to reduce violence within individual communities and among nations. Its library and archives house the world's largest collection of books and other materials documenting the civil rights movement, including Dr. King's personal papers and a rare 87-volume edition of *The Collected Works of Mahatma Gandhi,* a gift from the government of India. The library is open by appointment only for scholarly research. Equally important, the center is Martin Luther King, Jr.'s final resting place, a living memorial to an inspiring leader, which is visited by tens of thousands each year, including heads of foreign governments.

The tour, which is self-guided, begins in Freedom Hall, where memorabilia of King and the civil rights movement are displayed. Here, you can see his Bible and clerical robe, a hand-written sermon, a photographic essay on his life and work, and, on a grim note, the suit he was wearing when a deranged woman stabbed him in New York City. Also on display is the key to his room at the Lorraine Motel in Memphis, Tennessee, where he was assassinated. In an alcove off the main exhibit area is a video display on King's life and works. Additional exhibits include a room honoring Rosa Parks (whose refusal to give up her seat on a city bus led to the Montgomery bus boycott) and another honoring Gandhi.

Outside is Freedom Plaza, where Dr. King's white marble crypt rests, surrounded by a beautiful five-tiered Reflecting Pool, a symbol of the life-giving nature of water. The tomb is inscribed with his words: "Free at Last. Free at Last. Thank God Almighty I'm Free at Last." An eternal flame burns in a small circular pavilion directly in front of the crypt.

The Freedom Walkway, a vaulted colonnade paralleling the pool, will eventually be painted with murals depicting the civil rights struggle. Located at the end of Freedom Walkway is the Chapel of All Faiths, symbolizing the ecumenical nature of Dr. King's work and the universality of the basic tenets of the world's great religions.

A store on the premises offers King memorabilia and a wide selection of books and cassettes. Ranger talks focusing on the community and the civil rights movement take place frequently on Freedom Plaza.

449 Auburn Ave. (between Boulevard and Jackson sts.). © 404/524-1956. www.thekingcenter.com. Free admission. Daily 9am–5pm. Closed Thanksgiving, Christmas, New Year's Day. From I-75/85 south, exit at

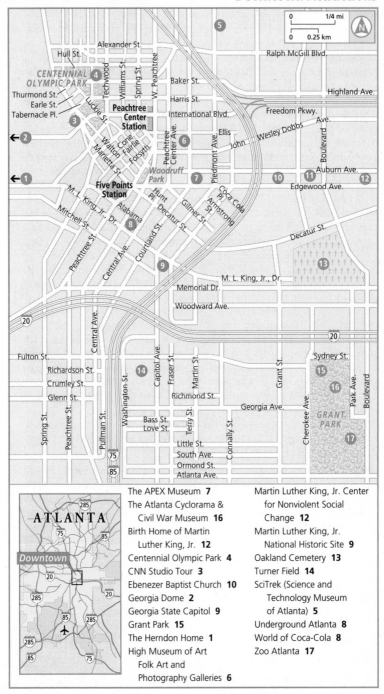

The APEX Museum **7**

The Atlanta Cyclorama & Civil War Museum **16**

Birth Home of Martin Luther King, Jr. **12**

Centennial Olympic Park **4**

CNN Studio Tour **3**

Ebenezer Baptist Church **10**

Georgia Dome **2**

Georgia State Capitol **9**

Grant Park **15**

The Herndon Home **1**

High Museum of Art Folk Art and Photography Galleries **6**

Martin Luther King, Jr. Center for Nonviolent Social Change **12**

Martin Luther King, Jr. National Historic Site **9**

Oakland Cemetery **13**

Turner Field **14**

SciTrek (Science and Technology Museum of Atlanta) **5**

Underground Atlanta **8**

World of Coca-Cola **8**

Zoo Atlanta **17**

Freedom Parkway/Carter Center. Turn right at first stoplight onto Boulevard. Follow signs to Martin Luther King, Jr., National Historic Site. MARTA: King Memorial Station is about 8 blocks away, or bus no. 3 east from the Five Points Station.

Martin Luther King, Jr., National Historic Site   Under the auspices of the National Park Service is an area of about 2 blocks around Auburn Avenue, designated as a National Historic Site and established to preserve the birthplace and boyhood surroundings of the nation's foremost civil rights leader. It includes King's boyhood home and the Ebenezer Baptist Church, where King's father and grandfather were ministers and King served as a co-pastor. King is often said to have been the pastor at Ebenezer, but in fact he never held that senior position. Free tours of King's birth home start at Fire Station No. 6, which was recently restored by the NPS; tickets are available on a first-come, first-served basis at the National Parks Service Visitor Center, 450 Auburn Ave. Other Auburn Avenue attractions, not under NPS auspices, include the Martin Luther King, Jr., Center for Nonviolent Social Change, where King is buried (see the previous listing), and the APEX Museum (p. 146). Several more surrounding blocks have been designated as a preservation district. This area is known as Sweet Auburn. John Wesley Dobbs, maternal grandfather of former Atlanta mayor Maynard Jackson, is the person who first called it such, after Oliver Goldsmith's *The Deserted Village,* the first line of which reads, "Sweet Auburn! loveliest village of the plains." Mayor Jackson says his grandfather called the area "sweet" because the keys to black liberation existed here in the form of "the three b's—bucks, ballots, and books." (See chapter 8 for tips on exploring the area.)

There is a visitor's center at 450 Auburn Ave., across from the King Center. It provides a complete orientation to area attractions and includes a theater for audiovisual and interpretive programs, interactive exhibits, and a bookstore. The visitors center is fronted by a beautifully landscaped plaza with a reflecting pool, King's crypt, which his wife had returned to the site several years ago, and an outdoor amphitheater for National Park Service programs.

450 Auburn Ave. ⓒ 404/331-6922. www.nps.gov/malu. Free admission. Labor Day to Memorial Day weekend, daily 9am to 5pm; Memorial Day weekend to Labor Day, daily 9am to 6pm. Closed January 1, Thanksgiving Day, and December 25. MARTA: Bus no. 3 from the Five Points MARTA station.

Michael C. Carlos Museum of Emory University   Emory University began its antiquities collection in 1875, and this intriguing museum dates to 1919, when it was founded to display the art and artifacts collected by Emory faculty in Egypt, Cyprus, Greece, Sicily, the Sea of Galilee, and the sites of ancient Babylon and Palestine. Today, the museum also maintains collections of ancient art and archaeology of Rome, Central and South America, the Near East, and Mesoamerica; works of the native cultures of North America; art of Asia and Oceania; and some 1,000 objects from sub-Saharan Africa. Additionally, a sizable collection of works on paper encompasses illuminated manuscript pages, drawings, and prints from the Middle Ages and the Renaissance to the 20th century. The museum is housed partly in a 1916 beaux-arts building that is on the National Register of Historic Places, its interior redesigned in 1985 by postmodernist architect Michael Graves. The remainder is in a 35,000-square-foot exhibition space (also designed by Graves) that opened in 1993.

The first-floor galleries feature exhibits from the extensive permanent collection—objects that were part of the daily life of people from five continents as early as the seventh millennium B.C. They include Bronze and Iron Age clay pots, jugs, loom weights, and oil lamps from Palestine; Egyptian mummies, pottery, cosmetic containers, and headrests; Greek and Cypriot pottery, flasks, and

Deering Rd.

85

Beverly Rd.

The Prado

McClatchey Park

Piedmont Way

Westminster Dr.

Inman Circle

1

2

8

W. Peachtree St.

Peachtree Circle

Peachtree St.

Westminster Dr.

Lafayette Dr.

Winn Park

3

MIDTOWN

4

Mecaslin St.

16th St.

15th St.

Holly St.

14th St.

Arts Center Station

Piedmont Park

5

Atlantic Dr.

Techwood Dr.

Spring St.

13th St.

12th St.

11th St.

Peachtree Walk

Crescent Ave.

Piedmont Ave.

Clara Meer Lake

10th St.

75

85

Midtown Station

6

10th St.

9th St.

8th St.

7th St.

Charles Allen Dr.

Vedado Way

Fowler St.

GEORGIA TECH

Ferst Dr.

Cypress St.

Juniper St.

Myrtle St.

Penn Ave.

Durant Pl.

St. Charles Way

4th St.

3rd St.

7

Ponce de Leon Av.

North Ave.

North Avenue Station

Peachtree St.

Civic Center Station

Piedmont Ave.

Argonne Ave.

Boulevard

■ **Atlanta Civic Center**

Simpson St.

Spring St.

Georgia Baptist Medical Center

ATLANTA

285

Midtown

75

85

20

Georgia Tech

285

Turner Field

20

85

285

285

85

75

Atlanta Botanical Garden **4**

Atlanta College of Art Gallery (Woodruff Arts Center) **3**

Center for Puppetry Arts **2**

Fox Theatre **7**

High Museum of Art **3**

Margaret Mitchell House and Museum **6**

Piedmont Park **5**

Rhodes Memorial Hall **1**

William Breman Jewish Heritage Museum **8**

statuary; and Mesopotamian pottery, coins, tools, sculpture, and cuneiform tablets inscribed with ancient writing. Also on this level: the Thibadeau Pre-Columbian collection, comprising over 1,300 objects spanning 2,000 years of creativity—gold jewelry, pottery, and statues, including many ceramic, volcanic stone, greenstone, and gold sculptures from ancient Costa Rica.

The upper floor is used for changing exhibits ranging in subject matter from Pueblo Indian pottery to Impressionist art. Throughout the museum, 210 plaster casts of ancient architectural elements—reliefs, friezes, column capitals, and decorative elements from temples and monuments—adorn hallway and lobby walls. Allow at least an hour to see the collections.

There are many interesting workshops, lectures, films, and gallery tours here; call to find out what's on during your stay. There's also a nice museum shop with a variety of educational books and gifts, as well as jewelry inspired by the collections. The museum's cafe, on the third floor, serves continental breakfast, lunch, coffee, and tea, and is open during regular museum hours.

571 S. Kilgo St. (near the intersection of Oxford and N. Decatur rds. on the Main Quadrangle of the Emory campus). (C) 404/727-4282. www.emory.edu/CARLOS. $5 donation suggested. Tue, Wed, Fri, and Sat 10am–5pm; Thurs 10am–9pm; Sun noon–5pm. Closed major holidays. Parking can be difficult on the Emory campus. Paid visitor parking is available in the Fishburne Parking Deck, at the B. Jones Center lot, and at the Peavine Parking Deck. MARTA: Bus no. 6 Emory from Candler Park Station or Lindbergh Station, or bus no. 36 N. Decatur from Avondale Station or Arts Center Station.

Oakland Cemetery *(Finds)* On the National Register of Historic Places, this outstanding 88-acre Victorian cemetery was founded in 1850. It survived the Civil War and remained the only cemetery in Atlanta for 34 years. Among the more than 48,000 people buried here are Confederate and Union soldiers (including five Southern generals), prominent families and paupers, governors and mayors, golfing great Bobby Jones, and *Gone With the Wind* author Margaret Mitchell. There's a Jewish section (consecrated by a temple), a black section (dating from segregation days), and a potter's field. Two monuments honor the Confederate war dead. And standing at the marker that commemorates the Great Locomotive Chase, you can see the trees from which the Yankee raiders were hanged (Confederate conductor Captain William Fuller is buried here). A 5-year $15 million restoration aimed at reviving the cemetery as a park got underway in early 2003.

Almost every grave has a story. Real-estate tycoon Jasper Newton Smith had a life-size statue of himself erected on his grave so he could watch the city's goings-on into eternity. (The sculptor originally gave Smith a tie, but Smith, who never wore one, refused to pay for the piece until the tie was chiseled off.) Dr. James Nissen, Oakland's first burial, feared being buried alive; his will stated that his jugular vein be severed prior to interment. And John Morgan Dye was a baby who died during the siege of Atlanta; his mother walked through the raging battle to the cemetery carrying the small corpse. The smallest grave, however, is that of "Tweet," a pet mockingbird buried in his family's lot. You'll also learn about graveyard symbolism on the tour: A lopped-tree-trunk marker indicates a life cut short or goals unachieved, rocks on a grave denote a life built on a solid foundation, and a shell means resurrection.

The cemetery is renowned not only for historical reasons, but also as an outdoor "museum" of Gothic and classical-revival mausolea, bronze urns, stained glass, and Victorian statuary.

Atlanta residents also view Oakland's rolling terrain as parkland; dozens of people jog and walk here every day, and picnickers are a common sight. Leashed pets are welcome. Every October, there's a celebration to commemorate the cemetery's founding, with turn-of-the-century music, food, and storytelling. Though you can visit whenever the cemetery is open, try to come when you can take a guided tour. It's fascinating.

248 Oakland Ave. SE (main entrance at Oakland Ave. and Martin Luther King, Jr., Dr.). © 404/688-2107. Free admission. Daily dawn to dusk; visitors center Mon–Sat 9am–5pm, Sun 1–5pm. Purchase an informative, self-guided walking-tour map brochure at the visitors center for $1. Guided walking tours available Mar–Nov Sat 10am–2pm, Sun 2pm. $5 adults, $3 seniors and children. Free parking inside the cemetery. MARTA: King Memorial.

World of Coca-Cola ★★ *Kids*   An exposition showcasing the world's most popular soft drink, World of Coca-Cola sounds like a huge Coke commercial. And it is. But it's also one of the biggest attractions in the city and a must-see for anybody who's ever had a taste of the Real Thing. (And who hasn't?) Its vast three-story pavilion houses a massive collection of Coca-Cola memorabilia, along with numerous interactive displays, high-tech exhibits, and video presentations. A self-guided tour begins on the third level, where visitors are greeted by a Rube Goldberg–like kinetic sculpture called a "Bottling Fantasy." Exhibits throughout trace the history of Coca-Cola from its 1886 debut at Jacob's Pharmacy in downtown Atlanta to its current worldwide fame.

Highlights include: a re-creation of a 1930s soda fountain (a jukebox on the premises plays Coke-themed pop songs of yesteryear like "Sweet Coca-Cola Bush" sung by Shirley Temple); diverse advertising campaigns over the years (Did you know that Maxwell House's "good to the last drop" was originally a Coke slogan?); a video on the making of the "Hilltop Reunion" Coke commercial (it kicked off the "I'd Like to Teach the World to Sing" campaign); print ads featuring screen stars such as Jean Harlow, Claudette Colbert, Clark Gable, and Cary Grant; and an interactive audio exhibit that lets you listen to Coke commercials sung by pop stars.

And, in case you've worked up a thirst by this time, you can sample unlimited amounts of 40 Coca-Cola Company beverages at Club Coca-Cola, including 20 international drinks that are not sold in the United States (for example, a pineapple/orange/banana beverage marketed only in Kenya). The kids will go wild, but the drinks are on the house, so what the heck. The tour ends in the first-floor gift shop, which sells a mind-boggling array of Coca-Cola logo items; everything from T-shirts to Coke polar bears. There's much, much more; this experience is a total immersion in Coca-Cola. Allow about 90 minutes to drink it all in; come on weekdays to avoid long lines. This attraction will be moving to downtown Atlanta, across from Centennial Olympic Park, sometime in 2005.

55 Martin Luther King, Jr., Dr. SW (at Central Ave., adjacent to Underground Atlanta). © 404/676-5151. Admission $6 adults, $4 seniors age 55 and over, $3 children age 6–11; under age 6 free with adult admission. Mon–Sat 9am–5pm, Sun noon–6pm. Closed Easter, Thanksgiving, and Christmas Day; abbreviated hours on Christmas Eve and New Year's Eve. Parking garage on Central Ave. off Martin Luther King Dr. MARTA: Five Points.

2 More Attractions

Atlanta College of Art Gallery   The Atlanta College of Art, housed in the Woodruff Arts Center complex, features an ongoing series of gallery shows. A recent example: "Light Over Ancient Angkor," a photo exhibition of Cambodian Angkor ruins. There are also faculty exhibitions, juried student shows, lectures, and concerts here. Call for details.

1280 Peachtree St. NE (in the Memorial Arts Building of the Woodruff Arts Center). © 404/733-5050. www.aca.edu. Free admission. Tues–Wed and Sat 10am–5pm; Thurs–Fri 10am–9:30pm; Sun noon–5pm.

Regional Atlanta Sights

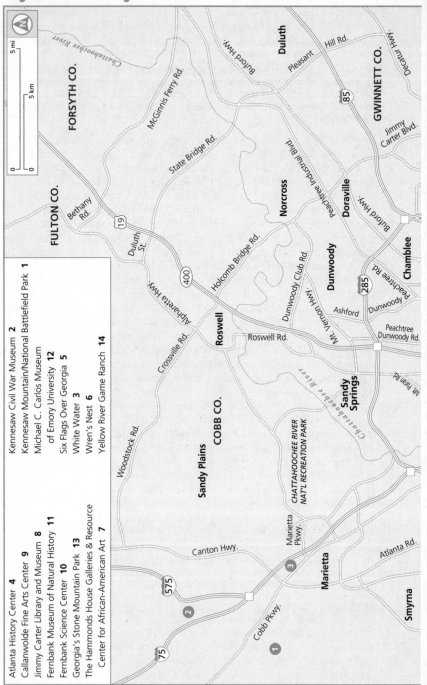

Atlanta History Center **4**
Callanwolde Fine Arts Center **9**
Jimmy Carter Library and Museum **8**
Fernbank Museum of Natural History **11**
Fernbank Science Center **10**
Georgia's Stone Mountain Park **13**
The Hammonds House Galleries & Resource
Center for African-American Art **7**

Kennesaw Civil War Museum **2**
Kennesaw Mountain/National Battlefield Park **1**
Michael C. Carlos Museum
of Emory University **12**
Six Flags Over Georgia **5**
White Water **3**
Wren's Nest **6**
Yellow River Game Ranch **14**

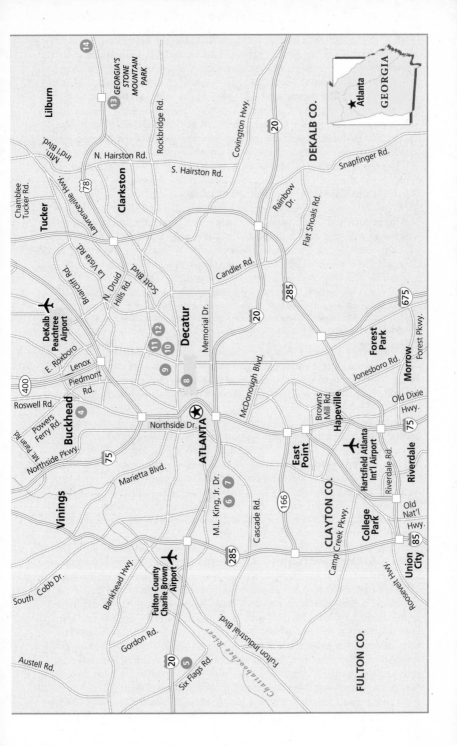

Callanwolde Fine Arts Center   A magnificent Gothic/Tudor–style mansion, built for Coca-Cola heir Charles Howard Candler in 1920, Callanwolde today serves as a fine-arts center for city residents. Classes are given in pottery, painting, photography, drawing, and more, and there are numerous workshops for adults and children. While touring the house, you may be surprised that most of the rooms are bare, and only Callanwolde's exquisite walnut paneling, beautifully carved ceilings and moldings, grand staircase, magnificent marble and stone fireplaces, and leaded-glass windows evoke its luxurious past. But this is a working arts center, not a museum, and the rooms are used for classes and workshops.

The estate occupies 12 acres (originally 27) in the Druid Hills section of Atlanta, an area planned by Frederick Law Olmsted, designer of New York's Central Park. Visitors are welcome to peruse shows of local artists in the Petite Hall gallery upstairs; enjoy the lawns and formal gardens, which are maintained by the county; and participate in the many events here—concerts, storytelling evenings, and dance performances. Especially memorable is Christmas at Callanwolde (see the "Atlanta Calendar of Events," in chapter 2), when the entire house is decorated for the season and shops are set up in different rooms. Attending a function here is the best way to experience the estate.

980 Briarcliff Rd. NE (north of Ponce de Leon Ave.). © 404/872-5338. www.callanwolde.org. Free admission, except for special events. Guided tours, by special appointment only, $1.50 adults, 50¢ children under age 12. Mon–Fri 10am–8pm; Sat 10am–3pm. Call to arrange guided tours as far in advance as possible. Self-guided tours are available at all times, except during special events.

Château Élan Winery & Resort   Château Élan is a hilltop winery that replicates a 16th-century French estate surrounded by verdant countryside. Its first wines were produced in 1985, and already they have garnered more than 200 awards. Guided tours are given daily between 11am and 4pm (call ahead for hours).

On view are the crushing and pressing machines, oak barrels used to age and flavor wines, the cask room, and the bottling area. The tours conclude with a wine tasting. Grapes ripen in July/August, so if you're here during harvesting in August and September, you'll actually see the winemaking procedure. More than 300 tons of grapes are harvested and processed each year. The interior of the château, a stage-set version of a Paris street, has a quarry-stone floor, wrought-iron fences, and street lamps. The building houses an art gallery offering monthly exhibits by regional and national artists, displays of antique European winemaking equipment, and a wine market.

There are also three on-premises restaurants, so plan to eat lunch or dinner here. **Café Élan,** open daily from 11am to 10pm, features sandwiches, salads, and light entrees. It's a charming setting, with seating under a green awning. **Paddy's Irish Pub,** open Saturday at noon, Sunday at 12:30pm, and the rest of the week at 2pm (closing hours vary), serves traditional Irish fare and spirits. The fancier **Le Clos,** with pale pink walls, lace-curtained French doors, and tables covered with crisp white linen, is open for dinner only Wednesday through Saturday evenings, with seatings from 6:30 to 9:30pm. A seven- or eight-course prix-fixe meal beginning at $78 or $88 features haute-cuisine entrees; appropriate Château Élan wines with each course are included. Reservations are imperative. Men are required to wear a coat and tie.

There are also four restaurants at the adjoining Château Élan resort. And there are picnic areas on the lovely grounds; custom picnic baskets can be purchased here.

You might also consider an overnight or longer stay at the 274-room **Inn at Château Élan,** a luxurious resort where facilities include four golf courses (three 18-hole and one par-3, 9-hole) and seven tennis courts (both offering pro shops and instruction), a full-service European-style health spa and salon (days of pampering are an option), an outdoor Olympic-size pool, an indoor heated pool, and a fitness center. Room rates begin at $180 double; call the numbers below for details and to inquire about golf, tennis, spa, and other packages.

100 Rue Charlemagne, Braselton, GA (30 miles north of Atlanta at Exit 126 off I-85). ℭ **800/233-WINE** or 678/425-0900 in Atlanta. www.chateauelan.com.

Georgia State Capitol   It wasn't until after the Civil War (1868) that Atlanta became, once and for all, the state capital; its present capitol building, completed July 4, 1889, was hailed as a testament to the city's recovery.

Modeled after the nation's Capitol, another neoclassical edifice atop a "crowning hill," its 75-foot dome, covered in gold leaf and topped by a Statue of Freedom, is a major Atlanta landmark. The building is fronted by a massive four-story portico with a pediment supported by six Corinthian columns set on large stone piers. In the rotunda, with its soaring 237-foot ceiling, are busts of famous Georgians, including signers of the Declaration of Independence and the Constitution. The capitol building's public spaces currently are being restored to their 1889 grandeur.

Tours begin on the main floor, and this level also serves as an information center for city and state attractions. The governor's office is off the main hall. The tours take 60 to 90 minutes; allow at least another 30 minutes to browse around on your own after the tour. Highlights of the grounds are detailed in a brochure available at the tour desk. *Note:* For security reasons, your bag will be searched when you enter.

Grand staircases in both wings rise to the third floor, where you'll enter the House of Representatives, and, across the hall, the Senate chambers. The legislature meets for 40 days, beginning the second Monday in January (it can also be called into special sessions); all of its sessions are open to the public. The fourth floor houses legislative galleries and the Georgia Capitol Museum, with exhibits on cotton, peach, and peanut growing; cases of mounted birds, fish, deer, insects, and other species native to Georgia; rocks and minerals; American Indian artifacts; and more. Note, too, museum displays on the first floor.

At Christmas, a beautifully decorated 40-foot tree adorns the rotunda. And on January 15, Dr. Martin Luther King, Jr.'s birthday, there's an annual memorial program. Local dignitaries, including the governor, give speeches, and King's family attends.

206 Washington St. (at Martin Luther King, Jr. Blvd.). ℭ **404/656-2844.** www.sos.state.ga.us. Free admission. Mon–Fri 8am–5pm. Tours given weekdays only Apr–Dec 10 11am and 1 and 2pm; Jan–Mar 9:30 and 10:30am and 1 and 2pm. Self-guided tours are possible at any time the capitol is open. Closed major holidays, including state holidays. Parking lot behind the capitol building on Capitol Ave. is closed to the public during legislative sessions; other lots are on M. L. King Jr., Dr. at Central Ave. and on Courtland St. between M. L. King Jr., Dr. and Central Ave. MARTA: Georgia State.

The Hammonds House Galleries & Resource Center of African-American Art   Occupying the 1857 Eastlake Victorian-style former home of Dr. Otis T. Hammonds, a black anesthesiologist and art patron, Hammonds House is a national center for the exhibition, preservation, research, and documentation of African-American art and artists. The Fulton County Commission purchased the house after Hammonds's death in 1985 with these aims in mind.

Hammonds' extensive collection included works by African-American and Haitian artists, as well as African masks and carvings. Along with later acquisitions—including works by Romare Bearden, William H. Johnson, Robert S. Duncanson, and Elizabeth Catlett—the permanent collection is shown on a rotating basis and is supplemented by exhibitions of renowned black artists from all over the world. The Resource Center on the premises, housing documents on African-American art and artists, is open to the public by appointment.

The house is located in the thriving West End neighborhood, declared a historic district in 1991. While you're in the area, take a look at the other lovingly restored Victorian bungalows and houses. A short walk away is the Atlanta University Center, the largest historically African-American education complex in the world, which includes Morehouse College. Dr. Martin Luther King, Jr. is its most famous alumnus, and a chapel there was built to honor his memory.

503 Peeples St. (at Lucile St., 2 blocks north of Ralph David Abernathy Blvd.). ☎ 404/752-8730. Admission $2 adults, $1 seniors and students. Tues–Fri 10am–6pm; Sat–Sun 1–5pm. MARTA: Bus no. 71 from the West End station.

The Herndon Home   Alonzo Herndon was born into the last decade of slavery in 1858. After emancipation, he worked as a field hand and sharecropper, supplementing his meager income by selling peanuts, homemade molasses, and axle grease. He arrived in Atlanta in the early 1880s, where he worked as a barber and eventually owned several barbershops of his own. He acquired real estate with earnings from these shops. By 1900, with only a year of formal education and less than 40 years out of slavery, Herndon was the richest black man in Atlanta. In 1905, he purchased a church burial association, which, with other small companies, became the nucleus of the Atlanta Life Insurance Company, today the nation's second-largest black-owned insurance company.

In 1910, Herndon built this elegant 15-room house in the beaux-arts neoclassical style with a stately colonnaded entrance. The tour begins in a receiving room with a 10-minute introductory video called *The Herndon Legacy.* Herndon and his wife, Adrienne McNeil, a drama teacher at Atlanta University, were the primary architects of the house, and construction was accomplished almost completely by African-American artisans. Because their son Norris occupied the home until 1977, much of the original furniture remains, and there are family photographs throughout. Adrienne died about a week after the house was completed.

The tour takes you through the reception hall; the music room, with rococo gilt-trim walls and Louis XV–style furnishings; the living room, with a frieze on its walls depicting the accomplishments of Herndon's life; the dining room, furnished in late Renaissance style with family china and Venetian glass displayed in a mahogany cabinet; the butler's pantry; and the sunny breakfast room. Upstairs, you'll see the bedroom used by Herndon's second wife Jessie, with its Jacobean suite and Louis XV–style furnishings; Herndon's Empire-furnished bedroom, where a book from a Republican National Convention displayed on a table lets you know his political bent; the collection room (Norris collected ancient Greek and Roman vases and funerary objects); Norris's bedroom; a sitting room; and a guest bedroom.

587 University Place (between Vine and Walnut sts.). ☎ 404/581-9813. Admission $5 adults, $3 students. Tues–Sat 10am–4pm, with tours on the hour. Closed New Year's Day, July 4th, Thanksgiving, Christmas Eve, and Christmas. MARTA: Vine City.

High Museum of Art Folk Art and Photography Galleries   Inside the impressive Georgia-Pacific Building near Five Points, this downtown branch of the High Museum of Art displays folk art and photography. Allow about an hour for your visit. Visitors can enter through an elegantly landscaped courtyard on John Wesley Dobbs Avenue, or from Peachtree Street via the imposing Georgia-Pacific lobby, itself the setting for Louise Nevelson's vast indoor environmental sculpture in white wood, *Dawn's Forest.* Spanning three levels, the museum has beautiful walls paneled in an African wood called angré, and pedestrian ramps afford visitors a view of the downtown skyline as they descend to the galleries.

The two levels of galleries provide approximately 5,000 square feet of exhibition space. The upper gallery has a barrel-vaulted ceiling with Plexiglas inserts allowing daylight to flood the space. In addition to exhibitions, the museum offers films, lectures, concerts, and gallery talks (call for details). The Georgia-Pacific Building, by the way, is built on the site of the Loew's Grand Theatre, where *Gone With the Wind* premiered in 1939.

133 Peachtree St. (at John Wesley Dobbs Ave.). ℂ **404/577-6940.** www.high.org. Free admission. Mon–Sat 10am–5pm. Closed Thanksgiving, Christmas, and New Year's Day. MARTA: Peachtree Center.

Kennesaw Civil War Museum   On this site began the wild adventure known as the "Great Locomotive Chase." The Civil War had been under way for a year on April 12, 1862, when Union spy James J. Andrews and a group of 21 Northern soldiers disguised as civilians boarded a locomotive called the *General* in Marietta, buying tickets for diverse destinations to avert suspicion. When the train made a breakfast stop at the Lacy Hotel in Big Shanty, they seized the locomotive and several boxcars and fled northward to Chattanooga. The goal of these daring raiders was to destroy tracks, telegraph wires, and bridges behind them, thus cutting off the Confederate supply route between Virginia and Mississippi.

Conductor William A. Fuller, his breakfast interrupted by the sound of the *General* chugging out of the station, gave chase on foot, then grabbed a platform car and poled along the tracks. With him were a railroad superintendent and the *General's* engineer. At the Etowah River, Fuller and crew commandeered a small locomotive called the *Yonah* and made better progress. Meanwhile, the raiders tore up track behind them, and when the pursuers got close, the raiders slowed them down by throwing ties and firewood onto the tracks. Andrews, a very smooth talker, managed to convince station attendants en route that he was on an emergency mission running ammunition to Confederate general Beauregard in Mississippi.

Fuller's chances of catching the *General* improved when he seized the southbound *Texas* and began running it backward toward the raiders, picking up reinforcements along the way and eventually managing to get a telegraph message through to Gen. Danville Leadbetter, commander at Chattanooga. The chase went on, with Andrews sending uncoupled boxcars careening back toward Fuller as obstructions. Fuller, however, who was running in reverse, merely attached the rolling boxcars to his engine and kept on. At the covered Oostanaula Bridge, the raiders detached a boxcar and set it on fire in hopes of finally creating an impassable obstacle—a burning bridge behind them. But the *Texas* was able to push the flaming car off the bridge. It soon burned out, and Fuller tossed it off the track and continued.

By this time the *General* was running low on fuel and water, the *Texas* was hot on its heels, and the raiders realized that all was lost. Andrews gave his final command: "Jump off and scatter! Every man for himself!" All were captured and imprisoned within a few days. Some escaped, others were exchanged for Confederate prisoners of war, and the rest were hanged in Atlanta, most of them at a site near Oakland Cemetery. Though the mission failed, the raiders, some of them posthumously, received the newly created Medal of Honor for their valor.

The museum, occupying a building that was once the Frey cotton gin, houses the *General* (still in running condition, but don't get any ideas), a walk-through caboose, exhibits of Civil War artifacts, memorabilia, and photographs relating to the chase and its participants. You can view a 20-minute narrated video about the chase, but if you really want the full story, rent the Disney movie, *The Great Locomotive Chase,* starring Fess Parker as the dashing Andrews. (You can also buy a copy in the museum gift shop.)

The museum is 3 miles from Kennesaw Mountain/National Battlefield Park (details below), so consider visiting both of these Civil War–related sights the same day.

2829 Cherokee St., Kennesaw, GA 30144. © 800/742-6897 or 770/427-2117. Admission $3 adults; $2.50 seniors, service people, and AAA members; $1.50 children age 7–15; age 6 and under free. Families pay a maximum of $12. Mar 15–Oct 15 Mon–Sat 9:30am–5:30pm, Sun noon–5:30pm; Oct 16–Mar 14 Mon–Sat 10am–4pm, Sun noon–4pm. Free parking. Take Exit 273 off I-75N and follow the signs.

Kennesaw Mountain/National Battlefield Park   This 2,884-acre park was established in 1917 on the site of a crucial Civil War battle in the Atlanta campaign of 1864. A very popular attraction, it draws some 2 million visitors annually.

The action began in June 1864. A month earlier, Gen. Ulysses S. Grant had ordered Sherman to attack the Confederate army in Georgia, "break it up, and go into the interior of the enemy's country as far as you can, inflicting all the damage you can upon their war resources." In response to this order, Sherman's army, 100,000 strong, had been pushing back Confederate forces composed of 65,000 men under Gen. Joseph E. Johnston. By June 19, Union troops had driven Johnston's men back to a well-prepared defensive position on Kennesaw Mountain. Southern engineers had built a line of entrenchments in its rocky slopes, allowing the Confederates to cover every approach with rifle or cannon. An Ohio officer later commented that if the mountain had been constructed for the sole purpose of repelling an invading army, "it could not have been better made or placed."

On June 27, following a few weeks of skirmishing, Sherman, underestimating the strength and still-feisty morale of the rebels, attempted to break through Confederate lines and annihilate them in a grand no-holds-barred assault from two directions. Confederate Gen. Samuel French described the onset of the attack: "As if by magic, there sprang from the earth a host of men, and in one long, waving line of blue the infantry advanced and the battle of Kennesaw Mountain began."

Sherman's men were repelled by massive bursts of firepower and huge rocks rolling down the mountain at them. Union casualties far outnumbered Confederate losses. Meanwhile, 8,000 Union infantrymen in five brigades attacked from another angle; in this battle, the Union lost 3,000 men, the Confederates 500. Weeks of torrential rain, which had turned these battlegrounds into a muddy mire, added significantly to the misery on both sides. There was no rain the day of the battle, but the day was swelteringly hot and muggy.

Allow at least 2 hours for exploring. Start your tour at the **visitors center,** where you can pick up a map, watch a 20-minute film about the battle, and view exhibits of Civil War artifacts, medicine, and memorabilia. On weekdays, you can drive or hike up the mountain to see the actual Confederate entrenchments and earthworks, some of them equipped with Civil War artillery. (On weekends, it may be too crowded to drive, but you can take a shuttle bus.) The steep trail is about 2 miles round-trip, so wear comfortable shoes. You'll find interpretive signs at key spots, and, on weekends and holidays Memorial Day through Labor Day, interpretive programs give further information about the battle. You'll also want to drive to **Cheatham Hill,** site of some of the fiercest fighting. There are 16 miles of hiking trails for those who want a more extensive tour (trail maps are available at the visitors center), and picnicking is permitted in designated areas, some with barbecue grills. The scenery is gorgeous, so even if Civil War battles are not your thing (that is, if you're reluctantly accompanying an enthusiastic spouse), it makes for beautiful hiking or driving.

Old Hwy. 41 and Stilesboro Rd., Kennesaw, GA. © 770/427-4686. www.nps.gov/kemo. Free admission. Park open daily dawn to dusk; visitors center open daily 8:30am–5pm. Closing hours can vary; please check the sign before you enter a gated area. Closed Christmas. Take I-75 north to Barrett Pkwy., then follow the signs.

Rhodes Memorial Hall   Rhodes Hall is one of a few remaining pre–World War I Peachtree Street mansions and is significant as a reminder that Peachtree was once a fashionable residential street. The house was designed shortly after the turn of the century by Willis Franklin Denny (at the time Atlanta's leading residential architect) as a home for affluent Atlanta businessman Amos Giles Rhodes and his family.

Its medieval baronial-cum–high—Victorian-Romanesque style was inspired by Rhineland castles. The Stone Mountain granite exterior is replete with arched Romanesque windows, battlements and buttresses, parapets, towers, and turrets. A large Syrian-arched veranda wraps the east and north facades. And the interior is grandiose, with maple- and mahogany-bordered oak parquet floors, mosaics surrounding the fireplaces, and a gracefully winding hand-carved Honduran mahogany staircase with nine stained-glass stairwell panels depicting "The Rise and Fall of the Confederacy." The house and stables originally occupied 150 acres of land and included servants' quarters, a carriage house, and other outbuildings. When it was built, this site was in suburbia, an afternoon's drive from downtown.

Upon Rhodes's death in 1929, his residence was deeded to the state of Georgia in keeping with his desire to preserve his home. The house was entered on the National Register of Historic Places in 1974. Today, it is headquarters for the Georgia Trust for Historic Preservation and is in an ongoing process of restoration. To date, the original dining-room suite and some other furnishings are in place, and all the mahogany woodwork and decorated ceilings on the first floor have been restored. Original landscaping—with white and red cedars, dogwoods, banana trees, and a circular flowerbed—has been re-created in the front yard.

1516 Peachtree St. NW (at Peachtree Circle). © 404/885-7800. Admission for self-guided tour $3 adults, seniors, and children; $5 adults, $4 seniors and children for guided tour; free for children age 6 and under. Mon–Fri 11am–4pm; Sun noon–3pm. Free parking in designated lot behind building on Spring St. MARTA: Arts Center.

Underground Atlanta ★★   The site of Underground Atlanta is the historic hub of the city, centered on the Zero Milepost that marked the terminus of the Western & Atlantic Railroad in the 1800s. For many years a flourishing locale, the area became so congested in the early 1900s that permanent concrete viaducts were constructed over it, elevating the street system and routing traffic over a maze of railroad tracks. Merchants moved their operations up to the new level, using the lower level for storage space. For most of the 20th century, it remained a deserted catacomb.

> (*Fun Fact* **Pricey Park Land**
>
> If you really, really, really had a good time at Centennial Olympic Park, you can have it all to yourself for a small fee. Though it's a public park, it's also a moneymaker managed by the Georgia World Congress Center, and parts of the park are sometimes rented for various business functions, parties, or other celebrations. There have even been a few weddings. You can rent the entire park for, um, $10,000. Call ℭ **404/223-4412** for details.

In 1969, a group of Atlanta businesspeople decided to create an underground entertainment complex of restaurants, shops, and bars in a setting that retained the historic feel of the area. The idea was great, but the complex declined and closed after a little over a decade. In 1989—after a public-private infusion of $142 million—a larger, livelier Underground reopened to much fanfare and for several years was once again an entertainment mecca and urban marketplace. Local civic leaders pinned their hopes for downtown revival on the complex, and for some time it looked as if the concept would work. But, beset by lease disputes, financial problems, and changes of management, Underground has failed to sustain its early promise, although the most recent management company may be making some progress. The complex is still worth a look if you're in the downtown area, but keep in mind that it's mostly a tourist attraction at this point. It's still struggling to find its place in the urban mix, perhaps because locals prefer the shopping and entertainment areas in Buckhead and Virginia-Highland.

Occupying 12 acres in the center of downtown, the complex is heralded by a beacon of oscillating searchlights emanating from a 138-foot light tower, an outdoor staging area used for performances and concerts, and the cascading waters of Peachtree Fountain Plaza. Underground offers nearly 100 retail operations and restaurants, many of them national chains. Humbug Square—where street vendors and con artists flourished in the early 1900s—has a colorful market with turn-of-the-century pushcarts and wagons displaying offbeat wares.

Markers throughout the complex indicate historic sites. Their origins are fascinating, so be sure to pick up an information sheet at the visitors booth and take your own self-guided tour. The **Atlanta Convention and Visitors Bureau** (ℭ **404/222-6688**) operates its most comprehensive center at 65 Upper Alabama St. Open Monday to Saturday 10am to 6pm, and Sunday noon to 6pm, it includes displays and interactive exhibits depicting the city's rich history. There's also **AtlanTIX!,** a ticket booth where visitors can purchase day-of-show half-price tickets to theater, dance events, and other live performances throughout the metro area.

50 Upper Alabama St. (bounded by Wall St., Central Ave., Martin Luther King, Jr., Dr., and Peachtree St.). ℭ 404/523-2311 or 877/859-4891. www.underatl.com. Free admission. Mon–Sat 10am–9:30pm; Sun noon–6pm. Some restaurants and clubs stay open until midnight (or later) nightly. Paid parking in the garages off Martin Luther King Dr. MARTA: Five Points Station has a short pedestrian tunnel that connects directly with Underground Atlanta.

William Breman Jewish Heritage Museum   This museum, the largest of its kind in the Southeast, offers a unique glimpse into Atlanta's history, exploring Jewish heritage with a special emphasis on the Atlanta Jewish experience. Two main galleries juxtapose the destruction of the Holocaust with the re-emergence of Jewish communities in Atlanta and throughout the world. The story is told through photographs, documents, and memorabilia uncovered in the attics and basements of local families and individuals. Holocaust survivors living in Atlanta generously shared their stories and their possessions to bear witness to their experiences.

In addition to the two main galleries, there's a Discovery Center with hands-on activities related to the exhibitions, a community archives, a genealogy center, a library, and a gift shop.

1440 Spring St. NW (in the Selig Center at 18th St.). © **404/873-1661.** Admission $5 adults, $3 seniors and students; free for children under age 6. Mon–Thurs 10am–5pm; Fri 10am–3pm; Sun 1–5pm. Closed major Jewish and some secular holidays. Free parking. MARTA: Arts Center.

PARKS
Refer to section 1, "The Top Attractions," earlier in this chapter, for full details on Georgia's Stone Mountain Park.

Piedmont Park, the city's most popular and centrally located recreation area (with its main entrance on Piedmont Ave. at Fourteenth St.), was once a farm and a Civil War encampment. Its first public usage was by the elite Gentlemen's Driving Club, which bought the property as a site for horseback riding and racing. It soon became a venue for state fairs, culminating with the spectacular Cotton States and International Exposition of 1895. In 1904, the property's 180-plus acres of woodsy meadow and farm acreage were transformed into a city park with a varied terrain of rolling hillsides, verdant lawns, and lush forest around Lake Clara Meer.

Today, Piedmont Park is the setting for many popular regional events such as concerts and music festivals. It contains softball fields, soccer fields, public tennis courts, a public swimming pool, and paths for jogging, skating, and cycling. The Atlanta Botanical Garden (see section 1, "The Top Attractions," earlier in this chapter) is next door.

The park gets a lot of use, and in some spots it can be downright scruffy-looking, but the Piedmont Park Conservancy and the City of Atlanta continue to upgrade the park's landscaping. A visitors center, where you can find information on the park and the surrounding area, is located at the Piedmont Avenue and Twelfth Street entrance. The park is closed to auto traffic, so it's a good spot to let the kids run around, throw a Frisbee, or have a picnic. The people-watching is superb, and the Midtown skyline beyond is magnificent. Don't let the kids miss PlayScape at the Twelfth Street entrance. Created by well-known sculptor Isamu Noguchi, it's a climbable series of brightly colored geometric shapes complete with ladders and slides.

Parking can be impossible, especially during special events, and authorities are quick to tow cars parked illegally. (All the activity in the park is a constant source of irritation to residents in surrounding neighborhoods.) It's easiest to take MARTA to the Arts Center station and walk the few blocks down Fourteenth Street. During special events, it's usually possible to take a shuttle to and from the station.

A great way to see the park and soak up some of its history is on a **walking tour** sponsored by the Piedmont Park Conservancy. The free tours depart from the visitors center at noon on Saturdays April through October. During the 1½-hour tour, guides will point out many historic areas, including remnants of the 1895 Exposition. Call © **404/875-8055** for information.

Named for Confederate captain Lemuel P. Grant, who helped build Atlanta's defense line, **Grant Park** (bordered by Sydney St. and Atlanta Ave., Boulevard and Cherokee aves.) still contains vestiges of his fortifications. Grant donated its 100 acres to the city for a park on this site. Near the intersection of Boulevard and Atlanta avenues, you can see the remaining earthwork slopes of Fort Walker, a commanding artillery bastion with its original gun emplacements. Its cannons and caissons can be seen in the museum area of Atlanta Cyclorama (see section 1, "The Top Attractions," earlier in this chapter), one of Grant Park's two major attractions. The other is Zoo Atlanta (see "Especially for Kids," below). The park is open daily from 6am to 11pm; it's best to visit during daylight hours.

3 Especially for Kids

Though the following attractions are great choices if you're traveling with kids, don't pass them up if you're not. Especially worthwhile are the Center for Puppetry Arts, SciTrek, Wren's Nest, and Zoo Atlanta (visit in conjunction with Atlanta Cyclorama and Oakland Cemetery). In addition, be sure to take the kids to the Fernbank Museum of Natural History and to the Birth Home of Martin Luther King, Jr., and the Center for Nonviolent Social Change (all described earlier in the chapter).

Center for Puppetry Arts ⭐ *Kids*   Don't miss this place if you're traveling with the kids. In fact, you might not want to miss it even without kids in tow. The center is dedicated to expanding public awareness of puppetry as a fine art and to presenting all of its international and historic forms. Opened in 1978, with Kermit the Frog cutting the official ribbon (he had a little help from the late Jim Henson), it contains a 300-seat theater, one smaller theater, gallery space, and a permanent museum. The puppet shows are marvelous—sophisticated, riveting, full-stage productions with elaborate scenery. Some are family oriented; others, with nighttime showings, are geared to adults. Call ahead to find out what's on; reservations are essential. You can also call a week or so in advance to enroll yourself or your kids in a puppet-making workshop.

In its permanent exhibit, "Puppets, The Power of Wonder," visitors can use joysticks to manipulate interactive puppets on their own. A video hosted by the late Jim Henson provides an overview of puppetry and takes visitors around the world to meet masters of the art. There's also a huge display of puppets ranging from ritualistic African figures to Punch and Judy to Henson's Pigs in Space. It's an excellent collection, one of the largest in North America, and it includes turn-of-the-century Thai shadow puppets, Indonesian *wayang golek* puppets used to tell classic stories (a centuries-old tradition), Chinese hand puppets, rod-operated marionettes from all over Europe, original Muppets, pre-Colombian clay puppets that were used in religious ceremonies circa A.D. 1200, and Turkish shadow figures made of dried animal skins. Reservations are required for guided tours of "Puppets, The Power of Wonder"; the tour lasts about an hour. Another gallery features visiting exhibits from all over the world.

The gift shop is like no other, with oodles of marionettes, one-of-a-kind handmade puppets, masks, videos, and other related items.

1404 Spring St. NW (at Eighteenth St.). © **404/873-3391.** www.puppet.org. Museum $5 adults; $4 children age 13 and under, students, and seniors; or $2 if you see a show or take a workshop. Show prices $8 adults; $7 children age 2–13, students, and seniors. Workshop $5; $4 when you see a show or visit the museum. Mon–Sat 9am–5pm; Sun 11am–5pm. Closed New Year's Day, Memorial Day, July 4th, Labor Day, Thanksgiving, and Christmas. Limited free parking. MARTA: Arts Center.

Fernbank Science Center *Kids*   Owned and funded by the DeKalb County School System, this museum/planetarium/observatory, located adjacent to the

65-acre Fernbank Forest, is an educational partner of the Fernbank Museum of Natural History (p. 154). Plan to visit the entire complex on the same day. There's a 1½-mile forest trail here, with trees, shrubs, ferns, wildflowers, mosses, and other plants marked for identification, and an extensive rose garden next door to the museum.

The indoor facility houses museum exhibits such as a video display on geological phenomena (volcanoes, earthquakes, mountain formation); a gem collection; an exhibit tracing the development of life in Georgia from 500 million years ago to a million years ago; a complete weather station; fossil trees; the original *Apollo 6* space capsule and space suit (on loan from the Smithsonian); computer games; a replica of the Okefenokee Swamp, complete with sound effects; and models of dinosaurs that roamed Atlanta in prehistoric times. There are planetarium shows, and, at the Observatory, which contains the largest telescope in the world dedicated to public education, an astronomer gives talks and helps visitors use the telescope.

156 Heaton Park Dr. NE (at Artwood Rd. off Ponce de Leon Ave.). ℂ 404/378-4311. http://fsc.fernbank.edu. Admission free. Planetarium shows $2 adults, $1 students; seniors free. *Note:* Children under age 5 not admitted to the planetarium, but there are special children's shows with an admission charge of 50¢. Mon 8:30am–5pm; Tues–Fri 8:30am–10pm; Sat 10am–5pm; Sun 1–5pm. Planetarium shows Tues–Fri 8pm; Wed and Fri–Sun 3:30pm. The Observatory is open Thurs–Fri 8 (or whenever it gets dark)–10:30pm, weather permitting. Live look at the night sky 11pm. Forest trails open Sun–Fri 2–5pm; Sat 10am–5pm. Closed most school holidays. From downtown, go east on North Avenue to Piedmont and turn left. Turn right on Ponce de Leon, drive 4 ½ miles and turn left at the light onto Atwood Road. Turn right on Heaton Park Drive and Fernbank is on the left across from Fernbank Elementary School.

SciTrek (Science and Technology Museum of Atlanta) *Overrated* *Kids*

This museum left a lot to be desired on our visit. Its purpose is to offer hands-on adventures for adults and kids in science, math, and technology, with over 150 interactive exhibits that transform alien concepts into user-friendly steps to learning. However, recent financial difficulties have seriously hurt this attraction. Many of the exhibits were either missing items or not working at all.

When all is in working condition at SciTrek, you can create a magnetic field to hurl a disc upward, change light into electricity, produce electric current using your own hand as a "battery," see how much electricity you can generate pedaling a bicycle (how many bulbs can you light up?), and test various metals for electrical conductivity.

A kinetic light sculpture lets you vary frequency, intensity, and revolutions to create an infinite variety of designs. You can also examine the range of your peripheral vision, step inside a kaleidoscope, watch yourself walking through a distorted room on video (demonstrating how the brain visually perceives things based on past experience), mix over 16 million colors (time permitting) on a computer, bend light beams, and look into infinity. An especially intriguing exhibit for kids of all ages is the frozen shadow room, in which you can "freeze" your shadow on a wall of light-sensitive phosphorous vinyl film; a bright flash causes the panel to glow except in the area your body shields from the light. It's lots of fun dancing and jumping to create shadow art on the wall.

KIDSPACE has simple exhibits geared to the 2- to 7-year-old set. Here the kids can paint their faces, squirt water to float toys downstream, construct a house, deliver news over closed-circuit television, play electronic instruments, make images on heat-sensitive liquid crystal with their hands, and produce a puppet show. There are also very easy computer games. "I Can Discover Nature" includes a huge ant farm and an aquarium that demonstrates the river system in simple terms.

Pulleys, levers, wheels, axles, and such are explored in another area. You can lift billiard balls with a screw auger, become a human gyroscope, and suspend a ball in the air using a Bernoulli blower.

In Mathematica, a history wall portrays the achievements of major mathematicians from the 12th century to the present. Other hands-on displays here demonstrate various aspects of mathematics, from the laws of planetary motion to probability theory.

Exhibits are supplemented by an ongoing series of lectures, demonstrations, workshops, and temporary shows. You can take some science home with you from the Science Store, which has a wonderful array of games, books, and activities. There's no snack bar unless you count the vending area, but you can take your lunch and park it in a locker for a nominal fee until you finish the exhibits. There's a picnic area inside.

Note: As mentioned before, SciTrek has been having financial difficulties, and the administration is contemplating closing its doors. At the very least, the museum may abbreviate its hours of operation, so be sure to call ahead before you visit.

395 Piedmont Ave. (between Ralph McGill Blvd. and Pine St.). ℂ 800/543-TREK outside Georgia or 404/522-5500. www.scitrek.org. Admission $9.50 adults; $7.50 seniors, students, and children age 3–12; free for children under age 3. Free parking. Mon–Sat 10am–5pm; Sun noon–5pm. Closed Easter, Thanksgiving, Christmas, New Year's Day. MARTA: Civic Center.

Six Flags Over Georgia (Kids)

One of the state's major family attractions, Six Flags offers a great day's entertainment. Arrive early (at least 30 min. before opening), note where you've parked in the vast lot, and take 10 minutes or so to plan out your show and ride schedule.

Nine of the park's 10 themed areas reflect the historical heritage of that region, from Southern (Cotton States, Confederate, Georgia, Lickskillet, and Promenade), to European (France, Britain, Spain), to American (U.S.A.). The tenth themed area, Gotham City, features Batman The Ride. The Promenade section, which showcases the heritage and charm of the South, includes a variety of dining and retail options, including a gazebo where guests can meet Bugs Bunny. The wascally wabbit is just one of many costumed Looney Tune characters (Sylvester, Daffy Duck, and others) that roam the park greeting kids.

Thrill rides include several wet ones, such as Splashwater Falls (plummet down a soaring 50-ft. waterfall), a log flume, and Thunder River (a simulated whitewater rafting adventure). White-knuckle coasters include the Georgia Scorcher (one of the Southeast's tallest and fastest stand-up roller coasters), the Viper (which goes from 0–60 mph in less than 6 sec. and has a 360-degree loop), Ninja (the "black belt" of roller coasters that turns riders upside down five times and offers thrilling loops, dives, and corkscrew turns), the Georgia Cyclone (a classic wooden roller coaster with 11 dramatic drops, patterned after Coney Island's famous thrill ride), the Great American Scream Machine (another classic wooden coaster), and Mind Bender (a triple-looper). Other highlights are Batman The Ride, Great Gasp (a 20-story parachute jump), Riverview Carousel (a merry-go-round from the early 1900s), and Free Fall (ever wonder what it would be like to fall off a 10-story building?). A less dizzying adventure is Monster Plantation, a Disneyesque boat ride through an antebellum mansion haunted by over 100 animated monsters. And there's much, much more.

Shows vary from year to year, but they usually include a major musical revue, a country music show, a golden-oldies show, thrill cinema adventures on a 180-degree screen, and an animated character show. In addition, headliners such as

Martina McBride play the 8,072-seat (with lawn seating for 4,000) Southern Star Amphitheatre.

There are restaurants and snack bars throughout the park, though you might consider bringing a picnic.

275 Riverside Pkwy. SW (at the Six Flags exit off I-20W), Austell, GA. ℂ 770/948-9290. www.sixflags.com. Admission $42 adults, $22 for seniors (age 55 and over) and for children 48 inches and under; free for under age 3. A nominal fee is charged for amphitheater concerts. Weekends only Mar to mid-May, Sept, and Oct; daily Memorial Day to Labor Day. Gates open 10am daily; closing hours vary. Parking $8.

White Water *Kids*   Forty acres of wet, splashy fun await you at White Water, one of the largest water-theme parks in the South. Its star attraction is the $1-million Tree House Island, a four-story fantasy tree house with over 100 different activities—curvy slides, net bridges, water cannons, chutes, etc. A giant 1,000-gallon bucket of water empties over the whole attraction every few minutes. Other park highlights include: Cliffhanger, a 990-foot free fall, one of the tallest such attractions in the world; the 735-foot Run-A-Way River, an enclosed tunnel raft ride; the "Atlanta Ocean," a 750,000-gallon wave pool; and a host of different slide and splash experiences. There's much more, including a special section for children 48 inches and under called Little Squirt's Island, offering 25 tot-size water attractions. Captain Kid's Cove, adjacent to it, has dozens of additional activities for kids age 12 and under. Restaurants and snack bars are on the premises, as are rental lockers and shower facilities. Swimsuits are essential.

Next to White Water is **American Adventures** (ℂ 770/424-9283), an indoor/outdoor family amusement park featuring children's rides in the Fun Forest (bumper cars, a small roller coaster, a tilt-a-whirl, and others); a classic carousel; a go-cart track; a penny arcade with over 130 games; Professor Plinker's Laboratory—a large children's play area with ball crawls and nets to climb; 18-hole miniature golf; and the Foam Factory, a huge, multilevel interactive play area featuring scads of foam ball activities. It's all geared to children age 12 and under. A family-style restaurant is on the grounds. Admission to American Adventures is $15 for children age 4 to 17, $4 for adults and children age 3 and under. To visit just the Foam Factory, admission is $3 for parents and children age 3 and under, $6 for children ages 4 to 17. The park is operated seasonally. Call for open dates and hours.

250 N. Cobb Pkwy NE (Exit 265 off I-75), Marietta, GA. ℂ 770/424-9283. www.sixflags.com. Admission $27 adults, $10 seniors, $17 children from age 3 and up to 48 in. tall; free for children under age 2. Parking $3. Weekends only starting in mid-May 10am–6pm; daily Memorial Day to late summer and Labor Day weekend 10am to late evening (closing hours vary). Closed early Sept to Apr.

Wren's Nest *Kids*   Named for a family of wrens that once nested in the family mailbox, Wren's Nest is the former home of Joel Chandler Harris, who chronicled the wily deeds of Br'er Rabbit and Br'er Fox. It's been open to the public since 1913, when his widow sold it to the Uncle Remus Memorial Association.

Harris's literary career began at the age of 13, when he apprenticed on the *Countryman,* a quarterly plantation newspaper. In 4 years spent learning journalism there, young Harris spent many an evening hanging about the slave quarters, drinking in African folk tales and fables spun by George Terrell, a plantation patriarch who became the prototype for Uncle Remus. Sherman's army put the *Countryman* out of business, and Harris went on to other newspapers, working his way up to editorial writer at the *Atlanta Journal-Constitution* by age 28. There, plagued by writer's block one gloomy winter afternoon, he remembered the plantation stories of his youth and evoked Uncle Remus to fill his column. Enthralled readers clamored for more, and the rest is history.

Impressions

*"I seem to see before me the smiling faces of thousands of children—
some young and fresh—and some wearing the friendly marks of age,
but all children at heart, and not an unfriendly face among them. And
while I am trying hard to speak the right word, I seem to hear a voice
lifted above the rest saying, "You have made some of us happy." And so
I feel my heart fluttering and my lips trembling and I have to bow
silently and turn away and hurry into the obscurity that fits me best."*
—Joel Chandler Harris, former owner of Wren's Nest,
died at the age of 62 on July 3, 1908.
He wrote these words, which later
appeared on his gravestone.

The house itself is an 1870s farmhouse with a Queen Anne–style Victorian
facade added in 1884. Harris lived here from 1881 until his death in 1908,
doing most of his writing in a rocking chair on the wraparound front porch. On
a 30-minute tour, including a slide presentation about Harris's life, you'll see a
good deal of Uncle Remus memorabilia. The stuffed great horned owl over the
study door was a gift from Theodore Roosevelt, whose White House Harris visited; the original wren's nest mailbox reposes on the study mantel; and all of
Harris's books, along with signed first editions of major authors of his day (Mark
Twain and others) are displayed in a bookcase.

The house is interesting, but the best part is the **storytelling.** Call ahead to
find out when storyteller-in-residence Akbar Imhotep will be telling stories
culled from African and African-American folklore; it's a real treat.

1050 Ralph David Abernathy Blvd. (2 blocks from Ashby St.). ⓒ **404/753-7735.** Admission $3 adults, $2 seniors and students age 13–19, $1 children age 4–12; free for under age 4. Tues–Sat 10am–4pm; Sun 1–4pm.
Closed on major holidays. Take I-20 West to Ashby St., turn left on Ashby, then right on Ralph David Abernathy Blvd.; Wren's Nest is 2 long blocks down on the left. MARTA: Bus no. 71 from West End rail station.

Yellow River Game Ranch *(Kids)*   This 24-acre animal preserve bordering the
Yellow River offers close encounters of the 4-legged kind—a chance to view, pet,
feed, and generally mingle with some 600 animals (always including quite a few
babies) living in open enclosures, or right out in the open, along a 1-mile oak-
and hickory-shaded forest trail. Owner Art Rilling knows every animal on the
ranch by name and can give you chapter and verse on each one's personality,
preferences, and in some cases, romantic history. The animals know they're
among friends here and are highly socialized, so you have a unique chance to
study them up close. Keep in mind before you visit that all these animals smell
like, well, animals. If a barnyard atmosphere bothers you, don't visit.

Inhabitants include donkeys named Rhett and Scarlett, Georgia black bears
that stand up and beg for marshmallows, goats, dozens of rabbits in Bunny Bur-
rows (kids can pet the bunnies), an assortment of interesting-looking chickens,
a herd of buffalo, sheep, burros, goats, ponies, a skunk named General Sherman
(we are in Atlanta, after all), and a groundhog named General Beauregard Lee
who lives in a white colonnaded Southern mansion complete with miniature
satellite dish.

Consider packing a picnic lunch. There are tables throughout the property,
and one especially nice picnic area overlooks the river.

4525 Hwy. 78, Lilburn, GA. © **770/972-6643**. Admission $6 adults, $5 children age 3–11; free for 1 child under age 3. Memorial Day to Labor Day daily 9:30am–5pm. Closed Thanksgiving and Christmas. Take I-85N to I-285E. Exit at State Hwy. 78, and follow it east for 10 miles.

Zoo Atlanta *(Kids)* This delightful 40-acre zoo dates from 1889, when George W. Hall (aka "Popcorn George") brought his traveling circus to town. Employee claims against Hall for back wages forced him to relinquish his menagerie, and the animal entourage was purchased by a prominent Atlanta businessman who donated the collection to the city as the basis for a zoological garden in Grant Park. It grew considerably over the years and was a popular local attraction, but it had fallen into disrepair by the mid-1980s. Director Terry Maple was brought in to rescue the zoo and oversee a still-ongoing multimillion-dollar renovation, and the turnaround has been dramatic.

Today, Zoo Atlanta is one of the finest in the country, with animals housed in large open enclosures that simulate their natural geographical habitats. The zoo participates in breeding programs, many of them focusing on endangered species, and is home to many of endangered animals, including Sumatran orang-utans, 19 western lowland gorillas, black rhinos, 3 African elephants, 2 Komodo monitors, and big-mouthed African dwarf crocodiles. The facility got a huge boost in popularity and respect late in 1999 with the arrival of Lun Lun and Yang Yang, two giant pandas, and it's hoped that the dynamic duo will produce offspring.

Currently the exhibit creating the biggest stir is the Asian Forest, home to the pandas. The two Chinese natives are a huge hit with adults and children alike. Although the pandas' rowdiest period is in the afternoon, the two put on quite a show most of the day: munching bamboo, tussling with each other, playing on their log swing, or climbing on the swinging ladder. Lun Lun might take a dip in the habitat pool, although Yang Yang has declined to take the plunge. (When Lun Lun has had enough of Yang Yang's roughhousing, she heads for the water.) In the summer, the two can be especially entertaining; if it's really sweltering, zoo officials give each of them a huge block of ice to help them cool off. Yang Yang likes to hug his until it melts.

Your first stop will probably be Flamingo Plaza. Farther on, Mzima Springs and Masai Mara house elephants, rhinos, lions, zebras, giraffes, gazelles, and other African animals and birds. The landscape resembles the plains of East Africa, with honey locust trees and yuccas; and the lion enclosure replicates an East African *kopje* (rocky outcropping). Frequent animal demonstrations, African storytelling, and educational programs take place under the Elder's Tree in Masai Mara.

The lushly landscaped Ford African Rain Forest—one of the most popular sections—centers on four vast gorilla habitats separated by moats. Studies on gorilla behavior take place here, and there are usually quite a few adorable babies. They're hard to spot sometimes, so be sure to ask if there are any to be seen. The zoo's longtime mascot, Willie B. (named after former Atlanta mayor William B. Hartsfield), died in 2000, but his daughters Kudzoo and Olympia

Fond Farewell

Willie B., the beloved Zoo Atlanta gorilla who died Feb. 2, 2000, had so many people come to his memorial service to pay their last respects that many had to be turned away. In all, there were close to 8,000 mourners who managed to attend live in the forest and usually put on a pretty good show. The best time to visit is around 2pm, when the gorillas are fed. Also in the section is a walk-through aviary of West African birds, an exhibit of small African primates, and the Gorillas of Cameroon Museum. Landscaping includes burned-out areas of forest and deadfall trees—gorillas do not live in manicured gardens.

In the Ketambe section, several families of high-climbing orangutans show off their skills among the trees and bamboo clusters of an Indonesian tropical rainforest. If you're lucky enough to be there at feeding time—around 2:30pm—you might see them swinging on ropes from tree to tree. In the Sumatran Tiger Forest, rare Sumatran tigers prowl a lush forest, sometimes dipping into a stream or waterfall. Nearby is a superb Reptile House—the zoo is home to one of the finest reptile collections in the country—and a special exhibit area, often used to house visiting animals.

Plan to catch entertaining and informative free animal shows in the Wildlife Theater during summer or at the African Elephant Demonstration given daily year-round.

A zoo train travels through the Children's Zoo area, where you'll find a playground and petting zoo where kids can get friendly with llamas, sheep, pot-bellied pigs, goats, and more. There are aviaries here, too.

There are snack bars (including a McDonald's) throughout the zoo. Or you can picnic in tree-shaded areas in Grant Park. The Zoo Atlanta Trading Company features zoo memorabilia and gifts.

800 Cherokee Ave. (in Grant Park). © 404/624-5600. www.zooatlanta.org. Admission $16 adults, $12 seniors, $11 children age 3–11; free for children under 3. Strollers can be rented. Daily 9:30am–4:30pm, until 5:30pm on weekends during daylight saving time. Visitors may stay on the premises 1 hr. beyond closing time. Closed New Year's Day, Thanksgiving, Christmas. Free but limited parking. Take I-75 south to I-20 east. Get off at the Boulevard exit (59A) and follow the signs to Grant Park. MARTA: Bus no. 105 from the West End rail station.

4 Special-Interest Tours

The **Atlanta Preservation Center,** a private, nonprofit organization headquartered at 537 Peachtree St. (© **404/876-2041**), offers a variety of 1- to 2-hour guided walking tours in the city. Cost of each tour is $5 for adults, $4 for seniors, students, and children, and free for children under age 5. Tours of the Fox Theatre District are given year-round; the remaining tours are offered as noted. Call or visit **www.preserveatlanta.com** for days, hours, and tour departure points.

During the **Fox Theatre District Tour,** you'll explore in depth this restored 1920s Moorish movie palace, a theater whose auditorium resembles the courtyard of a Cairo mosque and whose architecture and interior were influenced by the discoveries at King Tut's tomb (see p. 156 for a full description of the theater). This tour is subject to change due to special events or matinee performances.

Just added to the offerings in 2002, the **Grant Park Tour** takes you through Atlanta's history from the antebellum Grant Mansion and Confederate fortifications to the Victorian era and present day in Grant Park. The park, the centerpiece of this revitalized neighborhood, became a favorite spot because of its beautiful lake, numerous springs, and amusement area. It's now home to the Atlanta Cyclorama and Zoo Atlanta.

The **Historic Downtown Tour** (Mar–Nov) is an architectural survey of Atlanta's downtown, from Victorian buildings to modern high-rises. You'll learn about the architects, the businesspeople, and the prominent families who created the city's early commercial center. The tour includes peeks at historic interiors.

Run the Peachtree

The Peachtree Road Race is more than just the world's largest 10K road race. It's a social event in Atlanta, as thousands of spectators line Peachtree Street, Atlanta's main drag, to cheer the runners.

If you're lucky enough to be in town on July 4th, you can do the same. Pack a breakfast and station yourself just about anyplace along Peachtree from Lenox Square to Fourteenth Street. Or go straight to the finish in Piedmont Park and take part in the chaos of the finale. Be sure to arrive early. The wheelchair division of the race begins at 7am, and the official footrace begins at 7:30am. Peachtree is closed to traffic that morning, and you'll have difficulty crossing the street—even on foot—after 7am.

The race is quite a sight to behold, as 55,000 runners surge down Peachtree, a far cry from the 110 runners who gathered to run the first race July 4, 1970. (The only spectators then were a few surprised pedestrians walking their dogs.) The race is so large now that it takes 500 volunteers to coordinate the start and 50 minutes for the final group to pass the starting line. By then, the winner has already covered the 6.2-mile distance and rested for at least a quarter of an hour.

Don't even think about entering the race at the last minute. Many more applicants than can be accommodated vie for the available spots, and the event always closes out in a few days. You can, however, run the course other days of the year. There are sidewalks all the way down Peachtree, so it's a fairly safe course. Here's the route you should follow:

Start at the corner of Peachtree and Lenox roads, right across from Lenox Square. Proceed down Peachtree through Buckhead. Along the way, you'll pass by some of Atlanta's most elegant neighborhoods, and just after West Wesley Road, you'll have a magnificent view of the downtown skyline. Don't let the easy, downward trend of the first few miles fool you. This is a tough run, and just about halfway through the course, there's a fairly steep incline—appropriately dubbed Heartbreak or Heart Attack Hill. (Fortunately, the top of the hill is right in front of Piedmont Hospital.) In Midtown, proceed on Peachtree to Tenth Street, turn left, and continue to the end of the course, which is at the Charles Allen Drive entrance to Piedmont Park. To return to Lenox Square, backtrack to the Midtown station on Tenth Street a block off Peachtree and take MARTA to the Buckhead or Lenox station.

For more information, call the Atlanta Track Club at ℂ **404/231-9064.**

The **Inman Park Tour** (Mar–Nov) visits Atlanta's first trolley suburb, where you'll see preserved and restored Victorian mansions (exterior views only). Highlights include the homes of Coca-Cola magnates Asa Candler and Ernest Woodruff.

The **Sweet Auburn/MLK District Tour** (Mar–Nov) focuses on the area that 20th-century African-American entrepreneurs developed into a prosperous commercial hub. You'll also visit the church where Martin Luther King, Jr. preached and discover landmarks of the Civil Rights Movement.

Walking Miss Daisy's Druid Hills (Mar–Oct) explores the neighborhood that was the setting for the play and film *Driving Miss Daisy.* The gracious park-like area was laid out by noted landscapist Frederick Law Olmsted and contains many architecturally important homes.

The **Ansley Park Tour** (Mar–Nov) explores one of Atlanta's first garden suburbs (today a charming Midtown neighborhood), partly designed by Frederick Law Olmsted. Its broad lawns, majestic trees, parks, and beautiful houses make for a lovely tour. It's easy to get lost in Ansley Park, so if you want to explore the area, this tour is a good idea.

The following tours are not regularly scheduled, but special tours may be arranged:

The **Birth of Atlanta/Historic Underground Tour** (Mar–Nov) explores the historic Underground complex, the state Capitol, City Hall, the Fulton County Courthouse, and three inner-city churches with pre–Civil War roots.

The **Historic Midtown Tour** (Mar–Oct) explores the many faces of the booming Midtown area, from its bungalows and skyscrapers to its restaurants and churches.

5 Outdoor Pursuits

See also section 1, "The Top Attractions," earlier in this chapter, for a full description of **Georgia's Stone Mountain Park,** one of the best places in the region for all kinds of outdoor activities: picnicking, boating (rowboats, canoes, and sailboats), biking (rentals are available), fishing, hiking, golf, tennis, and swimming. Admission to the park (which includes parking) is $6 per car per day; an annual pass is $25.

BIKING
See the "In-Line Skating & Biking" section below.

FISHING
There's good trout fishing on the Chattahoochee River, in the North Georgia Mountains, about 1½ hours from downtown. Many lakes in the area are good for bass and striper, including **Lake Lanier,** a 38,000-acre reservoir about 45 minutes away. Fishing licenses, which can be bought at most sporting-goods stores, Wal-Marts, and Kmarts, are $3.50 for 1 day and $9 for 7 days. A trout-fishing stamp is $5.

The **Fish Hawk,** 279 Buckhead Ave. NE, between Peachtree and Piedmont roads (© **404/237-3473**), is an excellent and convenient supplier in Atlanta for quality tackle. It carries all kinds of fishing gear and outdoor clothing and can also supply the requisite license. The staff is extremely knowledgeable and can tell you where to find the fish you seek and anything you need to know about applicable state regulations. They're open Monday to Friday 9am to 6pm, and Saturday 9am to 5pm.

For additional information, serious anglers can call the **Georgia Department of Natural Resources,** License and Boat Registration Unit, at © **770/414-3333,** or visit **www.ganet.org/dnr/wild.** Fishing licenses can be purchased by calling © **888/748-6887** or visiting **www.permit.com.**

GOLF
Stone Mountain Golf Club (© **770/465-3278**) is nationally ranked. Robert Trent Jones, Sr., designed 18 of the 36 holes. It's a beautiful facility, some parts

of it adjacent to the park's lake. A pro shop is on the premises, and lessons are available. For weekends and holidays, reserve the Tuesday prior to the day you want to play; other times, reserve a week in advance. A restaurant/clubhouse has a large deck overlooking the lake. Greens fees are $47 Monday to Thursday, $57 Friday to Sunday and on holidays; prices may be lower in the off-season. There is a fee of $6 per car to enter the park. The course is open daily 7am to dark.

IN-LINE SKATING & BIKING

Piedmont Park is the place. **Skate Escape,** 1086 Piedmont Ave. NE, at Twelfth Street (© **404/892-1292**), is located close by. It offers all kinds of bicycles and skates for rent or sale, as well as helmets, bicycle locks, and accessories. You can also buy skateboards here. Conventional or in-line skates can be rented for $5 per hour, $15 per day; it's $6 per hour, $25 per day for a single-speed or children's bike. If you have an out-of-state driver's license, a major credit card is required for ID; or you can leave a deposit of $150 for skates, $250 for bikes. Skate Escape is open every day 11am to 7pm, and the folks here will give you good advice about routes through the park. MARTA: Midtown.

NATURE WALKS & SCENIC STROLLS

In addition to city strolls, Atlanta offers many wonderful places for quiet nature walks and easy day hikes.

The **Atlanta History Center,** 130 W. Paces Ferry Rd. (© **404/814-4000**), described fully on p. 147, stands on 32 woodland acres and offers self-guided walking trails and 5 gardens. You'll discover many plants native to the region along the forested mile-long Swan Woods Trail.

The **Chattahoochee River National Recreation Area** is a series of "units" or parklands that punctuate the 48 miles along the Chattahoochee River—from Buford Dam at Lake Lanier north of the city to Paces Mill at Vinings just outside Atlanta's northwestern limits. Along the way, there are trails that range from flat, easy walks to more strenuous ridge and valley hikes. It's an excellent way to enjoy some of the unspoiled parts of the scenic Chattahoochee River. There is no admission, but there is a $2 parking fee. For maps and more information, contact the **National Park Service** (© **770/399-8070** or www.nps.gov/chat).

Georgia's Stone Mountain Park, 16 miles east of downtown on U.S. 78, is also covered in this chapter (p. 156). It offers thousands of acres of beautiful wooded parkland and lakes. There's a walking trail that goes up and down the moss-covered slopes of the mountain; you'll be delighted by the wildflowers that bloom here each spring. There are also 20 acres of wildlife trails in the park, with natural animal habitats and a petting zoo, as well as more challenging hiking trails.

There are 16 miles of extensive hiking trails at **Kennesaw Mountain/ National Battlefield Park,** Old Highway 41 and Stilesboro Road, Kennesaw (© **770/427-4686**). The scenery is beautiful, and trail maps are available at the visitors center. See p. 176 for more information.

Piedmont Park, centrally located with its main entrance on Piedmont Avenue at Fourteenth Street, offers a glorious setting for strolls, jogging, and biking. The wonderful **Atlanta Botanical Garden** is next door. See p. 179 of this chapter for a full description of the park, and p. 146 for coverage of the botanical garden.

Château Élan, 30 miles north of Atlanta at Exit 126 off I-85 in Braselton (© **678/425-0900**), has nature trails along St. Emilion Creek (forested with tulip poplar, oak, hickory, and beech trees) and by Romanée–Conti Pond. There are picnic areas on the lovely grounds; custom picnics can be purchased at Café Élan. See p. 172 of this chapter for a complete description of its other attractions.

Described on p. 180 is the **Fernbank Science Center,** 156 Heaton Park Dr. NE (© **404/378-4311**), which has 1½ miles of paved trails with trees, wild-flowers, and plants labeled for identification. This unspoiled natural environment is home to many animals and birds, and a small pond teems with aquatic life.

The nonprofit **PATH Foundation** (© **404/355-6438**), which is dedicated to creating and maintaining a network of trails in metropolitan Atlanta for pedestrians and bicycles, has so far completed 18 miles of greenway trails. The most accessible is around **Chastain Park** in the northern part of the city. It's an easy, paved 2.6-mile loop around the rolling hills of the park and golf course. The **Atlanta–Stone Mountain trail,** which goes from the Carter Center to Stone Mountain Park, is another popular trek. Maps are available at most bicycle and sporting good stores. Call the above phone number for more information and advice about where to begin your journey.

RIVER RAFTING/CANOEING/KAYAKING

The **Nantahala Outdoor Center** (© **800/232-7238**) offers whitewater rafting adventures on the scenic Chattooga River in North Georgia (it's the one you saw in the movie *Deliverance*) and the Ocoee in Tennessee (which was an Olympic venue). Put-in points for both rivers are about a 2-hour drive from Atlanta. Trips vary in length (from a few hours to a few days) and difficulty.

The Chattooga offers Class II and III rapids in Section III and Class III, IV, and V in Section IV. The roller coaster Ocoee has Class III and IV rapids only. Kids must be at least 10 years old for easy trips, 12 or older for more difficult rapids. The company also offers canoeing and kayaking, and trips of varying difficulty on other rivers. All of the expeditions are immensely popular, so make reservations as far in advance as possible.

Prices vary depending on length and difficulty of the trip. Weekends are more expensive than weekdays. Half-day trips begin at about $35, full-day trips at about $62; both rates include equipment, a guide, and transportation from the outpost to the river. Rafting season is April 1 to October 31, with occasional trips in March and November.

The **Chattahoochee River National Recreation Area** (see "Nature Walks & Scenic Strolls," above) has several spots where canoers, kayakers, and rafters have access to the cold, slow-moving Chattahoochee River. Call the **National Park Service** (© **770/399-8070**) for more information. Watercraft can be rented from the **Chattahoochee Outdoor Center** (© **770/395-6851**) at the Johnson Ferry and Powers Island units in the recreation area.

SWIMMING

Almost every Atlanta hotel features a swimming pool. In addition, there is a sandy lakefront beach (complete with water slides) in Stone Mountain Park.

If you're *really* serious about getting wet, there's also **White Water,** Exit 265 off I-75 on North Cobb Parkway, in Marietta (© **770/424-9283**), a water theme park described in detail on p. 183.

TENNIS

The City of Atlanta Parks and Recreation Department operates 12 outdoor hard courts at **Piedmont Park,** all of them lit for night play (© **404/853-3461**). No reservations are taken; it's first-come, first-served. There's free parking at the courts, and showers and lockers are available on the premises. Hours are weekdays 10am to 9pm, and Saturday and Sunday 10am to 6pm. Fees are $2 per person per hour during the day, $2.50 per person per hour when courts are lit.

The city also has 13 outdoor clay courts and 10 outdoor hard courts (16 are lit) at the **Bitsy Grant Tennis Center,** 2125 Northside Dr., between I-75N and Peachtree Battle Avenue (*C* **404/609-7193**). Courts are available on a first-come, first-served basis. No reservations. There are showers and lockers available. The courts are open Monday to Thursday 8am to 9pm, Friday 8am to 8pm, and Saturday and Sunday 9am to 6pm. Hours from Labor Day to April are abbreviated; call ahead for details. Court fees are $2 to $3.50 per person per hour, depending on the type of court and the hour of play. There's a lot of team tennis played here; call ahead to check court availability. For information about other city courts, call the **Bureau of Recreation** (*C* **404/817-6766**).

The **Stone Mountain Tennis Center,** 5525 Bermuda Rd., Stone Mountain, GA 30087 (*C* **770/469-0108**), was built as the tennis venue for the Centennial Olympic Games and has some of the finest public courts in the state. There are 16 hard-surface courts, 15 of which are lit, located near Georgia's Stone Mountain Park, 18 miles east of downtown. Hours are Monday to Friday 9am to 9pm, and Saturday and Sunday 9am to 6pm. Cost is $3.50 per person per hour. Take U.S. 78 to Bermuda Road, one exit past the entrance of Stone Mountain Park.

6 Spectator Sports

Atlanta has four professional major league teams: the Braves, the Hawks, the Falcons, and the Thrashers (a new NHL team). Good tickets can be extremely hard to come by during a winning season. Tickets can be obtained from the individual teams, or you can charge tickets by contacting **Ticketmaster** (*C* **800/326-4000** or 404/249-6400; www.ticketmaster.com). A fee will be added to each ticket purchased through Ticketmaster.

AUTO RACING

From beginning to end, **Atlanta Motor Speedway** has race fans covered. Hosting two NASCAR Winston Cup races a year—one near the beginning of the season and one nearly dead last, as well as Bush Grand National, IMSA, and ARCA events, this track in Hampton, Georgia, 30 miles south of Atlanta, is where folks come to see the big boys run. The smart fans are those who can come in a day early and camp or RV; they get to avoid the traffic. The others aren't so lucky. Unreserved campsites are $30 during race week. Reserved camping for self-contained RVs is $75—there are no hookups. If you don't want to wait for a free parking space for your car, $75 reserved parking for vehicles is located directly behind the Champions Grandstand or Weaver Grandstand. Race tickets are usually available right up until the start of the race and some are quite reasonable. Tours of the speedway are available through the gift shop. Call *C* **770/946-4211** or visit the website at www.atlantamotorspeedway.com.

Situated on 700 scenic wooded acres about 45 minutes north of downtown Atlanta, **Road Atlanta** is one of the Southeast's premier road-racing motorsports facilities. Its 2.5-mile Grand Prix racecourse offers a challenging combination of turns, elevation changes, and high-speed straightaways. A year-round season includes sports car, motorcycle, truck, and vintage/historic racing, among others. Call *C* **800/849-RACE** or 770/967-6143, or visit www.roadatlanta.com

for information and a schedule of events. Tickets usually run $15 to $65, with higher prices for the Petit Le Mans, a 1,000-mile race. Infield parking is $5.

Road Atlanta is located in Braselton on Georgia Highway 53 between I-85 and I-985 (take I-85N to Exit 129, make a left, and follow the signs). If you're attending an event, you can rent a campsite for $25 a night; during special events, campsite prices may be higher. If you prefer a room to a tent, try The Lodge, a limited-service hotel owned by Château Élan, a nearby resort. Call ✆ 770/867-8100 for information.

BASEBALL

Although they've only won the World Series once in recent memory, in 1995, the **Atlanta Braves** consistently post a terrific record. In 1997, the team moved to **Turner Field,** a stadium built to host the Centennial Olympic Games that was later modified to become a world-class ballpark. (See "Stadiums," below, for details.) The regular season runs from the first week of April until the first week of October; post-season play is over by the end of October.

Advance-purchase seats run from $5 (Upper Pavilion) to $35 (Dugout Level), and ticket availability is proportional to the team's success. Call customer service (✆ 404/522-7630) for more information, or visit the website at www. atlantabraves.com. You can charge by phone through Ticketmaster (see number at the beginning of this section), or buy directly from the stadium box office, which is located at the northwest corner of the ballpark. It's open Monday to Friday 8:30am to 6pm, Saturday 9am to 5pm, and Sunday 1 to 5pm. Even if you can't get tickets in advance, it's sometimes possible to get $1 Skyline tickets (bleacher seats) and $5 standing-room-only tickets. Skyline tickets are available only on game day and go on sale 3 hours before game time. Fans are limited to one ticket per customer, and immediate entry to the ballpark is required. Standing-room-only tickets are sold on game day only and are available 1 hour before the first pitch, but only when all other tickets for the game have been sold. Check the designated ticket window in the main ticket area.

BASKETBALL

The **Atlanta Hawks** are the local NBA franchise, and their season runs from November to April. The Hawks play in Philips arena, which was built downtown on the site of the old Omni, adjacent to CNN Center, and opened in September 1999. Tickets range from $10 for a nosebleed seat to $65 for something up close and personal. Call Ticketmaster or ✆ 404/827-3865 for information.

On the college front, the **Georgia Tech Yellow Jackets** play in the highly competitive ACC. The season runs from mid-November to early March. Their home games are played in Alexander Memorial Coliseum, on the campus at Tenth and Fowler streets (see "Stadiums," below, for details). Tickets are usually $18, but they are difficult to come by. Available tickets go on sale at the Coliseum the day

---

(*Fun Fact* **Foul Play**

Kudzu, a prolific, fast-growing vine that smothers anything and everything in its path, once stopped an Atlanta Braves baseball game. On Aug. 29, 2000, in the ninth inning of a game between the Braves and the Cincinnati Reds, the lights abruptly went out at Turner Field. It seems that a kudzu vine had snaked around a critical terminal area, causing the 12-minute blackout. It was the first-ever kudzu delay in Major League Baseball. The Braves lost 4–2.

of the game. Call ℂ **888/832-4849** or 404/894-5447 for information.

FOOTBALL
The **Atlanta Falcons** are the city's NFL franchise, playing eight games (plus exhibition games) each season in the Georgia Dome (see "Stadiums," below, for details). Watching a game in the Dome is an interesting, noisy experience. The regular season begins in September and runs through December, with post-season games played in January. Pre-season games begin in August. Ticket prices are $25 to $41. Call ℂ **404/249-6400** for ticket information or visit www.atlanta falcons.com.

As for college football, the "Ramblin' Wrecks from Georgia Tech" have played their home games at 43,000-seat Bobby Dodd Stadium/Grant Field, on campus at North Avenue and Techwood Drive (MARTA: North Ave.), since 1913. The season runs from September to November. Call ℂ **888/832-4849** or 404/894-5447 for information. Tickets run $20 to $28 and are usually available, except for home games against the University of Georgia, which are always sold out. Games are played on Thursday nights and Saturday afternoons. Parking is limited; MARTA is the best option. Go early and stop at the Varsity for a hamburger or a hot dog; it's on North Avenue between the MARTA station and the stadium.

HOCKEY
The **Atlanta Thrashers,** an NHL team named after Georgia's state bird, took to the ice in October 1999, in Philips arena, which was built downtown on the site of the old Omni Coliseum. The season extends through May, and tickets run from $10 to $200. Call ℂ **404/584-PUCK** for information or visit www. atlantathrashers.com. Take MARTA to Omni/Dome/GWCC.

STADIUMS
Alexander Memorial Coliseum   This 10,000-seat stadium—renovated for the Olympics—is home to Georgia Tech's Yellow Jackets college basketball team. Parking is limited around the stadium; it's easiest to take MARTA.

Georgia Institute of Technology, Tenth and Fowler sts. ℂ **404/894-5400** for information. MARTA: North Avenue

Philips Arena   This spectacular new $213 million arena, home to the NHL Atlanta Thrashers and NBA Atlanta Hawks, was built on the site of the old Omni Coliseum. Tours of the arena are available every half hour daily 9am to 6pm on non-event days and 9am to 5pm on event days. The hour-long tours take in the Hawks and Thrashers locker rooms, the press box, and the luxury suites. Tickets are $7 adults, $5 seniors, and $4.50 children age 4 to 12; age 3 and under free.

A combination tour of the Philips Arena and the CNN Studio is available for adults only for $11. The Hawk Walk, which connects the CNN Center with Philips Arena, is worth a look if you're a sports fan. It's an indoor street that sells food and beverages and Atlanta Hawks and Atlanta Thrashers merchandise, and promotes TBS stations. There are huge video screens that show live action inside the arena or shows from one of the Turner networks, as well as giant billboards that flash ticker information from CNNSI and CNNfn.

100 Techwood Dr. NW (at Marietta St.). ℂ **404/827-2300**. www.philipsarena.com. MARTA: Omni/Dome/GWCC.

Fun Fact   **A Grand Golfer**

Robert Tyre "Bobby" Jones, who won golf's Grand Slam at the age of 28, never became a professional golfer. Jones, who rarely played in tournaments after 1930, went on to practice law in Atlanta. One of the city's public golf courses is named for him.

Georgia Dome   Atlanta's $214-million, 71,500-seat domed megastadium, which is the home of the Atlanta Falcons, hosted Super Bowl XXVIII in 1994, several Olympic events in 1996, and Super Bowl XXXIV in 2000. Its oval shape provides a good view of stadium action from every seat. It is the site of the annual Peach Bowl each January, and hosted the NCAA Men's Basketball Final Four in 2002. The Dome also hosts tennis matches, tractor pulls, college basketball, track and field events, and Supercross events. Check the papers or call the above number to find out what's on during your stay. Parking is extremely limited and expensive; take MARTA and walk to the Dome.

1 Georgia Dome Dr. (at International Blvd. and Northside Dr.). *C* **404/223-9200** for information. MARTA: Omni/Dome/GWCC.

Turner Field   This spectacular 50,000-seat ballpark started life as an 80,000-seat stadium built to host the Centennial Olympic Games in 1996. It was the site of the opening and closing ceremonies and numerous track and field events. After the Olympics, the north end of the stadium (with approximately 35,000 seats) was demolished and the stadium was modified to accommodate baseball. It's built in the style of old-time ballparks, but also includes a number of attractions besides the baseball game itself. The folks who run the stadium like to call it a baseball theme park, and it's not a bad idea to come to the game early and take in the various attractions, especially if you have children along. The **Braves Museum and Hall of Fame** features memorabilia commemorating legends and key moments in Braves history. (Take a gander at the bat Hank Aaron used to hit his 715th home run.) The museum is open to ticket holders on game days 3 hours before game time and 1 hour after the completion of the game. **Scouts Alley** is designed to teach fans about the fine art of scouting. Fans can also test their hitting and throwing skills, call up scouting reports on former and current Braves, play a trivia game, call a play-by-play inning of a game, learn about Hank Aaron's "hot" spot, and much more. At **The Cartoon Network's Tooner Field,** kids can hang out with Cartoon Network characters or play interactive games in the Digital Dugout. At **The East Pavilion,** fans can have their images inserted into a baseball card or a great moment in Braves history. **The Braves Clubhouse Store** is full of Braves-themed merchandise, some of which is available only at the stadium

If all this activity makes you hungry, head to **The West Pavilion,** where you can nosh on famous food items from other ballparks, or **The Braves Chop House,** a casual dining restaurant that overlooks the Braves' bullpen.

It's possible, and fun, to tour Turner Field. Tours depart every half hour Monday to Saturday 9:30am to 4pm and Sunday 1pm to 4pm on non-game days, and Monday to Saturday 9:30am to noon on game days. Prices are $7 adults, $4 children age 3 to 12; children under age 3 free. Call *C* **404/614-2311** for information. Tours include the museum, the dugout, the press box and broadcast booth, the clubhouse, Scouts Alley, and more. On non-game days, there's ample free parking in the north lot.

Museum-only tickets are $3 on non-game days; the museum hours vary according to the game schedule.

755 Hank Aaron Dr. SW. (C) **404/522-7630**. Parking $10, but extremely limited, in official lots. Handicapped parking in the South lot, east of I-75/85, on a first-come, first-served basis. MARTA: Park free at a MARTA rail station, ride the train ($1.50), and then take the free shuttle from the Five Points station to the stadium. Shuttle service begins 1 hr. before game time and continues for 1 hr. after the game ends. Or take MARTA to the Georgia State University station and walk several blocks to the stadium. Call MARTA at (C) **404/848-4711** for more information.

A Walking Tour of Sweet Auburn

You never really understand a city until you walk around it a bit. Atlanta's climate makes walking tours an option just about year-round.

In addition to the tour below, consider taking one of the guided walking tours listed in chapter 7. Also, note that certain attractions detailed in that chapter are walking tours in and of themselves: Georgia's Stone Mountain Park, Kennesaw Mountain/National Battlefield Park, Oakland Cemetery, and the Atlanta Historical Society in Buckhead.

Sweet Auburn includes the Martin Luther King, Jr. National Historic Site, which comprises about 2 blocks along Auburn Avenue, and the surrounding preservation district, about 10 more blocks. A neighborhood that nurtured scores of 20th-century black businesspeople and professionals, it contains the birthplace, church, and gravesite of Martin Luther King, Jr. The area was a vibrant commercial and entertainment district for black Atlantans from the late 1800s until the 1930s, when it went into a steep decline.

In the 1980s, the area where Martin Luther King, Jr., was born and raised was declared a National Historic Site, and now, under the auspices of the National Park Service, portions of Auburn Avenue are in an ongoing process of restoration. Although parts of the area are still in sad disrepair, new landscaping has beautified some of the street, and several homes on the "Birth Home" block have been restored to their 1920s appearance. (For more information about the National Historic Site, contact the **National Park Service** at © **404/ 331-6922** or visit the website at **www.nps.gov.malu**.) This walking tour provides insight into black history, the civil rights movement, and black urban culture in the South. If you're traveling with children, it's a wonderful opportunity to teach them about a great American. The major points of interest are covered in detail in chapter 7.

WALKING TOUR   SWEET AUBURN

Start:	The corner of Howell and Irwin streets. To get to this intersection, take I-75/85 south, then exit at Freedom Parkway/Carter Center. Turn right at the first stoplight onto International Boulevard. Follow signs to Martin Luther King National Historic Site: You can park in a lot on the north side of Irwin Street between Boulevard and Jackson Street. By MARTA: King Memorial Station is about 8 blocks away; or take bus no. 3 east from the Five Points Station.
Finish:	Auburn Avenue and Courtland Street.

Time: Allow about half a day to explore this area thoroughly. If you want to include a tour of Martin Luther King, Jr.'s Birth Home (stop no. 3)—and a visit to this area would not be complete without it—start out early in the day and obtain your tickets at the National Parks Service Visitor Center at 450 Auburn Avenue. Only a limited number are available each day.

Begin your stroll at:

1 Howell and Irwin Streets

Walk south along Howell Street, where renovated historic homes and recently built housing, designed to harmonize with the architecture of the neighborhood, provide testimony to the area's continuing renaissance. Note no. 102 Howell, built between 1890 and 1895, which was the home of Alexander Hamilton, Jr., Atlanta's leading turn-of-the-century black contractor. Its architectural details include Corinthian columns and a Palladian window.

Turn right on Auburn Avenue, and as you proceed, look for interpretive markers indicating historic homes (mostly Victorian and Queen Anne) and other points of interest en route to:

2 Martin Luther King, Jr., Center for Nonviolent Social Change

This institution is located at 449 Auburn Ave. (© **404/524-1956;** www.thekingcenter.com). The organization here continues the work to which King was dedicated—reducing violence within individual communities and among nations. Freedom Plaza, on the premises, is his final resting place. The center is open every day from 9am to 5pm. Here, you can take a self-guided tour of exhibits on King's life and the Civil Rights Movement. Admission is free. See p. 164 for more details.

Now double back a few blocks east to:

3 The Birth Home of Martin Luther King, Jr.

Free half-hour guided tours are given on a continual basis from 9am to 5pm at King's birthplace, located at 501 Auburn Ave. On weekends, especially, arrive early, since demand for tickets often exceeds supply. Tickets are obtained at the National Parks Service Visitor Center, 450 Auburn Ave. See p. 149 for more details on the birth home.

Walk back toward stop 2, noting the turn-of-the-century homes in the area such as:

4 The Double "Shotgun" Row Houses

Standing at 472–488 Auburn Ave., these two-family dwellings with separate hip roofs were built in 1905 to house workers for the Empire Textile Company. They were called "shotgun" because rooms were lined up in a row, and one could fire a shotgun straight through the whole house.

Continue west on Auburn Ave. At the corner of Auburn and Boulevard is:

5 Fire Station no. 6

This is one of Atlanta's eight original firehouses, completed in 1894. The two-story Romanesque-revival building was situated to protect the eastern section of the city. The station houses a museum, open daily from 9am to 5pm, where exhibits include restored fire engines and vintage fire-fighting paraphernalia. Admission is free. Note the Italianate arched windows on the second story.

Continuing west on Auburn Ave., a notable stop on your tour is:

6 Ebenezer Baptist Church

Situated at 407 Auburn Ave. (© **404/688-7263**), this church, founded in 1886, is where Martin Luther King, Jr., served as co-pastor from 1960 to 1968. The church is open Monday

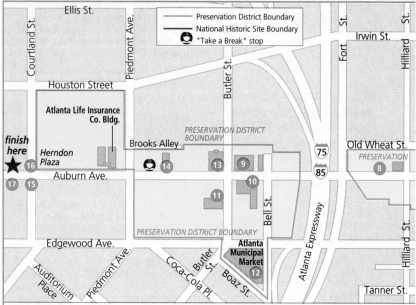

1 Howell & Irwin Streets
2 Martin Luther King, Jr.
  Center for Nonviolent Social Change
3 The Birth Home of Martin Luther King, Jr.
4 The Double "Shotgun" Row Houses
5 Fire Station No. 6
6 Ebenezer Baptist Church
7 Wheat Street Baptist Church
8 The Prince Hall Masonic Building
9 The Odd Fellows Building and Auditorium
10 The Herndon Building
11 The Butler Street YMCA

through Saturday 9am to 5pm. Here, you can listen to a taped message on the history of the church and enter the sanctuary and watch a videotape. The church has built a new sanctuary across the street, but the original building remains as a historic site under the auspices of the State Department of Parks & Recreation. See p. 154 for more details.

One block west at 365 Auburn Ave. is the:

⑦ Wheat Street Baptist Church

This church has served a congregation since the late 1800s. Auburn Avenue was originally called Wheat Street in honor of Augustus W. Wheat, one of Atlanta's early merchants. The name was changed in 1893.

Farther west, on Auburn between Hilliard and Fort streets, is:

⑧ The Prince Hall Masonic Building

This was an influential black lodge led for several decades by John Wesley Dobbs. Today, it houses the national headquarters of the Southern Christian Leadership Conference.

On the other side of the expressway, at 228–250 Auburn Ave., note:

⑨ The Odd Fellows Building and Auditorium

This is another black fraternal lodge, which originated in Atlanta in 1870. Completed in 1914, the building later became headquarters for an insurance company.

Across the street, at 231–245 Auburn Ave., is:

⑩ The Herndon Building

This building is named for Alonzo Herndon, an ex-slave who went on to

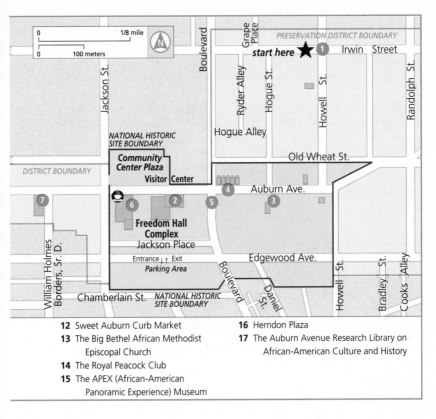

found the Atlanta Life Insurance Company. It was erected in 1924. By 1930, the Auburn business district supported 121 black-owned businesses and 39 black professionals.

Make a left on Butler Street and you'll see:

⓫ The Butler Street YMCA

Built in the early 1900s, this was a popular meeting place of civil rights leaders. Today, it's augmented by a modern YMCA across the street.

Continue south along Butler Street to the:

⓬ Sweet Auburn Curb Market

The market is located just below Edgewood Avenue. Formerly called the Municipal Market, this historic spot dates to 1924, when Atlanta was still a segregated city. Whites shopped within, but blacks were only permitted to patronize stalls lining the curb. The market's current name reflects that era. Today, it sells groceries and fresh produce—including many regional and ethnic items such as ham hocks and chitlins ("We sell every part of the pig here but the oink," says the owner). Fully cooked ethnic meals are available here, and there is seating so you can dig in right away. Open Monday through Thursday from 8am to 6pm, Friday and Saturday from 8am to 7pm.

Walk back to Auburn Avenue on Butler Street and turn left. To your right, at 220 Auburn Ave., is:

⓭ The Big Bethel African Methodist Episcopal Church

The church was originally built in the 1890s and then rebuilt in 1924 after a fire. In the 1920s, John Wesley Dobbs called the Bethel "a towering edifice to black freedom."

Fun Fact   **A Spot of History**

Dr. Martin Luther King, Jr., won the Nobel Peace Prize in 1964 at the age of 35, the youngest person ever to do so. He died 4 years later.

Farther along, at 186 Auburn Ave., is:

⑭ The Royal Peacock Club

This music club's walls are painted from floor to ceiling with peacocks. Closed for years, it presented top black entertainers such as Ray Charles, Aretha Franklin, and Dizzy Gillespie in its heyday.

TAKE A BREAK
The **Caribbean Restaurant**, 180 Auburn Ave., between Piedmont Avenue and Butler Street (℃ **404/658-9829**), has a plain but pleasant interior. Walls are hung with posters of Caribbean destinations and musicians, diners are seated on glossy white wooden benches at big picnic-style tables, and reggae and calypso music plays in the background. The low-priced menu lists authentic Caribbean foods such as oxtail stew, curried goat, spicy jerk chicken, red snapper stew, fried plantains (served with blue cheese dressing), and rôti skin (a pancake-like bread). All entrees come with rice and two vegetables. For dessert, try the homemade carrot cake or the red velvet cake. Major credit cards are accepted. Open Monday to Thursday from 11:30am to 9pm, Friday and Saturday from 11:30am to 10pm.

At 135 Auburn Ave., the corner of Auburn Avenue and Courtland Street, is:

⑮ The APEX (African-American Panoramic Experience) Museum

This museum features exhibits on the history of Sweet Auburn and the African-American experience, including a children's gallery with interactive displays. You can call ℃ **404/521-2739** to see if there's anything special happening at the museum while you're in town, See p. 146 for further details.

Cross the street to:

⑯ Herndon Plaza

Here, you can see exhibits on the Herndon family.

If you'd like to do further research on the history of Auburn Avenue—or on any aspect of African-American history and culture—continue on to 101 Auburn Ave.:

⑰ The Auburn Avenue Research Library on African-American Culture and History

This is the place to go for answers about African-American history. Operated by the Atlanta-Fulton County Library System, the library's collection includes literature, documents, rare records, and more. A Heritage Center on the premises features special exhibits, workshops, seminars, lectures, and events. Open Monday to Thursday 10am to 8pm, and Friday to Sunday noon to 6pm.

9

Atlanta Shopping

Atlanta is the shopping mecca of the Southeast. Period. Visitors might *say* they come to Atlanta to steep themselves in Southern history, take in a play or two, or contemplate the masterpieces in a museum. But what they really want to do is trot on over to Buckhead for a little retail therapy.

It's not just that there's a lot of shopping here; it's that it's so varied. There are chic boutiques that can hold their own with the best of Los Angeles or New York, flea markets bursting at the seams with antiques and collectibles, giant department stores, and interesting little browsable areas such as Virginia-Highland. And even if you don't want to buy anything, it's great fun to wander around the shopping areas, where you can check out the locals and take the pulse of the city.

1 Great Shopping Areas

BUCKHEAD

The stomping ground of well-to-do Atlantans, Buckhead is the ultimate shopping area, with two major malls and lots of little boutiques, antique shops, and galleries. If you're serious about shopping, this is the place to start. Even though the area has an upscale reputation, don't let that stop you. There's lots of variety, and the competition can mean excellent bargains.

The hot spot for the best of Buckhead is at the corner of Peachtree and Lenox roads, where two major malls—**Phipps Plaza** and **Lenox Square**—face off against each other (see section 2 of this chapter). If your time is limited, pick one of these malls and spend the morning.

If you have more time and are interested in art, antiques, or decorative accessories, head straight to **Bennett Street,** where you'll find a healthy concentration of stores in a 2-block strip. There are also many shops in **Buckhead West Village,** near the intersection of Peachtree and West Paces Ferry roads, and more establishments up and down Peachtree and scattered along smaller side streets.

BENNETT STREET

Located just off Peachtree on the south edge of Buckhead is a quaint little avenue that's become one of the most interesting shopping destinations in the city. Once a supply path that linked Atlanta to the surrounding countryside during the Civil War, Bennett Street evolved into a thriving warehouse district around the turn of the century. Several years ago, those same warehouses were transformed into a handy concentration of shops and galleries specializing in art, decorative accessories, and antiques. There are also two recommended restaurants, Fratelli di Napoli (p. 133) and Mick's (p. 106), and two small cafes in the area.

It all makes for a pleasant afternoon ramble, but if you don't have time to wander the whole street, check out The Stalls and the Interiors Market, both of which house many dealers in one location. Most shops are open Monday to Saturday from 10am or 11am to 5pm, and a few are open Sunday 1 to 5pm. Bennett Street—little more than a dead-end alley—is only a couple of blocks long, but it's built on a hill, so wear comfortable shoes. It's just off Peachtree Road between Collier Road and Peachtree Battle Avenue. To get there from downtown, take bus No. 23 from the Arts Center MARTA station to the 2100 block of Peachtree. Here's some of what you'll find:

Bennett Street Gallery   You'll find contemporary fine art, glass, ceramics, and jewelry, plus paintings in oil, acrylic, casein (a plasticky substance), and watercolor. 22 Bennett St. NW. ℂ **404/352-8775.**

Bittersweet Ltd.   The store directly imports English antiques and accessories, including a large collection of Blue Willow china and antique sporting items. 45 Bennett St. NW. ℂ **404/351-6594.**

Interiors Market   This is a large consortium of antique and art dealers all under one roof. Locals looking for just the right home accessory know to start here or at The Stalls rather than schlepping around to all the different shops in town. There's an ever-changing variety, with myriad booths featuring everything from fine antiques to old books. There's a tiny cafe amid all the plunder. 55 Bennett St. NW. ℂ **404/352-0055.**

Kilim Collection   An excellent source for old and new hand-woven flat-weave wool rugs and pillows, you'll also find vests, handbags, and upholstered pieces. 22 Bennett St. NW. ℂ **404/351-1110.**

Nottingham Antiques   Direct importers of European antique pine furniture. Some custom furniture is available here, too. 45 Bennett St. NW. ℂ **404/352-1890.**

Out Of The Woods Gallery   This shop offers unusual wooden gifts, accessories, and artwork from ancient and contemporary cultures. 22 Bennett St. NW. ℂ **404/351-0446.**

The Stalls   Just like the Interiors Market, this is a large assortment of dealers under one roof, which increases the odds that you'll find that special piece you've been searching for. The quality of the antiques and accessories is excellent and attracts designers from around the country. For lunch, you can stop at the Stalls Café, which serves an excellent grilled sandwich—pimento cheese with bacon and tomato. 116 Bennett St. NW. ℂ **404/352-4430.**

Tula   This large building near the end of the street houses about 10 to 12 galleries and artists' studios. There's an assortment of pottery, paintings, sculptures, textiles, and photographs. 75 Bennett St. NW. ℂ **404/351-3551.**

MIAMI CIRCLE

Most design centers are open to the trade only, and this street of showrooms and warehouses started out that way. But now, the majority of the nearly 100 merchants on Miami Circle in Buckhead are open to the public. It's a virtual smorgasbord of furnishings and accessories—from fine European and American antiques to country and primitive pieces. There's antique and reproduction pine, painted furniture, antique statuary, heirloom wicker, fine artwork, majolica, custom and antique rugs, antique books and bookcases, clocks, antique chandeliers, and at least one warehouse of designer fabrics.

This is not a quaint street suitable for a pleasant stroll, but it is a great place to browse for serious merchandise. Most establishments are open Monday to Saturday from 10am to 5pm, and some are open on Sunday. If you need something shipped home, it's not a problem. Miami Circle is off Piedmont Road, just a half-mile south of Peachtree and about a third of a mile north of the Lindbergh MARTA station.

WEST VILLAGE OF BUCKHEAD

The intersection of Peachtree and West Paces Ferry Road is the heart of the original Buckhead community. On the east side of Peachtree is the center of Buckhead night life, but the retail shops are on the west side of Peachtree, where you'll find everything from art and antiques to women's apparel. The West Village, as the area surrounding the intersection is called, is bounded by West Paces Ferry Road, Roswell Road, and East Andrews Drive. If you're navigating the city via public transportation, use the Buckhead MARTA station to access shopping in this area.

There are a couple of places to stop for a snack or lunch as you wander through the neighborhood. Or you can cross Peachtree to **Fado'** at 3035 Peachtree Rd. (✆ **404/841-0066**), an "authentic" Irish pub that serves commendable Gaelic fare; especially good is the *boxty* (filled Irish potato pancake) and the corned beef and cabbage. Here's some of what you'll see in the West Village:

Antiques & Home & Decorative Accessories

Boxwoods   It's hard to see everything in this delightful shop in one visit. There are intriguing gifts and serious gardening accessories, as well as numerous antiques, lamps, fresh flowers, and greenery. Open Monday to Saturday from 10am to 6pm. 100 E. Andrews Dr. NW. ✆ **404/233-3400.**

C'est Moi   This is probably one of the best shops in the West Village. Like many of the others, it has a French slant, and the stock is so well chosen that there's always something interesting to see, including tableware, fine linens, custom furniture, unusual picture frames, bath items, and jewelry. There's also a corner devoted to children's gifts and accessories. Open Monday, Tuesday, Friday, and Saturday 10am to 5pm, and Wednesday and Thursday 10am to 6pm. 3198 Paces Ferry Place NW. ✆ **404/467-0095.**

Foxglove Antiques   Foxglove Antiques is a charming old house filled with fine French and English antiques, accessories, and one-of-a-kind gifts. Open Monday to Saturday 10am to 6pm. 3188 Paces Ferry Place NW. ✆ **404/233-0222.** www.foxglovecottage.com.

Lush Life Home   This is the home decor offshoot of the popular Lush Life specialty nursery, located at 146 East Andrews Dr. It's stocked with sophisticated and witty Parisian-style decor, antiques, linens, fine milled soaps, and fragrances. The nursery is worth a visit, too. Open Monday to Saturday from 10am to 6pm. 3240 Roswell Rd. NW. ✆ **404/841-9661.**

Urban Frontier   Urban Frontier is jammed with rustic home furnishings, new and vintage linens, unusual Christmas ornaments, baby paraphernalia, tableware, and scores of interesting little one-of-a-kind knickknacks. One of its rooms is devoted entirely to accessories and fun stuff you might "need" to furnish a beach house. There's also a good selection of original folk art, including pieces by Jimmy Wright and Mary Proctor. Open Tuesday to Saturday 10am to 5:30pm. 3210 Paces Ferry Place NW. ✆ **404/240-0960.**

Art

Ann Jacob Gallery   This gallery blends fine contemporary art with works by emerging popular and folk artists. Open Tuesday to Saturday 10am to 5pm. 3261 Roswell Rd. NW. ✆ **404/262-3399.**

Lagerquist Gallery   The contemporary fine art in this gallery includes sculpture, paintings, watercolors, and works on paper by regional, national, and international artists. Open Tuesday to Saturday 10am to 5pm. 3235 Paces Ferry Place NW. ✆ 404/261-8273.

Signature Shop & Gallery   Everything here is one of a kind, handcrafted by contemporary American artists: dinnerware, turned wood bowls, decorative and functional ceramics, pewter vessels, sterling jewelry and utensils, quilts, furniture, and more. Open Tuesday to Saturday 10am to 5pm. 3267 Roswell Rd. NW. ✆ 404/237-4426.

Fashion Boutiques

Almanac   Almanac specializes in simple but fashionable women's clothing, especially separates. You'll also find handbags, shoes, and lingerie. Open Tuesday to Friday 10:30am to 6:30pm, and Saturday 10:30am to 6pm. 22A E. Andrews Dr. NW. ✆ 404/266-1188.

Moxie   Hip clothes for young women can be found here at affordable prices. The selection of costume jewelry is well priced. Open Monday to Saturday 11am to 7pm; summer hours vary. 3232 Roswell Rd. NW. ✆ 404/365-8819.

Nancy's   This store recently moved just up the street and continues to provide some of the best customer service I've ever experienced. A Buckhead favorite, with scores of repeat customers, the emphasis here is on comfortable, casual women's clothing and accessories. You'll find lots of linen and natural materials. The boutique staff is excellent at reinventing your look using a favorite piece in your current wardrobe paired with new items from the shop. Nancy's offers a personal shopper service via telephone. Open Monday to Friday 10:30am to 6pm, and Saturday 10:30am to 5pm. 3112 Roswell Rd. NW. ✆ 404/264-1333.

Peoples   The women's clothing in this friendly shop—suits, tops, skirts, dresses, jackets, swimwear—is contemporary, with clean, classic lines. It's a sleek, well-chosen collection you won't find in department stores. Open Tuesday to Friday 10am to 6pm, and Saturday 10am to 5pm. 3236 Roswell Rd. NW. ✆ 404/816-7292.

Razzle Dazzle   Razzle Dazzle has been on the Buckhead scene for more than 2 decades. Sportswear is the main staple here (great pants, sweaters, jackets, etc.), but there are also stunning little dresses, some eveningwear, hats, and a wonderful assortment of jewelry, some of it handmade. You'll find lines by Max Studio, Johnny Was, Michael Stars, and more. A big draw is the supply of vintage Levi's. Open Monday to Saturday 10:30am to 5pm. 49 Irby Ave. NW. ✆ 404/233-6940.

White Dove   White Dove is full of feminine, sexy, upscale clothing for day and evening. Many of the fabrics are delicate and antiquey—silky rayons, linens, chiffons, and gauzy cottons—and the hats are festooned with silk flowers. Open Tuesday to Saturday 11am to 6pm. 18 E. Andrews Dr. NW. ✆ 404/814-1994.

Sporting Goods

Patagonia   There's a lot here for outdoor enthusiasts, no matter what sport you enjoy—canoeing, paddling, skiing, cycling, climbing, surfing, and on and on. You'll find equipment, as well as boots, outerwear, and organic cotton clothing for men, women, and children. Open Monday to Friday 10am to 7pm, Saturday 10am to 6pm, and Sunday noon to 6pm. 34 E. Andrews Dr. NW. ✆ 404/266-8182.

Cool Coca-Cola Facts

The world's most popular soft drink, Coca-Cola, was invented in Atlanta. Here's just how much we love it:

- If all the Coca-Cola ever produced were to erupt from "Old Faithful" at its normal rate of 15,000 gallons per hour, the geyser would flow continually from 307 A.D. to the present.
- If all the Coca-Cola ever produced were in 8-ounce bottles laid end-to-end, they would reach to the moon and back 1,057 times. That's one round-trip per day for 2 years, 10 months, and 23 days.

CHAMBLEE'S ANTIQUE ROW

Antique Row, on New Peachtree Road at Broad Street and North Peachtree Road, is a quaint collection of shops located in historic buildings, some of which date as far back as the 1800s. Nearby, there are a few antiques malls, which house many dealers under one roof. The largest is the Broad Street Antiques Mall, 3550 Broad St. (© **770/458-6316**), which has around 100 dealers. In the assorted shops and malls, you'll find antique American and European furniture, glassware, pottery, Victoriana, Orientalia, wicker, collector toys, quilts, Coke memorabilia, jewelry, architectural antiques, Olympics collectibles, and crafts items. Hours vary with each store. Most are open Monday to Saturday 10:30am to 5pm, and Sunday 1 to 5pm. It's a little tough to get here if you don't have a car, but you can take a MARTA train to the Chamblee station, which is about three-fourths of a mile from the shops. On weekdays, take the no. 132 Tilly Mill bus from there; on weekends, walk or take a taxi.

VIRGINIA-HIGHLAND

This charming area of town, centered on North Highland Avenue between University Drive and Ponce de Leon Avenue, boasts antique shops, boutiques, and art galleries. There are three major concentrations: on North Highland just south of University Drive; at the intersection of North Highland and Virginia avenues; and just north of Ponce de Leon around St. Charles Place. From one end to the other, it's about a mile and a half, but it's a nice walk, and there are cafes where you can stop and take a break. If you only have a short time, go to North Highland and Virginia and take in the stores there. For lunch, try Murphy's (p. 136). This area is accessible by MARTA through the Five Points station.

Art

Aliya Gallery   This contemporary gallery showcases North American artists in many different media. Open Tuesday to Thursday 2 to 9pm, Friday 2 to 10pm, Saturday noon to 9pm, and Sunday noon to 6pm. 1402 N. Highland Ave. NE (at University Dr.). © 404/892-2835.

Modern Primitive Gallery   There's lots of the unexpected in this gallery, which specializes in folk, outsider, and visionary art from nationally known artists. Open Sunday, Tuesday, and Wednesday noon to 6pm, and Thursday to Saturday noon to 9pm. 1393 N. Highland Ave. NE (between University and Morningside drs.). © 404/892-0556.

Moments I Scream for Ice Cream

If you happen to be at the north end of the Virginia-Highland shopping district in the afternoon or evening, stop in for a divine gelato or sorbet at **What's the Scoop,** 1402 N. Highland Ave. It's open Monday and Tuesday noon to 10pm, Wednesday and Thursday noon to 11pm, Friday and Saturday noon to midnight, and Sunday noon to 10:30pm. Equally delicious is **Orange and Scarlett's** in Midtown at 814 Juniper Road. A combination coffee house/homemade ice cream shop, this new venture will please the palate with such frozen flavors as Sweet Jimmy, a vanilla and peanut brittle caramel swirl, named in honor of Georgia's Jimmy Carter; Gone with the Sin, featuring chocolate, almonds, pecans, walnuts and chocolate fudge; and Piedmont Perk, with toasted pistachios. Open 7 days a week, 7am to 11pm in fall and winter months, and 7am until midnight in the spring and summer.

Natural Body International   This appealing shop invites you to pamper yourself with all manner of skin treatments, oils, soaps, lotions, cosmetics, and an extensive line of aromatherapy products. All are natural and animal- and environment-friendly. There's also a day spa offering a full line of beauty treatments. Open Monday to Friday 9am to 8pm, Saturday 9am to 6pm, and Sunday noon to 6pm. There are several other Atlanta locations, including one in Buckhead at 2385 Peachtree Rd., Suite 3A (© **404/869-7722**). The hours vary. 1402-1 N. Highland Ave. (just below University Dr.). © **404/876-9642**.

Home & Decorative Accessories

Affairs   This shop offers many exquisite giftware items, an extensive collection of picture frames, dinnerware, French and Italian kitchenware, and bath products. There are even doodads for your favorite baby or pet. Delightful browsing. Open Monday to Thursday 9:30am to 9:30pm, Friday and Saturday 9:30am to 10pm, and Sunday 11am to 6pm. 1401 N. Highland Ave. (at University Dr.). © **404/876-3342**.

Delaware River Trading Co.   There's lots of cool stuff for your home or apartment here: furniture, dinnerware, luxury bedding, garden accessories, pillows, bath products, and so on. Open Sunday noon to 6pm, Monday to Thursday 11am to 8pm, and Friday and Saturday 11am to 9pm. 1198 N. Highland Ave. NE (at Amsterdam Ave.). © **404/874-5583**.

Metropolitan Deluxe   At first glance, it looks like nothing more than an interesting gift shop with lots of cards, candles, and unusual cut flowers. But downstairs, there's a fabulous assortment of linens (sheets, towels, comforters, etc.) and other home furnishings, including pillows, wooden tables, armoires, lamps, and upholstered pieces. There are also vases, glassware, products for bath and body, picture frames, dried flowers, wrapping paper, and many gift items. Open Monday to Thursday 10am to 10pm, Friday and Saturday 10am to 11pm, and Sunday 11am to 7pm. 1034 N. Highland Ave. NE (just north of Virginia Ave.). © **404/892-9337**.

20th Century   There's a wide-ranging inventory here: terrific jewelry, whimsical clocks, Art Deco items, unusual mirrors, and furnishings running the gamut from 19th-century reproductions to '50s Heywood-Wakefield blondwood pieces. Also in the mix: campy nostalgia items such as back issues of

Life magazine, Elvis trading cards, and antique radios and telephones. Open Monday to Thursday 10am to 9:30pm, Friday and Saturday 10:30am to 10pm, and Sunday 11am to 7pm. 1044 N. Highland Ave. (between Los Angeles and Virginia aves.). ℂ 404/892-2065.

Fashion Boutiques

Mitzi & Romano   Mitzi Ugolini carries cool and contemporary women's clothing, plus great jewelry and accessories, including Kate Spade handbags. Most of the selection is affordable. Don't miss the sale section at the back of the store. Open Monday to Thursday 10am to 9pm, Friday and Saturday 10am to 10pm, and Sunday noon to 7pm. 1038 N. Highland Ave. (between Virginia and Los Angeles aves.). ℂ 404/876-7228.

Mooncake   The ever-changing inventory of whimsical wearables for women here might include cloche and straw hats, flowing dresses, unusual silk separates, and handcrafted jewelry. The retro-style clothing looks vintage, but everything is new. You'll also find body and bath items, hair accessories, diaries, and greeting cards. Open Monday to Saturday 11am to 7pm. 1019 Virginia Ave. NE (just off North Highland Ave.). ℂ 404/892-8043.

Planetarian Ornaments   This shop is full of colorful women's apparel and accessories with an international connection. For example, there are patchwork jackets of Indonesian batik and dresses made of fabric inspired by aboriginal artwork. There's also a collection of furniture from around the world, with an emphasis on Asia. Open Sunday noon to 7pm, Monday and Tuesday 11am to 8pm, Wednesday through Friday 11am to 9pm, and Saturday 11am to 10pm and Sunday 12 to 7pm. 784 N. Highland Ave. NE (north of Ponce de Leon Ave.). ℂ 404/607-7694.

THE WESTSIDE

Atlanta's hottest new retail and restaurant destination is located in what is essentially an industrial section. The Westside, not to be confused with Buckhead's West Village, has been home for a few years to a small, pioneering group of home furnishings stores, artists' studios, and antiques shops. But the area gained instant legitimacy when Bacchanalia, one of Atlanta's most honored restaurants, decided to move there from its Buckhead home in January 2000.

So far, the district, which is housed in a collection of renovated warehouses and other motley buildings (Bacchanalia's building was once a meatpacking plant), has attracted two casual restaurants, an art gallery, a garden center, two furniture stores, and a handful of retail shops with the promise of more to come. Four times a year, there's a small outdoor festival featuring upscale antiques, clothing, art, produce, and refreshments. Call ℂ 770/481-0280 or visit www.westsideurbanmarket.com for dates and admission prices to the market.

⌒Finds   A Little Bit of Italy in Atlanta

A local chef's love of all things Italian has resulted in one of the country's hottest gourmet food lines. **Bella Cucina Artful Food** offers handmade pestos, fresh pasta sauces, coarse-grain and honey mustards, and fruit preserves prepared with farm produce and beautifully packaged right here in Hotlanta. Now you can buy the stuff at the company's first retail store, **Bella Cucina** (493 Peachtree St.; ℂ800/580-5674 or 404/881-0078; www.bellacucina.com; MARTA: Civic Center).

If you want to eat at Bacchanalia (p. 110), which is now open for lunch, be sure to call well in advance for reservations. You can, however, stop in at Mondo (p. 118), an upscale sandwich shop and bakery, or grab lunch at Taqueria del Sol (p. 118).

To reach the Westside, take I-75/85 from downtown, exit at Fourteenth Street, take Fourteenth Street west to Howell Mill Road, turn right, and go to the intersection of Howell Mill and Huff roads. Don't miss the additional stores on Foster Street, about a block down Huff Road, but note that the artists' studios at the end of the street are not open to the public. (And please don't feed the goats and chickens grazing in front of the studios.) Take MARTA to the Arts Center station to reach this area.

Bungalow   Simple, comfortable, elegant furniture is what you'll find here, as well as linens, books, lamps, and other home accessories. Open Monday noon to 5pm, and Tuesday to Saturday 11am to 7pm. 1198 Howell Mill Rd. NW, Suite 110. ✆ 404/367-8522.

Belvedere   Belvedere offers sleek, sophisticated furniture and decorative accessories. Open Tuesday to Saturday 11am to 5pm. 1200-A Howell Mill Rd. NW. ✆ 404/352-1942.

The Garden Path   This is a full-service nursery and landscape company with a selection of gardening paraphernalia and teak furniture. Open Tuesday to Saturday 10am to 6pm. 1198-B Howell Mill Rd. NW. ✆ 404/355-0788.

Macon & Co.   This large gallery has quite a variety under one roof. From sculpture to paintings to unique art furniture, the emphasis is on late-career artists, with a great percentage from the Southeast. There's also a location at 257 Trinity Ave. SW. Open Tuesday to Saturday 10am to 5pm. 1198 Howell Mill Rd. NW ✆ 404/603-9122.

Provenance   This store started out small a few years ago but recently expanded into a larger space that offers more room for its large and interesting collection of antiques, chandeliers, bed linens, rugs, tableware, and accessories. Open Monday to Saturday 10am to 6pm. 1157 Foster St. NW. ✆ 404/351-1217.

Scout   Casual, upscale men's and women's clothing and accessories co-exist with a large assortment of bath and beauty products by Bliss. Open Monday noon to 6pm, and Tuesday to Saturday 11am to 8pm. 1198 Howell Mill Rd. NW, Suite 114. ✆ 404/605-0900.

Star Provisions   Owned by Bacchanalia restaurant, Star Provisions is a cook's marketplace unlike any other in Atlanta. There's a small offering of locally grown organic produce, a cheese shop, a comprehensive wine shop, a bakery, and a specialty fish and meat market featuring Niman Ranch meats. There's also a large selection of unique tableware, cookbooks, and other gourmet-quality provisions such as olives, tea, coffee, olive oil, vinegar, and pasta. This place is nirvana if you're a serious foodie, but even if you're not, it's fun to look around and get a sample or two of cheese. And just try to sneak by the bakery with its fabulous array of goodies, including Bacchanalia's legendary Valrhona chocolate cakes, a divine confection with a gooey chocolate middle. Open Tuesday to Saturday 11am to 8pm. 1198 Howell Mill Rd. NW. ✆ 404/365-0410.

LITTLE FIVE POINTS

An area similar to Virginia-Highland (see above), though a lot funkier and much rougher around the edges, Little Five Points is as much a happening as an offbeat shopping area. There are still authentic hippies here and enough young people with wildly colored hair and pierced body parts to give you a '60s flash-back. In addition to the shops, there are a number of taverns and cafes. It is also close to Virginia-Highland, so if you crave additional browsing, both areas are easily covered in a few hours.

While you're shopping here, plan to have lunch at the Bridgetown Grill (p. 116), or at the Flying Biscuit Cafe (p. 139), which is about a mile up McLendon Avenue.

Begin your stroll on Moreland just north of Euclid, then proceed southwest along Euclid. Most shops are open Monday to Saturday 11am to 7 or 8pm, and Sunday noon to 6pm. But this is a very laid-back shopping district, and hours can change on a whim. Take MARTA to the Five Points station to access the stores reviewed below.

Abbadabbas's   If you're searching for comfortable shoes and don't care if they're a little offbeat, step into this wild little shoe store that's been a fixture for years. You'll find Birkenstocks, Doc Martens, and Converse, to name a few, as well as a great assortment of socks. There are four other locations around town. 421-B Moreland Ave. NE (between Euclid and North aves.). ✆ **404/588-9577.**

A Cappella Books   You'll discover new, used, and out-of-print books here, many of them relating to counterculture, literature, history, and the arts. Signed editions, too. 1133 Euclid Ave. (at Colquitt Ave.). ✆ **404/681-5128.**

The Clothing Warehouse   Vintage Levis are the main attraction here, but there's also a selection of other casual used clothing for men and women. 420 Moreland Ave. NE (between Euclid and North aves.). ✆ **404/524-5070.**

Identified Flying Objects   Just about everything in here is designed to be airborne—kites, Frisbees, golf discs, windsocks, boomerangs, darts, and juggling paraphernalia. There are also glow-in-the-dark stars for your bedroom ceiling and other nifty items suggesting that up is the best direction. Open daily 11am to 6:30pm. 1164 Euclid Ave. NE (at Moreland Ave.). ✆ **404/524-4628.**

Junkman's Daughter   This funky 10,000-square-foot mega-store looks like a transplant from New York's East Village. The merchandise includes inexpensive club clothing for men and women, including T-shirts, shoes, and other bizarre and totally tasteless wares. The staircase leading to the mezzanine is in the shape of a 20-foot red high-heeled shoe. 464 Moreland Ave. NE (between Euclid and North aves.). ✆ **404/577-3188.**

René René   *Atlanta* magazine once named René René the city's "best women's clothing" shop in the "funky club scene" category. It's true, but some of owner René Sanning's designs are also sophisticated—possibly even wearable for business. There's also a glamorous, Old Hollywood–style evening line that has attracted such customers as Faye Dunaway and Halle Berry. There are interesting accessories here, too. 1142 Euclid Ave. (between Moreland and Colquitt aves.). ✆ **404/522-RENE.**

Stefan's Vintage Clothing   Most of Stefan's merchandise is vintage clothing for men and women, from the early 1900s through the early 1960s, plus accessories like cigarette cases, cuff links, evening bags, hats, and period costume jewelry. There are cashmere overcoats, lingerie, cocktail and evening gowns, tuxedos, wedding gowns, Hawaiian shirts, bowling shirts, and suits. Prices are low, and merchandise is usually in impeccable condition. Definitely a cut above the other neighborhood shops. 1160 Euclid Ave. NE (between Moreland and Colquitt aves.). ✆ **404/688-4929.**

Wax n Facts Looking for that ancient Bob Dylan album that your college girlfriend got custody of when you broke up? It's probably here, along with all the other old vinyl everybody misses. 431 Moreland Ave. NE (between Euclid and North aves.). ✆ 404/525-2275.

STONE MOUNTAIN VILLAGE

Stone Mountain Village, just outside the West Gate of Georgia's Stone Mountain Park (bounded by Second and Main sts. north and south, Lucille St. and Memorial Dr. east and west; ✆ 770/879-4971; www.stonemountainvillage. com), is worth a visit. It has been developing since the 1800s, and many of the shops are housed in historic buildings. A lot of the stores specialize in antiques, crafts, and collectibles. Some examples: country furniture, imported toys, dolls, baskets, homemade jams, handmade patchwork quilts and quilting fabrics, handcrafted dulcimers, Civil War memorabilia, and out-of-print books.

It's great fun to wander about this quaint village, and there's usually some festive event going on—perhaps an arts-and-crafts fair or live entertainment. During Christmas season, the streets are candlelit and the village becomes a magical place populated by St. Nick, elves, carolers, and harpists. Hours for most shops are Monday to Saturday 10am to 6pm; many are also open Sunday 1 to 5pm.

Be sure to stop by the **Village Visitor Center,** housed in a restored 1915 caboose at the corner of Main and Poole streets, to find out about special sales and events. It's open Monday to Saturday from 10am to 4pm, and Sunday from 1 to 4pm. Parking is free at several lots in town.

Stop for a meal at the nearby **Village Corner Bakery, Tavern, and German Restaurant** at 6655 Memorial Dr., at Main Street (✆ 770/498-0329). For breakfast there are croissants, German apple pancakes, or ham-and-egg platters with homemade biscuits. At lunch, there are sandwiches, salads, quiche, soups, and home-baked desserts. And the dinner menu highlights European fare, especially German specialties such as Wiener schnitzel and sauerbraten. There are also many German-style beers available. Open Tuesday to Saturday 8am to midnight, and Sunday 10am to 8pm. Major credit cards (American Express, Diners Club, Discover, MasterCard, and Visa) accepted.

2 Department Stores & Malls

Discover Mills This is Atlanta's newest collection of specialty shops and outlets—200 in all—some of which offer up to 70% off on designer fashions and brand names. Just 30 minutes northeast of downtown, Discover Mills opened in late 2001 and features outlets and anchor stores include Bass Pro Shops Outdoor World; Burlington Coat Factory; Eddie Bauer Outlet; joan vass usa outlet; Last Call from Neiman Marcus; Limited Too; Mikasa Factory Store; OFF 5th (the Saks Fifth Avenue outlet); Off Broadway Shoe Warehouse; Osh Kosh B'Gosh Outlet; and Sun & Ski Sports. Open Monday to Saturday 10am to 9:30pm, and Sunday 11am to 7pm. 5900 Sugarloaf Parkway, Lawrenceville. ✆ 678/ 847-5201.

Lenox Square The vast upscale Lenox Square, which started out as a humble shopping center in 1959, has grown into one of the most popular shopping destinations in the Southeast. Its interesting mix of stores, many of them exclusive to the region, takes it beyond the usual cookie cutter mall, and the formula attracts locals and visitors alike. You can buy just about anything here, from hiking boots to an engagement ring, and even if you're not in the mood to buy, there's great people-watching.

Anchors include Neiman-Marcus, Macy's, and Rich's department stores, and there are 250 shops, restaurants, kiosks, and services in the mall, including 6 movie theaters and several fine dining restaurants. Two of the best restaurants are Prime (p. 127) and Brasserie Le Coze (p. 129). Among the best-known stores are Ann Taylor, Britches of Georgetown, Burberrys, Joan & David, J. Crew, Warner Bros. Studio Store, a Metropolitan Museum of Art store, BCBG, Cartier, Sharper Image, Laura Ashley, Brooks Brothers, Max Mara, Nicole Miller, St. John, Betsey Johnson, Coach, Polo/Ralph Lauren, Bally of Switzerland, F. A. O. Schwarz, Speedo, and Louis Vuitton. Pottery Barn and Crate & Barrel carry a selection of home furnishings and accessories, including many items usually available only by catalog.

Open Monday to Saturday 10am to 9pm, and Sunday noon to 6pm, with extended hours during the Christmas season. A few stores close early on Saturday night. There's valet parking ($3) and a free shuttle to Phipps Plaza at the main entrance on Peachtree. 3393 Peachtree Rd. NE (at Lenox Rd.). ℂ **404/233-6767.** MARTA: Lenox.

Macy's Peachtree   Opened in 1927, this downtown branch of Macy's is a department store in the grand tradition, its main floor featuring 30 lofty Corinthian columns, marble floors, and glittering, crystal chandeliers. However, it's perfectly up-to-date when it comes to merchandise. Open Monday to Saturday 9am to 8pm, and Sunday noon to 6pm. 180 Peachtree St. (between International Blvd. and Ellis St.). ℂ **404/221-7221.** MARTA: Peachtree Center.

Mall at Peachtree Center   Part of the vast Portman-designed Peachtree Center complex, this downtown mall offers around 70 shops, restaurants, and services on 3 levels. It's not exactly a shopping destination, but its location near major downtown hotels makes it convenient if you are in need of goods or services. There are a few apparel shops, including Brooks Brothers, and other stores offering gifts, jewelry, books, cards, and candy. Services include florists, hairstylists, Federal Express, UPS, a dry cleaner, and an optician. A food court dishes up everything from gyros to chocolate chip cookies, and full-service restaurants include some decent choices: Mick's (p. 106), Benihana, and Azio Pizza and Pasta. Most stores are open Monday to Saturday 10am to 6pm. Peachtree St. at International Blvd. ℂ **404/654-1296.** MARTA: Peachtree Center.

Phipps Plaza   Just across the street from Lenox Square is Phipps Plaza, Atlanta's most exclusive shopping venue and one of its prettiest, with spacious promenades and grand interior courts. Lord & Taylor, Parisian (a Birmingham, Alabama–based department store with a fantastic women's shoe department), and Saks Fifth Avenue anchor Phipps' 100-plus shops and restaurants. The exclusive Ritz-Carlton Buckhead hotel is just a few steps away.

Phipps Plaza's posh emporia (many of them area exclusives) include Gucci, Tiffany & Co., Jaeger, Jil Sander, Gianni Versace, Niketown, A/X Armani Exchange, Ross-Simons (jewelry, china, and silver), Origins, and Cole-Haan and Kenneth Cole for shoes. You'll also find chic boutiques selling ladies' and men's apparel, luggage, jewelry, home furnishings, and specialty gifts.

Services include valet parking ($3) and a free shuttle to Lenox Square at the Lenox Road entrance. There are several restaurants, including The Tavern at Phipps, which has a pleasant, clubby atmosphere. Also on the premises: a food court and a 14-screen movie theater. Stores are open Monday to Saturday 10am to 9pm, and Sunday noon to 5:30pm. 3500 Peachtree Rd. NE (at Lenox Rd.). ℂ **800/ 810-7700** or 404/262-0992. MARTA: Lenox.

Underground Atlanta   This 12-acre mix of shops and restaurants is not as vibrant as it was several years ago, but it still can be fun to browse if you're staying downtown. There are dozens of shops, plus vendors in Humbug Square selling merchandise off antique pushcarts. Shopping options include clothing stores for men, women, and children, running the gamut from lingerie at Victoria's Secret to sportswear at the Gap. Other interesting emporia include Art by God (fossils and rare mineral specimens), African Pride (gifts and apparel with an African-American theme), Kandlestix (where candlemakers display their wares), and Papier D'Couleur (papier-mâché birds, fruit, and animals). There are also novelty stores such as the bargain mecca Just a Dollar.

Of course, there's a food court and a couple of good restaurants, including Mick's (p. 106). For lunch, you might try Johnny Rockets, an entertaining 1950s-style hamburger joint the whole family will enjoy. If you're driving, there's parking in two garages off Martin Luther King, Jr. Drive. Open Monday to Saturday 10am to 9pm, and Sunday noon to 6pm. Alabama Street (between Peachtree St. and Central Ave.). ✆ 404/523-2311. MARTA: Five Points.

3 More Shopping Around Town

ANTIQUE/FLEA MARKETS

Atlanta is home to several permanent flea markets selling everything from custom furniture to antique toys, but the most exciting markets are those that set up shop once a month. The lineup of dealers—from all parts of the country—is ever-changing, so no matter how often you go, you'll always see something new and fresh.

If you're in search of real finds, shop on the first day as soon as the market opens. That's when local dealers swoop in to snatch up the best merchandise. Serious bargaining often takes place in the closing hours of the last day, when many dealers are anxious to avoid lugging their wares home with them. Be sure to keep your admission ticket; it's good for the whole weekend.

Lakewood Antiques Market   Held at the historic Lakewood Fairgrounds, this huge market has 1,500 dealer spaces, most of them in the huge old fair buildings. You'll find thousands of rare antiques and collectibles, old architectural treasures, books, glassware, tools, cookware, linens, jewelry, and so on. There's also some new merchandise, such as cut-rate garden pottery, wrought-iron sculpture, and custom wood furniture, as well as fruits and vegetables in summer and fall. There are several food stands throughout, some of them selling homemade baked goods. Because many of the stalls are outside, it's fun to browse this one when the weather is pleasant. The place is huge and fascinating, so plan to spend much of the day.

Open the second weekend of each month, Thursday noon to 6pm, Friday and Saturday 10am to 6pm, and Sunday 10am to 5pm. Admission is $3, except for Thursday, which is "dealer day" and costs $5. Some dealers will still be setting up their booths on Thursday, but you have the advantage of getting the first peek at all the merchandise. At the Lakewood Fairgrounds, between downtown Atlanta and the airport. Take I-75/I-85 south to Exit 243 (Langford Pkwy.) and go east to the fairgrounds. ✆ 404/622-4488. Free parking.

Pride of Dixie Antiques Market   This is the newest of the markets, and it is more of a true antique market than a flea market. There are spaces for 600 dealers, who have searched the countryside for fabulous finds. You'll see fine antique furniture as well as interesting primitive painted pieces, heirloom jewelry and silver, antique books, baskets, rugs, linens, roll-top desks, and much more. This market is held inside an air-conditioned building, so weather is not a factor. Open the fourth weekend of each month, Friday and Saturday from 9am to 6pm, and Sunday from 11am to 5pm. Admission is $4 for the weekend. At the North Atlanta Trade Center, north of Atlanta. Take I-85 north to the Indian Trail exit (about 25 min. from downtown), then follow the signs. © 770/279-9853. Free parking.

Scott Antique Markets   Scott is an immense and immensely popular market that has had so much success, it's had to open another location across the interstate from the original spot. There are spaces for 2,400 booths, all indoors, and the antiques and collectibles are some of the finest you'll see anywhere. This market is similar in atmosphere to Pride of Dixie, but much bigger, with loads of heirloom furniture, jewelry, silver, and so on, as well as a huge assortment of collectibles.

There's a free shuttle between the two Scott facilities, so it's easy to visit both locations. The market is held the second weekend of every month. If you're really ambitious, you can do Scott and Lakewood (see above) in one day. Open Friday and Saturday 9am to 6pm, and Sunday 10am to 4pm. Admission is $3. At the Atlanta Exposition Center south of the city. Take I-75 south to I-285. Go east on I-285 to Exit 55 (Jonesboro Rd.) and follow the signs. © 404/366-0833. www.scottantiquemarket.com. Free parking.

BOOKSTORES

In addition to the independent bookstores in Atlanta, the nationwide chain stores of B. Dalton, Waldenbooks, Borders, Doubleday, and Barnes & Noble are represented locally. Barnes & Noble's major store can be found in Buckhead, at 2900 Peachtree Rd., just a few minutes south of Lenox Square (© **404/261-7747;** MARTA: Lenox). The main Border's store is also in Buckhead, 3 blocks north of Lenox Square, at 3637 Peachtree Rd. (© **404/237-0707;** MARTA: Lenox).

Books & Cases & Prints Etc.   There are some used books here, but the big attraction is the vast collection of antique books, especially the complete leather-bound sets. There are also old Bibles, children's books, scholarly books, antique and reproduction bookcases, and rare prints. Open Monday to Saturday 10am to 5:30pm. 800 Miami Circle NE, Suite 100 (just off Piedmont Rd.). © **800/788-9107** or **404/231-9107.** MARTA: Buckhead.

Chapter 11—The Discount Bookstore   Based in Atlanta, Chapter 11 bookstores comprise the largest independent chain in the city. They take 30% off the cover price for the top 15 hardcover *New York Times* bestsellers, and all other books in the store are at an everyday discount of 11%. The staff—all serious readers—excel at answering questions and finding particular titles. Chapter 11 will special order books at no additional cost. Open Monday to Saturday 10am to 9pm, and Sunday noon to 6pm.

Besides the Ansley Mall store, there are several suburban locations and three other in-town stores: 3509 Northside Pkwy. (© **404/841-6338**), 1 block north of West Paces Ferry Road; 2091 North Decatur Rd. (© **404/325-1505**), near Emory University; and 2345-A Peachtree Rd. (© **404/237-7199**), in the Peachtree Battle Shopping Center at Peachtree Battle Avenue. Hours vary, but the Emory and Peachtree stores are open later. 1544 Piedmont Rd. (in the Ansley Mall at the corner of Monroe Dr.). © **404/872-7986.** MARTA: Lindbergh.

Engineer's Bookstore   The largest technical bookstore in Atlanta, Engineer's has an incredible selection of computer and engineering titles as well as the graduate and undergraduate texts for Georgia Tech. Relocated in 1993 to make way for the Olympic Village Dormitories, Engineer's Bookstore has been in business since 1954. Open Monday to Friday 9am to 5:30pm, and Saturday 10am to 2pm. 748 Marietta St. NW (at the corner of Means St., just off Tech Pkwy. and approximately 1 mile from Georgia World Congress Center). ℭ **800/635-5919** or 404/221-1669. MARTA: North Avenue.

Tall Tales Book Shop, Inc. This general bookstore in the Emory University area offers a large selection of mainstream titles with an emphasis on literary selections. All large publishers, as well as university and small presses, are represented. The staff is knowledgeable and will be happy to process special orders. Open Monday to Thursday 9:30am to 9:30pm, Friday and Saturday 9:30am to 10pm, and Sunday 12:30 to 6:30pm. 2105 LaVista Rd., No. 108. ℭ **404/636-2498.** MARTA: Lindbergh.

FACTORY & DISCOUNT OUTLETS

North Georgia Premium Outlets This 140-store center is a cut above most outlets, with designers and manufacturers such as Anne Klein, Donna Karan, Tahari, Calvin Klein, and Nike, to name a few. There are also outlets for Saks Fifth Avenue, Brooks Brothers, Crate & Barrel, Timberland, Bose, Williams-Sonoma, Kenneth Cole, Nine West, Pottery Barn, the Gap, and Lego. It's definitely worth the trip. Open Monday to Saturday 10am to 9pm, and Sunday noon to 6pm. 800 Hwy. 400 S. (35 min. north of Atlanta on Georgia 400), Dawsonville, GA 30534. ℭ **706/216-3609.** www.premiumoutlets.com.

FARMERS MARKETS

Atlanta State Farmers Market The State Farmers Market is a vast 146-acre outdoor facility where stall after stall is piled high with produce. There are also vendors of home-canned pickles, jams, and relishes; plants and flowers; and seasonal items such as pumpkins in October, holly and Christmas trees in December. It's a colorful spectacle. You can have a good meal at a restaurant on the premises. Open 24 hours daily except Christmas. 16 Forest Pkwy., Forest Park, GA. ℭ **404/366-6910.** Take I-75 south to Exit 23; the market is on your left.

DeKalb Farmers Market Even if you have no intention of purchasing, this incredible market, started in 1977 by Robert Blazer, merits a visit. A mind-boggling array of international food items is temptingly displayed in a 140,000-square-foot building. Tables are laden with mountains of produce from broccoli to bok choy, not to mention winter melons and water chestnuts, lily root, curry leaves, breadfruit, Jamaican jerk marinade, Korean daikon radish, a multiplicity of mushrooms, chick-pea miso, a vast beer and wine section, dried fruits, plants and flowers, seafood, meat, poultry, every imaginable fresh herb or hot pepper, fresh-baked breads and pastries, stalks of sugarcane, many varieties of cheese, frogs' legs, conch meat, quail, and on and on. As you shop, you can nibble whatever is offered at sample tables throughout the facility. There's also a small cafeteria on the premises. It's about a 20-minute drive from downtown. Open daily 9am to 9pm. 3000 E. Ponce de Leon Ave., Decatur, GA. ℭ **404/377-6400.** MARTA: Avondale.

Harry's Whole Foods Like the DeKalb Farmers Market, this megamarket must be seen to be believed. Under new ownership since 2001, Harry's is generally the same in concept—mountains of fresh produce, incredible selections of cheese, seafood, meats, gourmet items, wines, beers, and more exotica than you can imagine. There is a difference between the two, though. DeKalb attracts a more international clientele, although the selection of goods is not necessarily more international in scope. Harry's is a bit more upscale and polished, and attracts many suburbanites, probably because of its locations. DeKalb has a wider variety of organic foods and produce, while Harry's does better at baked goods, prepared foods, and cheese. Saturday and Sunday are crowded at all markets, but it seems to add to the fun if you don't have to do serious shopping. Open Monday to Saturday 9am to 8pm, and Sunday 10am to 7pm.

There are two other Harry's locations: 2025 Satellite Blvd., Duluth (ℂ 770/416-6900), and 70 Powers Ferry Rd., Marietta (ℂ 770/578-4400). 1180 Upper Hembree Rd., Alpharetta, GA. ℂ **770/664-6300.**

FASHION
See also sections 1 and 2 of this chapter for more stores.

The Bilthouse   Set in an old cottage in Buckhead, this shop is the place to go if you're looking for something casual that's a little out of the ordinary. Most of the clothing is designed for comfort—which is not to say that it doesn't also look great—and much of it is made of natural fabrics. There are linen shifts and separates, cotton sweaters, lots of one-of-a-kind dresses, tights, flowing skirts, and more for women of all ages. There's also unique furniture, jewelry, children's clothing, artwork by local artists, and little goodies for body and bath. Open Monday to Saturday 9:30am to 6pm. 511 E. Paces Ferry Rd. NE (5 blocks west of Peachtree Rd., on the corner of Maple Ave.). ℂ **404/816-7702.** MARTA: Buckhead.

K&G Men's Center   K&G is tucked away in an industrial area with a number of other discount stores, but it's definitely worth seeking out. It's a huge warehouse crammed with a large selection of top-quality men's clothing, men's shoes, and furnishings. You'll find truly excellent suits, even tuxedos. There are other K&G stores, all in the suburbs, but this is the original. To reach Ellsworth Industrial Dr., take I-75N, exit at Howell Mill Rd., go west to Chattahoochee Ave., turn right, and then take the next right. Open Friday 10am to 8pm, Saturday 10am to 7pm, and Sunday noon to 6pm. 1750 Ellsworth Industrial Dr. NW (at Chattahoochee Ave.). ℂ **404/352-3471.**

Luna   A good variety of strictly up-to-the-minute women's clothing and accessories here: sportswear, ultra-feminine evening wear, suits, jewelry, handbags, and cool shoes. Open Monday to Friday 11am to 8pm, Saturday noon to 6pm, and Sunday noon to 5pm. 3167 Peachtree Rd. (south of Piedmont Rd.). ℂ **404/233-5344.** MARTA: Lenox.

⟨Moments Fresh Market Fare

If your idea of fun is watching other people cook for you, stop in at the Morningside Farmers Market on Saturday morning. Each week at 9:30am, one of the city's top chefs (the likes of Guenter Seeger of Seeger's or Anne Quattrano and Cliff Harrison of Bacchanalia) gives a free cooking demonstration, and the lucky audience gets to sample the results. Afterward, browse the market, a small but beautiful array of organic, locally grown vegetables, fruit, herbs, and flowers. There are also handmade soaps, beeswax candles, primitive furniture, beaded jewelry, and other assorted artisanal items. The market, 1303 N. Highland Ave., is open on Saturdays, May through December, 8 to noon. Chefs appear May through October. Call ℂ **770/788-8707.**

A Pea In The Pod   This cleverly named shop features maternity clothes, but we're not talking T-shirts with an arrow pointing to your stomach. These are gorgeous clothes, from really chic sportswear to elegant business garb to eveningwear. Open Monday to Saturday 10am to 9pm, and Sunday noon to 5:30pm. In the Phipps Plaza mall, 3500 Peachtree Rd. (at Lenox Rd.). ℂ **404/261-0808.** MARTA: Lenox.

Potpourri   If you're in search of upscale traditional women's apparel, Potpourri will fit the bill. There are lots of lovely sportswear separates, as well as dresses, belts, costume jewelry, and other accessories. Open daily 10am to 6pm. 3718 Roswell Rd. NW. (just north of Piedmont Rd.). ℂ **404/365-0880.** MARTA: Buckhead.

Rexer-Parkes   This sophisticated shop offers cutting-edge American and European clothing for women who are looking for apparel with clean, classic lines that will not blend in with the crowd. You'll find sportswear, suits, dresses, and lingerie, and a good selection of the latest in jewelry, too. Open Monday to Friday 10am to 7pm and Saturday 10am to 6pm. 2140 Peachtree Rd. NE (in the Brookwood Square shopping center). ℂ **404/351-3080.** MARTA: Lindbergh.

GIFTS, ART & COLLECTIBLES

Also see the stores listed in the hot shopping neighborhoods that are detailed in section 1.

City Art Works   Tucked away in a strip shopping center, this place is pretty overwhelming. You'll find a huge array of one-of-a-kind quality gift items and artwork by local and national artists—jewelry, sculpture, pottery, lamps, frames, glassware, and so on. The mix is eclectic, ever changing, and hard to resist. Open Monday to Thursday 10am to 6:30pm, and Friday and Saturday 10am to 6pm and Sunday 1 to 5pm. 2140 Peachtree Rd. NW (in the Brookwood Square shopping center). ℂ **404/605-0786.** MARTA: Lindbergh.

Erika Reade   The emphasis here is on interesting home-related accessories and furnishings—paintings, antique and primitive furniture, mirrors, exquisite bed linens, and tabletop items. You'll find French soaps and candles, hand-blown glass, jewelry, wonderful gifts for adults and children, and much more. It's all absolutely up-to-date and extremely tasteful. Open Monday to Thursday 10am to 6pm, and Friday and Saturday 10am to 5pm. 3732 Roswell Rd. (just north of Piedmont Rd.). ℂ **404/233-3857.** MARTA: Lindbergh.

HARDWARE/WOODWORKING

Highland Hardware   This isn't a hardware store; it's an institution. Woodworkers come from all over the country to browse Highland's huge selection of woodworking supplies and tools, and still more order from its voluminous catalog. But even if you don't know a router from a bandsaw, it's fun to roam through the large, high-ceilinged store, which has an old-fashioned, neighborly feel. Highland also stocks regular hardware, gardening merchandise, annuals, and perennials. Call in advance if you're interested in attending one of the many woodworking programs or workshops. Open Monday to Saturday 8:30am to 6pm, and Sunday noon to 5pm. 1045 N. Highland Ave. NE (at Los Angeles Ave.). ℂ **404/872-4466.** www.tools-for-woodworking.com. MARTA: Five Points.

KITCHENWARE

Cook's Warehouse   There's everything you need here—except the kitchen sink—for setting up a gourmet kitchen: top-of-the-line cookware, dinnerware, quality knives, small appliances, cookbooks, chef's clothing, oodles of gadgets, a selection of olive oils and vinegars, and much more. There's a full schedule of cooking classes and demonstrations, too, so check the website. Open Sunday 12:30 to 5pm, Monday to Thursday 10am to 7pm, and Friday and Saturday 10am to 6pm. 549-1 Amsterdam Ave. NE (1 block west of Monroe Dr.). © **404/815-4993.** www.cookswarehouse.com. MARTA: Arts Center.

SPORTING GOODS

REI (Recreational Equipment Inc.)   This Seattle-based company has everything imaginable for the outdoor enthusiast: clothing, shoes, outerwear, and accessories for biking, hiking, camping, rock climbing, canoeing, kayaking, and so on. The staff is extremely knowledgeable, and the sales are frequent and fabulous. Open Monday to Friday 10am to 9pm, Saturday 10am to 7pm, and Sunday 11am to 6pm.

There's another REI just north of the city at 1165 Perimeter Center West NE (© 770/901-9200). 1800 Northeast Expressway (on the I-85 access road; take the Clairmont Rd. exit and go south). © **404/633-6508.** MARTA: Brookhaven.

Atlanta After Dark

This is a city that sizzles after dark, with numerous music clubs featuring jazz, rock, country, and blues. It also offers a comprehensive cultural scene, including symphony, ballet, opera, and theater productions. And major artists headline regularly at Atlanta's many large-scale performance facilities.

Nightlife turns up all over Atlanta, but the biggest concentration of clubs and bars is in Buckhead (near the intersection of Peachtree Rd. and E. Paces Ferry Rd.); in Virginia-Highland (at the intersection of Virginia and N. Highland aves., and on N. Highland just north of Ponce de Leon Ave.); in Little Five Points (near the intersection of Moreland and Euclid aves.); and downtown near Peachtree Center.

The Buckhead scene is like a huge, unruly fraternity party, with lots of people and cars cruising the streets. It gets rowdier as the night goes on and has been marked by violence on several occasions. In 2002, following scores of complaints from area residents, Atlanta Police began closing a couple of roads in the Buckhead area every Friday and Saturday night to discourage some of the cruising and traffic jams. Virginia-Highland is full of older young adults and professionals. Little Five Points is an eclectic mix of wildly, weirdly dressed folks and neighborhood regulars; downtown hosts a large component of out-of-town visitors and convention goers.

To find out what's on during your stay, consult the *Atlanta Journal-Constitution*. Its "Weekend Preview" section, published every Friday, highlights movies, plays, festivals, gallery openings, and other happenings for the upcoming weekend. There's also an extensive listing of live music. A calendar of events is published every other day of the week, but it's not as complete. The newspaper's website at **www.ajc.com** allows you to access a week's worth of newspaper features, including the events calendar and "Weekend Preview".

A free newspaper called *Creative Loafing,* available at hundreds of locations around town (hotels, restaurants, shops, MARTA stations, etc.), lists numerous events each issue and has special sections for "Gay and Lesbian Activities" and "Singles." Visit its website at **www.CreativeLoafing.com** or call ✆ **800/950-5623** for a copy of the paper before you visit.

Tickets to many performances are handled by Ticketmaster. Call ✆ **404/249-6400** (for popular performances) or ✆ **404/817-8700** (for cultural events) to charge by phone. Online, you can reserve tickets at **www.ticketmaster.com**. Ticketmaster also has more than 100 locations throughout Georgia, including all Publix Supermarkets, where customers can purchase tickets in person, though they must be paid for in cash. To avoid the Ticketmaster surcharge, it's often possible to purchase tickets directly from the box office where the event is taking place. If you are staying in a large hotel, the concierge service is usually able to obtain tickets to even the most popular events.

Day-of-show half-price tickets are available at the AtlanTIX! ticket booth at the Atlanta Convention and Visitors Bureau in Underground Atlanta. Customers can look over the show board to see what plays and other live performances have tickets available that day, purchase a voucher for the show, and pick up the ticket at the show's box office before curtain time. Vouchers must be paid for in person; phone sales are not available. Call ✆ **404/222-6688** for more information.

1 The Performing Arts

BALLET

The Atlanta Ballet   The oldest continuously operating ballet company in the United States, the Atlanta Ballet usually presents six productions each fall-through-spring season. Performances range from classics to new works and include *The Nutcracker* every December. Tickets are available through Ticketmaster (✆ 404/817-8700) or at the Fox Theatre box office on the day of the performance. Performing in the Fox Theatre, 660 Peachtree St. NE (at Ponce de Leon Ave.). ✆ 404/892-3303. www.atlantaballet.com. Tickets $10–$50. MARTA: North Avenue.

CLASSICAL MUSIC

Atlanta Symphony Orchestra   The Atlanta Symphony Orchestra performs under music director Robert Spano and principal guest conductor Donald Runnicles. Complementing the orchestra is the 200-voice Atlanta Symphony Orchestra Chorus, enabling performances of large-scale symphonic/choral works. The season runs from September to May in the Woodruff Arts Center, and there are summer concerts in Chastain Park Amphitheatre and in various parks and churches.

The ASO's annual schedule is extensive. The main offering is the **Master Season Series.** Master Season concerts, held on selected Thursday, Friday, and Saturday evenings in the plush 1,762-seat Atlanta Symphony Hall, feature renowned guest artists such as violinist Robert McDuffie, pianist Olli Mustonen, soprano Sylvia McNair, and mezzo-soprano Susan Graham. Also held during the season is a series of Sunday afternoon **Family Concerts** geared to children, **Casual Classics** on selected Saturday afternoons, holiday concerts during the Christmas season, and a tribute to Martin Luther King, Jr., in mid-January.

The ASO's **Classic Chastain Series** concerts are held in the 7,000-seat Chastain Park Amphitheatre from June to August. All except lawn seating is reserved. It's customary to bring elaborate picnics and wine to these events. The series features headliners such as Tony Bennett and Natalie Cole performing with the ASO. There are also free concerts in parks throughout the Atlanta area on summer evenings. These run the gamut from full symphony performances to light classical repertoires.

Tips Playing Southern

Want to talk like a Southerner? An easy way to start is with "y'all." But remember that "y'all" is always plural, NEVER singular. For instance, when talking to two or more people it's OK to say "Are y'all coming with me tonight?" But if you pose the same question to just one person who happens to know Southernspeak, he'll probably snicker (politely). And don't even think about saying "you all" instead of "y'all." Have y'all got that?

Note: At press time plans were underway for the construction of a $240 million Atlanta Symphony Center in Midtown. Performing in the Woodruff Arts Center, 1280 Peachtree St. NE (at Fifteenth St.). ☏ **404/733-5000** (box office) for information and tickets. www.atlantasymphony.org. Most tickets $19–$55. Box office open Mon–Fri 10am–8pm; Sat–Sun noon–8pm. Parking available in the Arts Center Garage on Lombardy Way between Fifteenth and Sixteenth sts. MARTA: Arts Center.

OPERA

Atlanta Opera   Under the artistic direction of William Fred Scott, the Atlanta Opera offers four fully staged productions during the spring and fall at the Fox Theatre. Principal performers are drawn from top opera companies from across the United States and Europe. Three performances are given of each opera. Recent productions included Verdi's *Otello* and Puccini's *Turandot*. Tickets can be difficult to obtain; charge them in advance if possible. Performing in the Fox Theatre, 660 Peachtree St. NE (at Ponce de Leon Ave). ☏ **800/35-OPERA** or 404/881-8801 for information. www.atlantaopera.org. Tickets $18–$126. Single tickets available through the Fox box office (☏ 404/881-2100) and Ticketmaster (☏ 404/817-8700). MARTA: North Avenue.

THEATER

The **Alliance Theatre Company** is the major theater company in Atlanta, but there are many other excellent companies with performances ranging from experimental to classic. Most are located near downtown and Midtown, but there are a number in the suburbs. Some of the notables include **Actor's Express** (☏ 404/607-7469), **Dad's Garage** (☏ 404/523-3141), **Horizon Theatre Company** (☏ 404/584-7450), **Jomandi Productions** (☏ 404/870-0629), **Neighborhood Playhouse** (☏ 404/373-5311), **7 Stages Theatre** (☏ 404/523-7647), **Shakespeare Tavern** (☏ 404/874-5299), **Theatrical Outfit** (☏ 404/577-5255)**, Theatre Gael** (☏ 404/876-9762), and **Theatre in the Square** (☏ 770/422-8369). Check the *Atlanta Journal-Constitution* on Friday and Saturday to see what's on during your visit. There are also performances by the **Georgia Shakespeare Festival** (☏ 404/264-0020) each summer and fall.

Alliance Theatre Company   The Alliance Theatre Company, under the direction of Kenny Leon, is the largest regional theater in the Southeast. On 2 stages, it produces about 10 plays a year (the season runs from Sept–June, with occasional productions during the summer). Many well-known actors have played these stages, among them Jane Alexander, Richard Dreyfuss, Esther Rolle, and Morgan Freeman. Recent seasons have included Dickens's *A Christmas Carol* (performed annually); *Medea,* starring Phylicia Rashad; and the world premiere of Elton John and Tim Rice's musical *Aida.* The Alliance Children's Theatre presents plays geared to youngsters from January to May. Tickets are $12.50 adults, $10 children. Performing in the Woodruff Arts Center, 1280 Peachtree St. NE (at Fifteenth St.). ☏ **404/733-5000** for information or to charge tickets. www.alliancetheatre.org. Tickets $16–$45. "Rush tickets" often available for $15 on the day of a performance; they must be purchased in person at the box office after 5pm. Box office open Mon–Fri 10am–8pm; Sat–Sun noon–8pm. Parking in the Arts Center Garage on Lombardy Way between Fifteenth and Sixteenth sts. MARTA: Arts Center.

MAJOR VENUES

In addition to the special places listed below, many of the stadiums listed in section 6, "Spectator Sports," in chapter 7, host major concerts from time to time. These include the Alexander Memorial Coliseum and Bobby Dodd Stadium/

Grant Field at Georgia Tech, Road Atlanta, Philips Arena, and the Georgia Dome.

Atlanta Civic Center   The Civic Center offers a wealth of entertainment options in its 4,600-seat auditorium. It hosts headliners, touring Broadway shows, traveling symphonies and opera companies, and fashion shows. 395 Piedmont Ave. NE (between Ralph McGill Blvd. and Pine St.). (C) **404/523-6275** for general information. MARTA: Civic Center (about 5 blocks away); buses go to the door.

Chastain Park Amphitheatre *Moments*   This delightful 7,000-seat outdoor facility offers concerts under the stars from May to October. Everyone brings food; a picnic on the grass or at your amphitheater seat is a tradition. Tables for up to six are available and people bring gourmet feasts, flowers, and even candelabra for an extra special experience. **Proof-in-the-Pudding** is an on-site caterer from which you can pre-order your meal if you choose. Menu selections come with enough food for four or more and are wonderful. For a fee, they'll even dress your table and have everything ready for you when you arrive; all you'll have to do is open the wine and light the candles. Big-name performers are featured. It can be difficult to get tickets at times, so order as far in advance as possible (months ahead if you can). The Atlanta Symphony Orchestra (see above) offers a summer series here. 449 Stella Dr. NW (in Chastain Park at Powers Ferry Rd.). (C) **404/233-2227** or 404/817-8700 for Ticketmaster. MARTA: Lenox.

Coca-Cola Lakewood Amphitheatre   The $15-million Lakewood Amphitheatre accommodates 19,000 people—7,000 reserved seats plus a sloping lawn that holds an additional 12,000. Needless to say, this is a vast facility used for major shows. Eric Clapton, Elton John, Pearl Jam, and Aerosmith have all performed here. There are picnic tables with umbrellas on the grounds, and though you can't bring in food or drink, a wide variety of refreshments is available, including beer, champagne, fruit and cheese, sandwiches, pizza, and, of course, Coca-Cola. 202 Lakewood Way (at the Lakewood exit of I-75/85, 3½ miles south of downtown). (C) **404/249-6400.** www.lakewoodamp.com. Take I-75 or I-85 south to Lakewood Freeway exit and follow the signs. MARTA: Lakewood/Fort McPherson (shuttle buses take patrons to and from the station).

Fox Theatre   Built in 1927, when movie theaters were conceived along lavish lines, the Fox is a Moorish-Egyptian extravaganza complete with arabesque arches, onion domes, and minarets. Its exotic interior reflects the Egyptomania of the '20s—a phenomenon resulting from archaeologist Henry Carter's discovery of the treasure-laden tomb of King Tut. Throne chairs, scarab motifs, and hieroglyphics are seen throughout the theater, and the auditorium evokes a Middle Eastern courtyard under an azure sky. See p. 156 for details on the Fox's history and architecture, as well as information on tours. The Fox is home to the **Atlanta Opera** and the **Atlanta Ballet** (see above). In addition, a wide spectrum of headliners plays the Fox, along with diverse entertainment ranging from Broadway musicals to rock 'n' roll. 660 Peachtree St. NE (at Ponce de Leon Ave.). (C) **404/ 881-2100** for information, or 404/817-8700 to charge tickets. Many paid parking lots nearby. MARTA: North Avenue.

Rialto Center for the Performing Arts   Located close to the center of downtown, this wonderful 900-seat facility is home to a variety of performances, from theater to dance to all types of music. It opened as a theater in 1916, then became the Rialto movie house, then was converted to a multi-purpose venue in the late 1990s. 80 Forsyth St. (C) **404/651-4727.** Paid parking in nearby lots. MARTA: Five Points or Peachtree Center.

Variety Playhouse   Built in Little Five Points in the 1930s as a neighborhood movie theater, the Variety today is an intimate concert hall offering an eclectic array of performances, from folk rock to jazz. There are frequent album-release parties here. It's definitely worth checking out. 1099 Euclid Ave. (near Washita St.). ℂ 404/521-1786 for information. Paid parking lot on Euclid Ave. near Colquitt Ave. MARTA: Inman Park or Bus 3.

2 The Club & Music Scene

Nightclubs come and go, so it's always a good idea to call ahead. Most clubs are open until 2, 3, or even 4am.

BLUES CLUBS

Blind Willie's   This well-known club features live blues from around the country, but local bands are part of the scene, too. The bar usually opens about 8pm, and there's a limited bar menu, but the big attraction is the music, which starts around 10pm. 828 N. Highland Ave. (just north of Ponce de Leon Ave.). ℂ 404/873-2583. Cover charge varies. MARTA: Five Points.

Fat Matt's Rib Shack   This barbecue joint packs them in every evening for a taste of smoky ribs, beer, and local blues. The food is as good as the sultry music, which starts every night at 8pm. 1811 Piedmont Ave. (a few blocks south of Cheshire Bridge Rd.). ℂ 404/607-1622. No cover. MARTA: Lindbergh Center.

Northside Tavern   Home of the locally and internationally acclaimed Mud-cats blues band, this hole in the wall was obviously a gas station in a previous life. Though the digs aren't anything to write home about and the location might look a bit shady, the music here is fantastic. The Mudcats play every Wednesday night and one weekend a month—when they aren't performing in Europe—yes, Europe. In between, there is plenty more live entertainment to keep you happy. Cold beer, a full bar, and a couple of pool tables round out the offerings. 1058 Howell Mill Rd. NW. ℂ 404/874-8745. Cover charge varies. MARTA: Arts Center.

A COMEDY CLUB

The Punchline   This popular suburban comedy club, about a 40-minute drive from downtown, features pros on the national comedy-club circuit—the comedians you see on Leno and Letterman. Jeff Foxworthy got his start here. Doors open an hour before showtime. Reasonably priced food is offered, along with a full bar. Thursday and early Friday shows are smoke-free. Though you can buy tickets at the club, they often sell out, so it's best to reserve by phone. You must be 21 and have a valid ID to get in. 280 Hilderbrand Dr. NE (off Roswell Rd. in the Balconies Shopping Center), Sandy Springs. ℂ 404/252-5233. Cover $8–$15, depending on the day of the week. Open Tues–Sun. MARTA: Sandy Springs.

DANCE CLUBS

Bell Bottoms   Dance the night away to your favorite tunes of the '70s and '80s at one of Atlanta's grooviest nightclubs, complete with go-go cages, bean bag chairs, and lava lamps. Located in the heart of Buckhead, just four doors down from "the big fish," Bell Bottoms does require patrons to abide by a "proper" dress code, whatever that means. 225 Pharr Rd. ℂ 404/816-9669. Open Wed–Sat. Cover $5–$10. MARTA: Buckhead.

Johnny's Hideaway   "Atlanta's Only Nightclub for Big Kids" has been one of Atlanta's top nightspots for the over-40 crowd for 20 years. Ebullient host

Johnny Esposito, always on hand to greet his guests, is a well-known Atlanta character. The music sweeps through the decades, from the big-band era to the '80s, attracting a crowd of all ages. The music gets "younger" as the night wears on, and the patrons do, too. This is a place for serious dancing, and though it's unpretentious, there are celebrities who drop by when in town (George Clooney and Robert Duvall). Check out the Frank Sinatra Room, filled with over 100 pieces of memorabilia. A reasonably priced menu lists items ranging from deli sandwiches to prime-rib main courses. Attire is dressy-casual. 3771 Roswell Rd. (2 blocks north of Piedmont Rd.). ℂ 404/233-8026. www.johnnyshideaway.com. No cover, but there's a 2-drink minimum after 8pm. MARTA: Buckhead.

Masquerade   Popular with the college-age crowd, Masquerade is housed in a century-old stone-walled Romanesque building—a former factory. Its interior, divided into three main areas: Heaven, Hell, and Purgatory, are all appropriately decorated. Up in Heaven is a concert hall featuring live local and national acts. Call the hot line at ℂ **404/577-2007** for information. Hell is a deejay dance party, and Purgatory is the game room, with pool tables and other non-music diversions. Sunday is Swing Night, when young and old groove to the tunes of the Big Band Era. Lessons begin at 8pm. 695 North Ave. NE (just east of Boulevard). ℂ **404/577-8178.** www.masq.com. Cover $5–$8 in Hell and Purgatory; $5–$20 (depending on the performer) in Heaven. Parking $3–$5. Usually closed Mon and Tues. MARTA: North Avenue.

Tongue & Groove   Really more of an elegant cocktail lounge than a dance club, Tongue & Groove attracts a chic upscale crowd—an older group than at many Buckhead establishments. The spacious interior is on the plush side, with glossy oak floors and lofty ceilings. The deejayed dance music has a different theme every night—everything from R&B to European pop to Latin dance tunes. The bar food is out of the ordinary (sushi, yakitori skewers, wontons, etc.), and there's also a wide selection of fine wines and champagnes. T & G enforces a strict dress code, so lose the jeans, caps, and sport shoes. You must be 23 to get in. **Note:** On Friday and Saturday nights, the Buckhead streets surrounding T & G are mobbed with revelers, and numerous nightspots in the area make this an ideal base for club-hopping. 3055 Peachtree Rd. (between E. Paces Ferry Rd. and Buckhead Ave.). ℂ **404/261-2325.** www.tongueandgroove-atl.com. Cover charge varies. Paid parking across Peachtree Rd. MARTA: Buckhead.

FOLK/ACOUSTIC/BLUEGRASS

Eddie's Attic   Eddie's Attic is a popular venue for acoustic singer/songwriters. The Indigo Girls, Billy Pilgrim, and Shawn Mullins started their careers here. The place is divided into three sections. The main bar is perfect for music lovers, with its small stage, intimate arrangement of seats, and excellent acoustics. Rowdier folks are invited into the poolroom or onto the covered patio, where there's a full bar and TV monitors playing the live performance from the main stage. The entire family is welcome for a 7pm nonsmoking show on Friday and Saturday. There is a full menu, mostly typical bar fare. 515–B N. McDonough St., Decatur (next to the old courthouse on the square). ℂ **404/377-4976.** www.eddiesattic.com. Cover $3–$10. Parking available on the square or at the lot on Church St., directly behind Eddie's. MARTA: Decatur.

Red Light Café   This classic San Francisco–style coffeehouse has a funky high-ceilinged interior decked with tables and comfy sofas, and offers a mix of art, music, conversation, and beverages. The big attraction is the music—local bluegrass, folk, rock, and jazz. You can order salads, fresh pastas, and sandwiches, and there's a good selection of bottled and draft beers, including some that are locally brewed. 553 W. Amsterdam Ave. (west of Monroe Dr.). © 404/874-7828. www.redlightcafe.com. Cover varies. Closed Mon. MARTA: Arts Center.

JAZZ CLUBS

Dante's Down the Hatch   This jazz supper club is the realm of Dante Stephensen, who mans the decks of this well-rigged schooner, a fantasy 18th-century ship (actually afloat in murky waters) in a colorful seaport village. It's a mix of antiques and nautical kitsch. There are many intimate seating areas, but the most romantic spot is in semi-enclosed private "cabins" on the lower deck, where a trio plays traditional jazz. Earlier in the evening, classical folk guitarists perform on the "wharf," and weekend nights, a solo pianist plays on the ship prior to the show. If you wish to have dinner during the show, the specialty is fondue, available by special reservation only. 3380 Peachtree Rd. NE (across the street from the Lenox Square mall). © 404/266-1600. Cover $6 for seating on the jazz ship; free on the wharf. MARTA: Buckhead.

Sambuca Jazz Café   Part restaurant, part jazz club, Sambuca is the third in a new chain of jazz cafes; the first two were in Texas. The bar is chic and large, and there's almost always a wait to get in, especially as the evening wears on. The big attraction here is the bar, not the restaurant, where there's a combo on the bandstand each night and a crowd on the dance floor. There are upscale couples and singles, often four-deep at the bar, and everyone is sharply dressed. Shows start at 7:30pm; there's a two-drink minimum in the bar, but no cover. If your main interest is the music, come early for a table near the bandstand. 3102 Piedmont Road NE (between Peachtree and E. Paces Ferry rds.). © 404/237-5299. No cover. MARTA: Lindbergh.

3 The Bar Scene

In addition to the neighborhood establishments listed here, there are a number of excellent bars in most of the major hotels, and many are mellow enough for friendly conversation. Two of the best are the **Lobby Lounge** at the Ritz-Carlton Buckhead, 3434 Peachtree Road (© **404/237-2700;** MARTA: Peachtree Center.), and **Park 75 Lounge** in the Four Seasons Atlanta Hotel, 75 Fourteenth St., in Midtown (© **404/253-3840,** ask for the Lounge; MARTA: Arts Center). The **Sundial Restaurant and Lounge,** high atop the Westin Peachtree Plaza Hotel, 210 Peachtree St. (© **404/589-7506;** MARTA: Peachtree Center.), and **A Point of View at Nikolai's Roof** in the Hilton Atlanta, 255 Courtland St. (© **404/874-6505;** MARTA: Peachtree Center.), have spectacular views of the city skyline. None of the places below charge a cover unless otherwise stated.

Atkins Park   Here you'll find a mix of casually dressed neighborhood regulars and young adults from other parts of town. The atmosphere is friendly and the ambience mellow and comfortable. Atkins Park began as a deli in 1922 (it holds the oldest existing tavern license in the city) and now includes a full-scale restaurant that stays open until 11pm on weeknights and midnight on Friday and Saturday. After that, better-than-average bar food is available. Atkins Park is known as the place to go for Jagermeister—it sells more than almost any other bar in Atlanta. Things get louder when the restaurant closes and the music (rock, blues, and jazz) is turned up. 794 N. Highland Ave. NE (at St. Charles Place, 1 block north of Ponce de Leon Ave.). © 404/876-7249. Some free parking in lot off St. Charles; paid parking in nearby lots. MARTA: Five Points.

> **Tips   Martinis & IMAX, Anyone?**
>
> For a different kind of action, check out Martinis & IMAX, a Friday night event for grownups at the **Fernbank Museum of Natural History.** From 6 to 10pm, enjoy a martini or other cocktail, have dinner, watch the films, and listen to a jazz group. Call the Martinis & IMAX hot line (© **404/370-1822**) for information on films, events, and music. To reserve tickets, call © **404/370-3060.** There is a $5 cover charge for non-members who do not purchase IMAX or special exhibition tickets, but it is redeemable toward a food or drink purchase.

Dark Horse Tavern   This tavern is primarily a neighborhood hangout during the week, but it attracts a mix of young professionals and college students on the weekend. There's live entertainment downstairs Wednesday to Saturday—mostly local bands, but occasionally a national group. Upstairs, there's a dining area serving American fare, where you can eat, drink, and socialize into the wee hours. For major sporting events, there's a big-screen TV. 816 N. Highland Ave. NE (2 blocks north of Ponce de Leon Ave.). © 404/873-3607. Cover $3–$5 for entertainment downstairs. Limited free parking in lot around back; paid lot across the street. MARTA: Five Points.

Fado'   If you haven't had a good glass of Guinness since your last trip to Dublin, Fado' (Gaelic for "long ago") is the place to pause for a pint or two. The interior is divided into five pub areas, each one distinct from the next: a cottage pub with a peat-burning fireplace, a Victorian pub with dark wood and stained glass, and so on. It's a pleasant, unhurried atmosphere, but only in the early evening before the serious revelers invade. After that, it's loud and crowded. There's traditional Irish or Celtic music several days a week, and the Irish fare is good, especially the *boxty* (the Irish version of a potato pancake) and the fish and chips in Guinness batter. 3035 Peachtree Rd. NE (at the corner of Buckhead Ave., just south of E. Paces Ferry Rd.). © 404/841-0066. Limited parking on neighboring streets; paid valet parking out back. MARTA: Buckhead.

Manuel's Tavern *Finds*   Not far from the yuppieness of Virginia-Highland and the funkiness of Little Five Points is an authentic neighborhood bar that's been a gathering spot for nearly 50 years. Owned by former DeKalb County chief executive officer Manuel Maloof, it's a regular watering hole for journalists, politicos, cops, students, and writers. Former President Jimmy Carter often drops by with the Secret Service in tow. The main bar, with its dark wood and large booths, is the best spot in the building, but there are two larger rooms with tables to accommodate the considerable crowds. It's lots of fun to watch the Braves here if you can't get tickets to the game. There's a full bar with 20 beers on tap, and 30 more bottled beers. Manuel's recently had a major menu expansion from the former bar food offerings to full home-cooking eats such as turkey and dressing, pork chops, and cordon bleu. 602 N. Highland Ave. NE (at North Ave.). © 404/525-3447. www.manuelstavern.com. MARTA: Five Points.

Mumbo Jumbo   If you're looking for a place to see and be seen, this is it. Downtown's hottest nightspot since it opened just before the Olympics, it's full of beautiful people, old and young, including professionals, high rollers, and creative types dressed in the very latest. Be sure to wear black or you'll stick out like a sore thumb. The crowd becomes louder and more avant-garde as the night rolls on, but it's high-energy posturing all evening. Consider having dinner here before you repair to the lounge; the food is good. 89 Park Place NE (at Woodruff Park). 𝒞 404/523-0330. Paid parking in nearby garages. MARTA: Peachtree Center.

The Park Tavern and Brewery This restaurant/bar on the edge of Piedmont Park has great views of the park and all its goings-on. There are two cozy, rustic bars inside, but the large patio is the best spot for sipping one of the brewery's handcrafted beers. 500 Tenth St. (at Monroe Dr.). 𝒞 404/249-0001. Limited parking. MARTA: Midtown.

Star Community Bar Housed in a former bank, this funky and cavernous club features the "GraceVault"—a small shrine filled with Elvis posters, an all-Elvis jukebox, Elvis clocks, and other memorabilia. Primarily a Little Five Points neighborhood hangout, it's very low-key and offbeat. Live music Wednesday through Saturday nights runs the gamut from rockabilly to rock 'n' roll and R&B. Most of the performers are local and regional, but occasionally bigger names play here as well. 437 Moreland Ave. NE (between Euclid and Mansfield aves.). 𝒞 404/681-9018. Cover $5–$10. Closed Sun. MARTA: Five Points.

SPORTS BARS

Champions Champions is the quintessential sports bar. The circular oak bar is plastered with thousands of baseball cards under a laminated surface, and more than two dozen TVs (including two large screens) air nonstop sporting events. If all the testosterone is too much for you, there's a patio with a full bar. Sports celebrities tend to stop in when in town. There's a serious Braves collection where you can buy autographed balls, bats, and more. At the Marriott Marquis, 265 Peachtree Center Ave. (between Baker and Harris sts.). 𝒞 404/586-6017. MARTA: Peachtree Center.

Jocks and Jills This is one of several Jocks and Jills around town, and it's also the one that attracts the most sports celebrities. If nobody famous shows up, you can still watch sporting events on 1 of the 20 televisions scattered around, or check out the sports memorabilia, which includes a pair of Evander Holyfield's boxing gloves. 1 CNN Center (on Techwood Dr. at Marietta St.). 𝒞 404/688-4225. Paid parking in nearby lots. MARTA: Omni/GWCC/Georgia Dome.

GAY & LESBIAN BARS

Also see the **Outwrite Bookstore and Coffeehouse** on p. 228.

Backstreet Ask any clubbing Atlantan about this multi-level nightclub and they'll tell you it's this city's premiere after-hours nightclub. Operating for more than 25 years, Backstreet is always open and always pouring. Patrons enjoy dancing, live entertainment and some of the best female impersonators around today. Call for showtimes. To comply with state law, Backstreet is actually a private club for which 3-month memberships are sold for $10. This allows the club to be open 24 hours a day. Admission is free Sunday through Thursday with proof of membership, and $5 on Friday and Saturday nights. If you're just in town for a few days and want to dance the night away at Backstreet, you can go on a Friday or Saturday night and get in with the purchase of the $10 membership. Be sure to take ID or you'll be turned away. 845 Peachtree St., NE. 𝒞 404/873-1987. Cover varies (see information in the review) MARTA: Midtown.

Blake's on the Park Not too far from Piedmont Park in Midtown you'll find a friendly, mostly gay bar that's popular with neighborhood denizens. A few doors away on Monroe Drive is Outwrite Bookstore and Coffeehouse, another pleasant gay and lesbian hangout. 227 Tenth St. (at Monroe Dr.). 𝒞 404/892-5786. Limited parking. No cover. MARTA: Midtown.

Eleven50 This elegant Miami-type club draws a mixed crowd. This club is very laid-back, with well-known DJs visiting on weekends. Regular cover is $10, but when the popular DJs are in the house, expect to pay $20. 1150-B Peachtree Rd. ✆ 404/874-0428. MARTA: Lenox.

Halo Lounge Halo is one of the most beautiful bars in Atlanta. Featuring a back-lit onyx bar, enjoy your favorite tunes spun by some of the coolest DJs in town. Halo is a favorite among all Atlantas no matter what their sexual preference. Thursday is the most popular day for the gay crowd. *Note:* Don't miss the entrance—the address is Peachtree Street, but the door is off 6th Street. 817 W. Peachtree St. NW ✆ 404/962-7333. No cover. MARTA: Midtown.

Red Chair Restaurant and Video Lounge Indoor and outdoor seating accommodates a cool crowd that fills up the large place. Mingle to music videos in this friendly lounge bedecked in crimson. Features weeknight performances of well-known acoustical music acts. 550-C Amsterdam Ave. ✆ 404/870-0532. No cover. MARTA: Arts Center.

A CABARET

Libby's: A Cabaret For anybody who yearns for the heyday of cabarets and supper clubs, there's an updated version that was recently opened by Atlanta native Libby Whittemore, a longtime performer on the local scene. The shows combine music, humor, and chat by the lively red-headed Ms. Whittemore, a talented, wisecracking diva who's funny as hell. Libby's seems to have filled a void in the night-life scene for grownups, but there's also a gospel brunch on Sunday afternoon for those who don't like to stay up late. 3401 Northside Parkway NW (just south of W. Paces Ferry Rd.). ✆ 404/237-1943. www.libbyscabaret.com. Cover charge varies. MARTA: Lenox.

4 Coffeehouses, Cafes & Late-Night Bites

Apres Diem This popular coffeehouse (formerly Café Diem) moved not too long ago from Virginia-Highland to this newer spot. Fortunately, the flavor of the original cafe has stayed the same. You can linger here undisturbed over an espresso or glass of wine on comfy couches inside or outdoors on the patio. There's a full bar and live music several nights of the week, but the atmosphere is still laid-back and casual. There are good desserts, a variety of French-style coffee drinks and teas, and an expanded menu if you want something substantial. 931 Monroe Dr. (south of Tenth St.). ✆ 404/872-3333. www.cafediem.com. MARTA: Arts Center.

Café Intermezzo Café Intermezzo, in South Buckhead, is a great place to stop after dinner or the theater, or if you just don't want the evening to end. In the tradition of a Vienna-style cafe, there's excellent coffee to go with the decadent desserts and pastries. Speaking of desserts, there are so many that each patron receives a private "tour" of the sweets cases to choose their poison. 1845 Peachtree Rd. (just south of Collier Rd.). ✆ 404/355-0411. MARTA: Lenox.

Majestic Food Shop Known simply as "the Majestic" to the locals, this 24-hour restaurant has been serving up diner food and a slice of life since 1935. You'll find obnoxious drunks, middle-class regulars, working girls, cops, street people, couples on dates, you name it. Sooner or later just about everybody comes to the Majestic for a late-night breakfast, a cup of coffee, or just to take in the scene. The late Nick Bitzis, a long-time owner who used to keep an aluminum baseball bat behind the register, once chased a group of customers with a butcher knife for smoking pot in one of the booths. The Majestic is open 24 hours, and things invariably get more interesting as the night wears on. 1031 Ponce de Leon Ave. NE (west of North Highland Ave.). ℂ 404/875-0276. MARTA: Inman Park.

Outwrite Bookstore and Coffeehouse   This casual spot caters to the gay and lesbian community and is a sort of clearinghouse for information on local issues and activities. The coffee and pastries are good, and the atmosphere is comfortable. Open until 11pm during the week, midnight on weekends. 991 Piedmont Ave. (at Tenth St.). ℂ 404/607-0082. MARTA: Midtown.

The San Francisco Roasting Company   It's hard to find a coffeehouse that's strictly local and not part of a national chain, but this is the real McCoy. A neighborhood spot that roasts its own coffee and bakes most of its own pastries, it has a lot of atmosphere and is great for just hanging out. 1192 N. Highland Ave. (at Amsterdam Ave.). ℂ 404/876-8816. MARTA: Five Points or Arts Station.

Appendix:
Atlanta in Depth

Atlanta has come a long way since it burned to the ground during Sherman's "March to the Sea" in 1864. This is the city from which Martin Luther King, Jr. launched his social revolution, and the city where Ted Turner launched his media empire. It is home to many of America's largest corporations and is one of the top convention cities in the country.

Atlanta may be best known, however, for hosting the 1996 Summer Olympics. The city went all out in its preparations for the 1996 Games, with new parks, hotels, and sports venues. In the center of downtown is Woodruff Park, which was spruced up to the tune of $5 million. The Olympic Village, erected just north of the central business district, now provides housing for Georgia State University students. South of the Olympic Village and stretching to CNN Center is the 21-acre Centennial Olympic Park—a major gathering place during the Olympics, with its dramatic Olympic Ring fountain, lawns, and gardens. (It was also the site of the bombing during the Olympics, which killed 1 person and injured 111.) Reopened in 1998, the park regularly hosts concerts, street festivals, and other cultural events, and anchors the city's efforts to revitalize commercial and residential development in this once-neglected corner of downtown. The Olympic Stadium, site of the opening and closing ceremonies as well as track and field events, has been reincarnated as Turner Field, home of the Atlanta Braves baseball team.

Since the Olympics, Atlantans have had a little time to think about their future and how to shape it. They've always been an optimistic bunch, but the recent breakneck development, which began with the Olympics and still continues, has many local citizens wondering if they have gotten too much of a good thing. Atlanta has had big-city problems like crime, urban blight, and clogged freeways for some time now. But the overall quality of life has been high. Currently, the spotlight is not on growth and how to encourage it, but on growth and how to manage it. Of great concern is traffic—horrendous by any standards—and the accompanying decline in air quality. There's still enormous development in the suburbs, but everyone is rethinking the role that the automobile plays, and there's much discussion of how to improve public transportation and make the metro area more pedestrian-friendly. Of great significance is the recent development in downtown. For years, city leaders have tried to encourage central city living, and it's finally beginning to take hold as developers are remaking old buildings into attractive apartments and lofts. The mark of a great city is an attractive and vital downtown area where people live as well as work, and Atlanta finally appears to be headed in that direction.

Perhaps the new introspection that has taken hold means that a brash young city is reaching maturity. Whatever the future holds for Atlanta, its heritage is one of cooperation, and that's one thing that's unlikely to change.

1 History 101

It is most fitting that Atlanta in the 21st century is an international gateway and transportation hub. The city was conceived as a rail crossroads for travel north, south, east, and west, and its role as a strategic junction has always figured largely in its destiny. It all began with a peach tree.

In 1826, surveyors first suggested this area of Georgia as a practical spot for a railroad connecting the state with northern markets. This was not yet the heyday of railroads, and the report was more or less ignored for a decade. But in 1837, the state legislature approved an act establishing the Western & Atlantic Railroad here. Today, a marker known as Zero Milepost in Underground Atlanta marks the W & A Railroad site around which a city grew. The new town was unimaginatively dubbed "Terminus." But future governor Alexander H. Stephens, visiting what was still dense forest in 1839, predicted that "a magnificent inland city will at no distant date be built here."

THE TRAIL OF TEARS

One aspect of the city's inception, however, was far from "magnificent." In the early 1800s, most of Georgia was still Native American territory. White settlers coveted the Cherokee and Creek lands because they wanted to expedite the building of the railroad and further expand their settlements. Throughout the 1820s, in order to keep the peace, native leaders signed numerous treaties ceding millions of acres. They adopted a democratic form of government similar to the white man's, complete with a constitution and supreme court; erected schools and shops; built farms; and accepted Christianity. But the white frontierspeople cared little whether the Native Americans adapted—they wanted them to leave.

With President Andrew Jackson's support, Congress passed a bill in 1830 forcing all Southern tribes to move to

Dateline

- **1782** Explorers discover Cherokee village of Standing Peachtree.
- **1820s** Cherokee and Creek leaders cede millions of acres to white settlers in hopes of keeping peace.
- **1837** The town, newly named Terminus, is selected as the site of a railroad terminus connecting Georgia with the Tennessee River. The same year, 17,000 Native Americans are forced to march westward on a "Trail of Tears."
- **1843** Terminus is renamed Marthasville.
- **1845** The first locomotive chugs into town; the city is renamed Atlanta.
- **1851** Georgia secedes from the Union, the Civil War begins, and Atlanta becomes a major Confederate supply depot and medical center.
- **1864** Union forces under Gen. William Tecumseh Sherman burn Atlanta.
- **1865** Civil War ends.
- **1877** Atlanta becomes the capital of Georgia.
- **1886** Newspaper editor Henry Grady inspires readers with vision of a "New South"; John S. Pemberton introduces Coca-Cola.
- **1900** Atlanta University professor W. E. B. Du Bois founds the NAACP.
- **1904** Piedmont Park designed.
- **1917** Fire destroys 73 square blocks of the city.
- **1929** Atlanta's first airport opens; Delta Air Lines takes to the skies and becomes Atlanta's home carrier.
- **1936** Margaret Mitchell's blockbuster novel, *Gone With the Wind*, is published.
- **1939** The movie version of *Gone With the Wind* premieres in Atlanta.
- **1952** The city of Atlanta incorporates surrounding areas, increasing its population by 100,000, and its size from 37 to 118 square miles.
- **1960** Sit-ins and boycotts protesting segregation begin; the million-square-foot Merchandise Mart is erected.
- **1961** Ivan Allen, Jr., defeats segregationist Lester Maddox in mayoral election. Atlanta's public schools and the Georgia Institute of Technology are peacefully desegregated.

lands hundreds of miles away on the other side of the Mississippi River. When the U.S. Supreme Court ruled against the order, Jackson ignored the ruling and backed the Georgia settlers. In 1832, the state gave away Cherokee farms in a land lottery; the white settlers assumed control over the land at gunpoint. The issue culminated in 1837, when 17,000 Native Americans were rounded up by federal soldiers, herded into camps, and forced on a cruel westward march called the "Trail of Tears." Some 4,000 died on the 800-mile journey to Oklahoma, and even those who survived suffered bitterly from cold, hunger, and disease.

Terminus and its surroundings were now firmly in the hands of the white settlers.

A CITY GROWS

Terminus soon began its evolution from a sleepy rural hamlet to a thriving city, a meeting point of major rail lines. In 1843, the town was renamed Marthasville, for ex-governor Wilson Lumpkin's daughter Martha. No one in Marthasville took note in 1844 when a 23-year-old army lieutenant, William Tecumseh Sherman, was stationed for 2 months in their area, but the knowledge he gained of local geography would vitally affect the city's history 2 decades later. The first locomotive, the *Kentucky*, chugged into town in 1845, and shortly thereafter the name Marthasville was deemed too provincial for a burgeoning metropolis. J. Edgar Thomson, the railroad's chief engineer, suggested Atlanta (a feminized form of Atlantic).

In 1848, the newly incorporated city held its first mayoral election, an event marked by dozens of street brawls. Moses W. Formwalt, a maker of stills and member of the Free and Rowdy Party, was elected over temperance candidate John Norcross. But if Atlanta was a bit of a wild frontier town, it also had civic pride. An 1849 newspaper overstated things poetically:

Atlanta, the greatest spot in all the nation, The greatest place for legislation, Or any other occupation, The very center of creation.

- 1964 Atlanta native Martin Luther King, Jr. wins Nobel Peace Prize.
- 1965 106 civic and cultural leaders die in plane crash at Orly Airport in Paris; Atlanta Fulton County Stadium is built.
- 1966 Baseball's Braves move from Milwaukee and the Falcons become a new NFL expansion team; the Beatles perform in Atlanta.
- 1968 Martin Luther King, Jr. is assassinated in Memphis.
- 1974 Atlanta's first black mayor, Maynard Jackson, is inaugurated; Atlanta Brave Hank Aaron hits his record-breaking 715th home run.
- 1976 Georgian Jimmy Carter elected president; Georgia World Congress Center, the nation's largest single-floor exhibit space, is completed.
- 1979 MARTA rapid-transit train system opens.
- 1980 New Hartsfield International Airport dedicated.
- 1983 Martin Luther King, Jr.'s birthday becomes national holiday.
- 1988 Atlanta hosts Democratic National Convention.
- 1989 Underground Atlanta opens with great fanfare.
- 1992 Atlanta completes the new 70,500-seat Georgia Dome.
- 1994 Atlanta hosts Super Bowl XXVIII at the Georgia Dome.
- 1995 On their third try, the Atlanta Braves win the World Series.
- 1996 Atlanta completes the 85,000-seat Olympic Stadium and hosts the Centennial Olympic Games.
- 1997 Atlanta reopens Olympic Stadium as the new Turner Field, home of the Atlanta Braves baseball team.
- 1998 A renovated Centennial Olympic Park opens as a major city gathering spot and a lasting legacy of the Centennial Olympic Games.
- 1999 Atlanta completes the Philips Arena, home to the Atlanta Hawks basketball team and Atlanta Thrashers hockey team.
- 2000 The city hosts Super Bowl XXXIV

> **Fun Fact** The Standing Peachtree
>
> Today, just about everything in Atlanta is called "Peachtree" something, but the first Peachtree reference dates back to 1782 when explorers discovered a Cherokee village on the Chattahoochee River called Standing Peachtree. Since peach trees are not native to the region, some historians maintain the village was actually named for a towering "pitch" tree (a resinous pine). Nevertheless, the Indian village became the location of Fort Peachtree, a tiny frontier outpost, during the War of 1812; a Peachtree Road connecting Fort Peachtree to Fort Daniel (in Gwinnett County) was completed by 1813.

STORM CLOUDS GATHER: ANTEBELLUM ATLANTA

By the middle of the 19th century, the 31-state nation was in the throes of a westward expansion, and the institution of slavery was the major issue of the day. In his 1858 debate with Stephen Douglas, Abraham Lincoln declared, "This government cannot endure permanently half slave and half free." A year later it was obvious that only a war would resolve the issue. In 1861 (a year that began dramatically in Atlanta—with an earthquake), Georgia legislators voted for secession and joined the Confederacy.

In peacetime, the railroads had fashioned Atlanta into a center of commerce. In wartime, this transportation hub would emerge as a major Confederate military post and supply center—the vital link between Confederate forces in Tennessee and Virginia. Early on, Federal forces saw the city's destruction as essential to Northern victory.

On a lighter note, Atlanta made the following ridiculous bid to become the capital of the Confederacy: "The city has good railroad connections, is free from yellow fever, and can supply the most wholesome foods and, as for 'goobers,' an indispensable article for a Southern legislator, we have them all the time." The lure of plentiful peanuts not withstanding, the Confederacy chose Richmond, Virginia, as its capital.

A CITY BURNS

Atlanta was not only a major Southern supply depot, it was also the medical center of the Confederacy. Throughout the city, buildings were hastily converted into makeshift hospitals and clinics, and trains pulled into town daily to disgorge sick and wounded soldiers. By 1862, close to 4,000 soldiers were convalescing here, and the medical crisis was further aggravated by a smallpox epidemic.

That same year, Union spy James J. Andrews and a group of Northern soldiers disguised as civilians seized a locomotive called the *General*, with the aim of blocking supply lines by destroying tracks and bridges behind them. A wild train chase ensued, and the raiders were caught and punished (most, including Andrews, were executed). The episode came to be known as the "Great Locomotive Chase," one of the stirring stories of the Civil War and the subject of two subsequent movies. The *General* is today on view at the Big Shanty Museum in Kennesaw.

The locomotive chase was an Atlanta victory, but the Northern desire to destroy the Confederacy's supply link remained intact. In 1864, Gen. Ulysses S. Grant ordered Major Gen. William T. Sherman to "move against Johnston's army to break it up, and get into the interior of the enemy's country as far as you can, inflicting all the damage you can against their resources."

Georgians had great faith that the able and experienced Gen. Joseph E. Johnston, whom they called "Old Joe," would repel the Yankees. As Sherman's Georgia campaign got under way, an overly optimistic editorial in the *Intelligencer* scoffed at the notion of Federal conquest, claiming "we have no fear of the results, for General Johnston and his great and invincible satellites are working out the problem of battle and victory at the great chess board at the front." Johnston himself was not as sanguine. Sherman had 100,000 men to his 60,000, and the Union troops were better armed.

By July, Sherman was forcing the Confederate troops back, and Atlanta's fall seemed a foregone conclusion; Johnston informed Confederate President Jefferson Davis that he was outnumbered almost two to one and was in a defensive position. His candid assessment was not appreciated, and Davis removed him from command, replacing him with the pugnacious 32-year-old Gen. John Bell Hood. The change of leadership only further demoralized the ranks, and Sherman openly rejoiced when he heard the news.

Some disgruntled Confederate soldiers deserted. Hood abandoned the defensive tactics of Johnston, aggressively assaulting his opponent. His policy cost thousands of troops and gained nothing. In the Battle of Peachtree Creek on July 20, 1864, Union casualties totaled 1,710; Confederate, 4,796. Throughout the summer, the city suffered a full-scale artillery assault. More than 8,000 Confederates perished in the Battle of Atlanta on July 22, while Union deaths totaled just 3,722. After hours of fierce fighting on July 28, the Confederates had lost another 5,000 men; the Yankees, only 600. The Yankees further paralyzed the city by ripping up train rails, heating them over huge bonfires, and twisting them around trees into useless spirals of mangled iron that came to be known as "Sherman's neckties." The most devastating bombardment came on August 9— "that red day . . . when all the fires of hell, and all the thunders of the universe, seemed to be blazing and roaring over Atlanta."

By September 1, when Hood's troops pulled out of the area, first setting fire to vast stores of ammunition (and anything else that might benefit the Yankees), the town was in turmoil: Its roads were crowded with evacuees, and its hospitals, hotels, and private residences were flooded with wounded men. Crime and looting were rife, and food was almost unavailable; the price of a ham-and-eggs breakfast with coffee soared to $25. Rooftops were ripped off houses and buildings, there were huge craters in the streets, and many civilians were dead. The railroads were in Sherman's hands.

On September 2, Mayor James M. Calhoun, carrying a white flag to the nearest Federal unit, officially surrendered the city. The U.S. Army entered and occupied Atlanta, raising the Stars and Stripes at city hall for the first time in 4 years. Claiming he needed the city for military purposes, Sherman ordered all residents to evacuate. Atlantans piled their household goods on wagons and, abandoning their homes and businesses, became refugees. Before departing Atlanta in November, Union troops leveled railroad facilities and burned the city, leaving it a wasteland—defunct as a military center and practically uninhabitable. The Yankees marched out of the city to the strains of "The Battle Hymn of the Republic."

In January 1865, there was $1.64 in the treasury, the railroad system was destroyed, and most of the city was burned to the ground.

A CITY REBUILDS

Slowly, exiled citizens began to trickle back into Atlanta. Confederate money was worthless. At the inauguration of his second term in 1865, Lincoln pledged "malice toward none, charity for all"—but after his assassination later that year, this policy was replaced with one of harsh Republican vengeance. It wasn't until 1876 that Federal troops were withdrawn and Atlanta was freed from military occupation.

Still, the city was making a remarkable recovery. Like the ever-resilient Scarlett O'Hara ("It takes more than Yankees or a burning to keep me down"), Atlanta rolled up its sleeves and began rebuilding. A Northern newspaper reported, "From all this ruin and devastation a new city is springing up . . . the streets are alive from morning till night with drays and carts and hand-barrows and wagons . . . with loads of lumber and loads of brick."

In the years after the war, Atlanta was filled with carpetbaggers (Northern adventurers and politicians who went South to take advantage of the unsettled postwar conditions) and other adventurers hoping to turn a quick buck, and with them came gambling houses, brothels, and saloons. But the city also boasted hundreds of new stores and businesses, churches, schools, banks, hotels, theaters, and a new newspaper, the *Atlanta Constitution.* Blacks chartered Atlanta University in 1867, today the world's largest predominantly black institution of higher learning. Moreover, the railroads became operative once again. Newspaper editor Henry Grady inspired readers with his vision of an industrialized and culturally advanced "New South." He was Atlanta's biggest civic booster. A new constitution in 1877 made Atlanta the permanent capital of the state of Georgia. Two years later, General Sherman visited the city he had destroyed and was welcomed with a ball and, lest he get any funny ideas, a grand military review.

In 1886, a new headache cure was introduced to the city—a syrup made from the cocoa leaf and the kola nut, which would eventually become the world's most renowned beverage, Coca-Cola. Atlanta adopted the symbol of a phoenix rising from the ashes for its official seal in 1888 and, the following year, dedicated the gold-domed state capitol and opened a zoo in Grant Park. Piedmont Park was built in 1904 as the site of the Cotton States and International Exposition—a $2.5-million world's fair–like extravaganza with entertainment ranging from Buffalo Bill and His Wild West Show to reconstructed "international villages". Former slave Booker T. Washington gave a landmark address, and John Philip Sousa composed the "King Cotton March" to mark the event.

THE TWENTIETH CENTURY

At the turn of the century, Atlanta's population was 90,000, a figure that more than doubled 2 decades later. Though a massive fire destroyed almost 2,000 buildings in 1917, the city was on a course of rapid growth. In 1929, Atlanta opened its first airport on the site of today's Hartsfield International, presaging the growth of a major air-travel industry. The same year, Delta Air Lines took to the skies and became Atlanta's home carrier.

Margaret Mitchell's blockbuster Civil War epic *Gone With the Wind,* which went on to become the world's second-best-selling book (after the Bible) and the basis for the biggest-grossing picture of all time, was published in 1936. Louis B. Mayer turned down a chance to make the film version for MGM, because "no Civil War picture ever made a nickel."

A more dire legacy of the Civil War and the institution of slavery was racial strife, and the early years of the 20th century were marked by violent race riots.

Impressions

No one goes anywhere without passing through Atlanta.
> —Francis C. Lawley, *London Times* reporter (1861)

I want to say to General Sherman, who is an able man . . . though some people think he is kind of careless about fire, that from the ashes he left us in 1864 we have raised a brave and beautiful city; that we have caught the sunshine in our homes and built therein not one ignoble prejudice or memory.
> —Henry Grady, *Atlanta Constitution* editor (1886)

Atlanta University professor W. E. B. Du Bois founded the NAACP in 1900. In 1939, black cast members were unable to attend the glamorous premiere of *Gone With the Wind* because the theater was segregated. And as late as 1960, segregation in Atlanta (as everywhere in the South) was still firmly entrenched and backed by state law. Unlike much of the South, though, the city has, for the most part, adopted a progressive attitude regarding race relations. Even before the civil rights movement, there were black advancements—the hiring of black police officers, the election of a black to the Atlanta Board of Education, the desegregation of a public golf course in 1955, and, in 1959, the desegregation of public transit. Mayor Bill Hartsfield (who held office for almost 3 decades) called Atlanta "a city too busy to hate." And his successor, Mayor Ivan Allen, Jr., called on Atlantans to face race problems "and seek the answers in an atmosphere of decency and dignity."

Atlanta peacefully desegregated its public schools and the Georgia Institute of Technology in 1961. Atlanta native Dr. Martin Luther King, Jr. headquartered his Southern Christian Leadership Conference here and made Ebenezer Baptist Church, which he co-pastored with his father, a hub of the civil rights movement. In 1974, Atlanta inaugurated its first black mayor, Maynard Jackson, and, following a term by another black mayor, Andrew Young, Jackson was reelected.

In 1966, Atlanta went major league when the Braves and the Falcons came to town. Atlantans went wild in 1974, when Hank Aaron broke Babe Ruth's home-run record here.

2 Famous Atlantans

Henry Louis "Hank" Aaron (b. 1934)   An outfielder with the Milwaukee (later Atlanta) Braves, Aaron broke Babe Ruth's record in 1974 with his 715th home run, in Atlanta–Fulton County Stadium. He remained cool and dignified in the face of the media frenzy surrounding his pursuit of the record, despite receiving countless death threats and bags of hate mail from bigots who felt that Ruth's achievement should never be surpassed by a black man. He retired in 1976 with 755 homers.

Henry W. Grady (1850–89)   Managing editor of the *Atlanta Constitution,* Grady preached post–Civil War reconciliation, and he worked passionately to draw Northern capital and diversified industry to the agrarian South. His name is synonymous with the phrase "The New South."

Joel Chandler Harris (1848–1908)   Called "Georgia's Aesop," he created Uncle Remus, the wise black raconteur of children's fables. His tales of Br'er Rabbit and Br'er Fox were the basis for Disney's delightful animated feature *Song of the South.*

Impressions

It stinks, I don't know why I bother with it, but I've got to have something to do with my time.

—Margaret Mitchell, author of *Gone With the Wind*

Gone With the Wind is very possibly the greatest American novel.

—*Publishers Weekly*

Robert Tyre "Bobby" Jones (1902–71)   The founder of the Masters tournament, Jones won golf's Grand Slam at age 28 and has been called the world's greatest golfer. He also held academic degrees in engineering, law, and English literature.

Martin Luther King, Jr. (1929–68)   Civil rights leader, minister, orator, and Nobel Peace Prize–winner, King preached Gandhi's doctrine of passive resistance.

Margaret Mitchell (1900–49)   Author of the definitive Southern blockbuster novel, *Gone With the Wind*. Originally a journalist, Mitchell began writing "the book" in 1926 when a severe ankle injury forced her to give up reporting. *GWTW* is, next to the Bible, the world's best-selling book.

John C. Portman (b. 1924)   Architect/developer who revolutionized hotel design in the United States with his lofty atrium-lobby concept and almost single-handedly designed Atlanta's skyline in the 1960s. He has been called "Atlanta's one-man urban-renewal program."

Robert Edward "Ted" Turner III (b. 1938)   Dubbed "the mouth of the South," America's most dynamic media mogul, Ted Turner, created 24-hour cable news networks CNN and Headline News, along with entertainment networks Superstation TBS and TNT. Turner is vice chairman of Time-Warner Inc., and owns a portion of MGM and the Atlanta Braves and Atlanta Hawks.

Alfred Uhry (b. 1936)   One of the winningest present-day playwrights (an Oscar, a Tony, and a Pulitzer Prize), Uhry, who was born and reared in Atlanta and spent much of his adult life here, has since moved away from the city. But he still has Atlanta on his mind. Many of his plays, the most notable of which are "Driving Miss Daisy" and "The Last Night of Ballyhoo," take place in Atlanta. As a student at Druid Hills High School in the mid-1950s, Uhry had early scripts produced there, including one about rural life that was upstaged by a boisterous live chicken.

Robert W. Woodruff (1889–1985)   Coca-Cola Company president, philanthropist, and leading Atlanta citizen for over half a century. He put Coca-Cola on the map worldwide; promoted civil rights; and gave over $400 million to Atlanta educational, artistic, civil, and medical projects, such as Emory University, the Woodruff Arts Center, and the High Museum.

Index

See also Accommodations and Restaurant indexes, below.

RESTAURANTS

FROMMER'S® COMPLETE TRAVEL GUIDES

Alaska
Alaska Cruises & Ports of Call
Amsterdam
Argentina & Chile
Arizona
Atlanta
Australia
Austria
Bahamas
Barcelona, Madrid & Seville
Beijing
Belgium, Holland & Luxembourg
Bermuda
Boston
Brazil
British Columbia & the Canadian
   Rockies
Budapest & the Best of Hungary
California
Canada
Cancún, Cozumel & the Yucatán
Cape Cod, Nantucket & Martha's
   Vineyard
Caribbean
Caribbean Cruises & Ports of Call
Caribbean Ports of Call
Carolinas & Georgia
Chicago
China
Colorado
Costa Rica
Denmark
Denver, Boulder & Colorado
   Springs
England
Europe
European Cruises & Ports of Call
Florida

France
Germany
Great Britain
Greece
Greek Islands
Hawaii
Hong Kong
Honolulu, Waikiki & Oahu
Ireland
Israel
Italy
Jamaica
Japan
Las Vegas
London
Los Angeles
Maryland & Delaware
Maui
Mexico
Montana & Wyoming
Montréal & Québec City
Munich & the Bavarian Alps
Nashville & Memphis
Nepal
New England
New Mexico
New Orleans
New York City
New Zealand
Northern Italy
Nova Scotia, New Brunswick &
   Prince Edward Island
Oregon
Paris
Philadelphia & the Amish Country
Portugal
Prague & the Best of the Czech
   Republic

Provence & the Riviera
Puerto Rico
Rome
San Antonio & Austin
San Diego
San Francisco
Santa Fe, Taos & Albuquerque
Scandinavia
Scotland
Seattle & Portland
Shanghai
Singapore & Malaysia
South Africa
South America
South Florida
South Pacific
Southeast Asia
Spain
Sweden
Switzerland
Texas
Thailand
Tokyo
Toronto
Tuscany & Umbria
USA
Utah
Vancouver & Victoria
Vermont, New Hampshire &
   Maine
Vienna & the Danube Valley
Virgin Islands
Virginia
Walt Disney World® & Orlando
Washington, D.C.
Washington State

FROMMER'S® DOLLAR-A-DAY GUIDES

Australia from $50 a Day
California from $70 a Day
Caribbean from $70 a Day
England from $75 a Day
Europe from $70 a Day

Florida from $70 a Day
Hawaii from $80 a Day
Ireland from $60 a Day
Italy from $70 a Day
London from $85 a Day

New York from $90 a Day
Paris from $80 a Day
San Francisco from $70 a Day
Washington, D.C. from $80 a Day

FROMMER'S® PORTABLE GUIDES

Acapulco, Ixtapa & Zihuatanejo
Amsterdam
Aruba
Australia's Great Barrier Reef
Bahamas
Berlin
Big Island of Hawaii
Boston
California Wine Country
Cancún
Charleston & Savannah
Chicago
Disneyland®
Dublin
Florence

Frankfurt
Hong Kong
Houston
Las Vegas
London
Los Angeles
Los Cabos & Baja
Maine Coast
Maui
Miami
New Orleans
New York City
Paris
Phoenix & Scottsdale

Portland
Puerto Rico
Puerto Vallarta, Manzanillo &
   Guadalajara
Rio de Janeiro
San Diego
San Francisco
Seattle
Sydney
Tampa & St. Petersburg
Vancouver
Venice
Virgin Islands
Washington, D.C.

FROMMER'S® NATIONAL PARK GUIDES

Banff & Jasper
Family Vacations in the National
   Parks
Grand Canyon

National Parks of the American
   West
Rocky Mountain

Yellowstone & Grand Teton
Yosemite & Sequoia/ Kings Canyon
Zion & Bryce Canyon

FROMMER'S® MEMORABLE WALKS

Chicago	New York	San Francisco
London	Paris	Washington, D.C.

FROMMER'S® GREAT OUTDOOR GUIDES

Arizona & New Mexico	Northern California	Vermont & New Hampshire
New England	Southern New England	

SUZY GERSHMAN'S BORN TO SHOP GUIDES

Born to Shop: France	Born to Shop: Italy	Born to Shop: New York
Born to Shop: Hong Kong,	Born to Shop: London	Born to Shop: Paris
Shanghai & Beijing		

FROMMER'S® IRREVERENT GUIDES

Amsterdam	Los Angeles	San Francisco
Boston	Manhattan	Seattle & Portland
Chicago	New Orleans	Vancouver
Las Vegas	Paris	Walt Disney World®
London	Rome	Washington, D.C.

FROMMER'S® BEST-LOVED DRIVING TOURS

Britain	Germany	Northern Italy
California	Ireland	Scotland
Florida	Italy	Spain
France	New England	Tuscany & Umbria

HANGING OUT™ GUIDES

Hanging Out in England	Hanging Out in France	Hanging Out in Italy
Hanging Out in Europe	Hanging Out in Ireland	Hanging Out in Spain

THE UNOFFICIAL GUIDES®

Bed & Breakfasts and Country
Inns in:
  California
  Great Lakes States
  Mid-Atlantic
  New England
  Northwest
  Rockies
  Southeast
  Southwest
Best RV & Tent Campgrounds in:
  California & the West
  Florida & the Southeast
  Great Lakes States
  Mid-Atlantic
  Northeast
  Northwest & Central Plains

  Southwest & South Central
    Plains
  U.S.A.
Beyond Disney
Branson, Missouri
California with Kids
Chicago
Cruises
Disneyland®
Florida with Kids
Golf Vacations in the Eastern U.S.
Great Smoky & Blue Ridge Region
Inside Disney
Hawaii
Las Vegas
London

Mid-Atlantic with Kids
Mini Las Vegas
Mini-Mickey
New England and New York with
  Kids
New Orleans
New York City
Paris
San Francisco
Skiing in the West
Southeast with Kids
Walt Disney World®
Walt Disney World® for Grown-ups
Walt Disney World® with Kids
Washington, D.C.
World's Best Diving Vacations

SPECIAL-INTEREST TITLES

Frommer's Adventure Guide to Australia &
  New Zealand
Frommer's Adventure Guide to Central America
Frommer's Adventure Guide to India & Pakistan
Frommer's Adventure Guide to South America
Frommer's Adventure Guide to Southeast Asia
Frommer's Adventure Guide to Southern Africa
Frommer's Britain's Best Bed & Breakfasts and
  Country Inns
Frommer's Caribbean Hideaways
Frommer's Exploring America by RV
Frommer's Fly Safe, Fly Smart
Frommer's France's Best Bed & Breakfasts and
  Country Inns
Frommer's Gay & Lesbian Europe

Frommer's Italy's Best Bed & Breakfasts and
  Country Inns
Frommer's New York City with Kids
Frommer's Ottawa with Kids
Frommer's Road Atlas Britain
Frommer's Road Atlas Europe
Frommer's Road Atlas France
Frommer's Toronto with Kids
Frommer's Vancouver with Kids
Frommer's Washington, D.C., with Kids
Israel Past & Present
The New York Times' Guide to Unforgettable
  Weekends
Places Rated Almanac
Retirement Places Rated